T0344523

Cases on Security, Safety, and Risk Management

Aleksandra Zając
American Institute of Applied Sciences in Switzerland, Switzerland

Giuseppe Catenazzo
American Institute of Applied Sciences in Switzerland, Switzerland & ICN Business School, France

Emmanuel Fragnière
University of Applied Sciences of Western Switzerland, Switzerland & University of Bath, UK

IGI Global
Publishing Tomorrow's Research Today

Published in the United States of America by
  IGI Global
  701 E. Chocolate Avenue
  Hershey PA, USA 17033
  Tel: 717-533-8845
  Fax: 717-533-8661
  E-mail: cust@igi-global.com
  Web site: https://www.igi-global.com

Library of Congress Cataloging-in-Publication Data

CIP Data Pending
ISBN: 979-8-3693-2675-6
eISBN: 979-8-3693-2676-3

Vice President of Editorial: Melissa Wagner
Managing Editor of Acquisitions: Mikaela Felty
Managing Editor of Book Development: Jocelynn Hessler
Production Manager: Mike Brehm
Cover Design: Phillip Shickler

British Cataloguing in Publication Data
A Cataloguing in Publication record for this book is available from the British Library.

All work contributed to this book is new, previously-unpublished material.
The views expressed in this book are those of the authors, but not necessarily of the publisher.

Editorial Advisory Board

Table of Contents

Detailed Table of Contents

Chapter 1

  Shilpy Verma, Amity University, Noida, India

The rapidly growing digitization has positively contributed to economic growth, social development, and increased environmental protection. At the same time, it has also made socio-technical systems and its associated ecosystems more susceptible to cyber-threats. The rapid increase of technological adoption raises the need to provide a secure and sustainable cyberspace for internet users. A key concern of today's technology driven economies is cybersecurity issues. It is essential to build cyber security ecosystem and resistance to cyber threats. It should also be emphasised that sustainability, data regulation, and cybersecurity will be key to the digital transformation in the years to come. Given this, it is important to have measures (regulatory, organisational, and legal) to curb cyberattacks. This chapter intends to examine the need, strategies to follow to fight against digital threats and future steps in the building sustainable cyber security ecosystem.

Chapter 2

Ankur Biswas, Adamas University, India

Abhishek Roy, Adamas University, India

Priyadarshini Tikader, Vidyasagar University, India

Dharmesh Dhabliya, Vishwakarma Institute of Information Technology, India

Kirti H. Wanjale, Vishwakarma Institute of Information Technology, India

Sabyasachi Pramanik, Haldia Institute of Technology, India

Ankur Gupta, Vaish College of Engineering, India

The industrial sector has emerged as a hub for research on the quickly emerging field of smart technology throughout the last few decades. Smart technology (ST) included a wide range of cutting-edge technologies, such as block chains, artificial intelligence, cyberphysical production systems, internet of things, industrial internet of things (IOT), and systematic data analysis. The authors provide an overview of numerous smart technologies that may be used to control the complex properties of computer and sensor technologies, with the goal of reducing the gap between people and robots. This chapter presents the whole literature evaluation on the use of ST to enhance the production and maintenance of machinery and equipment, as well as potential risks to ST. This chapter also includes the survey report that compares the adoption rate of the current technology to that of the previous five years in an effort to lower the amount of human labor needed in the industrial sector by utilizing a variety of sensors, affordable techniques, and real-time results.

P. Suresh, Vellore Institute of Technology, India
P. Keerthika, Vellore Institute of Technology, India
Manjula Devi R., KPR Institute of Engineering and Technology, India
S. Maheswaran, Kongu Engineering College, India
Kishor Kumar Sadasivuni, Qatar University, Qatar
N. Anusha, Vellore Institute of Technology, India
Shreeya Sanjeev Gokhale, Vellore Institute of Technology, India

The interconnection of less secure devices in a network is known as the internet of things (IoT). Data and systems may be better protected with the aid of cyber security in the IoT. Cyber security violations occur most frequently when an attacker uses many systems connected to multiple networks or systems to conduct an offence. These cyber dangers can do more than just steal or corrupt data; they can also temporarily or permanently disable network infrastructure. Because it is always changing, manually detecting cyber-attacks becomes expensive and tiresome. Therefore, they may be identified and categorized using machine learning methods. Internet of things devices may now maintain connections for long durations without any intervention from a person. This chapter extensively covers cyberattack detection and categorization in IoT systems using machine learning approaches.

Sureyya Yigit, New Vision University, Georgia

This chapter evaluates European and African security risks, aiming to contribute to the multidimensional understanding of security that is much needed in today's world. The term "security" has an intriguing etymology, deriving from the Latin word securitas, which conveys a state of being "without care". In the modern context, it denotes the absence of risks or dangers and is closely intertwined with trust and proactive measures. Security encompasses diverse facets of life and is associated with geopolitical, criminal, social, anti-competitive, extrajudicial criminal, and cyber risks. In this chapter, an analysis of the Swiss police's methods for detecting and responding to radicalisation, extremism, and violence, with a specific focus on how these tactics are applied in the Vaud Canton and Neuchatel regions, are explored alongside the specific strategies employed in West Africa to assess the risk of youth radicalisation. Furthermore, the chapter carefully assesses the comprehensive approach used to address psychosocial risks and enhance the capabilities of young individuals.

This study explores the complex relationship between corporate governance, risk management, and social responsibility, focusing on the impact of regulatory and market changes. It assesses the influence of the Sarbanes-Oxley Act of 2002 and the Committee of Sponsoring Organisations (COSO) Enterprise Risk Management framework on corporate governance. Through a comparative analysis of risk management across countries, the chapter highlights the role of legal frameworks and industry standards. The study also examines technology's role in enhancing transparency and accountability, particularly through data analytics and cybersecurity. A Greek case study provides a detailed national perspective. By synthesising literature, regulatory reports, and the Greek case, the research offers a comprehensive overview of current practices and future trends, emphasising the importance of transparent risk disclosure and strong governance in building corporate resilience and stakeholder trust.

Risk assessment as the need of the hour is what managers agree upon unanimously in today's competitive environment. The main objective of this research study is to examine the aspects of risk and risk assessment in organizational setup and further analyze the relationship between risk assessment tools and organizational effectiveness in the Indian automobile industry. The study will give managers a perspective of how risk assessment tools are different from one another in terms of their perceived benefits as managers have plenty of risk assessment tools to choose from within an industry and the contributions of this study will render great insight to risk managers and future entrepreneurs in managing risk innovatively. The present study is among the first few to identify and explore the impact of risk assessment tools on organizational effectiveness via perceived benefits. These findings advance the understanding of risk assessment tools upon organizational effectiveness and help risk managers assess and control risk in a better way.

  Danuta Kaźmierczak, *University of the National Education Commission,
     Poland*
  Stanisław Kowalkowski, *War Studies University, Poland*
  Marek Wrzosek, *War Studies University, Poland*

Although every protracted crisis is unique, they often share several characteristics: long duration, conflict, weak governance or public administration structures, unsustainable livelihood systems, poor food security outcomes, and breakdown of local institutions. The Directorate-General for European Civil Protection and Humanitarian Aid Operations reports difficulties in cooperating with national and local authorities and the existence of double coordination structures. This chapter discusses the need for humanitarian units in national DRM structures, consisting of the representatives of all sectors providing security to citizens—police, social services, healthcare, border guards, fire service, armed forces, NGOs, local governors, and fellow citizens—would ensure higher effectiveness due to their fractal structures. Advantages include accurate decision-making, assigning tasks and assets to proper personnel, supporting multi-actor teams in action, communicating with international organizations and avoiding task duplication, and interoperability across teams and flexible response.

    Jorge Vareda Gomes, *Universidade Lusófona, Portugal*
    Mário Romão, *ISEG, Universidade de Lisboa, Portugal*
    Ricardo Simplício, *ISEG, Universidade de Lisboa, Portugal*

In times of major technological changes with ever shorter production cycles, subject to strong global competition, it is vital for organizations to optimize resources and benefit from their investments to achieve the expected successes. One of the main difficulties that organizations face is the high number of projects in their portfolio. Selecting and prioritizing projects is essential to ensure the maximum return on investment and the sustainability of the organization. The analysis and selection of projects is carried out using different approaches, each with advantages and disadvantages that need to be considered. The selection and prioritization of projects depends largely on the nature and profile of managers, organizational culture, and techniques that best fit the organization's environment. This study intends to confront the pilot model of selection and prioritization developed by the Portuguese Navy and establish a bridge with the academic literature.

    Lyudmila Bovsh, State University of Trade and Economics, Ukraine
    Tetiana Tkachuk, Kyiv State University of Trade and Economics,
        Ukraine
    Nataliia Zikii, Kyiv State University of Trade and Economics, Ukraine
    Kamel Mouloudj, University of Medea, Algeria
    Ahmed Chemseddine Bouarar, University of Medea, Algeria

Hospitality entities face ongoing pressures at a macro level, necessitating effective strategic approaches to business security management. Therefore, the aim of this chapter was to explore the essential elements of strategic security management in hospitality, influenced by macro trends. This involved examining the origins of risks and threats, as well as key components in developing a security management strategy, including metrics, key risk indicators (KRIs), objectives and key results (OKRs), and foresight capabilities. The analysis employs an analytical approach and underscores that effective security strategies not only mitigate risks but also foster a secure and trustworthy environment for guests and staff. Additionally, staying abreast of technological advancements and industry trends enables hospitality entities to adapt their security measures proactively. In conclusion, it is emphasized that implementing robust security protocols such as access control measures, surveillance systems, and emergency response plans is crucial for proactive risk management.

    Elen Paraskevi Paraschi, University of Patras, Greece

As environmental pressures increase globally, the need arises to understand and manage present and emerging environmental risks. The purpose of this chapter is to introduce a new Environmental Risk Assessment (ERA) approach to identify, assess, and report the level of environmental risks that can lead to significant interruptions, infrastructure damages, safety threats, and long-term effects on airport operations. ERA evaluates the quantitative and qualitative characteristics of environmental hazards, which involve physical, chemical, and biological factors that can imperil humans and infrastructure. The presented ERA framework is deployed in six phases, namely airport preparation, definition of the assessment scope and parameters, data collection and development of projection scenarios, risk assessment, mitigation and adaptation strategies, report, monitor, and review. In essence, the outlined ERA approach serves as a managerial tool to facilitate policy assessment and sustainable decision-making.

Sustainability practices at airports encompass a spectrum of environmental impacts stemming from airport operations and assets, as well as digital, social, and economic factors. The significance of sustainability practices, particularly within airport operations, is underscored by the intrinsic connection between sustainability and aviation. This significance arises from both international regulations and the demands of investors and stakeholders within the industry. This study employed a longitudinal case study approach to examine Istanbul Airport in Turkiye. The study aims to examine the quantity and quality of sustainability reporting by the Istanbul Airport through its sustainability report. It uses content analysis to examine the use of the Global Reporting Initiative (GRI) standards, and United Nations (UN) Sustainable Development (SD) goals. Furthermore, GRI reporting principles were used as the basis for the analysis of the quality of the sustainability report in the research. The findings were reported and discussed.

This case study explores the tumultuous journey of Go First, an airline marred by allegations of recurrent engine failures. Investigating the aftermath of these accusations, the case scrutinises the intricate interplay between safety, regulatory compliance, and financial viability in the aviation industry. Drawing from qualitative research and a comprehensive review of secondary sources, the narrative delves into the operational disruptions, safety concerns, financial strains, and reputational damage faced by the airline. The study contributes unique insights into crisis management, offering educators, researchers, and industry professionals a real-world context for understanding and addressing operational challenges within the aviation sector.

Preface

In the ever-evolving landscape of business and societal operations, the importance of robust security and effective risk management cannot be overstated. It is within this context that we present "Cases on Security, Safety, and Risk Management," a comprehensive collection of research-based case studies that delve into practical problems and their innovative resolutions. Our goal is to illuminate the multifaceted challenges of security issues and risk factors, offering valuable insights into their management and mitigation.

Risk management is a critical discipline that extends far beyond the confines of financial institutions. It encompasses the identification, analysis, evaluation, mitigation, and control of risks across all sectors, enabling businesses to not only survive but thrive. This book is designed to be a versatile resource, providing an interdisciplinary perspective that bridges the gap between theory and practice. We have curated contributions from a diverse range of experts, including engineers, lawyers, social scientists, and policymakers, to ensure a holistic approach to the subject matter.

The relevance and urgency of effective risk management in today's business environment cannot be overstated. By emphasizing the centrality of security and safety as core components of business strategy, this book seeks to shift the perception that these are peripheral concerns. The case studies within illustrate that addressing these issues head-on is essential for the sustainability and success of any organization.

Our intended readership is broad, reflecting the diverse applications of risk management. Undergraduate and postgraduate students in management, business administration, law, and security studies will find these cases invaluable for deepening their understanding of security in business contexts. Academics and researchers can use these cases to inspire and inform their research, as well as to enrich their teaching with real-world examples. Business professionals and decision-makers will benefit from the practical insights provided by these case studies, enhancing their analytical and decision-making skills.

Key topics covered in this book include risk identification, risk analysis, risk evaluation, risk mitigation, risk control, risk management in various contexts (private and governmental organizations, non-profits), health and safety policies in workplaces, work safety training for crews and workers, insurance, safe products, services, and infrastructure, environment-friendly solutions, addressing new social security needs, and social stability and sustainability.

We believe that this interdisciplinary approach, coupled with the depth of analysis provided by our contributors, will make "Cases on Security, Safety, and Risk Management" a pivotal resource for understanding and addressing the complex challenges of risk in today's interconnected world.

ORGANIZATION OF THE BOOK

Chapter 1: Harnessing the Strength of Digital Technologies for Cybersecurity

Shilpy Verma from Amity University, Noida Campus, Uttar Pradesh, India, explores the dual-edged nature of rapidly growing digitization, which, while fostering economic growth, social development, and environmental protection, also makes socio-technical systems more vulnerable to cyber-threats. With technological adoption accelerating, the need for a secure and sustainable cyberspace is paramount. Cybersecurity is a critical issue for today's technology-driven economies, necessitating the development of resilient ecosystems against cyber threats. This chapter examines the strategies needed to combat digital threats and outlines future steps for building a sustainable cybersecurity ecosystem. Emphasizing the importance of sustainability, data regulation, and cybersecurity in digital transformation, Verma highlights the necessity of regulatory, organizational, and legal measures to curb cyberattacks.

Chapter 2: Security of Tomorrow's Cyber Physical Systems

In this chapter, Ankur Biswas, Abhishek Roy, Priyadarshini Tikader, Dharmesh Dhabliya, Kirti H. Wanjale, Sabyasachi Pramanik, and Ankur Gupta, representing various institutions in India, provide an extensive overview of smart technology (ST) in industrial settings. They discuss the integration of cutting-edge technologies such as blockchains, artificial intelligence, cyber-physical systems, IoT, and data analysis to bridge the gap between humans and robots. This literature review covers the use of ST in enhancing the production and maintenance of machinery and equipment while also addressing potential risks. A survey compares the adoption rate of current technologies to those of the past five years, aiming to reduce human labor in the industrial sector through sensors, cost-effective methods, and real-time results.

Chapter 3: A Contemporary Survey on Effectiveness of Machine Learning for Detection and Classification of Cyber Attacks in IoT Systems

Keerthika P., Suresh P., Manjula Devi R., Maheswaran S., Kishor Kumar Sadasivuni, Anusha N., and Shreeya Gokhale, from various institutions in India and Qatar, present a comprehensive survey on the application of machine learning techniques to detect and classify cyber-attacks in IoT systems. With IoT devices becoming more prevalent and vulnerable to network attacks, cybersecurity in IoT is crucial for protecting data and systems. The chapter discusses the challenges of manually detecting cyber-attacks, which evolve constantly, and highlights how machine learning can automate this process. The survey covers various machine learning methods that enhance the security of IoT devices, enabling them to remain connected with minimal human intervention.

Chapter 4: European and African Evaluation of Security Risks

Sureyya Yigit from New Vision University, Georgia, delves into the concept of security, derived from the Latin "securitas," meaning "to be without care." Yigit explains that security involves the containment of risks within acceptable levels, given that absolute elimination of risk is impossible. This chapter focuses on various types of security, including geopolitical, criminal, societal, anti-competitive, extra-judicial criminal, and cyber risks. Security, intertwined with trust and prevention, is defined legally in some national contexts to protect freedom, life, property, and democratic institutions. Yigit's analysis emphasizes the interdisciplinary nature of security sciences and the necessity of maintaining acceptable risk levels.

Chapter 5: Navigating the Nexus of Corporate Governance, Risk Management, and Social Responsibility While Unveiling Responsibility Dilution and Embracing Risk

Yianni Doumenis and Emmanuel Fragnière explore the evolving landscape of risk management and corporate governance, shaped by market dynamics, regulatory changes, and emerging trends. They focus on the impact of the Sarbanes-Oxley Act of 2002 on corporate risk management frameworks, emphasizing transparency and materiality. The chapter highlights the need for companies to manage risks effectively and disclose relevant mitigation strategies to stakeholders. By integrating robust risk management practices and advocating for openness in disclosure, companies can foster sustainable growth. This chapter underscores the importance of holistic risk management in building trust and meeting regulatory and market demands.

Chapter 6: Extrapolating the Influence of Risk Assessment Tools on Organizational Effectiveness within the Automobile Industry: An Empirical Study

K. Madhu Kishore Raghunath, S. Tulasi Devi, and P. Sheela investigate the critical role of risk assessment in the competitive environment of the Indian automobile industry. This empirical study examines the relationship between risk assessment tools and organizational effectiveness, providing managers with insights into the perceived benefits of different tools. The study emphasizes the importance of innovative risk management and offers valuable findings for risk managers and entrepreneurs. By identifying and exploring the impact of risk assessment tools, the authors advance the understanding of how these tools can enhance organizational effectiveness.

Chapter 7: Fractally Organized Units May Increase Organizational Effectiveness in Protracted Crises

Danuta Kazmierczak, Stanislaw Kowalkowski, and Marek Wrzosek discuss the unique characteristics of protracted crises, such as long duration, conflict, weak governance, and poor food security outcomes. They propose the integration of humanitarian units within national disaster risk management structures to enhance organizational effectiveness. These units, comprising representatives from various sectors including police, social services, health care, border guards, fire service, armed forces, NGOs, local governors, and citizens, can ensure accurate decision-making, task allocation, and multi-actor team support. The chapter emphasizes the advantages of such units in improving interoperability, avoiding task duplication, and providing flexible responses in crisis situations.

Chapter 8: Projects Selection and Prioritization in the Portuguese Navy

Jorge Gomes and Mário Romão address the challenges of project selection and prioritization in the Portuguese Navy amidst rapid technological changes and global competition. They explore different approaches to project selection, considering the advantages and disadvantages of each method. The chapter highlights the importance of aligning project selection with organizational goals and the role of managerial perspectives and organizational culture in this process. By examining the pilot model developed by the Portuguese Navy, the authors establish a connection with academic literature and provide insights into optimizing resource allocation for maximum return on investmen

Chapter 9: Strategic Management of Hospitality Security Under the Influence of Macro Trends

Lyudmila Bovsh, Tetiana Tkachuk, Natalia Zikii, Kamel Mouloudj, and Ahmed Chemseddine Bouarar explore the strategic management of security in the hospitality industry, influenced by macro trends. The chapter examines the origins of risks and threats, and key components of a security management strategy, including metrics, Key Risk Indicators (KRIs), Objectives and Key Results (OKRs), and foresight capabilities. The authors emphasize the importance of proactive security measures, such as access control, surveillance systems, and emergency response plans, in mitigating risks and fostering a secure environment for guests and staff. Staying abreast of technological advancements and industry trends is crucial for adapting security measures effectively.

Chapter 10: A Proposed Framework for Environmental Risk Assessment (ERA) in Airports

Elen Paraschi introduces a new Environmental Risk Assessment (ERA) approach to address the increasing environmental pressures on airports. The chapter outlines a six-phase ERA framework to identify, assess, and report environmental risks that can disrupt airport operations, damage infrastructure, and pose safety threats. The phases include airport preparation, defining the assessment scope, data collection, risk assessment, mitigation and adaptation strategies, and monitoring. This framework serves as a managerial tool to facilitate policy assessment and sustainable decision-making in airport operations.

Chapter 11: Sustainability Reporting on Istanbul Airport: Analyzing Risks and Best Practices

Seda Ceken examines sustainability practices at Istanbul Airport, focusing on environmental, digital, social, and economic impacts. The chapter analyzes the airport's sustainability reporting using Global Reporting Initiative (GRI) standards and United Nations Sustainable Development goals. By employing content analysis, Ceken evaluates the quantity and quality of the airport's sustainability report, discussing best practices and areas for improvement. The findings highlight the importance of comprehensive sustainability reporting in meeting international regulations and stakeholder demands.

Chapter 12: Flight to Crisis, Navigating Operational Challenges: A Case Study on Go First's Alleged Engine Failures

Baranidharan S., Chandrakala G., and Sonal Devesh present a case study on the operational challenges faced by Go First airline due to alleged engine failures. The chapter investigates the interplay between safety, regulatory compliance, and financial viability in the aviation industry. Through qualitative research and secondary sources, the authors examine the impact of engine failures on the airline's operations, safety concerns, financial strains, and reputation. This study offers unique insights into crisis management, providing a real-world context for educators, researchers, and industry professionals to understand and address operational challenges in aviation.

CONCLUSION

As we bring this exploration of risk management and security to a close, it is evident that the landscape of risk is ever-evolving, shaped by technological advancements, geopolitical shifts, and emerging societal trends. This collection of chapters highlights the critical importance of adaptive and resilient approaches to managing risk across various domains, from cybersecurity to corporate governance, and from industrial settings to humanitarian responses.

The insights provided by our esteemed contributors underscore the necessity of a holistic and interdisciplinary approach to risk management. As digital technologies continue to permeate every aspect of our lives, the dual-edged nature of these advancements becomes increasingly apparent. The promise of economic growth, social development, and environmental sustainability is tempered by the growing vulnerability of our socio-technical systems to cyber threats.

In the realm of cybersecurity, as Shilpy Verma eloquently discusses, the development of a secure and sustainable cyberspace is paramount. The strategies outlined for combating digital threats and building a resilient ecosystem are essential for protecting our digital future. Similarly, the extensive review of smart technologies in industrial settings by Ankur Biswas and colleagues highlights the potential and risks associated with the integration of cutting-edge innovations.

Security, in its many forms, remains a cornerstone of societal trust and functionality. Sureyya Yigit's analysis of security risks reinforces the idea that while absolute elimination of risk is unattainable, maintaining acceptable levels of risk through robust security measures is vital. The application of machine learning for detecting and classifying cyber-attacks in IoT systems, as explored by Keerthika P. and her team, exemplifies how technological advancements can be harnessed to enhance security and reduce human intervention.

Corporate governance and risk management, as Yianni Doumenis and Emmanuel Fragnière elucidate, are increasingly intertwined with social responsibility and regulatory compliance. Their insights into the Sarbanes-Oxley Act and its implications for risk management frameworks highlight the importance of transparency and materiality in fostering sustainable corporate growth.

The empirical study on the automobile industry by K. Madhu Kishore Raghunath and colleagues, along with the detailed examination of the Bank of Bhutan's risk landscape by Soumya Pandey, provide practical perspectives on the application of risk assessment tools and resilience strategies in specific sectors.

The integration of humanitarian units in protracted crises, as proposed by Danuta Kazmierczak and her co-authors, offers a novel approach to enhancing organizational effectiveness in complex and prolonged emergency situations. Similarly, the strategic management of hospitality security amidst macro trends, as explored by Lyudmila Bovsh and her team, underscores the necessity of proactive measures in ensuring guest and staff safety.

Environmental risk assessment in airports, as introduced by Elen Paraschi, and sustainability reporting at Istanbul Airport, analyzed by Seda Ceken, provide crucial frameworks for addressing environmental pressures and aligning with international standards. Lastly, the case study on Go First's operational challenges by Baranidharan S. and colleagues offers a real-world context for understanding crisis management in the aviation industry.

In conclusion, the diverse perspectives and rigorous analyses presented in this book offer a comprehensive understanding of the multifaceted nature of risk and security in our interconnected world. It is our hope that these insights will inspire further research, inform policy decisions, and guide practical applications in risk management and security across various sectors. As we navigate the complexities of the digital age, the principles and strategies outlined herein will serve as a beacon for building a safer, more resilient, and sustainable future.

Aleksandra Zajac

American Institute of Applied Sciences in Switzerland, Switzerland

Giuseppe Catenazzo

American Institute of Applied Sciences in Switzerland, Switzerland & ICN Business School, France

Emmanuel Fragnière

University of Applied Sciences of Western Switzerland, Switzerland & University of Bath, UK

Chapter 1
Harnessing the Strength of Digital Technologies for Cybersecurity

Shilpy Verma

Amity University, Noida, India

EXECUTIVE SUMMARY

The rapidly growing digitization has positively contributed to economic growth, social development, and increased environmental protection. At the same time, it has also made socio-technical systems and its associated ecosystems more susceptible to cyber-threats. The rapid increase of technological adoption raises the need to provide a secure and sustainable cyberspace for internet users. A key concern of today's technology driven economies is cybersecurity issues. It is essential to build cyber security ecosystem and resistance to cyber threats. It should also be emphasised that sustainability, data regulation, and cybersecurity will be key to the digital transformation in the years to come. Given this, it is important to have measures (regulatory, organisational, and legal) to curb cyberattacks. This chapter intends to examine the need, strategies to follow to fight against digital threats and future steps in the building sustainable cyber security ecosystem.

1. INTRODUCTION

In recent years information technology has emerged as one of the most significant growth drivers for sustainable economic and social development. With this development, cyber security is now seen as one of the most important factors in maintaining global sustainable development. It has been noted that the United Nations Sustainable development goals (UNSDG) give priority to cyber security in

DOI: 10.4018/979-8-3693-2675-6.ch001

the form of trusted and safe cyber environment. To achieve the objectives outlined in the United Nations Sustainable Development Goals, trust in ICT or cyber space is essential. The goals of sustainable development would be challenging to attain in the absence of a secure cyberspace.

According to Cybersecurity Ventures official cybercrime report published in 2022, cybercrime is estimated to cause USD 8 trillion damages in 2023 and will grow to USD 10.5 trillion by 2025, (Yeo and yeo, n.d.). It can be the third-largest nation after China and the USA if these damages were measured as an economy. According to the 2023, Global Risks Report of the World Economic Forum, cybercrimes and cyber insecurity are among the top global risks, (Taddeo & Bosco, 2019). As the world becomes more interconnected through technologies, this ever-increasing risk will certainly spread to all corners of the world. It is therefore imperative that challenges associated with cyberspace are treated and recognised so that a reliable cyber security ecosystem can be formed. A sustainable cybersecurity ecosystem is a pre requite for securing digitally connected world from exploitation or suffering data breaches, (Walsh, 2019). The foremost cornerstone of the National Institute of Standards and Technology (NIST) Cybersecurity Framework (CSF) is to assess and mitigate cyberspace risks before controlling them. According to the Deloitte's report "the interconnected nature of Industry 4.0-driven operations and the pace of digital transformation mean that cyberattacks can have far more extensive effects than ever before." Furthermore, the number of end-to-end interconnected devices are expected to grow manifold in coming years, to reach 25.44 billion by 2030, (Sataloff, Johns, & Kost, 2019). This is expected to bring about the proliferation of cyberattacks on the government organisations, private institution and individuals associated with cyberspace. It should also be emphasised that sustainability, data regulation and cybersecurity will be foremost element to the digital transition in the years to come. Given this, it is imperative to have regulatory, organisational, and legal measures in first place to curb cyberattacks.

In the mitigation of potential risks of cybercrime, the latest cybersecurity technologies can play a key role. By adopting these technologies, organisations and individuals can safeguard themselves from potential threats and protect their information. As cybercrime landscape continues to evolve, developing an emerging technologies-based cybersecurity strategy is no longer an option, it is a necessity to prevent cyberattacks and protect sensitive data. Since, cybersecurity is a continuously evolving process, it is essential to be aware of latest cybersecurity technologies.

Machine learning, big data analytics, cloud computing, artificial intelligence and blockchain are some of the technologies helps in the prevention of cyberattacks. By utilising these technologies, potential threats can be identified and prevented on timely basis. These technologies analyse the concerned data, learn from patterns, and make predictions about these threats.

2. WHAT IS SUSTAINABLE CYBERSECURITY?

As you are already aware environmental sustainability is concerned with conservation of natural resources so that we can meet the needs of present generation without compromising the needs of the future generation. To understand the term sustainable cybersecurity, you need to consider entire data environment equivalent to physical environment. Just like environment sustainability, which focuses on protection of physical environment, sustainable cybersecurity is concerned with the protection of digital environment. Just like industrial waste pollute the river, in a similar way hacker, phisher, malware, spam messages and distributed denial-of-service attacks (DDoS) contaminate your database. For instance, a river can be polluted beyond it carrying capacity, in a similar way overuse of cyberspace, such as when limited bandwidth is consumed by too many spam messages can cause targeted websites to crash through too many requests for site access. Hence, maintaining physical and digital environment sustainability requires development of sustainable ecosystem to ensure that resources remain accessible to both current and future generation.

As we all know renewable energy sources, eco-friendly regulations and waste reductions are the foundation of sustainability. Attacks on cybersecurity often leads to operational disturbances, wastage of resources and undermines the efforts to optimize resource consumption and reduce wastage. Businesses may direct valuable resources towards remediation and recovery. Hence, concentrated efforts towards environmental sustainability and cybersecurity are crucial to make real progress towards a greener society with firm digital foundations.

Digital technology such as Internet of Things is essential to collect data and monitor environmental analytics to identify sustainable practices. If hackers attack the security of these systems, the progress gets compromise. For example, if a hacker targets a digitally equipped waste management system of a city, it can lead to waste accumulation on streets, resulting from missing pickups. By targeting critical infrastructure such as water processing facilities and power plants, cyberattacks hampers the environment sustainability efforts. Many carbons reduction plans rely on automated systems and digital technologies that manage and monitor the energy consumption, distribution, and production. At the same time, these types of solutions call for a high level of data protection and cybersecurity to mitigate potentials cyberattacks. Cyber attackers have found new means to breach security of cloud services and data centres to misappropriate valuable resources. These kinds of attacks jeopardize the creation and implementation of environmental projects that leads to inefficiencies. To safeguard their critical infrastructure against cyberattacks on their interconnected and advanced technology, many organisations need robust infrastructure.

To ensure cybersecurity sustainability, organisations need to invest in ecosystem in a way that minimizes cost, mitigates risk, and maximizes effectiveness both today and in the long run. While there is cost associated measures to mitigate cybersecurity risks, there is a bigger cost if we do not and that cost is measured not only in monetary terms, but in public safety and national security. The cyber ecosystem like natural environment comprises a variety of diverse participants, individuals, governments, non-profit firms, private organisation, cyber devices (digital technologies, software, and computers, etc) interconnected to each other. Unlike physical environment, cyberspace does not exist in any physical form. It is a complex environment that arises from the interaction of technological devices, software, people, and networks connected to it. Mainly, cybersecurity is concerned with preservation of integrity and confidentiality of information available in the cyberspace. The most significant feature of cyberattacks is that it is constantly evolving, and it is essential to develop strategies for the prevention of cyberattacks and protecting the sensitive information and data. Many attackers constantly develop new strategies and techniques to disrupt essential services, steal sensitive information or data and breach security systems.

3. CYBERCRIME AND SECURITY CHALLENGES

3.1 Internet of Things Privacy and Security: Challenges and Solutions

The term "Internet of Things" (IoT) refers to a notion of connected devices and objects of all kinds over Internet wireless or wired. It is used for various purposes such as business expansion, transportation, communication, and education. IoT introduced the concept of hyperconnectivity through which businesses and individuals may easily communicate with one another from remote locations seamlessly. According to the "State of IoT – Spring 2023" report released by IoT Analytics, worldwide the IoT networks increased by 18% in 2022, reaching a whopping 14.3 billion active IoT endpoints. Which is further expected to grow by 16% to reach 16 billion connected IoT devices by 2023 and projected to surpass 29 billion by 2027, (Sinha, 2023). The IoT has seen instant evolution during the past few decades. Although IoT has benefited many individuals, organisations are able to solve many problems in various sectors but with it comes data privacy and security challenges. Traditionally data security has been implemented at device level be it a any smart devices such as laptop or smartphone connected to the IoT network. However, today security and privacy measures would be implemented at multiple layers between IoT endpoints. The Mirai botnet attack on Dyn in 2016 is a most prominent example where vulnerabilities in IoT was exploited to flood a network or server with massive traffic to begin an extensive distributed denial of service (DDoS) attack. Which, in turn, resulted in website outages across the eastern USA, causing damage of an estimated $110 million.[1]

The issues and challenges associated with IoT are summarised in Table given below:

Table 1. Issues and challenges in IoT

Issues	Challenges
Privacy Concerns	Absence of data protection collected by IoT devices
	Inability to recognize the privacy expectations of users and lack of privacy protection models for IoT
	No strict rules against data collection and use
Security Issues	There is lack of resources to train future generations in secure IoT design
	Lack of standardise metrics to identify the security of IoT devices
	Lack of an optimally controlled role in the communication models of IoT devices to prevent the risk of hijacking and cyber attacks
	Development of IoT device or software without the security laws

3.2 Phishing Attacks

Phishing attacks are among the most prevalent kinds of cyberattacks that are usually done with intention of stealing the confidential information like login details, personal data, credit card information for financial gains or to install malware on victim's machine. It is a type of cybersecurity attack which starts with fraudulent message or email received by victim from malicious actors. The message is written to look as though it comes from trusted entity or sender. These messages are designed to coax the recipient, causing them perform actions like clicking malicious link, installing a malicious file and divulge their confidential information such as access credentials. A most common example of phishing attack involves tricking a recipient into clicking a malicious website link from his designated email. The scammers then ask for login information which the receiver readily provides, believing that it is from a trusted source. In this way, the scammers or hackers ensures that they obtained the information they needed.

In January 2021, according to Statista (2021), there were approximately 245,771 phishing attacks were recorded These days attackers around the world are getting more tricks and ideas for planning their attacks. There is a need to develop processes or techniques to promote cyber security against attacks. One of those cyber security strategies are AI driven. Many organisations have achieved great results by investing in AI-based cyber security systems through which employees are given training to protect sensitive information from phishing attacks, (Alhashmi, Darem, & Abawajy, 2021). AI-based cyber security measures focus on promoting more security by educating individuals on the cyber security this reduces their chance of getting attacked as compared to individual who lacks awareness. Therefore, more organisations should implement AI-based cyber security awareness measures to prevent phishing attacks, thereby reducing the number of phishing attacks globally.

3.3 Ransomware Attacks

Ransomware attacks involve transmitting malicious software that can cause irretrievable damage to victim's data and computer. By encrypting the files stored on it and locking the device, it revokes your access to your data. To restore access to your data or unlock your computer, ransomware attackers demand payment for doing it. This is frequently done through anonymous websites or emails that demand payments in bitcoin or cryptocurrency. Unfortunately, despite paying the ransom access to data and device is not guaranteed and victims may lose not only their money but also any sensitive data they may have stored on their devices.

Furthermore, there is no foolproof defence against ransomware attacks, and even the finest security precautions may not be adequate if hackers are persistent enough. Additionally, a lot of new ransomware variations are always being created, so keeping up with these developments is essential for protection against such attacks. There are certain recommendations that are not exhaustive but provide best strategy for securing systems and networks, which are as follows:

- Consider restricting internet access: consider restricting access to the most common ransomware entry points, such as social media accounts or personal email. Also, use a proxy server to access the internet and consider using an ad blocker.
- Use a backup system that lets you save multiple copies of the backups, even if one copy contains encrypted or malicious files. Test your backups for functionality and integrity on a regular basis.
- Use anti-spam and antivirus solutions. Perform regular scans of your system and network with anti-virus programs turned on so signatures can be updated automatically. Use an anti-spam solution to block phishing emails before they can reach your network. Consider adding a spam alert to all emails received from unknown sources that warn you of the risks of clicking on a link and opening an attachment.
- Provide phishing and social engineering training to employees. Encourage them to avoid opening suspicious emails, to avoid clicking on the links or

attachments in emails, and to exercise caution before visiting unfamiliar websites.

3.4 Cloud Attacks

Cloud computing is the on-demand delivery of computing services-including software, database storage system, servers, networks, information and analytics-over the internet ("the cloud"), without proper user control and direct management. Organisations can rent access to everything from database storage to applications from a cloud service owners instead of managing their own data centres or computing infrastructure. Cloud computing has evolved over the years to offer number of benefits to users. One benefit includes reduce complexity and cost of maintaining and purchasing their own IT infrastructure, instead organisations can simply pay for services when they use it. By offering the similar services to many customers, cloud computing service providers can achieve significant economies of scale in its operations and maximise efficiency.

Cloud computing, which was first introduced only as a simple backup storage option, has now evolved into a broad computing platform that has completely transformed the way businesses store, handle and exchange data. Therefore, it's crucial to understand what a cloud attack entails so that your business can develop a defence mechanism against them. A cloud attack involves targeting an off-site service platform that provides software, computing, storage, and hosting services through its cloud infrastructure through malicious activities. The adoption of cloud computing services by an organisation means that a significant part of the data, network, applications, and systems are under the control of third-party. The cloud computing top threat includes the following:

- Denial of Service: This kind of attack on the cloud makes the data services applications inaccessible to the intended user. In this attack regular traffic becomes challenging to process as attackers flood service or application or a targeted machine with lots of requests resulting in denial-of service to requesters, (Iwendi *et al.*, 2021).
- Data Loss: A situation in information systems in which data is lost due to transmission, processing, or storage failure, (Mell & Grance, 2011).
- Account Hijacking: In this cloud account of organisation or individual is hijacked by attacker. A sort of identity theft in which the attackers engage in unauthorized activity using the stolen account information, (Mell & Grance, 2011).

- Data Breaches: It is a risk involving breach of security where confidential, private or sensitive information is stolen, copied, sent, viewed, taken, or used by anyone who does not have the authority to do so, (Abazari *et al.,* 2019).

To protect against cyber-attacks, it is essential to keep data backups for facilitating recovery on account of any disaster. To guarantee data availability, it must be regularly backed up and maintained in accordance with security standards to ward off any kind of attack like hacking and unauthorized access.

4. CYBERSECURITY BREACHES IN THE PAST

4.1 Department of Health Care Policy and Financing, USA

In August 2023, in one of the biggest data leaks and hacks to have hit the USA, the personal and healthcare data of over 10 million people was stolen by group of hackers, targeting IBM. "The data was hacked because the IBM, a third-party vendor uses the MOVEit file transfer software application to move Colorado Department of Health Care Policy and Financing (HCPF) data files in the normal course of business. Clop, a Russian-speaking cybercriminal group, has claimed responsibility for breaching dozens of organisations by exploiting the vulnerability and many have confirmed that they were affected. Information the unauthorized actor may have accessed includes, full names, social security numbers, Medicaid identification numbers, Medicare ID numbers, Date of Birth, home address and contact information, demographic or income information, clinical and medical information such as diagnosis, condition, lab results, medication or other treatment information, health insurance information."

4.2 Yahoo! Inc.

Marking the one of the largest data breaches ever, Yahoo in 2016 first announced publicly that theft of data and information of over 0.5 billion users accounts had taken place during 2014. The state sponsored hackers accessed the information like names, hashed passwords, email address, telephone numbers, birthdays and, in some cases unencrypted or encrypted security questions and answers. Yahoo further disclosed that the hacked data "did not include bank account information, payment card data or unprotected passwords, (Trautman & Ormerod, 2016). The hack of Yahoo users accounts was claimed by hackers Canadian Karim Baratov and Latvian Alexey Belan. A series of phishing emails containing malware download link was sent by hackers Baratov and Belan to Yahoo! Employees. All it took was one employee click to allow hackers access to the company's network. Once within the network, their goal was to locate the user database and any internal tools that may be used to change the data. Both objectives of this significant cyberattack were swiftly achieved. They made a back door on a Yahoo! server so they wouldn't lose network access.

4.3 Aadhaar Card: Cybersecurity Issues

In 2009, Aadhaar card was issued to all Indian residents, which is a 12-digit unique identity number that was developed to ease the transfer of money to citizens of the country from government schemes. The process of issuing the 'Aadhaar Card' involves retina and face scan as well as the collection of citizens' fingerprints. With almost 1.2 billion enrolments, it is one of the largest biometric databases on the world and accounts for about 89% of India's population. The world's largest ID database, Aadhaar, (The Financial Express, 2018), was breached by malicious actors in the year 2018, revealing information on more than 1.1 billion Indian individuals, including their biometric information like iris scans and fingerprint, emails, names, addresses and phone numbers. The problem exacerbated to such a level, that one could access confidential Aadhaar database simply by Googling it.

The malicious actors hacked into the Aadhaar database through the website of state utility Indane, which is connected to the government database through an API that allows apps to retrieve data stored by other apps or software. Unfortunately, Indianan's API lacked access control, which made its data vulnerable. Hackers sold access to the data through a WhatsApp group for just $7. Despite warnings from security researchers and technology groups, it took until March 23, 2018, for Indian authorities to take the vulnerable access point offline.

4.4 LinkedIn Data Breach

LinkedIn is a social networking platform, where individuals and business professionals connect with each other. In 2021, a Dark Web forum hacker exposed database of 700 million LinkedIn members for sale. It contained information such as profile picture, name, phone numbers, email-Id, and gender. This data breach affected nearly 92% of LinkedIn members out of the total 756 million users accounts, (Bhadouria, 2022). This massive amount of data containing personal information allowed other bad actors to launch social engineering attacks against targeted users. To extract personal information data, hackers utilised the LinkedIn API. Combining this data with other API sources allowed an adversary to create a master list of data that is maliciously sold over the Internet. Since most of the LinkedIn users are of business type, attackers greatly benefit from this theft.

4.5 Facebook Data Breach

The social media network giant was involved in a large-scale data breach scandal in March 2018, in which Cambridge Analytica the British political consulting firm obtained the personal data of about 87 million users for political purposes without their permission and utilised it for political campaign purpose such as US presidential elections of 2016 and Brexit Vote Leave campaign, (Duarte, 2020). Cambridge Analytica uses the data to determine voter behaviour and personality traits, which, in turn, was utilised to help conservative campaigns target online messaging and advertisements, (Rosenberg *et al.,* 2018). In this era of digital global economy, cybersecurity attacks, identity theft, ransomware and data breaches have become ubiquitous. The leaked data often provide confidential information to cybercriminals who use the personal information to scam and impersonate individuals into handing over confidential login credentials.

5. STRATEGIES FOR SUSTAINABLE CYBERSECURITY ECOSYSTEM

Environmental sustainability and cybersecurity sustainability can occasionally coincide with each other, particularly when it comes to the technology selected to promote the cybersecurity. For example, consider the cloud provider that power their data centres with renewable energy or business firm that responsibly recycle the laptops, servers, IoT and other electronic devices when they reach end of life. Cybersecurity promotes environmental sustainability by encouraging the responsible usage of technology, safeguarding the vital infrastructure and tackle new issues in the digital sphere.

Cybersecurity awareness and education programs are vital in promoting responsible digital practices within the environmental community. By educating stakeholders about potential cyber risks, best practices for data protection, and privacy breaches, cybersecurity helps individuals and organizations make informed decisions when implementing sustainable solutions. The awareness programs empower the individuals to mitigate cybersecurity risks at the same time ensuring the positive environmental influence of their initiatives.

Cybersecurity promotes environmental sustainability by educating individuals to make more environment sensitive decisions, fostering the development of environmentally friendly technologies, protecting critical infrastructure, addressing cybersecurity risks in sustainable technologies. It includes systems that control and monitor smart grids, waste management networks, renewable energy generation. By preserving the integrity and ensuring the availability of these systems, cybersecurity helps overcome the interruptions that contributes towards environmental deterioration and could hamper the sustainability efforts.

Cybersecurity aims to protect data from attackers, which is essential for all private and public organisations as well as to all individuals, it is an integral part of mitigation of cyber threat strategies. It contributes towards more resilient and safer environment by ensuring the availability of confidential and integral digital ecosystem. It broadly covers the preservation and inception of processes concerned with detection of forthcoming cyberthreats and the minimisation of associated costs, (Ahmed, 2019). Cyberthreats are rapidly increasing due to complex and menace plans and motives to attack the information system. Given current scenario, it is in everyone's best interest to work to achieve cyberspace sustainability and protect the data environment from malware, ransomware attacks and hackers, (Penzenstadler *et al.*, 2014). In fact, the development of sustainable cybersecurity ecosystem is a prerequisite for efficient functioning of contemporary technology-based society. The essence of sustainable cybersecurity is to deliver outcomes or maintain productivity despite any attack that occurs. Moreover, be prepared rather than being unrealistic by expecting cyberattacks to be completely avoidable. As a part of a robust cybersecurity strategy, it is critical to have competent people everywhere to identify the threat and build the cybersecurity ecosystem responses and defences, (Evans & Reeder, 2010).

5.1 Cyber Risks and Preventive Strategies

5.1.2 Artificial Intelligence (AI) and Machine Learning (ML) for Sustainable Cybersecurity

By utilizing technologies such as Artificial Intelligence and Machine Learning, cybersecurity experts can identify and respond to threats more accurately and faster than ever before. These technologies analyse vast amounts of data, learn from patterns, and predict potential threats. The cyberthreat landscape is constantly changing. Digital technologies such as AI and ML can be used by both cybersecurity experts and data hackers to enhance their capabilities. While cybersecurity experts can use it to detect and prevent these attacks, data hackers can use these technologies launch cyberattacks. MI and AI can be used to design extremely convincing phishing emails that can launch personalised and targeted attacks. These emails are designed in a way that can trick even the most vigilant users into downloading infected attachments or clicking on malicious links. "To triggers false negatives in antivirus software or to create sophisticated malware that mimics benign software attackers would use machine learning algorithms. These technologies can also be used by attackers to commit fraud. Machine learning algorithms can be used to manipulate transaction data, such as creating fake credit card transactions. These fraudulent transactions may be difficult to distinguish from legitimate transactions, causing direct financial losses to organisations and individuals".

Although AI and ML can be utilised to escape traditional cybersecurity measures but at the same time it can also be used to leverage and strengthen those measures. These technologies can be used to identify any suspicious activity that may indicate any type of cyberattack. To identify unauthorised access, failed logins and other anomalies, AI and ML specifically uses User Entity and Behaviour Analytics (UEBA) platforms. For instance, sophisticated antivirus software may utilize AI and ML to quickly identify the behaviour of malicious software and develop an attack profile that may be used to detect similar activity, perhaps elimination further action of the same kind. Antivirus programs and firewalls can use AI and ML to learn from prior attacks and instantly adjust to new threats.

Moreover, AI and ML can be applied to Security Orchestration, Automation and Response (SOAR) solutions for cyberthreat mitigation, detection, and prevention, (Kinyua & Awuah, 2021). To increase the effectiveness of physical and digital security operations, SOAR platforms are used. SOAR is a software program that many organisations use to respond to security breaches and collect data about security threats with no or little human assistance. Machine learning, for instance, can be used to categorize warnings and decide which ones demand quick attention. It can also be used to examine previous occurrences and the measures taken in response to automate tedious operations that might improve speed, be more accurate, and accelerate incident response, (Rapid 7, 2020).

The role of AI and ML in cybersecurity is rapidly evolving. Both defenders and attackers are prompted to enhance their capabilities by harnessing the full potential of these technologies.

5.1.3 Machine Learning in Phishing and Malware Detection

One of the most common social engineering attacks are phishing attacks targeting users' email to deceptively steal sensitive and confidential information. To mitigate and detect these attacks, a numerous anti-phishing techniques have been developed over the last few decades, which still inaccurate and inefficient. Hence, to counter these attacks, there is a need for developing an accurate and efficient detection technique. Machine learning tends to learn the features of phishing websites and predict whether the websites are legitimate or phishing, (Alswailem *et al.,* 2019). Phishers use several approaches, such as phishing Uniform Resource Locators (URL), email, text messages, telephone calls and forum postings to steal users' information. The conventional method of detecting malicious URLs involves creating blacklist of such URLs based on manual opinions or user reports. However, malicious URLs not on the blacklist are continuously increasing. Thus, to identify an exhaustive blacklist of malicious URLs is almost impossible, (Wu, Kuo, & Yang, 2019). Machine Learning (ML) techniques based on the learning of computer can be used to identify malicious URLs, (Zamir *et al.*, 2019). The optimum mapping between the d-dimensional vector space and the output variable is found during the training phase of the ML method. Compared to the blacklist approach, this method offers a significant generalization capability to detect unknown malicious URLs, (Almseidin *et al.*, 2019).

5.1.4 Intrusion Detection System (IDS) and Prevention System (IPS)

Intrusion detection system is a software designed to monitor a system or network to detect any kind of potential threat or malicious activity. Any intrusion or anomalous activity is recorded centrally using a security information and event management system, which is notified further to an administration. Intrusion prevention system takes this detection one step forward, acts own it's on to block any intrusion and shuts down the network to prevent any movement in it. Whenever a configuration error, virus or security breach is notified, an IDS send an alert to organisation security staff and may remove malicious intruder from the network.

Intrusion detection and prevention is one of the main concerns for today's organisation cybersecurity, which is accomplished by IDS. Which when combined with Machine learning solutions is likely to improve the effectiveness of IDS, (Frontiers Media, n.d.). To detect threats against endpoint devices, cloud, IoT, IDS can exploit ML, (Almseidin *et al.*, 2017).

5.1.5 Big Data Analytics in Cybersecurity

About 51 percent of surveyed organisations based on a survey of 1,296 business leaders across 53 countries have experienced fraud or some form of economic crime, according to PWC's Global Economic Crime and Fraud Survey 2022 (2022). It was also revealed by the survey that cybercrime was the foremost source of fraud in technology, media, and telecommunication sector (50 percent), followed by health (40 percent), government and public sector (36 percent) and industrial manufacturing (32 percent).

Due to increasing engineered threats (advanced persistent threats, malware, phishing, etc) and rapidly growing complexity of networks (wireless connections, Internet of Things, smart devices, etc), cybersecurity is experiencing big data challenge. The emerging technology, big data analytics offers the capability to process, store, collect, and visualize enormous cybersecurity data, which are so complex and large that traditional data processing techniques are inadequate to deal with them. Unlike traditional technologies which focuses on analysing logs and alerts generated by web application firewalls, firewalls, and proxy servers. The big data analytics detects the cyberthreat more quickly and respond to it effortlessly. These tools can identify emails and attachments that contain suspicious content, unusual login attempts, recurrent large-volume financial transactions or any other learned suspicious behaviours. It outlines the severity and the nature of a problem, provide detailed reports and alerts to mitigate future digital threat, which requires minimal manual intervention.

Cyber experts can detect vulnerabilities by creating a baseline scenario for normal activities. Any variation from normal activity can be detected with the help of big data analytics, which, in turn, will enable to predict cyber-attacks beforehand. Big data analytics facilitate continuous monitoring of the cyberspace through automated monitoring and real time detection of threat. Using big data analytics, cyber experts across the world are building a network which can effectively analyse large scale data to combat advance cyber threat, (Kshetri, 20210. Automation of entire work-flow system using ML and AL technologies combined with big data analytics will enable real-time identification of data security and privacy breaches.

5.1.6 Blockchain Technology

Blockchain is a digital ledger for storing digital asset data in a way that it is impossible to change or hack the data. It is basically a digital ledger of transactions which are distributed throughout the electronic device that maintain the duplicated copies of the chain. An important feature of this technology is decentralisation as no one organisation or computer can own the chain. A record of transaction is added to all the network of computers whenever a new transaction occurs on the chain. The decentralised database managed by several networks or devices is termed as distributed ledger technology (DLT). This technology has in-built transparency and enhanced security as every action in the digital ledger can be easily traced, viewed, and checked, which is expected to solve today's cybersecurity breaches. Today blockchain technology is used by multiple industries such as education, energy, logistics, etc, as its decentralised network ensures that data is verified and stored on multiple networks, making it effective cybersecurity solution.

Another benefit of blockchain technology in cybersecurity is its ability to maintain records of cyber-attacks and threats. Security professionals can harness the potential of blockchain technology to identify attack patterns and implement enhanced security measures by analysing the stored and recorded information about attacks on a blockchain network. This can enable swift incident response and mitigate potential threats.

6. EMERGING TRENDS AND POTENTIAL AREAS FOR FURTHER RESEARCH

In the post COVID-19 era, many researchers have examined the role of cyber-security in digital transformation. Many other studies have focused on the role of cybersecurity in the Internet of things, (Rudenko *et al.*, 2022), machine learning, (Aiyanyo, Samuel, & Lim, 2020), big data analytics, (Rawat, Doku, & Garuba, 2021), and blockchain-based systems, (Schlatt *et al.*, 2022). Several studies examined the components of cybersecurity such as cyber risk management, cybercrime, cyber-attack, and cyber threat. Despite these studies, there is apparent need for comprehensive research that outlines a clear understanding of digital technologies that contributes towards cybersecurity. The landscape of cybersecurity ecosystem is constantly evolving, from new defense mechanisms, techniques and attacks, it's continuously changing. Thus, future research needs to fill the gap in the literature and examine how emerging digital technologies such as AI, cloud computing, internet of things and blockchain technologies can strengthen the cybersecurity ecosystem.

7. CONCLUSION

As we all are aware that increasing number of individuals across the globe are becoming more reliant on digital infrastructure and information communications technology for seamless access to communication, information, and efficient service delivery. This interconnectivity creates vulnerabilities in the form of cyberattacks such as phishing, malware, ransomware, and cloud attack, etc. The rapid prevalence of cybercrime exhibits the significance and need of cybersecurity against such attacks. The absence of fully secured cyberspace would make it difficult to fully acquire the benefits of digital transformation.

As the cybercrime landscape continues to evolve, the complete prevention of cybercrime is an impossible task. For instance, one cannot prevent the creation of socially engineered phishing webpage, but such a threat can be mitigated by detecting that a given webpage is compromised and warning the users before they fall victim to phishing. Hence, most cybersecurity technologies focus on threat detection.

In the mitigation of potential risks of cybercrime, the latest cybersecurity technologies can play a key role. By adopting these technologies, organizations and individuals can protect themselves from potential threats and safeguard their information. As cybercrime landscape continues to evolve, developing an emerging technologies-based cybersecurity strategy is no longer an option, it is a necessity to prevent cyberattacks and protect sensitive data. Since cybersecurity is a continuously evolving process, it is essential to be aware of the latest cybersecurity technologies.

Artificial intelligence, machine learning, cloud computing, big data analytics and blockchain are some of the technologies helps in the prevention or detection of cyberattacks. By utilizing these technologies, potential threats can be identified and prevented on a timely basis. These technologies analyze the concerned data, learn from patterns, and make predictions about these threats. These technologies can be used to identify any suspicious activity that may indicate any type of cyberattack. To identify unauthorized access, failed logins, and other anomalies.

Security professionals can harness the potential of blockchain technology to identify attack patterns and implement enhanced security measures by analyzing the stored and recorded information about attacks on a blockchain network. Cyber experts can detect vulnerabilities by creating a baseline scenario for normal activities. Any variation from normal activity can be detected with the help of big data analytics, which, in turn, will enable us to predict cyber-attacks beforehand. Big data analytics facilitate continuous monitoring of cyberspace through automated monitoring and real time detection of threats.

The cyberthreat landscape is constantly changing. Digital technologies such as AI and ML can be used by both cybersecurity experts and data hackers to enhance their capabilities. While cybersecurity experts can use it to detect and prevent these attacks, data hackers can use these technologies to launch cyberattacks. Although AI and ML can be utilized to escape traditional cybersecurity measures but at the same time it can also be used to leverage and strengthen those measures. These technologies can be used to identify any suspicious activity that may indicate any type of cyberattack.

REFERENCES

Aadhaar Now World's Largest Biometric Database. (2018). *5 Facts from UIDAI CEO's Presentation in Supreme Court You Must Know*. The Financial Express.

Abazari, F., Analoui, M., Takabi, H., & Fu, S. (2019). MOWS: Multi-objective workflow scheduling in cloud computing based on heuristic algorithm. *Simulation Modelling Practice and Theory*, 93, 119–132. DOI: 10.1016/j.simpat.2018.10.004

Ahmed, M. (2019). Data summarization: A survey. *Knowledge and Information Systems*, 58(2), 249–273. DOI: 10.1007/s10115-018-1183-0

Aiyanyo, I. D., Samuel, H., & Lim, H. (2020). A Systematic Review of Defensive and Offensive Cybersecurity with Machine Learning. *Applied Sciences (Basel, Switzerland)*, 10(17), 5811. Advance online publication. DOI: 10.3390/app10175811

Alhashmi, A., Darem, A., & Abawajy, J. (2021). Taxonomy of Cyber security Awareness Delivery Methods: A Countermeasure for Phishing Threats. *International Journal of Advanced Computer Science and Applications*, 12(10). Advance online publication. DOI: 10.14569/IJACSA.2021.0121004

Almseidin, M., Zuraiq, A. A., Al-kasassbeh, M., & Alnidami, N. (2019). Phishing detection based on machine learning and feature selection methods. International Journal of Interactive Mobile Technology, 13(12), 171–183. DOI: 10.3991/ijim. v13i12.11411

Alswailem, A., Alabdullah, B., Alrumayh, N., & Alsedrani, A. (2019). Detecting Phishing Websites Using Machine Learning. 2nd International Conference on Computer Applications & Information Security (ICCAIS).

Bhadouria, A. S. (2022). Study of: Impact of Malicious Attacks and Data Breach on the Growth and Performance of the Company and Few of the World's Biggest Data Breaches. *International Journal of Scientific and Research Publications*, 10(10), 1–11. DOI: 10.29322/IJSRP.X.2022.p091095

Big Data Analytics for Cyber Security and Advance Persistent Threat Intelligence. (n.d.). Frontiers Media. https://www.frontiersin.org/research-topics/37830/big-data-analytics-for-cyber-security-and-advance-persistent-threat-intelligence

Duarte, R. P. G. M. (2020). Case Study: Facebook in face of crisis (Doctoral dissertation).

Evans, K., & Reeder, F. (2010). *A human capital crisis in cybersecurity: Technical proficiency matters*. CSIS.

Iwendi, C., Rehman, S. U., Javed, A. R., Khan, S., & Srivastava, G. (2021). Sustainable Security for the Internet of Things Using Artificial Intelligence Architectures. *ACM Transactions on Internet Technology*, 21(3), 1–22. DOI: 10.1145/3448614

Kinyua, J., & Awuah, L. (2021). AI/ML in Security Orchestration, Automation and Response: Future Research Directions. *Intelligent Automation & Soft Computing*, 28(2), 527–545. DOI: 10.32604/iasc.2021.016240

Mohammad, A., Maen, A., Szilveszter, K., & Mouhammd, A. 2017. Evaluation of machine learning algorithms for intrusion detection system. In *Proceedings of the IEEE 15th International Symposium on Intelligent Systems and Informatics (SISY'17)*. IEEE.

Nir, K. (2021). Economics of artificial intelligence in cybersecurity. *IT Professional*, 23(5), 73–77. DOI: 10.1109/MITP.2021.3100177

Penzenstadler, B., Raturi, A., Richardson, D., & Tomlinson, B. (2014). Safety, security, now sustainability: The nonfunctional requirement for the 21st century. *IEEE Software*, 31(3), 40–47. DOI: 10.1109/MS.2014.22

PM. Mell, T.Grance, NIST Definition of Cloud Computing. (2011). (pp. 800–145). National Institute., DOI: 10.6028/NIST.SP.800-145

PWC's Global Economic Crime and Fraud Survey. (2022). Protecting the perimeter: A new frontier of platform fraud. https://www.pwc.com/gx/en/forensics/gecsm -2022/pdf/PwC%E2%80%99s-Global-Economic-Crime-and-Fraud-Survey-2022.pdf

Rapid 7. (2020). Catching modern threats: InsightIDR detection methodologies. Available: https:// www.rapid7.com/resources

Rawat, D. B., Doku, R., & Garuba, M. (2021). Cybersecurity in Big Data Era: From Securing Big Data to Data-Driven Security. *IEEE Transactions on Services Computing*, 14(6), 2055–2072. DOI: 10.1109/TSC.2019.2907247

Rosenberg, M. (2018). How Trump Consultants Exploited the Facebook Data of Millions. *The New York Times*. https://www.nytimes.com/2018/03/17/us/politics/ cambridge-analytica-trump-campaign.html

Rudenko, R., Pires, I. M., Oliveira, P., Barroso, J., & Reis, A. (2022). A Brief Review on Internet of Things, Industry 4.0 and Cybersecurity. *Electronics (Basel)*, 11(11), 1742. Advance online publication. DOI: 10.3390/electronics11111742

Sataloff, R.T., Johns, M.M., & Kost, K.M. (2019). Industry 4.0 and cybersecurity Managing risk in an age of connected production. Academic Press.

Schlatt, V., Guggenberger, T., Schmid, J., & Urbach, N. (2022). Attacking the Trust Machine: Developing an Information Systems Research Agenda for Blockchain Cybersecurity. *International Journal of Information Management*. Advance online publication. DOI: 10.1016/j.ijinfomgt.2022.102470

Sinha, S. (2023). State of IoT 2023: Number of connected IoT devices growing 16% to 16.7 billion globally. IoT Analytics. https://iot-analytics.com/number-connected -iot-devices/

Statista. (2021). Potential scenarios of AI-enabled cyberattacks worldwide as of 2021. https://www.statista.com/statistics/1235395/worldwide-ai-enabled-cy berattackscompanies/

Taddeo, M., & Bosco, F. (2019). We Must Treat Cybersecurity as a Public Good: Here's Why. Accessed at https://www.weforum.org/agenda/2019/08/we-must-treat -cybersecurity-like-public-good/

Trautman, L. J., & Ormerod, P. C. (2016). Corporate directors' and officers' cyber-security standard of care: The Yahoo data breach. *The American University Law Review*, 66(5), 1231.

Walsh, K. (2019). Continuous Monitoring Drives Sustainable Cybersecurity. Accessed at https://www.zeguro.com/blog/continuous-monitoring-sustainable-cybersecurity

Wu, C. Y., Kuo, C. C., & Yang, C. S. (2019). A phishing detection system based on machine learning. *2019 International Conference on Intelligent Computing and its Emerging Applications (ICEA)*, 28–32. DOI: 10.1109/ICEA.2019.8858325

Yeo and yeo. (2023). Cybercrime to cost the World 8 trillion annually in 2023. Accessed from https://www.yeoandyeo.com/resource/cybercrime-to-cost-the-world -8-trillion-in-2023

Zamir, A., Khan, H. U., Iqbal, T., Yousaf, N., Aslam, F., Anjum, A., & Hamdani, M. (2019). Phishing web site detection using diverse machine learning algorithms. *The Electronic Library*, 38(1), 65–80. DOI: 10.1108/EL-05-2019-0118

KEY TERMS AND DEFINITIONS

Distributed Denial-of-Service (DDoS): It is a malicious attack attempted to disrupt the normal traffic of a targeted server, service or network by overwhelming the target or its surrounding infrastructure with a flood of Internet traffic.

Intrusion Detection System: It is a device or software application that monitors a network for malicious activity or policy violations. Any malicious activity or violation is typically reported or collected centrally using a security information and event management system.

Intrusion Prevention System: It is a network security tool (which can be a hardware device or software) that continuously monitors a network for malicious activity and takes action to prevent it, including reporting, blocking, or dropping it, when it does occur.

Mirai: Mirai is malware that turns networked devices running Linux into remotely controlled bots that can be used as part of a botnet in large-scale network attacks. It primarily targets online consumer devices such as IP cameras and home routers.

Security Orchestration, Automation, and Response (SOAR): It is a group of cybersecurity technologies that allow organizations to respond to some incidents automatically.

User Entity and Behaviour Analytics: It is a security software that uses behavioural analytics and machine learning to identify abnormal and potentially dangerous user and device behaviour.

Uniform Resource Locators: A URL (Uniform Resource Locator) is a unique identifier used to locate a resource on the Internet. It is also referred to as a web address..

ENDNOTE

[1]   *What is the Mirai Botnet?* Cloudflare. Available from: https://www.cloudflare.com/learning/ddos/glossary/mirai-botnet/

Chapter 2
Security of the Tomorrow's Cyber Physical Systems

Ankur Biswas
Adamas University, India

Abhishek Roy
Adamas University, India

Priyadarshini Tikader
Vidyasagar University, India

Dharmesh Dhabliya
https://orcid.org/0000-0002-6340 -2993
Vishwakarma Institute of Information Technology, India

Kirti H. Wanjale
https://orcid.org/0000-0003-4271 -504X
Vishwakarma Institute of Information Technology, India

Sabyasachi Pramanik
https://orcid.org/0000-0002-9431 -8751
Haldia Institute of Technology, India

Ankur Gupta
https://orcid.org/0000-0002-4651 -5830
Vaish College of Engineering, India

EXECUTIVE SUMMARY

The industrial sector has emerged as a hub for research on the quickly emerging field of smart technology throughout the last few decades. Smart technology (ST) included a wide range of cutting-edge technologies, such as block chains, artificial intelligence, cyberphysical production systems, internet of things, industrial internet of things (IOT), and systematic data analysis. The authors provide an overview of numerous smart technologies that may be used to control the complex properties of computer and sensor technologies, with the goal of reducing the gap between people and robots. This chapter presents the whole literature evaluation on the use of ST to enhance the production and maintenance of machinery and equipment, as well as

DOI: 10.4018/979-8-3693-2675-6.ch002

potential risks to ST. This chapter also includes the survey report that compares the adoption rate of the current technology to that of the previous five years in an effort to lower the amount of human labor needed in the industrial sector by utilizing a variety of sensors, affordable techniques, and real-time results.

INTRODUCTION

Numerous themes are causing major change in CPSs: increased integration of the IoT. The IoT, that is the technique of linking physical objects to the internet via the use of sensors and other devices, is becoming more integrated with it. One of the most significant future advances in cybersecurity is the usage of AI and ML technology. Large data sets may be analysed by these clever algorithms, which can also spot patterns or abnormalities that can point to a possible cyberthreat. CPSs combine sensing, computing, and network to attach physical architecture and entities to the Internet and to each other. NSF is at the forefront of driving advancements in the fundamental knowledge and abilities required to implement cyber-physical systems. The three main components of a CPS are a distributed cyber system, a networking and transmission element, and a physical system, as seen in Figure 1. The architecture of CPSs consists of distributed hardware, software, and network components integrated in physical systems and surroundings. They combine cyber (computation and communication) and physical (sensors and actuators) capabilities. CPS is used in almost every sector and environment, including building systems, manufacturing, aerospace, electric power grids, healthcare, and automobiles. The three Cs of ideal security are coordinated, integrated, and all-encompassing. Cybercriminals are always devising new tactics to prey on huge organizations, governments, and compact and mid-extension organizations. The protection of data, software, and hardware on internet-connected devices against cyberthreats is known as cybersecurity.

Figure 1. Distributed components of a cyber system

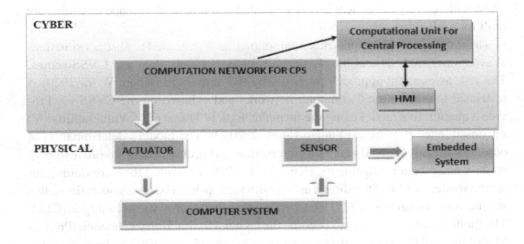

The technique is utilized by both people and organizations to prevent unlawful entry to data centres and various digital infrastructures. The event is bringing together the four Ps of cyber security: people, process, policy, and partners in order to establish a culture that is aware of cyber risk. Reaction times can be accelerated, early failure detection can be achieved, and bandwidth can be utilized effectively using CPS. CPS is a component of cloud computing that may provide users with resources based on their need. Physical security and cybersecurity have always been seen as two separate endeavours. However, integrating cybersecurity with physical security may also improve threat detection and response capabilities, boost overall security posture, and save costs. Physical assaults may breach or destroy information systems, but cyberattacks pose significant risks and can cause physical components to fail.

LITERATURE REVIEW

The field of cybersecurity is highly wide, and it may be difficult to identify hostile activity on a network. It is often harder to assess and model cybersecurity since cyber defenders have less resources and knowledge.

On the other side, the widely used IoT applications add a lot of uncertainty to the CPS; unforeseen or poorly managed risks result in a highly competitive infrastructure for a cyber defence. In the case of the medical and healthcare industries, compromised security may result in both financial loss and human peril. The hostile actors use socially engineered assaults or take advantage of system weaknesses. Vulnerability detection, reporting, and repair may be a time-consuming and laborious procedure. Reducing or eliminating the effects of cyberattacks is mostly dependent on how effectively dependencies are modelled and how well defence measures are built for each cyber-terrain.

(Mittal, S. et al. 2020) presents a paradigm that is restricted to abstract situational awareness analysis and mostly depends on past assault data and CVSS scores. The risk assessment approach proposed by the authors in (Khan, W. Z. 2020) is restricted to conventional computer networks and is based on the CVSS v3. Provide a quantitative model using the formula "Risk = Threat (T) x Vulnerability (V) x Consequence (C)" as in (Yuqian Lu et al. 2020). The model's determination of outcomes mostly depends on SME interaction and previous data. In order to help readers make better judgements, (Kusiak, A. 2019) presented their continuing research model that links the digital assets with the top-level business operations. In a similar vein, researchers at MITRE Corporation propose crown jewel analysis (CJA). The model is later upgraded to become the Cyber Mission Impact Business Process Modelling tool (CMIA), with the representation of cyber interdependence between assets being its primary achievement. Additionally, the authors of (Thomas D et al. 2019) provide a comprehensive solution that objectively assesses cybersecurity threats and offers recommendations for implementing the best protection possible against such risks. In order to strengthen overall security posture, (Yao, X. et al. 2019) presents Cauldron, a modelling and visualisation tool that maps the whole network and possible cyber-attacks using scenarios. Government agencies only have access to the CMIA model and other models recommended by MITRE Corporation that are more theoretical in nature and lack implementation specifics. Cauldron is also a component of military-funded research that is lacking in granularity and more oriented towards application.

WHERE THESE SECURITY TECHNOLOGIES CAN BE USED

Combining information and control systems into cyber-physical systems exposes them, for the most part, to threats of attacks on their information systems as well as the possibility of environmental and public health risks from physical systems controlled by failed or malfunctioning control systems. For this reason, it is especially crucial to consider the risks associated with combined information and control systems. Let's use the rapidly expanding example of autonomous automobiles as an illustration of how information and control systems might be combined, and consider the liability implications for a business-like Google that is leading the way in this field of study. Google is a provider of software. Software usage agreements clearly indicate in capital letters that the seller disclaims all responsibility for the software's proper operation and for any resultant damages. That is to say, most software producers will only agree to repair the issue (typically with a patch) or reimburse the purchase price of the product if it malfunctions or fails (or if a software-based service fails). Compare this to the responsibilities taken on by automakers. The manufacturer is required to make a concerted effort to recall and repair all impacted cars in the event of a safety issue. Vehicle control software has already had problems; Toyota's uncontrollably high acceleration problems were one such instance, however the involvement of software bugs was never established.

It is important to highlight that the frameworks being examined in the Toyota instance fall within the "control and administrative software" classification in Figure 2, not the "data processing software" group on the left of the figure.

But when its data-processing navigation system is interfaced with control systems—like which that regulate the vehicle's speed, braking, turning, etc.—a serious liability problem suddenly emerges since a malfunction might result in a deadly collision. This issue is starting to be discussed and it may prevent autonomous cars from being used on the present road network.

a. Reducing the Whole Risk

The information above makes it clear that the risks associated with creating cyber-physical systems are higher than the summation of the threats associated with each of the lone component frameworks. For this reason, even if we were to suppose that tools and mitigation strategies were in place to reduce the risks associated with each individual system—that they are not—the authors would further need to mark the enhanced threat associated with combined frameworks.

Enhancing Component System Quality Enhancing the calibre of the component framework's testing and design is one way to start reducing the total threat for a CPS. Just the increased responsibility alone justifies this. Now, a data processing system mistake, or a hack of these systems, might cause damage to people and/or the environment. As mentioned in (Yao, X. et al. 2019), integrating security into the expansion lifecycle and introducing better thorough testing of the data-processing framework are undoubtedly important initial steps. Such design and testing considerations must take into account an environment where control systems are impacted by the data-processing system's outputs. On the control systems front, a concurrent effort must be made. The knowledge that data would be initiated from external frameworks (from and to the managerial and control systems running the physical architecture) must be taken into account throughout the design and testing phases. This will enhance the security requirements and the associated verification and validation attempts.

b. Integration Testing Is Essential

Moreover, as previously said, new situations are created by the merging of systems, even when the security and safety of the component systems have been reinforced. This necessitates the creation of a separate process for the requirements, design, and testing of the integrated frameworks. Moreover, there are a lot more ways for the integrated CPSs to be attacked go wrong—means that are unlikely to be seen when looking at each system separately. As stated in (Qi, Q. et al. 2019), cooperation between the many security and safety software developers is crucial for this.

c. Needs for Both Fail-Safe and Fail-Secure Systems

The behaviour of the individual and coupled systems during malfunctions and failures requires special attention. With the decrease in manual control by skilled human operators, this is becoming more and more crucial.

Furthermore, the complexity and interconnectivity of contemporary systems are increasing to the point that it is almost impossible for any one person to understand every facet of them. Therefore, relying on human responses to peculiar and unanticipated occurrences influencing or being influenced by these systems is not rational. As a result, it is essential to make sure that security and safety requirements are spelt out in detail early on in the development life cycle, integrated into the systems, and thoroughly tested under a range of conditions. There are situations were failing secure and failing safe are incompatible. In the event of a malfunction, security professionals may choose a closed building entrance system, which would prevent unauthorised individuals from entering. Conversely, safety engineers would prefer an open system, which would allow anyone inside to escape in the event of a fire.

d. How to Include People in Cyber-Physical Systems

As mentioned in (Khan S. et al. 2020), the human element in CPSs has to be recognised and taken into consideration. For instance, it is necessary to evaluate how people fit into "driverless" cars and make sure the systems support suitable human overrides and other forms of interaction. Unfortunately, human input to the loop is either ignored entirely or studied very little in much of the literature.

CPS PROTECTION

Consequently, CPSs must implement and adhere to rules that protect the digital and physical environments of their foundations for essential infrastructure. In 2023, cloud computing and cyber security were more intertwined, suggesting a growing dependence. The potential for and hazards related to digital security have expanded with the growing usage of cloud services. CPS is assemblies of physical components and computers which cooperate to manage an activity in a safe and efficient manner. Instances of CPS consist of industrial control systems, water systems, and smart grids. Security of Cyber-Physical Systems (CPSs) Depending on the situation, the CPS may do great damage by failing to provide the proper protection. For example, if the use of CPS by a nuclear power plant has jeopardized its safety, the whole community may be at risk (Khanh, P. T. et al. 2023).

Types of Online Crime Application security protects related data and applications from unauthorized access and illicit use. Data security, cloud security, mobile security, network security, IoT security, and so forth are examples of security measures.

Steps to achieving cyber security • A risk management system. Assess the risks to your company's data and systems by putting in place an appropriate risk management strategy that is • securely configured. Monitoring, preventing malware, handling incidents, educating and informing users, network security, controlling user rights, and so on.

CYBER-PHYSICAL PRODUCTION SYSTEMS

A smart technology called the Cyber Physical Production System (CPPS) is being proposed for artificial intelligence (Veeraiah, V. et al. 2023). It is an accumulation of innovations that work together with the global standards and its continuing processes based on the advancement of Computer and Communication Technologies (CCT), which is what, is driving the fourth generation of industry, known as Industry 4.0. The vast amount of unprocessed data gathered from various sensors for industrial production is very beneficial in identifying malfunctions or predicting equipment wear. The CPPS has five distinct level architectures that work together to create an effective and productive system. The following graphic, seen in Figure 2, describes the five C levels of architecture.

Figure 2. Cyber physical production system architecture

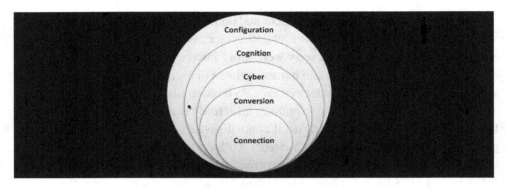

The intimate connection between the first and fifth levels is shown by the CPS's five 5C surface levels. While all levels begin at C, the CPPS begins with the self-senses connected and the data collected from this system to be used on the network in order to generate products that save costs. Figure 3 displays the primary architecture of the CPPS.

Figure 3. How CPPS framework functions

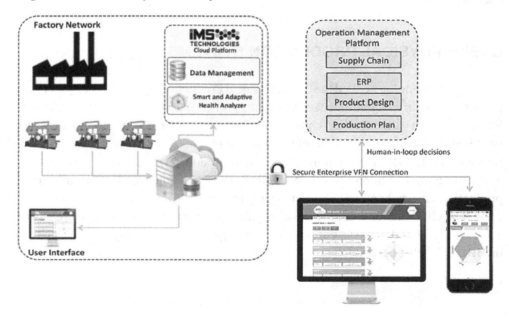

AUTOMATIC IDENTIFICATION AND SENSORS

Many categories of sensors are utilized in automated identification of various components, such as cost, temperature, motion, and environmental conditions. The widely used sensor in automation is RFID (Radio Frequency Identification), which is used in manufacturing sectors to ensure that products meet full quality standards. Though each product is labelled differently, the tags are utilized in RFID technology to operate wireless technological equipment. These tags may be used for a variety of specific tasks, such as storing and retrieving data, as seen in Figure 4. RFID is always fraught with privacy and cyber security concerns. The RFID tags used in these sensors have a limited range and are quickly compromised by tags from other RFID sensors (Jain, V. et al. 2023). The industrial and automation sectors employ a wide variety of sensors, including motion, torque, temperature, pressure, and MEM (micro-electro-mechanical) sensors.

Figure 4. Type of sensors

ACTUATORS AND SENSORS

Sensors and actuators are two essential technologies for robotics and the Internet of Things. These elements are necessary for the correct operation of IoRT systems because they provide fundamental features and clear interfaces for identification and response. The functioning of IoRT building elements is dependent on sensors and actuators, as opposed to IoT. Robotic Interaction Services (RoIS) abstract the hardware in service robots and specify HRI functions and the use of external building elements. Radar, lidar, cameras, microphones, and other sensors and actuators are necessary for HRI capabilities like face recognition and wheel control. These elements enable logical functional characteristics like human detection and identification by being physically executed on the robot or in the surrounding areas. Apps for HRI that work with both devices and gateways may be created thanks to this standard. A key component of robotics (Bansal, R. et al. 2022) is actuator, which allows objects to be moved, people and goods to move, and even automated doors to operate. In the realm of robotics, several actuation techniques have been developed, such as automated planning and execution by many robots.

NEW IORT TECHNOLOGY DEVELOPMENTS

IoRT applications need inexpensive, proactive-illuminated solid-state semi-conductor (CMOS) photographic sensors to function well in a range of weather conditions, such as sunshine, darkness, rain, fog, and dust. For both horizontal road surface scanning and vertical item detection, these sensors need to have a high level of accuracy and resolution. Sensor fusion is mostly detached with 2D description since the majority of sensors nowadays only supply 2D sensing data. To improve IoRT initiatives in the future, additional height data, 3D visualization, and the fusion of actuators and sensors are required. LIDAR systems offer 360-degree vision to autonomous robotic devices and autos by using a rotating, scanning mirror to deliver a full view. LIDAR systems provide accurate 3D information about the local environment to autonomous robotic vehicles. This information may be used for collision prediction, obstacle avoidance, motion vector analysis, and object identification. Due to its tiny size, low power consumption, and reduced potential for mutual interference, radar technology is a useful tool for preventing collisions in environments with dust, smoke, or other weather-related pollutants.

Figure 5. Annual change in IoT vs non-IoT devices

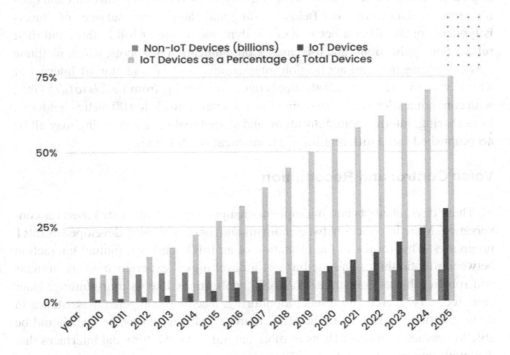

Globally, IoT devices are replacing non-IoT equipment. The top IoT markets include the United States, China, and the industrialized nations of the Asia-Pacific area and the European Union. According to preceding APAC-related trends, the region is expected to dominate in spending and adoption in the global market. As seen in Fig. 5, market forecasts indicate that by 2025, China will have a 2/3rd share of the IIoT market in the APAC area.

Technologies Of Communication

For enabling virtualization of activities on existing computing engines and enable the use of these infrastructures in many domains, the communication infrastructure of IoRT requires new approaches. These techniques should enable internal communication, edge computing, and the sharing of data streams—all crucial for 3D awareness and imaging systems. Collider avoidance dramatically reduces accidents and collisions, and it requires time-critical communication. IoRT often uses networking technologies to control local robots and specific white spectrum frequencies to control faraway robots. IoT uses 4G, WiFi, Bluetooth, and new protocols like LoRa and SIGFOX in addition to machine-to-machine communication. This degree of service creation and interoperability, however, is more difficult and calls for semantic data from other fields. Finding and categorizing services of objects is typically quite difficult because of the dynamic nature of IoRT states and their reliance on applications, and use cases. Communication protocols, which facilitate network connection and application interaction, are the foundation of Internet of Things systems. These standards supply data rates ranging from 1 Mb/s to 6.75 Gb/s, with communication ranges spanning from 20 metres inside to 100 metres outdoors. Data sharing, internal communication, and shared real-time computing may all be accomplished using different IoRT communication strategies.

Voice Control and Recognition

These days, chatbots and microphone-equipped gadgets are often used for conversation. More interfaces between humans and robots are being developed as IoRT progresses. This results in the formation of an IoRT mesh via mutual interaction between robotic things and the birth of a novel digital experience where humans and robotic objects cooperate. For IoRT applications like as tour-guiding, elder care, recovery, search and rescue, monitoring, teaching, and general assistance in daily situations as well as in factories, homes, and workplaces, people should be able to interact with robot fleets in more natural ways. Multimodal interfaces that deal with movement detection, auditory localization, people monitoring, users (or other person/robot) localization, and the blending of several modalities are crucial for developing IoRT applications. Robust noise-reduction methods may be leveraged for voice control and speech recognition by using the robot's motions and postures. The quality of the microphone is important for automated speech recognition in order to eliminate background noise.

Using Machine Learning to Facilitate Adaptive

The IoT community understands that in order to handle the large and varied amounts of sensory data produced by network nodes efficiently, it is critical to integrate Machine Learning (ML) algorithms into IoT devices. IoRT solutions may adapt to various contexts thanks to this connection, and IoRT applications can take in knowledge from their experiences and surroundings. For the ML service to cover all IoRT nodes, including the edge nodes in the network, it must be sufficiently distributed and intelligent. This distributed and embedded intelligence may provide high-level cumulative knowledge from the low-level data collected by the device/sensor via early data fusion and predictive analytics. These predictions may be sent onto a new learning algorithm on a different network node, which would do more forecasts and data fusion operations. As a consequence, a sophisticated network of ML algorithms will be created, capable of gradually compiling the observed data.

IoRT Ecosystem Marketplace

Encouraging participation and the growth of an IoRT ecosystem requires techniques for the monetization of service components and data. AnIoRT ecosystem has to be built around a marketplace. A marketplace makes it easier to register, find offers, and access the information or characteristics which services provide. These services can operate independently via IoRT platforms, or they can directly affect robots or objects. Products and services are bought and sold in the marketplace that serves as a hub for transactions. Offering discovery is the process by which a consumer uses a marketplace search interface to look for offers. Offering authentication is the process by which an offering's provider submits a metadata description for the marketplace to ingest and index. Creating shared ontologies for the semantic description of data is necessary to make data registration and discovery easier.

One possible way to protect access to the market is via role and privilege control. Secure access to the marketplace may also be achieved via permission and authentication. ● Reputation management, which entails customer assessments of vendors and their products; these assessments might be taken into account when choosing search results and doing further research. accounting and auditing, in which a user's utilization of a service is tracked and service providers have the option to charge a fee for this use. This feature is essential for enabling IoRT monetization and providing growth engines for the ecosystem. It is intimately associated with the administration of various data-providing licenses.

ANALYTICS USING BIG DATA

A highly productive computing system is also needed to handle the massive amount of data that must be collected and analysed. The smart manufacturing technique uses specific data collection techniques to reduce costs, time constraints, and budgetary issues. Accurate raw data collection is also necessary, and big data analytics have a major responsibility in the manufacturing sector. He created the term Manufacturing Internet of Things (MIOT) and conducted investigation on the big data analytics sectors and their issues. Utilize big data analytics technologies, provide in-depth analyses of various big data sources for smart manufacturing, and provide improved guidance on achieving successful outcomes.

Use of Blockchain Technology

Blockchain is a fundamental component of the newest smart technologies, which are driving IIOT and the manufacturing industry's transition to the next generation. Block chain technology affects not only the manufacturing industry but also the supply chains for banking, healthcare, and auto insurance. Block chain technology is the hottest smart technology in the Internet of Things because of its distinctive qualities, which include its open nature, discoverability, trust, security, and cost-effectiveness. The name "Ethereum" is explained by the researcher Blockchain platform; users may sign the ethereum, which is governed by peers as well as by one person and is decentralised.Additionally, the Ethereum virtual machine is constructed, mostly consisting of the ork nodes. According to recent study, Blockchain technology may be used to create Digital Twins (DTs) that are legitimate, secure, and efficient in production.

AI

AI is a fundamental component of ST; without AI, Industry 4.0 may not have existed. The triumph of a smart technology is based on the degree to which AI is applied to that methodology; the terms AI and ML are synonymous. The goal of combining AI and ML with SNA (Social Network Analysis), which is based on social network theories, is to accelerate the technique of analysis and decision-making. 2018 saw MHI and his colleagues conduct a lengthy five-year assessment of various ST that are used worldwide, as shown in Table 1.

Utilizing Serverless Technology

The technology is still evolving as serverless providers figure out how to get around few of the issues with serverless computing. A drawback is cold starts. If a serverless service isn't utilized for a time, the provider usually deactivates it to save energy and prevent over-provisioning. That function will need to be restarted by the serverless provider when a user runs a request which uses it later. "Cold start" describes the significant latency that this early phase adds. Succeeding requests would be fulfilled much more rapidly (warm starts) once the function is operational; but, if it is not utilized again for a while, it will ultimately go inactive. For more on how to utilize Cloudflare Workers, see our developer guide. When the drawbacks of serverless architecture are overcome and edge computing becomes more popular, we can expect to see more of it. streamlined the backend code Programmers may use FaaS to develop simple apps that each individually carry out a certain task, such sending a request to an API.

Quicker turnaround: The time to market might be largely shortened with serverless architecture. Developers may add and change code as required, without having to go through a tedious deploy method, in order to provide bug fixes and new features.

A Serverless Computing Example

Business leaders over the world have been offering their customers high-availability, high-performance online services by using serverless computing. Among the notable examples are:

MLBAM: Advanced Media for Major League Baseball

Of the bigger and more reputable sports leagues in the United States is the Major League Baseball Association. The business provides clients with accurate and current sports analytics using a program called Statcast. On the Statcast website, you can do complex searches using parameters like pitch velocity, pitch category, season category, and player names. With serverless computing, it can facilitate precise statistics and assist users in making judgments regarding baseball games.

Working with Autodesk

Autodesk offers reliable software for the mission-critical and bandwidth-intensive engineering, architecture, and construction industries. It unveiled Tailor, a new tool that could quickly create distinctive Autodesk accounts for companies that have all the necessary configurations. Using a serverless architecture, Autodesk launched Tailor in two weeks with only two FTES managing the service.

Netflix

One of the largest over-the-top (OTT) video providers in the globe, Netflix, is an advocate of serverless computing. It used serverless to build a platform which can handle various revisions per day from 2017 and before. To manage how the platform responds to user requests and system requirements, Netflix developers just need to specify the adapter code. A key component of Netflix's unique Dynamic Scripting Platform is its serverless architecture that controls end-user delivery, provisioning, and platform updates.

CURRENT AND UPCOMING DIFFICULTIES

Owing to the complexity and diversity of ST resulting from the variety of network intelligence and communication, this industry has several problems that need to be solved. A few of these difficulties are listed below:

Technical Staff: The technical staffs is necessary to operate the intricate and compatible framework; but, they also need to process effective machine learning, comprehend communications networks, and ensure that these topologies operate smoothly over the network with a good knowledge of operating systems and quick data-driven techniques. Technical personnel will find it simple to manage data management plans and machine aggregation with software techniques to fulfil the security and sustainability requirements of computer-based outcomes while achieving efficient results in the ST IN manufacturing industry.

Tough to Manage Massive Data Analysis and Organizing Methods

Numerous data analytic approaches are available to address data gathering, sensing, and decision-making processes based on these data management strategies. These techniques also enable various IIOTs to operate efficiently by managing and retrieving vast amounts of data.

System Integration: In order to ensure that various smart technologies and ML are compatible; the newer manufacturing framework needed IPV6 connection to enable various interfaces to function properly. In the last several decades, a multitude of technologies and platforms were utilized to achieve productive outcomes for the industrial industry; nevertheless, integrating these platforms together may be challenging. From mechanical manufacture to human production, technology advanced to information technology (IT), and today's CPPS is utilized.

Big Data Analytic Tools: managing vast amounts of data and doing analysis on it may be challenging. A lot of data analytic tools are utilized, and the key problem with these tools is sharing and preserving records across various networks.

Utilizing Various Protocols and Wireless Technologies

It is difficult to utilize various technologies with wireless technology; instead, all computer-human communication occurs across networks with varying topologies, whether they are dispersed or centralized. It is difficult to decide which communication network is best for a productive framework since there are several communication networks and wireless technologies in use. Communication networks are subject to several technological problems, such as latency, capacity, and other variables.

Development of a particular operating system

Certain operating systems are required for usage in the industrial industry. The most widely used OS which satisfy the needs of smart manufacturing processes are TinyOS and ConTiki. An operating system that is capable of handling heavy traffic, a smart grid, an intelligent communication framework, bandwidth usage, and interoperability must be designed.

The Supply Chain Is Difficult

The smart manufacturing sectors employ a wide range of heterogeneous systems that are integrated with one another and with a lengthy supply chain of suppliers, systems, and stakeholders. The challenge of the smart manufacturing framework is managing global supply chains involving multiple stakeholders and technologies attached to ST. Additionally, it is necessary to eliminate any communication conflicts between the various platforms utilized by the smart industrial manufacturer.

Customer Trust Involvement

System integrated, dependable, and long-lasting approaches are required for the product which must result from smart manufacturing. Numerous wireless technologies, including several issues found in IOT and Industrial 4.0.By creating efficient software models that are machine-to-human orientated, the client should be granted access to these technologies.

CONCLUSION

This study provides an overview of intelligent technologies that provide lucrative and dynamic goods. These technologies include wireless connectivity via various operating systems with dependable and efficient systems and communication protocols. To lessen the effort and engagement of human machines, smart technologies are also moving towards robotics. Utilizing sensor technology, digital twins provide many advantages for lowering product costs and raising product quality.

REFERENCES

Bansal, R., Jenipher, B., Nisha, V., Makhan, R., Dilip, K., Pramanik, S., Roy, S., & Gupta, A. (2022). Big Data Architecture for Network Security. In Cyber Security and Network Security. Wiley. DOI: 10.1002/9781119812555.ch11

Hedberg, T. D., Bajaj, M., & Camelio, J. A. (2019). Using Graphs to Link Data Across the Product Lifecycle for Enabling Smart Manufacturing Digital Threads. *ASME Journal of Computing and Information Science in Engineering*, 1, 213–224.

Jain, V., Rastogi, M., Ramesh, J. V. N., Chauhan, A., Agarwal, P., Pramanik, S., & Gupta, A. (2023). FinTech and Artificial Intelligence in Relationship Banking and Computer Technology. In Saini, K., Mummoorthy, A., Chandrika, R., Gowri Ganesh, N. S., & Global, I. G. I. (Eds.), *AI, IoT, and Blockchain Breakthroughs in E-Governance*. DOI: 10.4018/978-1-6684-7697-0.ch011

Khan, W. Z., Rehman, M. H., Zangoti, H. M., Afzal, M. K., Armi, N., & Salah, K. (2020). Industrial internet of things: Recent advances, enabling technologies and open challenges. *Computers & Electrical Engineering*, 81, 1–13. DOI: 10.1016/j.compeleceng.2019.106522

Khanh, P. T., Ng c, T. H., & Pramanik, S. (2023). Future of Smart Agriculture Techniques and Applications. In Khang, A., & Global, I. G. I. (Eds.), *Advanced Technologies and AI-Equipped IoT Applications in High Tech Agriculture*. DOI: 10.4018/978-1-6684-9231-4.ch021

Kusiak, A. (2019). Fundamentals of smart manufacturing: A multi-thread perspective. *Annual Reviews in Control*, 47, 214–220. DOI: 10.1016/j.arcontrol.2019.02.001

Lu, Liu, Wang, Huang, & Xu. (2020). Smart manufacturing: Connotation, reference model, applications and research issues. Robotics and Computer-Integrated Manufacturing, 61, 1-14.

Mittal, S., Khan, M. A., Purohit, J. K., Menon, K., Romero, D., & Wuest, T. (2020). A smart manufacturing adoption framework for SMEs. *International Journal of Production Research*, 58(5), 1555–1573. DOI: 10.1080/00207543.2019.1661540

Mondal, D., Ratnaparkhi, A., Deshpande, A., Deshpande, V., Kshirsagar, A. P., & Pramanik, S. (2023). Applications, Modern Trends and Challenges of Multiscale Modelling in Smart Cities. In *Data-Driven Mathematical Modeling in Smart Cities*. IGI Global. DOI: 10.4018/978-1-6684-6408-3.ch001

Qi, Q., & Tao, F. (2019). A Smart Manufacturing Service System Based on Edge Computing, Fog Computing, and Cloud Computing. *IEEE Access : Practical Innovations, Open Solutions*, 7, 86769–86777. DOI: 10.1109/ACCESS.2019.2923610

Veeraiah, V., Talukdar, V., Manikandan, K., Talukdar, S. B., Solavande, V. D., Pramanik, S., & Gupta, A. (2023). Machine Learning Frameworks in Carpooling. In Handbook of Research on AI and Machine Learning Applications in Customer Support and Analytics. IGI Global.

Yao, X., Zhou, J., Lin, Y., Li, Y., Yu, H., & Liu, Y. (2019). Smart manufacturing based on cyber-physical systems and beyond. *Journal of Intelligent Manufacturing*, 30(8), pp2805–pp2817. DOI: 10.1007/s10845-017-1384-5

KEY TERMS AND DEFINITIONS

Cyber Physical System: A complex network of embedded systems, sensor networks, and actuation systems under the direction of a computational and communication core is called a cyber-physical system (CPS). CPSs have physical input and output, and they are intended to function similarly to a network of numerous variables.

Cyber-Physical Production System: A CPPS is a manufacturing environment system that integrates digital and physical technologies to carry out production operations. Distributed computing capabilities, embedded computer hardware, and standard industrial equipment comprise CPPSs.

IoT: A network of devices known as the IoT may transmit and share data with different frameworks and devices over the internet or other communication networks. Sensors, processing power, software, and other technologies are all included in IoT devices.

Smart Technology: The capacity of a technology to interact and cooperate with other networked technologies, as well as to provide remote accessibility or operation from any location, automatic or adaptive functioning, and other features, is what distinguishes a technology as "smart."

Chapter 3

A Contemporary Survey on the Effectiveness of Machine Learning for Detection and Classification of Cyber Attacks in IoT Systems

P. Suresh

https://orcid.org/0000-0001-9815
-2982

Vellore Institute of Technology, India

P. Keerthika

https://orcid.org/0000-0002-9420
-6389

Vellore Institute of Technology, India

Manjula Devi R.

https://orcid.org/0000-0002-9319
-8874

*KPR Institute of Engineering and
Technology, India*

S. Maheswaran

https://orcid.org/0000-0002-1836
-1117

Kongu Engineering College, India

Kishor Kumar Sadasivuni

Qatar University, Qatar

N. Anusha

Vellore Institute of Technology, India

Shreeya Sanjeev Gokhale

Vellore Institute of Technology, India

EXECUTIVE SUMMARY

The interconnection of less secure devices in a network is known as the internet of things (IoT). Data and systems may be better protected with the aid of cyber security in the IoT. Cyber security violations occur most frequently when an attacker uses

DOI: 10.4018/979-8-3693-2675-6.ch003

many systems connected to multiple networks or systems to conduct an offence. These cyber dangers can do more than just steal or corrupt data; they can also temporarily or permanently disable network infrastructure. Because it is always changing, manually detecting cyber-attacks becomes expensive and tiresome. Therefore, they may be identified and categorized using machine learning methods. Internet of things devices may now maintain connections for long durations without any intervention from a person. This chapter extensively covers cyberattack detection and categorization in IoT systems using machine learning approaches.

1. INTRODUCTION

Connected to an IoT platform, which collects and analyses data from a wide variety of devices, are objects and gadgets having built-in sensors. Those sensors you could see in stores are a great example. Customers' average time spent in each section of the store, most-returned-items, and preferred shopping routes can all be tracked by these systems. Trends, suggestions, and potential issues can be identified with the use of this data prior to their occurrence (Trilles et al., 2024). Every day, more and more, people's social lives and habits are being shaped by the internet. A direct result of globalization is the ever-increasing societal impact of the Internet. A key component of critical governmental infrastructure, the Internet is quickly rising to the position of most significant social and economic engine. The Internet's dynamic and complex design leaves us vulnerable to a never-ending stream of new threats. Locating these weaknesses inside network traffic is a critical concern in modern cyber-security. The original intent of cybersecurity was to prevent illegal access to and manipulation of computer systems, software, and data stored in computer networks.

Cyber security is of utmost importance in IoT applications as these applications are highly interconnected and involve sensitive data. IoT devices are integrated into various industries, including healthcare, transport, manufacturing, and more. The importance of cyber security in IoT applications is highlighted by the fact that all these industries rely on confidential information, such as Personal Identifiable Information (PII), medical records, financial data, and confidential company data (Alharthi & Rastogi, 2020).

A cyber-attack refers to a deliberate and malicious effort to undermine the information system of an individual or entity. Usually, the assailant exploits the interruption of the target's network to gain an advantage (Verma & Shri, 2022). The incidence of cybercrime has consistently risen each year as individuals exploit the vulnerabilities present in commercial systems for personal gain. Frequently, assailants are seeking a ransom: Approximately 53% of cyber-attacks led to financial losses amounting to $500,000 or more. A cyber-attack refers to the deliberate act of cybercriminals targeting and compromising one or more computers or networks using one or more computers (Luna et al., 2016). A cyber-attack can use a compromised computer to initiate more attacks, pilfer data, or deliberately incapacitate equipment. Cyber-criminals utilize several methods, including ransomware, phishing, malware, and denial of service, to begin a cyber-attack. Cybercriminals, who possess knowledge about the most recent advancements in corporate cybersecurity, have adapted their strategies to surpass and overwhelm existing defensive measures. Contemporary cyberattacks include polymorphic code and several routes to avoid being detected. Consequently, it has become increasingly challenging to recognize hazards and respond accordingly. The endpoint, which refers to the devices used by individuals to access a network remotely, is the primary focus of cybercriminals and the initial line of defense for organizations in the context of remote work. It is crucial to comprehend the prevalent cyber threats encountered by employees and possess endpoint security solutions capable of detecting, halting, and neutralizing these assaults in order to protect the remote workforce effectively (Abdullahi et al., 2022).

There are several distinct types of cyberattacks. Cybercriminals employ a variety of techniques to carry out various attacks, such as phishing, exploiting compromised passwords, and cyberattacks. This first access provides cybercriminals with a multitude of aims, including but not limited to: ransomware, data theft, denial of service assaults, malware infections, and more. Unauthorised access, data theft, denial-of-service (DoS) attacks, and hacking are some of the security dangers facing Internet of Things (IoT) applications. Damage to physical property, money, legal trouble, regulatory penalties, brand equity, and consumer confidence can all ensue from a successful cyberattack on an Internet of Things system (Al-Mhiqani et al., 2019).

An IoT cyberattack specifically targets either an IoT device or an IoT network. The hacker can get administrative access, steal data, or form a botnet with other infected machines with distributed denial of service (DDoS) attacks. Considering the projected significant growth in the number of linked devices, cyber security experts anticipate a corresponding increase in IoT infections. Moreover, the implementation of 5G networks, which will stimulate the utilization of interconnected gadgets, might potentially result in an increase in cyber threats.

Importance of cyber security in IoT applications are:

- **Protecting Confidential Information:** IoT devices often collect and manage confidential data, including patient health records, financial data, and personal identifiable information. By ensuring cyber security, manufacturers of IoT devices can guarantee the protection of this confidential information from theft, unauthorized access, or unlawful disclosure.

- **Ensuring Physical Safety:** Cyber-attacks on connected and autonomous vehicles, drones, or medical devices can result in physical harm, putting human lives at risk. Cyber security measures help reduce the risk of potential attack, ensuring physical safety.
- **Protecting Financial Loss:** Cyber security measures can help protect the organization's financial losses resulting from a cyber-attack. Organizations that fail to implement adequate cyber security measures are likely to pay hefty fines for failure to protect sensitive data.
- **Building Customer Trust:** IoT device providers must ensure their devices' cyber security to gain customer trust. Customers trust companies that provide secure IoT devices to prevent hackers from accessing their personal information.

Figure 1. Types of attacks in IoT systems

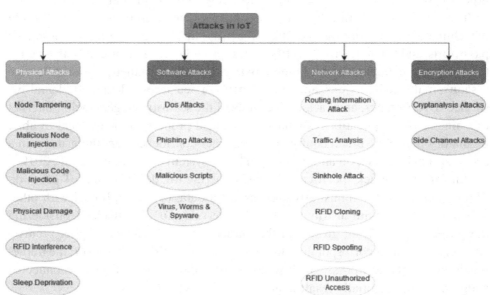

Figure 1 depicts the many categories of assaults that occur in Internet of Things (IoT) systems. Typically, Internet of Things (IoT) systems are susceptible to several types of assaults, including physical, software, network and encryption attacks. Physical assaults are directed on the hardware of IoT devices. Adversaries have the ability to induce malfunctions or illicitly access data via altering equipment, interfering with sensors, or obtaining unauthorised physical access to the devices.

Physical assaults occur when individuals have physical access to Internet of Things equipment. IoT devices should be located in a secure environment, however this may not always be feasible, as a significant number of cyber security assaults are initiated from within a company. To disseminate malicious code, an assailant frequently initiates physical cyber security attacks by inserting a USB drive. Therefore, it is imperative, particularly at this moment, to incorporate artificial intelligence (AI) driven security measures in order to safeguard your devices and data.

IoT systems might be vulnerable to compromise as a result of defects in web apps and the corresponding software for Internet of Things devices. Web applications can be used to acquire malicious firmware upgrades or user credentials (Rashid et al., 2020). An IoT assault refers to a form of cyber-attack that specifically targets internet-connected devices, including computers, vehicles, buildings, and other physical objects that are equipped with software enabling communication or data collection. Cryptanalysis attacks in the Internet of Things aim to obtain private information shared by sensors, control devices, and gateways through encrypted connections, without requiring the knowledge of the encryption keys. An unencrypted IoT device allows an attacker to sniff data and store it for later use. Moreover, malevolent individuals can deploy their own algorithms and assume command of your machine after encryption keys are decrypted. Encryption is crucial for ensuring the effectiveness of your cybersecurity measures in the IoT environment.

Every industry that uses IoT devices is particularly vulnerable to potential cyber-attacks. By implementing appropriate security measures to protect sensitive data, organizations and manufacturers can reduce the risks of cyber-attacks and ensure customer trust.

2. MACHINE LEARNING IN CYBER ATTACKS DETECTION

Machine learning algorithms are essential in the field of cyber security, namely in the identification and classification of cyber-attacks in IoT. These algorithms provide efficient answers to security issues and have enabled the development of strong systems for detecting and categorizing abnormalities. The process of identifying and classifying cyber-attacks in IoT systems requires the application of various ML techniques such as decision trees, random forests, deep learning neural networks, and unsupervised clustering methods like k-means (Suresh et al., 2022).

- **Decision Trees:** These algorithms create a decision-making model that uses a tree-like structure by splitting various features to provide a target value. Decision trees are used in cyber security to detect specific cyber-attacks and classify them.

- **Random Forests:** Combining many decision trees into one improved prediction model is the goal of random forests, an ensemble machine learning approach. They are used to classify different types of cyberattacks and assess how serious such attacks are.
- **Deep Learning Neural Networks:** These machine learning algorithms can learn and recognize complex patterns in datasets and are widely used in cyber security for identifying unknown attacks. They are capable to recognize subtle patterns in the data that other algorithms miss (Lin et al., 2020).
- **K-Means Clustering:** This approach may cluster data points that share similar features into groups. It is an unsupervised machine learning algorithm. When it comes to identifying new dangers and suspicious activity in IoT devices, K-means clustering is a lifesaver.

Machine learning algorithms offer various benefits in detecting and classifying cyber-attacks in IoT devices. They can work in real-time with minimal manual intervention and process large volumes of data at high speeds. These algorithms also offer high accuracy and efficiency in identifying and classifying new types of cyber-attacks and can alert on potential intrusions quickly. These algorithms constantly evolve, learning and adapting to new changes, providing increased security as the security threats continue to grow.

Machine learning (ML) techniques have employed mathematical models for various tasks such as classification, clustering, regression, and others (Ahmetoglu & Das, 2022). To build a machine-learning model, data samples are processed during training. There are therefore many potential applications for this approach. The characteristics chosen from the educational data and the machine learning method used determine the model's effectiveness. A machine learning model is considered effective if it can reliably organize, predict, or categorize data according to predefined criteria. To enhance the accuracy of the model, one may either increase the amount of data or convert the existing data into other forms (Farooq et al., 2022).

The raise in use of internet has led to the emergence of several security vulnerabilities. To address these security vulnerabilities, a range of technologies are utilized, including as firewalls, data encryption, and user authentication. These security methods protect against different types of attacks. Unfortunately, many security technologies lack the capability to do thorough packet analysis. Consequently, they are incapable of detecting assaults at the intended level. In order to address the deficiencies of existing security measures, the intrusion detection and prevention systems are developed. These systems, using techniques such as artificial intelligence, machine learning and deep learning has the capability to conduct more comprehensive data analysis compared to previous security systems (Kilincer et al., 2021).

Machine learning's powerful capabilities are also available for cyber security. Machine learning is employed in the field of cyber security to enhance the identification of malicious software, prioritize events, and detect breaches. ML approaches may also be employed to notify organizations about security concerns and potential attacks. Machine learning identifies sophisticated dangers and focus on specific targets, such as analyzing an organization's characteristics, identifying weaknesses in its architecture, and detecting possible vulnerabilities and methods of exploitation that are interconnected (Fraley & Cannady, 2017).

Finally, ML algorithms have transformed the way cyber security works in IoT. These algorithms provide an efficient and accurate method to detect and classify various threats for IoT devices and help in developing modern security solutions. As cyber attackers become more sophisticated, ensuring that technologies used in cyber security stay ahead of the threat is tedious. Machine learning algorithms are the tools that bring about this change (Sarker, 2021).

3. ELEMENTAL STUDY OF CYBER ATTACKS

The integration of IoT into our daily lives has posed a significant risk owing to the occurrence of Denial of Service (DoS) and Distributed Denial of Service (DDoS) attacks. A DoS attack is a type of cyberattack in which the attacker sends an overwhelming number of spam requests to the network, preventing the server from processing legitimate requests. A DoS attack involves the deliberate and temporary or permanent disruption of a resource or device, preventing its intended users from accessing it (Wehbi et al., 2019). During a DDoS assault, the resource or device being targeted is overwhelmed by a large volume of incoming traffic that originates from several sources, making it challenging to identify the specific source of these attacks. After the initial instance of spread DDoS, the bulk of DoS assaults have been spread in nature (Lima Filho et al., 2019). . Table 1 provides a breakdown of the qualities and problems associated with the IoT.

Due to the increasing sophistication of cyberattacks, network traffic anomaly detection has become an essential component of cyber defence in the age of the Internet of Things (Boukerche & Coutinho, 2021). In fact, the sophistication of assaults grows in tandem with the development of new Internet-related technology. When it comes to modern, advanced assaults, dictionary-based brute-force attacks (BFA) rank high on the list of difficulties. For this reason, we employ machine learning techniques to provide efficient ways of real-time detection and mitigation of such brute-force assaults (Alsamiri & Alsubhi, 2019). A whole new computer environment has emerged as a result of developments in ICT (Hossain et al., 2020). These advancements allowed for the establishment of the Internet of Things (IoT) communication. The IoMT, or Internet of Medical Things, is a system wherein different pieces of medical equipment communicate and exchange private data (Saheed & Arowolo, 2021).

Table 1. IoT – challenges and characteristics

Characteristics of IoT	Challenges in IoT Cyber Security
Massive deployment	The dispersion of data and information across several devices makes it imperative to safeguard each device separately. Nevertheless, the network overhead may rise with this configuration.
Heterogeneity	To guarantee the safety of devices with varying degrees of capability, several approaches are necessary.
Low power and low cost communications	Networking protocols that guarantee dependable communication are required due to the high energy consumption of IoT devices. Nevertheless, shaky dialogue may emerge from deploying decentralized cybersecurity solutions.
Low latency	Implementing complicated cybersecurity solutions might cause delays, which could affect IoT applications already under time restrictions.

Security is a major challenge in the Internet of Things (IoT) due to several factors:

- **Large-scale deployment:** IoT involves connecting a vast number of devices, ranging from consumer products to critical infrastructure. The sheer scale of deployment makes it challenging to ensure the security of each device and the overall system.
- **Heterogeneity:** IoT encompasses diverse devices from different manufacturers, running various operating systems and software platforms. This heterogeneous nature makes it difficult to establish standardized security measures and creates compatibility issues between different devices.
- **Limited resources:** In terms of processing speed, memory, and battery life, many IoT devices are severely lacking. These limitations make it hard to install strong security measures, making them open to assaults.
- **Inadequate updates and patches:** Internet of Things (IoT) devices frequently lack adequate procedures for implementing security upgrades and fixes. Manufacturers might not give priority to security or offer extended support, resulting in equipment being left vulnerable and unpatched to all the known vulnerabilities.
- **Lack of secure communication:** The devices of IoT frequently communicate with each other and with cloud services. This raises data privacy and confidentiality as concerns. Inadequate encryption, weak authentication mechanisms, and insecure communication protocols can compromise these concerns.

- **Physical vulnerabilities:** These devices are physically distributed across various locations that makes them susceptible to physical tampering and theft. Threat actors can compromise devices, steal important information, or alter their behaviour without the owner's knowledge.
- **Lack of security awareness:** Users and manufacturers often lack awareness about the security risks in IoT and the best practices. Weak passwords, default configurations, and improper device management further contribute to security vulnerabilities.
- **Data privacy concerns:** Given the vast amounts of sensitive information that networked devices gather, transmit, and store, data privacy is a big concern in IoT security. Implementing robust encryption, secure communication protocols, and stringent access limits are crucial to ensure the security of user data. Further complicating matters is the fact that personal data may be difficult to secure across different devices and platforms due to the decentralised nature of IoT networks, which may prevent the adoption of standard privacy methods.
- **Emerging attack vectors:** IoT introduces new attack vectors that were not prevalent in traditional computing systems. Attacks like botnets, distributed denial-of-service (DDoS), and manipulation of interconnected devices can disrupt critical services and infrastructure.

To tackle these security problems, the stakeholders such as manufacturers, legislators and consumers need to work together in partnership. The process include applying safe design methodologies, creating strong authentication and encryption methods, providing prompt security upgrades, and fostering security awareness and education within the IoT ecosystem (Singh et al., 2022).

4. APPLICATIONS OF ML TECHNIQUES FOR CYBER SECURITY

4.1 Intrusion Detection in IoT

Machine learning is employed for the detection of intrusions in IoT to recognise and alleviate possible security problems. Several methodologies were devised to identify unauthorised access in IoT systems. Anomaly detection is the initial method employed, where a training dataset is evaluated using five classifiers: K-nearest neighbour, Support Vector Machine, Neural Network, Decision tree, and Random Forest it is inferred that the accuracy rates varied from 0.991 to 0.999. An alternative method involves employing machine learning algorithms to identify DDoS attacks by utilizing Software-defined Networks (SDN). The third strategy employed artificial neural networks, resulting in a greater false-negative rate. The accuracy rates of all the above said three models were similar, but the neural networks showed greater promise in detecting them. The models exhibited a high rate of both false positives and false negatives. In order to enhance the accuracy, the training data can be augmented. Machine learning-based intrusion detection systems necessitate a meticulously annotated and representative dataset for training. Additionally, continuous monitoring and continuous maintenance are necessary to guarantee the system's efficacy in promptly identifying and responding to developing threats.

4.2 Detection of Cyber-Attacks in Cyber-Physical Systems

When digital and physical components work together, it's called a cyber-physical system (CPS). The assaults are directed against it. Data will be extracted from the CPS database and subsequently normalised to eliminate mistakes and duplicate entries. To further optimise the system's Hidden Markov Model based on Fuzzy Logic, it is utilised in tandem with the Heuristic Multi-Swarm Ant colony Optimisation procedure. One way to make numerical data more consistent is to normalise it. The capacity of machine learning to sift through mountains of data in search of patterns—and, by extension, anomalies—makes it an ideal tool for the detection of cyber-attacks. Normalisation using the Min-Max and Z-score methods are two of the most used options.

Min-Max Normalization: The Min-Max normalization formula scales the data to a specific range (typically between 0 and 1) as per equation 1.

$$X_{normalized} = \frac{(X - X_{min})}{(X_{max} - X_{min})} \tag{1}$$

Z-score Normalization (Standardization): The Z-score normalization formula transforms the data to have a mean of 0 and a standard deviation of 1 as per equation 2.

$$X_{normalized} = \frac{(X - X_{mean})}{X_{std}} \tag{2}$$

4.3 Detection of Cyber Attacks in Smart Grid System

Cyber-attack detection in a smart grid system using machine learning algorithms involves leveraging data from various sources within the smart grid infrastructure to identify potential malicious activities or anomalies (Mane et al., 2020). Initially, data is collected from different sources in the smart grid system, including SCADA (Supervisory Control and Data Acquisition) systems, sensor readings, network traffic logs, control signals, and historical attack data if available. This data provides information about the normal behaviour and characteristics of the smart grid system (Mane et al., 2020). Then, clean and pre-process the collected data and extract meaningful features from the pre-processed data that capture relevant information about the smart grid system, such as power consumption patterns, network traffic characteristics, sensor readings, control commands, and system behaviour (Park & Kwon, 2022). Next, choose an appropriate machine learning algorithm for cyber-attack detection, such as anomaly detection algorithms (e.g., clustering, auto encoders) or supervised classification algorithms (e.g., Decision trees, Random forests, SVM or neural networks).

It's important to consider the unique characteristics of the smart grid system, such as real-time requirements, resource constraints, and interpretability of model decisions, when applying machine learning for cyber-attack detection. Collaboration between machine learning experts, domain experts, and cyber security professionals is crucial to develop robust and effective cyber-attack detection systems for smart grids.

4.4 Reliable Network Attack Detection in SCADA Systems

Due to the proliferation of connected devices and the standardisation of open SCADA protocols, malicious breaches are growing in frequency and variety. Conventional intrusion detection systems can't pick up on new types of database threats. This research assesses the efficacy of machine learning for SCADA intrusion detection using real-time data sets derived from gas pipeline system data made available by Mississippi State University. There are two methods for data normalisation and four for estimating missing data. With an F1 score above 99%, the results show that Random Forest is able to identify intrusions successfully (Lopez Perez et al., 2018) . Previous studies have shown that random forests are biased when dealing with categorical data. Training it takes too long, and it doesn't work well with linear algorithms that include a lot of sparse information. Using KPCA and the Support Vector Data Description are both viable options.

4.5 Cyber-Attack Method and Perpetrator Prediction

One of the world's most pressing issues now is cyber-attacks. They have a daily negative impact on people's and nations' budgets. As the number of cyberattacks rises, so does the prevalence of cybercrime. The system used machine learning methods to assess cybercrimes in two separate models and forecast how defined features will affect the identification of cyber-attack strategies and attackers. Here, it utilised a strategy that relied on eight different machine learning approaches and found that the accuracy ratios were rather close. With an accuracy rate of 95.02%, Support Vector Machine Linear emerged as the top approach for detecting cyberattacks.

The initial model demonstrated a remarkable ability to accurately forecast the sorts of attacks that potential victims are susceptible to. The next approach, Logistic Regression, demonstrated the most efficacy in identifying attackers, achieving an accuracy rate of 65.42%. The second model utilised a comparative analysis of the features of offenders to determine their identifiability. The findings indicated that there is a negative correlation between the occurrence of a cyber-attack and the educational attainment and income levels of the individuals targeted. This paper presents a methodology that utilises machine learning algorithms and historical cybercrime data to forecast and identify cyber-attacks (Bilen & Özer, 2021).

Support vector machine methods are unsuitable for handling huge data sets. The performance is poor when the dataset contains a significant amount of noise, especially when the target classes overlap. If the number of attributes for each data point exceeds the number of training data specimens, the performance of the support vector machine will be suboptimal. Since the support vector classifier assigns data points to either side of the classifying hyperplane, there is no provision for probabilistic explanation of the classification. An innovative method using a sparse-coding kernel to address the issue of overfitting in Support Vector Machines (SVM). The Gene-Switch-Marker (GSM) utilises Support Vector Machine (SVM) overfitting on individual genes to accurately identify and capture significant biomarkers.

4.6 Cyber Attack Detection and Notifying System

The prevalence of cybercrime is growing globally, with criminals taking advantage of various loopholes in computer networks. The area of cyber security is in dire need of new, effective approaches. Due to the complexity and ever-changing nature of cyberattacks, the majority of the strategies employed by contemporary Intrusion Detection Systems (IDS) fall short. Recent years have seen machine learning emerge as a key component in the fight against cyber security risks. Several important issues in cyber security have been addressed using machine learning techniques, including intrusion detection, spam detection, malware classification and detection, and phishing detection (Ahsan et al., 2022). Ultimately, we want to make it so the intrusion detection community has a hard time using machine learning well by utterly upending the current attack detection process.

The majority of the strategies employed in contemporary Intrusion Detection Systems (IDS) are inadequate in dealing with the ever-changing and intricate characteristics of cyber-attacks on computer networks. Hence, the use of efficient adaptive approaches, such as diverse machine learning methodologies, can result in improved rates of detection, reduced rates of false alarms, and manageable computational and communication expense (Annam Pranitha, 2023). This text presents an overview of numerous prominent intrusion detection algorithms that are based on different machine learning approaches. ML approaches possess attributes that enable the creation of Intrusion Detection Systems (IDSs) with a notable capacity for detecting intrusions accurately and minimising the occurrence of false positives. Additionally, these systems are capable of swiftly adjusting to evolving harmful behaviours. Intrusion Detection Systems (IDS) employ a range of machine learning approaches, including Random Forest, Decision Tree, and Logistic Regression, to enhance performance across several parameters. An Intrusion Detection System (IDS) should offer the optimal solution that is in line with the specified requirements (Malathi & Padmaja, 2023). It is impossible to have complete control over when, when, or how an attack may occur, and it is not yet possible to ensure perfect prevention against them. Predict forthcoming assaults. Examine methods used to safeguard data integrity and confidentiality through an audit process. Maximise efficiency and minimise expenses, identify unfamiliar risks, and uncover unidentified hazards.

5. CONCLUSION

Early detection of cyberattacks on the physical system was the primary focus of this research, which aimed to employ machine learning (ML) approaches. We investigated and considered many alternate approaches of initiating a cyberattack. In recent years, there has been a remarkable shift in the techniques utilized to initiate cyber-attacks. Because cybercriminals are infinitely creative, they are always developing new detection techniques to circumvent existing ones. The implementation of ML approaches was necessary for the detection of cyber attackers because of the massive amount of data that had to be collected from various sources.

REFERENCES

Abdullahi, M., Baashar, Y., Alhussian, H., Alwadain, A., Aziz, N., Capretz, L. F., & Abdulkadir, S. J. (2022). Detecting Cybersecurity Attacks in Internet of Things Using Artificial Intelligence Methods: A Systematic Literature Review. In *Electronics (Switzerland)* (Vol. 11, Issue 2). DOI: 10.3390/electronics11020198

Ahmetoglu, H., & Das, R. (2022). A comprehensive review on detection of cyber-attacks: Data sets, methods, challenges, and future research directions. In *Internet of Things (Netherlands)* (Vol. 20, p. 100615). Elsevier. DOI: 10.1016/j.iot.2022.100615

Ahsan, M., Nygard, K. E., Gomes, R., Chowdhury, M. M., Rifat, N., & Connolly, J. F. (2022). Cybersecurity Threats and Their Mitigation Approaches Using Machine Learning—A Review. In *Journal of Cybersecurity and Privacy* (Vol. 2, Issue 3, pp. 527–555). DOI: 10.3390/jcp2030027

Al-Mhiqani, M. N., Ahmad, R., Abidin, Z. Z., Ali, N. S., & Abdulkareem, K. H. (2019). Review of cyber attacks classifications and threats analysis in cyber-physical systems. *International Journal of Internet Technology and Secured Transactions*, 9(3), 282–298. DOI: 10.1504/IJITST.2019.101827

Alharthi, Z. S. M., & Rastogi, R. (2020). An efficient classification of secure and non-secure bug report material using machine learning method for cyber security. *Materials Today: Proceedings*, 37(Part 2), 2507–2512. DOI: 10.1016/j.matpr.2020.08.311

Alsamiri, J., & Alsubhi, K. (2019). Internet of things cyber attacks detection using machine learning. *International Journal of Advanced Computer Science and Applications*, 10(12), 627–634. DOI: 10.14569/IJACSA.2019.0101280

Annam Pranitha, A. P. (2023). Detection Of Cyber Attack In Network Using Machine Learning Techniques. *Journal of Science and Technology*, 8(7), 133–139. DOI: 10.46243/jst.2023.v8.i06.pp133-139

Bilen, A., & Özer, A. B. (2021). Cyber-attack method and perpetrator prediction using machine learning algorithms. *PeerJ. Computer Science*, 7, 1–21. DOI: 10.7717/peerj-cs.475 PMID: 33954249

Boukerche, A., & Coutinho, R. W. L. (2021). Design Guidelines for Machine Learning-based Cybersecurity in Internet of Things. *IEEE Network*, 35(1), 393–399. DOI: 10.1109/MNET.011.2000396

De Lima Filho, F. S., Silveira, F. A. F., De Medeiros Brito, A.Junior, Vargas-Solar, G., & Silveira, L. F. (2019). Smart Detection: An Online Approach for DoS/DDoS Attack Detection Using Machine Learning. *Security and Communication Networks*, 2019(1), 1574749. DOI: 10.1155/2019/1574749

Farooq, U., Tariq, N., Asim, M., Baker, T., & Al-Shamma'a, A. (2022). Machine learning and the Internet of Things security: Solutions and open challenges. *Journal of Parallel and Distributed Computing*, 162, 89–104. DOI: 10.1016/j.jpdc.2022.01.015

Fraley, J. B., & Cannady, J. (2017). The promise of machine learning in cybersecurity. *Conference Proceedings - IEEE SOUTHEASTCON*. DOI: 10.1109/SECON.2017.7925283

Hossain, M. D., Ochiai, H., Doudou, F., & Kadobayashi, Y. (2020). SSH and FTP brute-force attacks detection in computer networks: Lstm and machine learning approaches. *2020 5th International Conference on Computer and Communication Systems, ICCCS 2020*, 491–497. DOI: 10.1109/ICCCS49078.2020.9118459

Kilincer, I. F., Ertam, F., & Sengur, A. (2021). Machine learning methods for cyber security intrusion detection: Datasets and comparative study. *Computer Networks*, 188, 107840. Advance online publication. DOI: 10.1016/j.comnet.2021.107840

Lin, E., Chen, Q., & Qi, X. (2020). Deep reinforcement learning for imbalanced classification. *Applied Intelligence*, 50(8), 2488–2502. DOI: 10.1007/s10489-020-01637-z

Lopez Perez, R., Adamsky, F., Soua, R., & Engel, T. (2018). Machine Learning for Reliable Network Attack Detection in SCADA Systems. *Proceedings - 17th IEEE International Conference on Trust, Security and Privacy in Computing and Communications and 12th IEEE International Conference on Big Data Science and Engineering, Trustcom/BigDataSE 2018*, 633–638. DOI: 10.1109/TrustCom/BigDataSE.2018.00094

Luna, R., Rhine, E., Myhra, M., Sullivan, R., & Kruse, C. S. (2016). Cyber threats to health information systems: A systematic review. In *Technology and Health Care* (Vol. 24, Issue 1, pp. 1–9). IOS Press. DOI: 10.3233/THC-151102

Malathi, C., & Padmaja, I. N. (2023). Identification of cyber attacks using machine learning in smart IoT networks. *Materials Today: Proceedings*, 80, 2518–2523. DOI: 10.1016/j.matpr.2021.06.400

Mane, N., Verma, A., & Arya, A. (2020). A Pragmatic Optimal Approach for Detection of Cyber Attacks using Genetic Programming. *20th IEEE International Symposium on Computational Intelligence and Informatics, CINTI 2020 - Proceedings*, 71–76. DOI: 10.1109/CINTI51262.2020.9305844

Park, J. H., & Kwon, H. Y. (2022). Cyberattack detection model using community detection and text analysis on social media. *ICT Express*, 8(4), 499–506. DOI: 10.1016/j.icte.2021.12.003

Rashid, M. M., Kamruzzaman, J., Hassan, M. M., Imam, T., & Gordon, S. (2020). Cyberattacks detection in iot-based smart city applications using machine learning techniques. *International Journal of Environmental Research and Public Health*, 17(24), 1–21. DOI: 10.3390/ijerph17249347 PMID: 33327468

Saheed, Y. K., & Arowolo, M. O. (2021). Efficient Cyber Attack Detection on the Internet of Medical Things-Smart Environment Based on Deep Recurrent Neural Network and Machine Learning Algorithms. *IEEE Access : Practical Innovations, Open Solutions*, 9, 161546–161554. DOI: 10.1109/ACCESS.2021.3128837

Sarker, I. H. (2021). CyberLearning: Effectiveness analysis of machine learning security modeling to detect cyber-anomalies and multi-attacks. *Internet of Things : Engineering Cyber Physical Human Systems*, 14, 100393. DOI: 10.1016/j.iot.2021.100393

Singh, J., Wazid, M., Das, A. K., Chamola, V., & Guizani, M. (2022). Machine learning security attacks and defense approaches for emerging cyber physical applications: A comprehensive survey. *Computer Communications*, 192, 316–331. DOI: 10.1016/j.comcom.2022.06.012

Suresh, P., Logeswaran, K., Keerthika, P., Devi, R. M., Sentamilselvan, K., Kamalam, G. K., & Muthukrishnan, H. (2022). Contemporary survey on effectiveness of machine and deep learning techniques for cyber security. In *Machine Learning for Biometrics: Concepts, Algorithms and Applications* (pp. 177–200). Academic Press. DOI: 10.1016/B978-0-323-85209-8.00007-9

Trilles, S., Hammad, S. S., & Iskandaryan, D. (2024). Anomaly detection based on Artificial Intelligence of Things: A Systematic Literature Mapping. In *Internet of Things (Netherlands)* (Vol. 25). Elsevier B.V. DOI: 10.1016/j.iot.2024.101063

Verma, A., & Shri, C. (2022). Cyber Security: A Review of Cyber Crimes, Security Challenges and Measures to Control. *Vision (Basel)*. Advance online publication. DOI: 10.1177/09722629221074760

Wehbi, K., Hong, L., Al-Salah, T., & Bhutta, A. A. (2019). A Survey on Machine Learning Based Detection on DDoS Attacks for IoT Systems. *Conference Proceedings - IEEE SOUTHEASTCON, 2019-April.* DOI: 10.1109/Southeast-Con42311.2019.9020468

Chapter 4
European and African Evaluation of Security Risks

Sureyya Yigit

https://orcid.org/0000-0002-8025-5147

New Vision University, Georgia

EXECUTIVE SUMMARY

This chapter evaluates European and African security risks, aiming to contribute to the multidimensional understanding of security that is much needed in today's world. The term "security" has an intriguing etymology, deriving from the Latin word securitas, which conveys a state of being "without care". In the modern context, it denotes the absence of risks or dangers and is closely intertwined with trust and proactive measures. Security encompasses diverse facets of life and is associated with geopolitical, criminal, social, anti-competitive, extrajudicial criminal, and cyber risks. In this chapter, an analysis of the Swiss police's methods for detecting and responding to radicalisation, extremism, and violence, with a specific focus on how these tactics are applied in the Vaud Canton and Neuchatel regions, are explored alongside the specific strategies employed in West Africa to assess the risk of youth radicalisation. Furthermore, the chapter carefully assesses the comprehensive approach used to address psychosocial risks and enhance the capabilities of young individuals.

DOI: 10.4018/979-8-3693-2675-6.ch004

INTRODUCTION

This chapter focuses on a multidimensional understanding of security and related to this concept, investigates the following dimensions: risk identification, risk analysis, risk evaluation, risk perception, risk control and the state's management risk when facing security threats. Since the beginning of the 1990s, under the dual effect of the technological and geopolitical revolution, the international environment has experienced profound upheavals. Public opinion is generally aware of the major conflicts destabilising the world. That being the case, it does not perceive the other risks threatening to destabilise the world.

States, societies, and commercial enterprises are faced with six new types of risks, which are essential to consider so that they do not disrupt their stability, future, and the development of their activities.

1. GEOPOLITICAL

These risks result from increased terrorism, international insecurity and multiplication of risk areas. The resulting phenomena (political instability, attacks, guerrillas, kidnappings of expatriates, maritime piracy) considerably disrupt the internationalisation of activities. Non-governmental organisations (NGOs) and companies that export or establish abroad find themselves in situations where they no longer have local contacts to ensure the security of their environment or territory. This imposes an increase in the cost of their operation or the obligation to leave certain markets. Likewise, today, many more countries than at the beginning of the millennium are virtually forbidden to tourists, an illustration of a generalised deterioration in the internal security of many countries.

"Grey zones" are regions that are not or no longer controlled by states, having come under the control of terrorist or criminal entities (Hughes, 2023). The lack of control at state borders allows the free movement of armed gangs responsible for violence, crime and looting. Today, "grey zones" exist in almost all African countries in the Middle East (Syria, Iraq, Yemen, Afghanistan) and Latin America (Mexico, Colombia). In these spaces, warlords, clans or radical religious movements ensure control of part of the territory. Military interventions to re-establish a semblance of order are confronted with infinite difficulties, as witnessed in Somalia or Afghanistan. However, it must be recognised that "grey zones" are not a particularity of regions at war: certain suburbs of European metropolises also present all such characteristics (insecurity, trafficking, violence).

2. CRIMINAL

These risks illustrate the eruption of criminal organisations (mafias, cartels) in the legal economy. Illicit actors infiltrate states and the traditional activities of companies by multiple means (real estate investments, financial participations, buyouts of SMEs, counterfeiting, extortion, money laundering, fraud, corruption, cybercrime) in order to develop their businesses or recycle their funds, this phenomenon increasingly affects the functioning of the international economy.

Indeed, globalisation has benefited not only traditional economic players but also many criminal networks that have seized this opportunity to develop and expand their activities, mainly taking advantage of the acceleration of cross-border flows, deregulation policies and the generalisation of liberal capitalism on a global scale (Yigit, 2021). Criminals, mafias and cartels have been able to take advantage of globalisation much more quickly than businesses and states. They make better use of technologies, bank transfers, and market openings.

3. SOCIETAL

These risks are the expression of deviant behaviours that characterise 21st-century societies, marked by the loss of religious, philosophical, and ideological benchmarks, as well as by the search for meaning and the rise of extremism and fundamentalism. There are two types of societal risks: sectarian excesses and protest phenomena. Both come from the same desire to call into question liberal societies and to destabilise businesses in the name of a belief that some seek to impose (radical Islam, Scientology, as well as other sects) or of a cause that others defend with great violence (anti-capitalist movements, radical ecologists, animal rights defenders). Beyond the classic social protest, these phenomena have increasingly serious repercussions on the cohesion of nations, public order and business activity. States are thus faced with the multiplication of disputes of all kinds (Yigit, 2023). Companies are increasingly influenced by opinion movements – legitimate or not – who want to be heard and impose their ideas for change. These opinion movements take full advantage of the hypermedia coverage of modern societies, constantly looking for novelty and news to the detriment of balanced information. Fake news is a good illustration of where this has led to.

Even if the protest movements are far from constituting a new risk; in that case, they are nevertheless distinguished by a double evolution that occurred from the 1990s: on the one hand, they have changed their goals and aims, now primarily attacking economic targets (large businesses and the power of money) and no longer only state symbols; on the other hand, they are characterised by increased violence, sometimes going as far as terrorism. Indeed, certain protest movements have frequently resorted to violence to achieve their objectives quickly. Under their leadership, in Seattle (United States, 1999) and Genoa (Italy, 2001), the protests during the G8 summits took the form of an urban guerrilla war. For these, the main idea became one that hitting a policeman is not violence but revenge against illegitimate institutions. Some of these extremist groups had no other reason for existing than these brutal and occasional demonstrations; they were at the origin of looting and damage on the sidelines of the demonstrations, and they deliberately sought confrontation with the police.

4. ANTI-COMPETITIVE

These risks are the consequence of tougher economic competition (increase in competitive intensity, frantic race for innovation and conquest of markets), which leads many players to resort to hostile, unfair or illegal practices to acquire information (espionage), circumvent market access rules (corruption, influence, political pressure) or overcome competition (destabilisation, sabotage). If the victory of liberal democracy over communist central planning has allowed the market economy to establish itself, this success paradoxically led to the return of the role of the economy as the main area of competition between nations (Pietrzak, 2021). The war between states and companies for global market control has been increasing.

The all-out search for information continues to expand, and new methods of capturing information become widespread. For some particularly aggressive players, the priority objective is no longer to satisfy market needs but to psychologically destroy competitors' offers and reputations in customers' minds. Such processes distance themselves from traditional ethics and legality. They are largely inspired by knowledge from the world of intelligence and clandestine operations, even if the connection with these is rarely mentioned. These methods pose enormous risks to the countries and companies that are victims, which can go so far as to call into question their existence. Some developed states objectively contribute to perverting the law of supply and demand through clandestine interventions (employment of intelligence services) and political pressure to ensure their companies win markets against their competitors, even if they officially advocate respect for world trade laws.

5. EXTRAJUDICIAL CRIMINAL

These risks result from the extraterritorial application of American law regarding export rules (embargoes), anti-corruption standards and the fight against terrorism (renditions). Since the end of the Cold War, the United States has developed a formidable strategy to ensure its political and economic supremacy (Pietrzak, 2017). This strategy is mainly based on imposing legal rules on all their rivals. The United States has spent much effort attracting and coercing other states to agree upon its legal measures in three decades. The laws enacted in Washington today are considered to impose themselves on the rest of the world to the detriment of the rights and interests of other nations. The American authorities have thus built an arsenal of repressive legislation, giving them the means to fight against the economic expansion of their competitors or the desire for their partners' independence. Moreover, if these countries refuse to comply, the United States may take unilateral retaliatory measures. Thus, their policy of extraterritorial sanctions has largely developed since the beginning of the 1990s. This translates into criminal proceedings and significant financial sanctions for companies and their managers.

6. CYBER THREATS

They illustrate that the digital revolution has opened new spaces for conflict, crime and protest. This revolution has superimposed on the physical environment a virtual environment in which the five risks presented above manifest themselves. However, rather than evoking a new specific type of threat, it is more appropriate to consider that all malicious activities are now deployed on both the physical and cyber levels: cyber war, cybersabotage, cybercrime, cyber activism, cyber propaganda, and cyber espionage (Yigit, 2021, December 10).

This chapter will identify and examine the security risks evaluated by several states, offering insights into several governments' threat perceptions, the steps taken to analyse and evaluate such risks, and recommendations for future planning and strategy. The focus will be on Swiss policies to assess security risks and how to tackle them. Attention will be turned to the issue of youth radicalism in West Africa and the transnational criminal and terror organisations destabilising the region. Finally, the International Labour Organisation's mechanism to identify and reduce psychosocial risks is extensively explored to shed light on improving risk analysis.

LITERATURE REVIEW

In a recent study authored by Zhou et al, it was argued that the conflict in Ukraine has had substantial and urgent implications for global energy and food security (Zhou et al., 2022). However, the precise nature of these effects, including key vulnerabilities and mechanisms of influence, remains incompletely elucidated. Their study introduced an enhanced model of cascading failures that incorporates overload limitations to appraise the repercussions of the Russian-Ukraine War on global energy and food security. Additionally, the researchers proposed a methodology for assessing network structure characteristics, encompassing robustness and resilience, through model simulations across various scenarios. The primary findings of the study are as follows:

i.   The upper limit of node load holds the most substantial sway over global energy and food security, whereas the lower limit parameter of node load exerts a more limited effect.

ii. Most networks exhibit consistent recovery and resilience vis-à-vis the Russian-Ukraine conflict and global perturbation, except the barley network.

iii. An important observation is that the countries experiencing failure are not necessarily those with the largest trade flow but countries with lower economic and political standing.

iv. The findings underscore the importance of expanding production capacity and diversifying energy sources to mitigate the risks associated with the Russian-Ukraine conflict. Furthermore, global organizations should take on a more substantial role in balancing the global demand for energy and food security between larger and smaller nations. This highlights the importance of your role as policymakers, researchers, and global organizations in addressing these critical issues.

Mishra et al regard water as an essential element in both natural ecosystems and human societies (Mishra et al., 2021). However, human activities on both land and water have significantly altered the environment. Global changes such as urbanization, population growth, economic shifts, changing energy needs, and climate change have put immense pressure on water resources. Achieving global water security is crucial for sustaining development and addressing the challenges presented by these changes. Their study aims to offer a comprehensive understanding of water security and its evolution in response to recent environmental changes like urbanization and socioeconomic shifts. It delves into the implications of these changes and presents sustainable solutions for achieving water security. Water security ensures reliable access to sufficient, safe water for everyone at a reasonable cost, enabling a healthy and productive life for present and future generations. However, considering both quantity and quality, meeting various water needs requires more focused efforts.

While strides have been made in developing new strategies, practices, and technologies for water resource management, there needs to be concerted efforts to disseminate and implement these solutions. Addressing water security challenges requires a comprehensive, sustainable approach that integrates social, economic, and environmental systems at various scales. Their paper seeks to capture the evolving dimensions and new paradigms of water security, emphasizing the significance of a holistic view that encompasses a wide range of sustainable solutions to address water challenges.

Liaw et al underscore the security landscape presenting formidable challenges to the national security of all states, irrespective of their standing in the global arena Liaw et al., 2021). Security studies have evolved from a focus on state-centric security to encompass non-traditional security concerns, marking a significant paradigm shift. Sri Lanka, as a maritime nation, occupies a strategic position at the confluence of the Indian Ocean, rendering it susceptible to a myriad of internal and external threats. The government's role in addressing these non-traditional security challenges is crucial, as decisive action is needed to fortify national security and stimulate economic growth.

Their article conducts an exhaustive exploration of Sri Lanka's security environment and its national security perspective. It identifies non-traditional security threats and critically evaluates their impact on the country's security. Furthermore, their article delineates pragmatic mitigation methods aimed at securing the nation. Their study's methodological framework encompasses primary and secondary data obtained through a qualitative research approach, including an ethnographic study.

The findings of their study underscore the proactive role that Sri Lanka must play in shaping its security environment. This involves a pragmatic and astute evaluation of its national interests, prioritizing political stability, maintaining a sustained state of preparedness, fostering active cooperation and coordination both regionally and internationally, and cultivating an enduring process of confidence-building. Their study also advocates for the adoption of a model-based approach as an effective avenue for Sri Lanka to overcome its security challenges, with a strong emphasis on tailoring the application of any model to align with Sri Lanka's specific contextual requirements.

Bove, Rivera & Ruffa situate their research within the theoretical framework of comparative politics and international relations, offering a unique and novel perspective (Bove, Rivera & Ruffa, 2020). While extensive research has traditionally focused on military involvement in politics through coups, they redirect attention to a broader scope of military engagement in politics, arguing that terrorist violence and the looming threat of terror attacks present an opportunity for military intervention without the overt seizure of state institutions. The impact of terrorism on military involvement in politics can be understood through two primary mechanisms. Firstly, government authorities often turn to military expertise to effectively address terrorism, bolster national security, and navigate military involvement in political matters. Additionally, state armed actors leverage their informational advantage over civilian authorities to influence political decision-making. Panel data analysis demonstrates that both domestic terror attacks and perceived threats from domestic and transnational terrorist organizations can result in heightened military participation in politics. The authors provide detailed cases from France (1995–1998 and 2015–2016) and Algeria (1989–1992) to illustrate these theoretical mechanisms.

In their recent 2021 publication, Albert, Baez, and Rutland delve into the persistent discussions surrounding the potential impact of infectious diseases on national and international security (Albert, Baez & Rutland, 2021). With the advent of COVID-19 prompting a thorough reconsideration of the relationship between infectious diseases and global security, the authors explore the specific security ramifications of COVID-19. Their analysis is underpinned by an exploration of the theoretical frameworks of human security and biosecurity. They assert, with compelling evidence, that COVID-19 represents a substantial threat to global security. They assert that the pandemic poses a fundamental challenge to individual well-being, as articulated by human security theory, and raises overarching concerns within high-level politics, as evidenced by biosecurity considerations. Their analysis emphasizes that viewing security threats from both individual and state perspectives underscores the significance of recognizing infectious diseases as a critical international security concern. Additionally, their article includes a comprehensive review of relevant literature, ensuring that the audience is well-informed, and applies the theoretical framework to conduct a case study analysis centred on the United States.

Alcaraz & Lopez assert that Industry 4.0 is playing an increasingly positive role in revolutionizing the value chain through the modernization and optimization of production and distribution processes (Alcaraz & Lopez, 2022). At the forefront of this transformation is the digital twin (DT), a state-of-the-art technology that offers simulation capabilities for forecasting, optimising, and estimating states and configurations. While these capabilities drive industrial stakeholders to invest in this new paradigm, focusing on the associated risks is crucial. The deployment of a DT relies on integrating various technologies such as cyber-physical systems, the Industrial Internet of Things, edge computing, virtualization infrastructures, artificial intelligence, and big data. However, these technologies' convergence and interaction with the physical world pose significant security threats that require further investigation. Their paper examines the current state of the DT paradigm, classifies potential threats, and considers the functionality layers and operational requirements for a comprehensive classification. Additionally, their paper offers a preliminary set of security recommendations and approaches to ensure the secure and trustworthy use of DT technology.

Boulton identifies a cross-disciplinary research project delved into reframing climate and environmental change (CEC) as a unique form of threat, termed a hyper-threat (Boulton, 2022). The project utilized conventional military analytical methods to assess the hyperthreat and its context, aiming to develop innovative approaches to address it. In contrast to existing literature and established geopolitical discourse cautioning against securitizing CEC, Boulton argues that neglecting to incorporate CEC into mainstream geopolitical and national security strategies now carries greater risk. The research uncovered new pathways toward stability by foregrounding the hyperthreat of CEC as the primary focus and examining its interconnectedness with other threats. Introducing a new theoretical framework termed "entangled security," the study lays the groundwork for an initial "grand narrative" and "grand strategy". Her work illustrates how reconceptualizing military theory can play a vital role in shaping new policy directions and security priorities.

Kruck & Weiss underline the prevalence of the "regulatory state" significantly influencing European public policy in various sectors (Kruck & Weiss, 2023). While conventional security provision is closely associated with the "'positive state'" and its reliance on political authority and independent capabilities, they argue that exper-tise and regulations also play a crucial role in shaping European security provision within national and supranational "regulatory security states," notably the European Union. Their framework offers a comprehensive analysis of the emergence of these regulatory security states, delving into the driving forces and constraints of security state reforms and their impact on the effectiveness and democratic legitimacy of European security policymaking. Their research aims to enhance our understanding of security governance in Europe's multi-level political system, exploring the actors involved, the methods they employ, and the foundations for their operations.

Kim, Panton and Schwerhoff suggest that the ongoing energy crisis has prompt-ed essential policy inquiries concerning the reinforcement of short-term energy security while upholding a steadfast commitment to the green transition (Kim, Panton & Schwerhoff, 2024). This challenge has been further accentuated by the recent agreement at COP28 to shift away from reliance on fossil fuels. Their paper delves into the historical determinants of energy supply security and scrutinizes the ramifications of the green transition on energy security. Retrospectively, it is apparent that the diversification, or lack thereof, of energy trade partners has wielded substantial influence on energy security dynamics within and between nations over the past two decades. The green transition is anticipated to augment energy security predominantly, if investments are strategically directed to address the emerging challenges posed by the escalated dependence on renewable energy sources. The inferences drawn from their research are as follows:

i. The prevailing energy crisis has underscored the significance of striking a harmonious balance between meeting short-term energy requisites and pursuing enduring energy security.

ii. in conjunction with the escalating export shares of principal energy producers, the mounting concentration of fossil fuel imports has profoundly shaped energy security trends in recent decades.

iii. Despite the substantial surge in coal production in China, most of it is domestically consumed, thus enabling Indonesia and Australia to dominate the global coal export market.

iv. There exists a pivotal interplay between climate policy and energy security.

v. The rapid proliferation of renewable energy presents fresh challenges for energy security, yet comprehensive solutions are already considerably advanced.

vi. Besides the principal considerations, energy security is influenced by myriad supplementary elements.

SWITZERLAND: POLICE DETECTION OF RADICALISATION, EXTREMISM AND VIOLENCE

Switzerland, located in the centre of Europe, is surrounded by France, Germany, Italy, Liechtenstein, and Austria. The country is made up of 26 cantons. Its national Security Network (SNN) brings together all the security policy instruments of the Swiss Confederation, cantons and municipalities (Hagmann et al., 2018). Its bodies - the political and operational platforms - manage the consultation and coordination of decisions, means and measures constituting security policy issues concerning the Confederation and the cantons. The emphasis is placed on internal security, where coordination is more important than external security, which falls under the competence of the Confederation.

In the context of the fight against terrorism, the SSN has been mandated to develop a National Action Plan to Prevent and Counter Radicalisation and Violent Extremism, which is aimed at all prevention stakeholders (Eser Davolio, 2019). The latter was adopted in December 2017 by the relevant political bodies of the Confederation, cantons and municipalities (Merz, 2021). When viewing the context of terrorism in Switzerland, the country has been spared from terrorist acts for almost 50 years. However, since 2012, similar to other European countries, it has had to face the departure of people residing on its territory to join Islamist terrorist organisations, particularly in Syria and Iraq.

Due to a growing threat, the Federal Council adopted, in September 2015, Switzerland's first strategy for the fight against terrorism (Naji & Schildknecht, 2021). This strategy falls into four areas:

1. Prevention;
2. Repression;
3. Protection;
4. Crisis Preparation.

The first three areas are intended to prevent terrorist attacks in Switzerland as well as the export or support of terrorism from its territory. Since it is not possible to exclude that such attacks will take place in Switzerland, the preparedness measures for a crisis must guarantee that the country will be able to control a terrorist attack by strengthening its resistance capacity.

The National Action Plan constitutes the main measure implemented in prevention. The work was coordinated by the SSN, which, to do this, brought together the main stakeholders (social, education, police, integration) from the Confederation, cantons, and municipalities. The terrorist threat launched a challenge to federalism in the area of security. However, the various actors were able to meet this challenge by demonstrating pragmatism and innovation, thus demonstrating that it is possible, through well-structured and coordinated network work, to provide the expected responses to a major challenge for the country's security.

The plan's primary objective is to develop various measures aimed primarily at facilitating early detection of people in the process of radicalisation. Its scope of action is as upstream as possible and is part of a real network with all actors in the penal and judicial chain until the final stage of reintegration and disengagement.

The plan includes five areas of action:

I. Knowledge and expertise;
II. Collaboration and coordination;
III. Fight against ideologies and extremist groups;
IV. Disengagement and reintegration;
V. International collaboration.

In total, 26 concrete measures have been developed and must be implemented within five years. At the heart of this action plan is the principle of institutional and interdisciplinary collaboration, which is based on the following requirements:

i. Exchanges of information and experiences between the different actors;
ii. Defined working procedure (and appropriate instruments);

iii. Integration of and support for civil society.

To guarantee the implementation of the various measures, the local level (cantons and large towns) must set up a coordination structure at its level, bringing together the main actors such as the police, schools, social services, those responsible for integration or even the health field, to name just a few. This structure must be supported by the political authority which designates the leading service. It is then up to this round table to develop general prevention measures and, above all, to examine the different situations presented to it by those in the field. In broad terms, each case must be handled with the stakeholders concerned, who will be responsible for consulting on the measures to be taken. These may remain in the field of prevention in the broad sense or fall within the competence of the intelligence services or the police when it is considered that the person could present a security risk. Indeed, only support as early as possible can reduce, as much as possible, the risk of acting out.

Concerning the role of the police in the prevention of radicalisation, they are one of the key players. However, it is not their role to be the driving force. Indeed, in the early detection phase, it is important to differentiate from the legal process, which will be triggered when the risk of committing the act has been detected. For this reason, arguments recommend that other organisations (integration, social services) take responsibility for implementing the various measures. Several strategies have been implemented in several cantons according to this principle, proving effective.

Two measures of the plan were specifically devoted to the police, briefly presented below.

A) Intensification of Work Policy Network Implementation

Networking, building good relationships and trust with foreign communities and associations must be intensified in municipal and cantonal police forces. Particular attention should be paid to contact with (cultural) associations and organisations, for example, organisations working in the field of asylum. This way, mutual trust can be established, networks maintained, and security policy issues discussed. The "Brückenbauer" model implemented by certain police forces can be useful to promote the execution of these tasks (Kersten & Budowski, 2016).

This measure fully aligns with the vision of community policing, which is dear to the Anglo-Saxon world. The first step is to create a bond of trust between the police officers in the field and the different communities or associations active in their engagement sector. This contact work and information must facilitate intervention as upstream as possible. The Zurich cantonal police, which has implemented this concept for several years, were able to measure its positive effects in preventing radicalisation thanks to contacts established with representatives of different communities (Davolio et al., 2015). Therefore, the training offer of the Swiss Police Institute, which is responsible for the continuing training of employees, has been expanded with a course specifically dedicated to this type of activity, which the police forces of several cantons have already taken up.

B) Establishment and Introduction of Threat Management Concept

Cantonal threat management on an institutional level, most often placed under the direction of the police, must identify sufficiently early the potential danger that people or groups may present, evaluate it and finally defuse it by appropriate means. All attention must be paid to ensuring that radicalisation and violent extremism are integrated into the concept of threat management. For radicalisation and violent extremism to be addressed in an interdisciplinary manner, additional partners or knowledge must be integrated if necessary.

The concept of threat management developed in Switzerland in the context of domestic violence and the increase in quarrelsome people in administrations is based on the use of various risk assessment tools and relays in various administration services and other affiliated institutions. In this context, processes implemented in another context are effective in the fight against radicalisation. Experiences carried out in regions where the concept was already in place prove that, in several situations, people in care were able to be stopped in their radicalisation process, or such a possibility could be ruled out. For this measure, training was also offered by the Swiss Police Institute (Ajil & Staubli, 2023).

Even if the police are not responsible for coordinating measures to prevent radicalisation and violent extremism, they nonetheless remain one of the pillars. Indeed, through its numerous collaborations in its daily activity, it can be confronted with feedback, allowing it to take the first steps. To do this, it must establish relationships of trust with its partners through networking and not repression. The phenomenon of radicalisation poses new challenges in the field of prevention. One must, therefore, seize this opportunity to develop, through the proposed measures, new skills for the police, which can be part of a more global framework.

VAUD CANTON

The canton of Vaud has Lausanne as its capital and a population of 800,000. It has an area of 3,212 km^2. The Vaud Gendarmerie is an integral part of the cantonal police, and it brings together General Services, the Vaud Gendarmerie, and the Security Police. Switzerland has the particularity of a federal state in which responsibility for public security falls under cantonal jurisdiction. Each canton develops police strategies, which are then discussed, compared, and unified across the Swiss territory.

In terms of the risk level in Switzerland, for several years, it has also been the target of several highly violent events, the deadliest of which was perpetrated in the hall of the Grand Council in Zug, in central Switzerland. Between 1986 and 2012, across the entire territory, there were at least ten deadly situations in which citizens were seriously injured or died. Whilst there has not been any noticeable rise in attacks perpetrated on Swiss territory, preparatory acts have been foiled.

Particularly attentive to the numerous attacks in the United States and Europe, whether in terms of terrorism or mass killings, Switzerland cannot ignore that this type of attack could also occur on its territory. This risk constantly evolves with authors demonstrating inventiveness, determination, and total self-sacrifice. It was therefore necessary to study, analyse, reflect, and think about how to develop, but above all deploy, effective operational means to understand and deal with such situations for the Vaud canton. The other cantons do the same for their territories.

From real-life experiences, one of the key elements for managing such crises is the ability of law enforcement to gain the upper hand as quickly as possible over the opposing party. This involves, in particular, an increase in firepower linked to specialised weaponry and adapted tactics. Similar to other Western police forces, it has been noted that the action of first responders is essential in containing or stopping a terrorist threat. The standard procedures and equipment of police patrols and the gendarmerie are adapted, both in the fight against medium and serious crime and in their role as first responders during a terrorist attack. They are the subject of constant reflection and consolidation.

The hypothesis of equipping all first responders with weapons of war and modifying the criteria for engaging the weapon of all collaborators raises questions of proportionality, economy of means, image, ethics, and doctrine for all employees working in the canton of Vaud. The tactical intervention groups, for their part, provide essential expertise in this area. However, to be efficient, these groups must be able to prepare thoroughly. An implementation deadline must then be accepted. Therefore, the availability of a means of intervention with an intermediate profile between first responders and tactical intervention groups or support units arises as a rational response to the state of the latent threat in our regions. This intermediate means is equipped with weapons adapted and trained in the related engagement tactics.

One tool with which to combat serious security risks is utilising the tactical intervention groups and the objective of intermediate means between first responders and tactical groups are as follows:

i.   Increases firepower

ii.   Allows you to fix and neutralise the threat
iii. Available 24 hours a day
iv.   Capable of main effort over time
v.   Discreet
vi.   Rational
vii. Flexible
viii. Proportionate to the threat in the regions

Such operators are trained in the use of assault rifles and the corresponding tactics relating to them; they are available daily or upon mobilisation. They act within the framework of their patrol or in formed units. In the event of commitment, the special operators position themselves in the same state of mind and in addition to the first-time speakers. They use their firepower and tactical knowledge to regain the upper hand and end the threat.

To align with new threats, these operators must undergo three days of basic training and four and a half days per year of continuing training in collaboration with the army and the Swiss Police Institute. The training is mainly based on the mastery of progression techniques and tactics and the handling and shooting of long weapons. Each year, a test validates the skills of these operators and thus authorises their operational commitment. In order to optimise this concept, requirements are imposed on each employee wishing to integrate this means. To be an operator, one must demonstrate great self-control, a developed sense of responsibility and recognised shooting skills. In addition, perfect knowledge of the procedures applicable to cases of mass killing will be required.

Regarding possible deployments, most employees are integrated into the operational units of the gendarmerie, thus contributing to 24-hour availability. Every day, in their standard field of activity, the validated operators work with the weapons and equipment specific to their mission. In the event of an impromptu event and when they are in the canton, the operators converge in order to contribute to the main effort. During an attack by a sniper or a terrorist, it is the implementation of this trained operational process which happens in the first minutes, just after the first responders. In the meantime, specialised response groups are preparing and will be ready to deploy.

As mentioned, on the whole, Switzerland has been spared attacks from terrorist types. Every tragedy, whether in France, Belgium, Germany, Sweden, or the United States, no matter how dramatic, requires them to study the methods used relentlessly (DeVore & Stähli, 2011). They have aimed to seek to understand them to develop and refine new strategies. These will have to evolve as quickly as a society and its potential dangers. It is clear that in mass shootings, violent cases or terrorist attacks, the first minutes are decisive, even momentous (DiGiovanni, 2003). There is, therefore, a need for a concept which offers rapid action, allowing intervention as quickly as possible depending on the location of the attack. The operators being armed accordingly, their interventions will respond effectively to the threat as soon as they arrive at the locations chosen by the attack.

NEUCHATEL (MPV): THREAT MANAGEMENT AND PREVENTION OF VIOLENCE

Instances of people threatening public figures, serious and repeated interpersonal and domestic violence, the rise of extremism, people adopting obsessive harassment behaviour (stalking), young people suggesting their intention to attack their establishment school and other troubled people turning up in anger in one or other of the State services (contributions, social services, courts) have risen. A good example is the violence demonstrated in the Zug parliament, which was preceded by clues that could have been detected. In this instance, a disturbed person killed 14 elected officials, including three state councillors, and injured 15 other people in 2001 in the parliament of the canton of Zug in Switzerland.

It is important for the cantons to have a structure in place that can recognise warning signs, assess the risk potential and work to defuse the threat. A threat management service is also a skills centre that can offer training and support to state service employees who, in their role, must make decisions that are only sometimes accepted by citizens. Preventing every act is not possible, but the risks can be mitigated. Indeed, the targeted acts of the police regularly deal with potentially dangerous and mentally disturbed people.

Similar to two dozen other Swiss cantonal police forces, the Neuchâtel police established a Threats & Violence Prevention (MPV) group (République et canton de Neuchâtel, 2024). They focus especially on the following issues:

i.   Serious domestic violence
ii. Death threats
iii. Stalking
iv. Potential Amok cases
v.   Radicalization

They carry out proactive police work with the following missions:

i.   Develop police resources to identify the warning signs of an act;

74

ii. Assess the risk and the imminence of a possibility of taking action by speaking in particular with the author and using evaluation instruments designed for this purpose;
iii. Defuse the risk of escalation of violence, in particular by speaking with people concerned – perpetrator and victim – or by setting up meetings with the network (Child and Adult Protection Authority, public prosecutor, psychiatric hospital) to find medium and long-term solutions by integrating criminal and non-criminal preventive dimensions;
iv. Ensure monitoring of people at risk by centralising information concerning them.

The size of the police force, the irregularity of situations requiring treatment and the means at our disposal have led us to favour the option of a flexible structure which can be reinforced if necessary. Under the responsibility of the head of the Psychological Department of the Neuchâtel Police, the group comprises six police officers specialising in the field of threats. Particularly competent in interpersonal communication, the MPV workers have all completed a three-week internship in psychiatry, followed continuing training, and benefited from threat assessment and management supervision. The speakers work part-time on MPV missions. Regarding time investment, support for the MPV group totals two 100% positions over the year. To support the MPV group, gendarmes are recruited in the various local police stations and trained in the "MPV antenna" function (République et canton de Neuchâtel, 2023, October 16). Aware of the theme, they take charge of situations linked to threats, make an initial assessment, and, if necessary, transmit it to the MPV group.

MPV interviews are not criminal hearings, whether the result of a proactive approach or the consequence of a problematic fact. Even if the participation of a member of the MPV team may be required as part of the hearing of a victim, a witness, or a perpetrator, more broadly for a shared perspective in the context of an official criminal procedure, the MPV interview is part of a framework, but above all a somewhat different logic. Where the police inspector seeks to establish and contextualise constitutive facts, the MPV speaker aims to understand the reality of the people encountered. In the context of MPV interviews, it is, above all, a question of creating a sufficient bond with the person in order to be able to achieve the objectives below.

Objectives of MPV interviews with the person targeted by the threats:

a. Collect information contributing to an initial assessment
b. Provide support through proposed strategies for the safety of potential victims

c. When the targeted person is the source of information, maintain a position of "healthy scepticism" and evaluate the issues as well as the underlying motivations (conscious or not) for their comments

d. Create a sufficient bond of trust so the targeted person can continue sending information about the author

Objectives of MPV interviews with the author of threats or inappropriate behaviour generating fear of passage to the act of violence:

a. Collect the information necessary for assessment of the risk of acting out
b. Exercising influence over the person by seeking to reduce the potential danger they represent
c. Gather information on possibilities to help the person in order to reduce the risk of violence
d. Inform the perpetrator of the consequences of his behaviour and set limits
e. Create a sufficient bond of trust for, in the event where appropriate, facilitate monitoring subsequently

Traditionally, when a police officer assesses the risk of a citizen reoffending or committing an act - for example when s/he is required to advise a victim of obsessive harassment (stalking) - s/he will base his judgment on his experience and capacity for discernment. Although intuition is certainly important in assessing whether a situation is serious, the evaluator is always biased by their preconceptions and will tend to perceive the situation in a way that confirms their beliefs. To avoid these biases and increase the reliability of risk assessment, different policies, particularly in Anglo-Saxon countries and Germany, use more or less complex instruments, computerised or not, some indicating the degree of risk by a number - alternatively, a colour, others determining risk management strategies based on the recorded data.

An example of an in-depth assessment instrument is the Octagon, which was developed in 2016 and used by several Swiss police forces; the Octagon allows a common language during discussions between the different threat management (Yeung, 2004). For an initial assessment of a threat, there are so-called screening instruments. For example, the Pyramid of risk of committing an act of violence (Souder & Bethay, 1993). Whether conducted by telephone or during an interview with the author or target of threats, this instrument allows one to ask the right questions. It ensures the collection of targeted information on the presence or absence of relevant risk factors. It makes it possible to structure information on the author's personality of the threats, background, current context, observable behaviours and events that could trigger the act.

It is not a simple checklist in which the counting of a certain number of factors would automatically indicate that the person is dangerous, but rather an aid to collecting information, taking the distance necessary for an overall analysis of the situation and, if necessary, transmit the right impulse to the appropriate department. Such a screening instrument complements the participant's experience, intuition, and common sense.

Effective threat management relies on early detection and networking at the cantonal level. The medium-term vision is to train contact persons in the various state services, particularly those who regularly deal with dissatisfied citizens (e.g., the tax, employment, prosecution and bankruptcy, adult and youth protection, consumer and veterinary affairs, and automobiles). These employees will be trained to assess a threat situation and to advise their colleagues or department managers. These contact persons will then transmit situations assessed as significant risk to MPV and work closely together to manage the crisis.

At the Swiss level, the existence, since 2017 of training in threat management organised by the Swiss Police Institute makes it possible to train police officers from all police forces wishing to set up and develop such a service. This training promotes a common language and tools (e.g., the Octagon) for police responders from different police forces. On the other hand, from 2019-2020, some bases on assessing a threat (in particular, the risk pyramid) began to be taught in the different police cadet schools. At the European level, the Association of European Threat Assessment Professionals organises a yearly congress, allowing discussions between professionals in the field - police officers, university researchers, and security managers of multinationals.

WEST AFRICA: RISK OF YOUTH RADICALISATION

One can observe that violent radicalisation in West Africa seems to have an exogenous character if judged by the fact that it began in this region. One can list Maghreb- the Sahel since 1991; Algeria, with the crisis of the Islamic Salvation Front in 1991; the birth of the Armed Islamic Group in 1992; the split from them and birth of the Salafist Group for Preaching and Combat in 1998; reconversion of them into Al-Qaeda in the Islamic Maghreb in 2007; birth, more than 20 years later, in 2011, of the Movement for Unity and Jihad in West Africa in Mali. All this heralds the emergence of pseudo-jihadist groups in the Sahel, except the Boko Haram group, which was created in 2002.

West African countries, particularly those of the G5 Sahel, have an institutional framework that facilitates the coordination of regional cooperation in development policies and security matters in West Africa. They are, however, not without fault and also constitute fertile ground conducive to radicalisation for the following reasons: extreme poverty - with 50% of the population living below the poverty line, and more in rural areas; the lowest human development indices in the world; chronic food insecurity; a high rate of acute malnutrition (15% of children under five are in a situation of global malnutrition; difficulties in accessing basic social services (education, health, drinking water, sanitation); climatic shocks (drought, flooding, silting and drying up of watercourses, locust danger and invasion of grain-eating birds, desertification); livelihoods (agriculture, livestock breeding, fishing) affected by the harmful effects of climate); land insecurity and intercommunity conflicts; youth unemployment, lack of professional training and lack of job opportunities; illiteracy.

Moreover, despite everything, radicalisation in West Africa still needs to be better documented. Indeed, the research field is inaccessible, and only qualitative data are predominant. The phenomenon is new and poorly studied, and general information is not always accessible. The constant is that illiteracy, rare opportunities for employment and self-employment, poor knowledge of religion, religious indoctrination, the feeling of injustice, ignorance of the law, local conflicts as well as weak national sentiment constitute the main factors of radicalisation, especially among young people.

Moreover, despite the lack of statistical data, it is proven that acts of violence are committed, in the vast majority of cases, by young people and sometimes by very young people, including a significant number of "child soldiers" and enlisted teenagers. This youth - without any distinction of social status, standard of living or education - must be taken into account and be on the front line of this fight because of their creativity, energy, endurance and determination.

This role of young people is today widely recognised by international and regional institutions, notably in United Nations Resolution 2250 focusing on youth in terms of decision-making (United Nations, 2015, December 9). The Niamey Declaration of 2015 on smuggling of migrants and trafficking in persons signed by interior and foreign ministers from Europe and West Africa is also a relevant regional agreement (IOM, 2018). Therefore, to carry out this, it will be necessary to act on three levers: 1) skills, 2) motivation, and 3) the environment; at the institutional, socio-economic, and cultural levels.

1. Strengthening the Skills of Young People

As a prerequisite, to take care of young people from the formal and traditional education system. The education systems must be reformed with the objectives of:

i.   Developing a culture of excellence, competence, expertise and innovation in training
ii. Promoting a school that produces young people who are "legal" models of success for the younger children
iii. Modernising Koranic schools and creating bridges with the formal system
iv. Promoting education adapted for nomadic communities linked to the preservation of their way of life
v.   Developing "second chance schools"
vi. Developing extracurricular and leisure activities (citizen holidays, work of common interest) as tools for strengthening national cohesion

2. Motivating Young People to Fight Against Radicalization

i.   Start from situations that young people experience and reinforce, gradually build their abilities and knowledge of their reality, and equip them to manage it
ii. Use a participatory and democratic approach to detect issues that seem important to them and help them find solutions
iii. Create the conditions for their commitment to security based on a partnership with the police based on an awareness of the interest in collaborating (taking into account the grievances of their community)
iv. Identify credible interlocutors and establish widely inclusive procedures and methods of action (e.g., involving young women) that can create trust
v.   Support young people in their actions (e.g., awareness, information)
vi. Make disengaged people and victims active players in the fight against violent extremism
vii. Promote evaluation monitoring tools to measure, with young people, the progress made, and the regresses of the two educational systems

3. Promoting the Environment

The institutional level

i.   Review, where necessary, all the provisions which limit the participation of young people in the development of public policies
ii. Ensure that the legal framework guarantees young people the full enjoyment of their fundamental rights, in particular, their freedom to organise, express themselves and undertake projects

iii. Create mechanisms for making available public resources in municipalities that can enable young people to develop local strategies to combat violent extremism

iv. Promote a national civic service (fight against illiteracy, protect the environment, strengthen civic culture and democracy)

THE SOCIO-ECONOMIC LEVEL

i. Create employment and training opportunities, professional support and internships for young people, taking into account geographical equalisation

ii. Firmly fight corruption, in particular against tax evasion (police, customs and gendarmerie)

iii. Develop transparent mechanisms for access to employment that are credible and convincing

THE SOCIO-CULTURAL AND SPORTING LEVEL

i. Develop subsidy mechanisms (public usefulness) for youth organisations such as Scouts and Pioneers

ii. Create multi-purpose cultural-cultural complexes (places of prayer, auditoriums, libraries, multimedia rooms, music classes, sports halls)

iii. Establish sports and cultural infrastructures equipped with quality equipment and teams of facilitators

iv. Design sports competitions and cultural activities between young people at the local, sub-regional, and national levels

Countering violent extremism is challenging. This is a coordinated action between the three levers mentioned above, and to guarantee its success, there is a need

i. To strengthen the democratic and economic governance of the States

ii. To mobilise resources from partners, which will be directed towards national priorities.

Under these conditions, one can hope to have young people – a shield against violent extremism – equipped with a healthy mind and body and evolving in a conducive environment.

SOLVE: INTEGRATED APPROACH TO MANAGING PSYCHOSOCIAL RISKS

Psychosocial issues require a very different approach from traditional efforts. They constitute major threats to organisational performance. The combined factors can result in a significant number of workplace accidents and illnesses, leading to disability, sickness, and even fatalities. As a result, these issues deeply impact productivity, increase costs, and threaten the organisation's existence. These problems affect almost all countries, regardless of their level of development, all sectors, and all categories of workers. The International Labor Office (ILO) designed the SOLVE method to integrate health promotion into occupational health and safety policies (Probst, Gold & Caborn, 2008).

The SOLVE approach is therefore designed to offer an integrated response in the workplace to problems of stress, drugs, alcohol, violence, AIDS, and smoking, which often manifest themselves there. By directly linking occupational health and safety issues to organisational management and development issues, SOLVE offers the tools for autonomous policy and immediate action in the workplace to reduce and prevent difficulties in question. This approach thus makes it possible to improve working conditions on a psychosocial level.

In this context, SOLVE is a tool that can help address the issue of work-related dangers and psychosocial risks. The ILO's experience in social dialogue has enabled it to successfully implement certain initiatives dealing with this issue, both in the workplace and within communities, by bringing together employers, workers, prevention officers, governments, decision-makers, politicians, public services, and non-governmental organisations.

Indeed, the management of emerging problems related to occupational health must be considered from a holistic point of view, taking into account an approach that examines both the levels of influence and the negative synergistic effects caused by multiple causes and effects. These problems significantly affect productivity, direct and indirect costs, and the organisation's very existence.

In general, workplace issues such as violence, drug use, smoking, alcohol abuse, family tensions, depression, and even suicide can have a significant impact. The costs associated with these issues can be enormous in terms of human distress and economic burden. According to the International Labour Organization, health promotion at work is effective when it complements occupational safety and health measures by integrating health promotion activities into OSH management practices to prevent accidents and illnesses and protects and improves the health and well-being of men and women at work (Wilson et al., 2006).

The workplace is, therefore, the ideal place to address the issue of emerging psychosocial risks, thanks to the joint action of employers, workers and public authorities. This approach requires the implementation of an occupational health policy consisting of:

1. Prevent occupational diseases and other work-related pathologies, as well as work accidents;
2. Improve working conditions and the organisation of work;
3. Integrate psychosocial risks into measures of risk assessment;
4. Determine the specific needs of the organisation by studying the interactions inherent to it, those which interest individuals and associated individuals and organisations when evaluating the conditions necessary for workers' health.

The job of a police officer is undeniably stressful, as they are constantly exposed to risks and violence, often feeling powerless when dealing with challenges such as alcoholism or mental illness due to a lack of support systems. Along with the pressure to be prepared for emergencies, police officers face various organizational and management challenges, which they often find more stressful than actual police operations.

The most stressful operations for police officers typically involve witnessing sudden deaths, arresting violent individuals, attending to victims, and informing their families. In the United States, where violent crimes are prevalent, many police officers fear for their lives, leading to a belief that they need to prioritize their safety, sometimes resulting in less hesitation to use force.

Police union representatives suggest that current stress levels have increased due to issues such as drug trafficking, leading to fatigue, alcoholism, and family problems among officers. In the United States, about three-quarters of heart attacks experienced by police officers are linked to stress, and courts have ruled that any police officer who suffers a heart attack, even when off duty, is entitled to compensation.

In this context, a global OSH management system should include the inclusion of psychosocial risks in order to be able to effectively manage their effects according to the same management principles as those applied to other occupational risks and to integrate measures to promote health and improve prevention practices. Indeed, the promotion of health at work has the potential to improve working life, which constitutes an important factor in stimulating productivity and performance at work.

Incorporating health promotion into OSH policies benefits both workers and employers by enhancing the long-term well-being of workers and their families and reducing the burden on health, social protection, and security systems. Integrating measures to promote health into OSH management systems improves occupational health practices and fosters a culture of prevention. The first edition of SOLVE, published in 2002, was specifically developed to address the needs of ILO constituents in safeguarding workers from emerging psychosocial risks and promoting their health and well-being in the workplace.

The second edition has undergone extensive revision and expansion to meet the evolving challenges of today's dynamic work landscape. The original five themes have been re-examined in light of scientific advancements and proven best practices. The updated version now encompasses additional facets of health promotion, including nutrition, sleep, and physical activity. Managing and mitigating stress during shifts in work organization and workplace culture necessitates understanding psychosocial factors. It is also crucial to explore new scenarios that may contribute to economic stress during times of change.

The innovative SOLVE method training comprehensively covers nine crucial topics related to workplace health promotion. This highly interactive method is designed to equip participants with the essential knowledge and skills needed to seamlessly integrate these themes into an occupational safety and health policy and an effective program of action to promote health in the workplace.

To achieve these objectives, the SOLVE method is deliberately:

1) People-cantered. It is increasingly clear that workers represent a decisive asset for the success of any organisation. Their well-being is essential to developing the "new" business, which must be healthy, flexible, competitive, knowledge-based and quality-driven.

2) Preventive purposes. Prevention is a much more effective mode of action regarding costs and success than reacting to a problem afterwards. A healthy work organisation and professional environment are prerequisites for the success of a productive organisation.

3) Sensitive to gender differences. The conditions for which psychosocial risks affect both men and women are considered. During its training and promotional activities, SOLVE seeks gender balance while avoiding assigning a specific role to each.

4) Focused on results. Success can only be measured by results achieved in the workplace. Acting to promote change in the workplace must be a natural extension of the SOLVE approach.

5) Adaptable. The situations are complex, and the solutions are multiple. A one-size-fits-all approach to a given problem does not provide answers tailored to every environment and culture. Several approaches and options are presented and discussed so that users can develop programs and actions that will meet their own needs in their particular situation.

6) Autonomous. Programs and policy measures developed to meet the needs of employers and workers must provide positive results, be adaptable to changing circumstances and be economically justified. The training program aims for a lasting action that can easily be continued within the company while remaining profitable.

Ultimately, SOLVE presents a groundbreaking approach to integrating workers' health, safety, and well-being into the organization's development and economic sustainability. This enhances productivity and competitiveness in the global economy and equips one with effective tools to proactively address emerging workplace risks.

CONCLUSION

Generally speaking, the fight against terrorist action requires speed in the response and a good operational capacity to support a large-scale intervention. Therefore, the findings of this research recommend:

1. Increased strengthening of operational intelligence
2. Joint definition of intervention modalities with all the forces
3. The reorganisation of specialised units to be able to intervene as quickly and effectively as possible
4. The production of a checklist to determine the responsibility of each stakeholder and the intervention procedure
5. An organisation that surrounds everyone when there is a terrorist attack
6. Anticipation of interventions, allowing list places likely to be attacked and training yourself to react better to study how to be most effective possible

In the field of cybercrime, the recommendations are:

1. The creation of technological crime training centres
2. The provision of specialised units with the latest generation of technological equipment
3. Capacity building training for investigators specialising in the field of cybercrime

Regarding irregular migration and its consequences, the recommendations are:

1. Full commitment to the fight against this criminal activity
2. The creation of jobs for young Africans who try by all possible means to migrate to Europe
3. To plan a professional reintegration plan for those who made a living from this activity of illicit migrant trafficking (particularly in the case of Niger, which has already taken measures criminalising this fact)
4. Finally, in the area of psychosocial risk management, the recommendations are to those responsible, given the enormous risks surrounding police activities, to analyse and evaluate the consequences that could arise before implementing any police activity always carefully. It is also recommended to conduct a relevant analysis with all the experts in the field before committing, as this could reduce the risks

Public or private security officials' concern is now broadening to new areas added to their traditional missions – the fight against terrorism, crime, and illegal immigration – which impose new operating conditions on them. In an environment in perpetual upheaval, these managers can no longer free themselves from an approach to monitoring these new threats under the penalty of being victims of surprises and ultimately losing control of the situations. Henceforth, why training and mobilising all security players around continental research, active and dynamic intelligence is essential.

Exploring the transformation of the security concept from its traditional realist roots to more holistic perspectives, in-depth analyses evaluate the relevance of traditional security studies, specifically realism, in the post-Cold War era. The primary focus is examining how societal security interacts with national security, which has received limited attention in academic circles. Multiple studies argue that internal societal dynamics pose a more significant threat to a state's security than external pressures.

As digital reliance expands globally, countries with technological leadership positions are increasingly susceptible to cybersecurity threats. The path of cybersecurity is influenced by various factors, including the economic incentives driving the protection of digital economies, the intertwining of cybersecurity policies with geopolitical disputes, and the competition among major powers for supremacy in surveillance technologies and advanced communication systems such as AI and 5G. Furthermore, examining the role of states in regional and international governance mechanisms and the potential trade-offs between enhancing digital security and upholding privacy and human rights yields valuable insights into the intricate realm of cybersecurity.

The UN's introduction of the new global youth, peace, and security agenda in 2015 has been an important development. Moreover, it is important to understand this agenda in the larger context of the securitisation of development, with an increasing focus on youth as a security subject and actor, shaped by three interconnected sets of global security concerns:

1. The concept of the "youth bulge" refers to the issue of growing surplus populations worldwide.
2. Presenting young people as peacebuilders can help gain their support for the current global social and economic system.
3. Concerns about globally connected young people being radicalized by extremist organizations have led to collaborative efforts between governments and the private sector, which are taking on a more prominent role in monitoring the online activities of young individuals around the world.

Based on an analysis of the core of the global youth and security agenda, there is a need for more critical reflection when considering the growing focus on youth as a social category in global development and policy discussions. Considering the broader implications of counter-radicalisation partnerships and the interconnectedness between state and non-state entities in security is crucial. These partnerships should not lead to a retreat of the state; rather, they should amplify state oversight over activities that may otherwise be perceived as private or voluntary endeavours in crime control. Significantly, they foster informal crime control, which complements and extends the formal control exerted by the criminal justice system. In conclusion, youth work is pivotal in averting and advancing positive radicalisation through lawful and democratic political engagement. However, youth work agencies must exercise prudence when engaging in counter-radicalisation programs primarily influenced by security considerations. To effectively achieve their objectives of integration and fostering a sense of belonging, youth work should endeavour to maintain a clear demarcation from security-related interventions.

REFERENCES

Ajil, A., & Staubli, S. (2023). Predictive policing and negotiations of (in) formality: Exploring the Swiss case. *International Journal of Law, Crime and Justice*, 74, 100605. DOI: 10.1016/j.ijlcj.2023.100605

Albert, C., Baez, A., & Rutland, J. (2021). Human security as biosecurity: Reconceptualizing national security threats in the time of COVID-19. *Politics and the Life Sciences*, 40(1), 83–105. DOI: 10.1017/pls.2021.1 PMID: 33949836

Alcaraz, C., & Lopez, J. (2022). Digital twin: A comprehensive survey of security threats. *IEEE Communications Surveys and Tutorials*, 24(3), 1475–1503. DOI: 10.1109/COMST.2022.3171465

Boulton, E. G. (2022). PLAN E: A grand strategy for the twenty-first century era of entangled security and hyperthreats. *Journal of Advanced Military Studies*, 13(1), 92–128. DOI: 10.21140/mcuj.20221301005

Bove, V., Rivera, M., & Ruffa, C. (2020). Beyond coups: Terrorism and military involvement in politics. *European Journal of International Relations*, 26(1), 263–288. DOI: 10.1177/1354066119866499

Davolio, M. E., Banfi, E., Gehrig, M., Gerber, B., Luzha, B., Mey, E., ... Wicht, L. (2015). School of Social Work Research and Development Background to jihadist radicalisation in Switzerland.

DeVore, M. R., & Stähli, A. (2011). From armed neutrality to external dependence: Swiss security in the 21st century. *Schweizerische Zeitschrift für Politikwissenschaft*, 17(1), 1–26. DOI: 10.1111/j.1662-6370.2011.02003.x

DiGiovanni, C.Jr. (2003). The spectrum of human reactions to terrorist attacks with weapons of mass destruction: Early management considerations. *Prehospital and Disaster Medicine*, 18(3), 253–257. DOI: 10.1017/S1049023X00001138 PMID: 15141866

Eser Davolio, M. (2019). Background of Jihadist radicalisation and measures for prevention and intervention in Switzerland. Sozialpolitik. ch, 2(2.2).

Hagmann, J., Davidshofer, S., Tawfik, A., Wenger, A., & Wildi, L. (2018). The programmatic and institutional (re-) configuration of the Swiss national security field. *Schweizerische Zeitschrift für Politikwissenschaft*, 24(3), 215–245. DOI: 10.1111/spsr.12304

Hughes, G. (2023). War in the grey zone: Historical reflections and contemporary implications. In Survival: Global Politics and Strategy June-July 2020 (pp. 131-157). Routledge.

IOM. (2018). About the Niamey declaration. Niamey Declaration. https://www .niameydeclarationguide.org/#:~:text=ABOUT%20THE%20NIAMEY%20 DECLARATION&text=At%20the%20meeting%2C%20a%20joint,migrants%20 and%20victims%20of%20trafficking

Kersten, A., & Budowski, M. (2016). A gender perspective on state support for crime victims in Switzerland. *International Journal of Conflict and Violence*, 10(1), 127–140.

Kim, J. J., Panton, A., & Schwerhoff, G. (2024). Energy security and the green transition.

Kruck, A., & Weiss, M. (2023). The regulatory security state in Europe. *Journal of European Public Policy*, 30(7), 1205–1229. DOI: 10.1080/13501763.2023.2172061

Liaw, J., De Silva, N., Ibrahim, N., Moiden, A. H., Razak, M. A., & Abd Khalil, A. (2021). The Impact on Non-Traditional Security Threats in Sri Lanka. Akademika, 91(3).

Merz, F. (2021). Improving National PVE Strategies: Lessons Learned from the Swiss Case. Researching the Evolution of Countering Violent Extremism, 22.

Mishra, B. K., Kumar, P., Saraswat, C., Chakraborty, S., & Gautam, A. (2021). Water security in a changing environment: Concept, challenges and solutions. *Water (Basel)*, 13(4), 490. DOI: 10.3390/w13040490

Naji, N., & Schildknecht, D. (2021). Securing Swiss Futurity: The Gefährder Figure and Switzerland's Counterterrorism Regime. *Social Sciences (Basel, Switzerland)*, 10(12), 484. DOI: 10.3390/socsci10120484

Pietrzak, P. (2017). The US Foreign Policy towards Syria under the Donald Trump Administration. RESEARCH GATE. https://www. researchgate. net/pub-lication/310599117_The_US_Foreign_Policy_towar ds_Syria_under_the_Donald_Trump_Administration

Pietrzak, P. (2021). Immanuel Kant and Niccolò Machiavelli's Traditions and the Limits of Approaching Contemporary Conflicts—The Case Study of the Syrian Conflict (2011–Present). *Statu Nascendi Journal of Political Philosophy and International Relations*, 2, 53–84.

Probst, T. M., Gold, D., & Caborn, J. (2008). A preliminary evaluation of SOLVE: Addressing psychosocial problems at work. *Journal of Occupational Health Psychology*, 13(1), 32–42. DOI: 10.1037/1076-8998.13.1.32 PMID: 18211167

République et canton de Neuchâtel. (2023, October 16). *Antennes MPV - neuchâtel.* Police Neuchâteloise Antennes MPV. https://www.ne.ch/autorites/DESC/PONE/GCM/Documents/Antennes.pdf

République et canton de Neuchâtel. (2024). La Gestion Cantonale des menaces (GCM). https://www.ne.ch/autorites/DESC/PONE/GCM/Pages/accueil.aspx

Souder, W. E., & Bethay, D. (1993). The risk pyramid for new product development: An application to complex aerospace hardware. *Journal of Product Innovation Management*, 10(3), 181–194. DOI: 10.1111/1540-5885.1030181

United Nations. (2015, December 9). Security Council, unanimously adopting resolution 2250 (2015), urges member states to increase representation of youth in decision-making at all levels | meetings coverage and press releases. https://press .un.org/en/2015/sc12149.doc.htm

Wilson, D. J., Takahashi, K., Smith, D. R., Yoshino, M., Tanaka, C., & Takala, J. (2006). Recent trends in ILO conventions related to occupational safety and health. *International Journal of Occupational Safety and Ergonomics*, 12(3), 255–266. DOI: 10.1080/10803548.2006.11076688 PMID: 16984785

Yeung, A. B. (2004). The octagon model of volunteer motivation: Results of a phenomenological analysis. *Voluntas*, 15(1), 21–46. DOI: 10.1023/B:VO-LU.0000023632.89728.ff

Yigit, S. (2021). The Concept of Citizenship and the Democratic State. *Electronic Journal of Social and Strategic Studies*, 2, 5–25.

Yigit, S. (2021, December 10). Hybrid war: Addition to the IR lexicon. Retrieved February 29, 2024, from https://www.geopolitic.ro/2021/12/hybrid-war-addition -ir-lexicon/

Yigit, S. (2023). Multi-Dimensional Understandings of Migration: Threats or Opportunities? In Handbook of Research on the Regulation of the Modern Global Migration and Economic Crisis (pp. 239-256). IGI Global.

Zhou, X., Lu, G., Xu, Z., Yan, X., Khu, S., Yang, J., & Zhao, J. (2022). Influence of Russia-Ukraine War on the Global Energy and Food Security. *Resources, Conservation and Recycling*, 188, 106657. DOI: 10.1016/j.resconrec.2022.106657

KEY TERMS AND DEFINITIONS

Extremism: The promotion or advancement of an ideology based on violence, hatred, or intolerance, that aims to negate or destroy the fundamental rights and freedoms of others.

Police: The official organization that is responsible for protecting people and property, making people obey the law, finding out about and solving crime, and catching people who have committed a crime.

Radicalization: The process by which people come to support terrorism and extremism and, in some cases, to then participate in terrorist groups.

Risk: The chance or probability that a person will be harmed or experience an adverse health effect if exposed to a hazard. It may also apply to situations with property or equipment loss, or harmful effects on the environment.

Security: The state of being or feeling secure; freedom from fear, anxiety, danger, doubt, etc.; state or sense of safety or certainty.

State: The political organization of society, or the body politic, or, more narrowly, the institutions of government. The state is a form of human association distinguished from other social groups by its purpose, the establishment of order and security; its methods, the laws, and their enforcement; its territory, the area of jurisdiction or geographic boundaries; and finally, by its sovereignty.

Threat: An avowed present determination or intent to injure presently or in the future.

Violence: The intentional or unintentional use of force whether physical or psychological, threatened, or actual, against an individual, oneself, or against a group of people, a community, or a government.

Chapter 5

Navigating the Nexus of Corporate Governance, Risk Management, and Social Responsibility While Unveiling Responsibility Dilution and Embracing Risk

Yianni Doumenis
University of West London, UK

Emmanuel Fragnière
University of Applied Sciences Western Switzerland, Switzerland

EXECUTIVE SUMMARY

This study explores the complex relationship between corporate governance, risk management, and social responsibility, focusing on the impact of regulatory and market changes. It assesses the influence of the Sarbanes-Oxley Act of 2002 and the Committee of Sponsoring Organisations (COSO) Enterprise Risk Management framework on corporate governance. Through a comparative analysis of risk management across countries, the chapter highlights the role of legal frameworks and industry standards. The study also examines technology's role in enhancing transparency and accountability, particularly through data analytics and cybersecurity. A Greek case study provides a detailed national perspective. By synthesising literature, regulatory reports, and the Greek case, the research offers a comprehensive

DOI: 10.4018/979-8-3693-2675-6.ch005

overview of current practices and future trends, emphasising the importance of transparent risk disclosure and strong governance in building corporate resilience and stakeholder trust.

1. INTRODUCTION: ACTUAL CONTEXT OF CORPORATE RISK MANAGEMENT

Corporate governance and risk management are critical to the sustainability and ethical behaviour of organisations. Integrating these disciplines mitigates potential risks and enhances the organisation's ability to adapt to regulatory changes and market dynamics. Recent global financial crises and corporate scandals have underscored the necessity for robust governance structures and transparent risk management practices, with the G20/OECD Principles of Corporate Governance offering a comprehensive framework to enhance these practices globally (OECD, 2015). This paper provides a thorough analysis of the evolving landscape of corporate governance and risk management, focusing on the interplay between regulatory frameworks, market forces, and technological advancements.

1.1 Overview of the Evolution ff Risk Management and Corporate Governance

Market conflicts at the turn of the 21st century led to sweeping regulatory measures, most notably the Sarbanes-Oxley Act of 2002, which significantly reshaped corporate governance by mandating rigorous financial reporting and internal controls (Sarbanes-Oxley Act, 2002). This act mandated the inclusion of risk management responsibilities within the Board of Directors' purview, particularly through the Independent Auditing Committee. Subsequently, the Committee of Sponsoring Organizations (COSO) introduced the Enterprise Risk Management (ERM) framework, aiming to integrate risk management practices into corporate governance structures (COSO, 2017).

Contemporary risk management governance emphasizes transparency and materiality, expecting companies to disclose pertinent risks and mitigation strategies to stakeholders. The OECD's 2020 report on State-Owned Enterprise (SOE) corporate governance highlights significant advancements in global governance practices (OECD, 2020). This evolution underscores the necessity for corporations to stay informed about emerging trends and regulatory changes to excel in the contemporary business landscape.

1.2 Frameworks for Risk Management in Key Economies

The integration of risk control and transparency at the corporate level is evident in European Corporate Governance Standards, including the UK Corporate Governance Code (Financial Reporting Council, 2014) and the Hellenic Corporate Governance Code (Hellenic Corporate Governance Council, 2021), both of which emphasize the importance of risk management within corporate governance. Both codes place risk management at the heart of governance as a central feature of the Board of Directors.

A comparative analysis of risk management's linkage to the regulatory frameworks of France, Germany, Japan, the UK, and the US is provided in the Table 1, with the OECD Corporate Governance Factbook 2019 offering a comprehensive overview of these practices across different countries (OECD, 2019).

Table 1. Companies' risk management approach is linked to the country's regulatory framework

Country	Board Responsibilities for risk management	Implementation of the Internal Control and Risk Management Systems	Board level Commitment – Risk as part of the Audit Committee
France	By Law	Code	By Law
Germany	Law/Code	Law/Code	Law/Code
Japan	Law	Law	---
UK	Code	Code	Code
US	Stock Exchange	Law/Stock Exchange	Law/Stock Exchange

Source: OECD Corporate Governance Factbook (OECD, 2023)

The landscape of risk management practices varies across different countries, with notable differences in regulatory frameworks and approaches. France and Germany adopt a dual approach, combining legal requirements with industry codes. Japan relies predominantly on legal mandates, while the UK follows a principles-based approach with governance codes providing guidance. In the US, practices are influenced by stock exchange regulations and federal laws.

Figure 1. Risk management and internal control committees (British Business Bank, 2023)

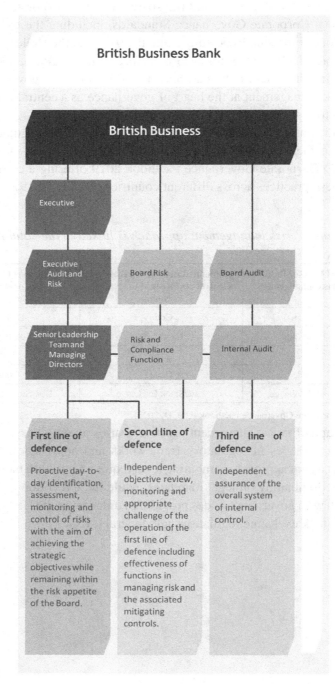

From this overview, countries can be grouped into those adopting a prescriptive, law-based approach (France, Germany, Japan, and the US) and those following a principles-based approach (UK). Notably, the requirement for a specific risk committee outside the audit committee is limited across most countries. The diagram of Figure 1 illustrates the interplay of risk awareness and transparency through robust risk governance and clear accountabilities, as highlighted in the British Business Bank's 2023 report, which outlines the necessary structures and processes for effective risk management (British Business Bank, 2023). This diagram depicts the interplay between risk awareness, transparency, robust risk governance, and clear accountabilities within corporate structures. At the core of effective risk management is a culture of awareness, where stakeholders at all levels are cognizant of potential risks and their implications. Transparency is vital for fostering trust and confidence among stakeholders, as it involves open communication and disclosure of relevant risk information.

Robust risk governance frameworks provide the structure and processes necessary for identifying, assessing, and mitigating risks effectively. These frameworks typically involve the establishment of risk management committees or structures within organisations to oversee risk-related activities.

Clear accountabilities ensure that individuals or teams within the organisation are responsible for managing specific risks and are held accountable for their actions. This accountability fosters a sense of ownership and ensures that risk management efforts are coordinated and effective.

These committees play a crucial role in driving effective risk management and internal control practices within organisations. The Risk Management Committee focuses on the organisation's overarching risk strategy, including risk identification, assessment, mitigation, and monitoring. On the other hand, the Internal Control Committee is responsible for ensuring the effectiveness of internal control systems, including regular evaluations, reviews, and addressing any deficiencies or gaps in control processes.

By establishing and empowering these committees, organisations can enhance their resilience to various risks and strengthen their overall governance framework.

1.3 Regulatory Impact and Global Trends in Risk Management: Objectives of the Study

The primary purpose of this study is to explore the evolving landscape of risk management within corporate governance frameworks, focusing on the critical role of regulatory measures and global trends. Specifically, the study aims to:

1. **Examine the Influence of Regulatory Measures:** Investigate how landmark regulations, particularly the Sarbanes-Oxley Act of 2002, have shaped the incorporation of risk management responsibilities within corporate governance structures, highlighting their impact on board-level oversight and the establishment of risk committees.

2. **Emphasize the Importance of Transparency and Materiality:** Analyse the contemporary emphasis on transparency and materiality in risk management governance. This involves assessing how companies are required to disclose relevant risks and mitigation strategies openly, ensuring that stakeholders are well-informed about potential risks and the company's responses.

3. **Highlight Global Adaptation and Progress:** Review significant global advancements in governance practices, using insights from the OECD and other sources to demonstrate how different countries are adapting their corporate governance frameworks to meet emerging trends and regulatory changes. The study underscores the importance of staying current with these developments to achieve excellence and resilience in the rapidly evolving business environment.

The following is a description of the structure of the paper: Section 2 examines the implementation of the Enterprise Risk Management (ERM) framework, with a particular focus on methodologies and case studies that assess its effectiveness. Section 3 presents a comparative analysis of corporate governance and risk management regulations across different countries, elucidating the variations and commonalities in their approaches. Section 4 presents a case study of corporate governance and risk management practices in Greece, offering a comprehensive analysis within a specific national context. Section 5 examines the role of technology in facilitating transparency and accountability within corporate governance frameworks. Section 6 synthesizes the findings from the preceding sections, and Section 7 discusses the implications for future research and practice in the fields of corporate governance and risk management.

2. ASSESSING THE EFFICACY OF ENTERPRISE RISK MANAGEMENT (ERM) FRAMEWORK IMPLEMENTATION

Evaluating the effectiveness of Enterprise Risk Management (ERM) frameworks, especially those developed by COSO, is vital in contemporary corporate governance for enhancing organizational risk management and governance practices (Deloitte, 2014). This study addresses several gaps in existing literature, providing a comprehensive assessment of ERM implementation.

Research Aims

1. **Evaluate the Effectiveness of ERM Frameworks in Enhancing Corporate Governance:** Previous research lacks comprehensive assessments of COSO's ERM frameworks and their impact on corporate governance practices.
2. **Assess ERM Implementation Methodologies**: A structured approach is needed to evaluate best practices and challenges in ERM implementation across organizations.
3. **Analyse Key Performance Indicators (KPIs) for ERM Effectiveness**: Identifying and analysing relevant KPIs is essential to measure the success of ERM frameworks and understand their impact on risk management and governance.
4. **Conduct Comparative Case Studies Across Different Industries**: Existing literature lacks detailed comparative analyses of ERM implementation across sectors. Examining case studies will highlight the practical challenges and successes in adopting ERM practices.
5. **Provide Recommendations for Tailoring ERM Strategies to Industry-Specific Challenges**: Companies face unique operational contexts and industry-specific challenges, requiring customized ERM strategies to address these effectively.

By focusing on these aims, the study will aim to address significant gaps in current research and offer actionable insights for practitioners, providing a comprehensive evaluation of ERM frameworks and their impact on corporate governance.

2.1 Methodologies for Evaluating Erm Framework Implementation

To rigorously assess the effectiveness of ERM framework implementation, we propose employing a combination of qualitative, quantitative, and mixed methods:

1. **Qualitative approaches:** We recommend conducting in-depth interviews and focus groups with stakeholders involved in ERM implementation, including risk managers, board members, and other key personnel. These qualitative methods will offer rich, contextual insights into the practical challenges and successes encountered during ERM adoption. For instance, interviews can reveal specific difficulties in integrating ERM into existing processes or highlight improvements in risk communication and management.
2. **Quantitative methods:** We propose using surveys and data analysis to objectively measure the impact of ERM on risk management outcomes. Surveys can gather broad data on how ERM has influenced organizational risk practices, while

statistical analysis can quantify changes in risk metrics, such as the frequency and severity of risk incidents. For example, a decrease in the number of risk events or financial losses post-ERM implementation can be directly linked to the framework's effectiveness.

3. **Mixed methods:** To achieve a comprehensive evaluation, we suggest integrating qualitative and quantitative methods. This approach allows for a deeper understanding of trends observed in quantitative data through qualitative insights. For example, qualitative feedback can explain why certain risk mitigation strategies were effective, while quantitative data can provide validation. Combining these methods will offer a more holistic view of ERM's impact.

2.2 Case Studies of Companies Implementing ERM

We advocate for an analysis of case studies from companies across various industries to derive actionable insights into ERM implementation:

1. **Industry-specific applications:** We propose examining ERM implementation in different sectors to understand how the framework is adapted to address industry-specific risks. For instance, financial services might focus on compliance and credit risks, whereas manufacturing might emphasize operational and supply chain risks. These industry-specific studies will reveal how ERM can be customized to fit different organizational contexts and risk environments.

2. **Successful implementations:** We recommend focusing on case studies of companies that have successfully implemented ERM frameworks. These examples can showcase best practices and strategies that led to improved risk management and organizational resilience. For example, successful cases might demonstrate significant reductions in risk exposure or enhanced response capabilities, providing valuable lessons for other organizations.

3. **Comparative analysis:** We propose comparing successful and less successful ERM implementations to identify common factors contributing to effective risk management. This comparative approach can uncover best practices, such as strong senior management support or effective risk assessment processes and highlight challenges that need to be addressed. By analysing these factors, organizations can learn how to enhance their ERM implementation strategies.

2.3 Measuring Impact on Risk Mitigation and Corporate Governance

To gauge the impact of ERM framework implementation, we suggest focusing on the following areas:

1. **Impact on risk mitigation:** We propose evaluating how ERM implementation enhances risk identification, assessment, and mitigation. By comparing risk profiles before and after ERM adoption, researchers can measure improvements in risk management outcomes. For instance, successful ERM implementation should result in a better understanding of risk exposure and a more proactive approach to managing risks, leading to fewer unanticipated risk events.
2. **Influence on corporate governance:** We recommend assessing how ERM frameworks influence corporate governance practices, including decision-making, board oversight, and accountability. By evaluating ERM's integration into governance structures, researchers can determine improvements in transparency and accountability. For example, the presence of an effective ERM framework might lead to more informed strategic decisions and enhanced oversight by the board.
3. **Key Performance Indicators (KPIs):** We suggest identifying and tracking KPIs related to risk management and corporate governance to measure ERM implementation success. Relevant KPIs may include reductions in risk exposure, compliance with regulatory requirements, and levels of board engagement in risk oversight. Monitoring these KPIs over time will provide insights into the long-term impact of ERM on organizational resilience and governance practices.

In summary, we propose a comprehensive approach to assessing ERM framework implementation by employing a mix of methodologies, analysing case studies, and measuring impact through KPIs. This structured approach will offer valuable insights into the effectiveness of ERM frameworks and their contributions to enhanced risk management and governance practices.

3. COMPARATIVE ANALYSIS OF THE REGULATORY LANDSCAPE ACROSS COUNTRIES

Understanding the regulatory landscape across different countries is essential for grasping how corporate governance frameworks are shaped by legal and regulatory environments. This section provides a comparative analysis of corporate governance regulations in select countries, explores how these regulations adapt to market dynamics, and examines their impact on businesses and investor confidence. We will also identify key findings and implications from this analysis to provide a comprehensive overview of the global regulatory environment.

The discussion on regulatory frameworks includes an in-depth examination of how different countries approach corporate governance and risk management. The study compares prescriptive, law-based approaches with principles-based frameworks, highlighting their respective strengths and weaknesses. For example, while the United States' Sarbanes-Oxley Act enforces stringent reporting and accountability standards, the UK's principles-based approach offers more flexibility, allowing companies to adapt governance practices to their specific needs. This section also explores the implications of these frameworks on investor confidence, corporate transparency, and global competitiveness.

3.1 Regulatory Landscape Across Countries

To understand the variations in corporate governance regulations, it is crucial to examine the legal frameworks, regulatory bodies, and key principles guiding practices in different countries.

1. **United States:** In the U.S., corporate governance is primarily guided by regulations such as the Sarbanes-Oxley Act (SOX), which mandates rigorous financial reporting and internal controls. The Securities and Exchange Commission (SEC) oversees compliance, while principles such as shareholder rights, board independence, and executive compensation play critical roles. The emphasis on transparency and accountability is a hallmark of the U.S. regulatory framework.

2. **United Kingdom:** The UK's corporate governance framework is influenced by the UK Corporate Governance Code, which provides principles and provisions for best practices in governance. Corporate governance practices in the UK are guided by principles outlined by SpencerStuart (2019) and the UK Corporate Governance Code, overseen by the Financial Reporting Council, which provides principles and provisions for best practices in governance (Financial Reporting Council, 2018). The Financial Reporting Council (FRC) oversees the implementation of these standards. Key principles include board leadership, effectiveness, and accountability, with a strong focus on ensuring that boards are both diverse and independent.

3. **Germany:** Germany follows a dual board system with the Supervisory Board and the Management Board, each with distinct roles. The German Corporate Governance Code outlines principles for transparency, control, and responsible management. The Code emphasizes stakeholder interests and long-term sus-

tainability, with the Deutsches Institut für Normung (DIN) playing a key role in setting standards.

4. **Japan:** Japan's corporate governance practices are guided by the Corporate Governance Code, which focuses on enhancing transparency and accountability. The Tokyo Stock Exchange (TSE) enforces compliance, and principles such as board diversity and stakeholder engagement are integral to the framework. Recent reforms have aimed at improving board effectiveness and shareholder rights.

5. **France:** In France, corporate governance is influenced by the AFEP-MEDEF Code, which emphasizes the role of independent directors, transparency, and executive pay. The Autorité des Marchés Financiers (AMF) regulates compliance, and there is a strong focus on aligning corporate governance practices with European Union directives.

3.2 Adaptations to Market Dynamics

Regulatory frameworks across countries evolve in response to shifting market dynamics, including economic fluctuations, technological advancements, and geopolitical changes. In response to economic fluctuations, regulatory frameworks have evolved, as seen in the updated guidance by the Financial Reporting Council (Financial Reporting Council, 2020).

1. **Economic fluctuations:** In response to economic crises, such as the 2008 financial crash, many countries have introduced reforms to strengthen corporate governance. For example, the U.S. Sarbanes-Oxley Act was enacted to address accounting scandals and enhance financial transparency. Similarly, the European Union introduced the Markets in Financial Instruments Directive (MiFID II) to improve market stability and investor protection.

2. **Technological advancements:** Technological changes, such as the rise of digital finance and fintech, have prompted regulatory updates to address new risks and opportunities. Technological advancements have prompted regulatory updates, such as the General Data Protection Regulation (GDPR) by the European Commission (2018). For instance, the General Data Protection Regulation (GDPR) in Europe addresses data privacy concerns arising from digital transformations. Countries are also adapting their regulations to include provisions for cybersecurity and digital assets.

3. **Geopolitical changes:** Geopolitical events, such as Brexit, have led to adjustments in regulatory practices. The UK's departure from the EU necessitated changes in its corporate governance regulations to align with new trade agreements

and regulatory standards. Similarly, trade tensions and international sanctions influence how countries shape their corporate governance and compliance requirements.

3.3 Impact on Businesses

Regulatory variations have significant implications for businesses operating across different countries, affecting decision-making, risk management, and transparency.

1. **Decision-making:** Regulatory differences can influence corporate strategies and decision-making processes. For example, stringent regulations in the U.S. might lead to higher compliance costs, affecting corporate budgeting and strategic planning. In contrast, more flexible regulations in other regions might allow for greater operational freedom but may also pose higher risks.
2. **Risk management:** The regulatory environment shapes how businesses approach risk management. For instance, comprehensive regulations in countries like Germany and France may lead to more robust risk management practices, while less stringent frameworks might result in varying levels of risk exposure. Businesses must adapt their risk management strategies to comply with local regulations and mitigate potential legal and financial risks.
3. **Transparency and accountability:** Regulations impact the level of transparency and accountability within organizations. Countries with rigorous disclosure requirements, such as the U.S. and the UK, generally see higher standards of corporate transparency. This, in turn, affects investor trust and corporate reputation.

3.4 Influence on Investor Confidence

The effectiveness of corporate governance regulations is closely linked to investor confidence. Regulatory variations across countries influence investor perceptions and behavior in several ways, as highlighted in McKinsey & Company's 2020 report on the impact of corporate governance on investor confidence (McKinsey & Company, 2020):

1. **Transparency:** Strong regulatory frameworks that enforce transparency and disclosure foster greater investor confidence. For example, high standards of financial reporting and board accountability in the U.S. and the UK can enhance investor trust and attract investment.

2. **Disclosure requirements:** Countries with stringent disclosure requirements typically offer investors more comprehensive information, reducing uncertainty and increasing confidence in the market. Conversely, weaker disclosure standards may lead to investor scepticism and reduced investment.
3. **Enforcement of governance standards:** Effective enforcement of corporate governance standards is crucial for maintaining investor confidence. Regions with robust regulatory bodies and strict enforcement mechanisms, such as the SEC in the U.S. or the AMF in France, tend to have higher levels of investor trust compared to regions with less rigorous enforcement.

3.5 Key Findings and Implications

Our comparative analysis of corporate governance regulations across countries highlights several key findings:

1. **Regulatory Trends:** There is a growing trend towards enhanced transparency and accountability in corporate governance, driven by both local and international pressures. Regulatory frameworks are increasingly incorporating principles related to board diversity, executive compensation, and stakeholder engagement.
2. **Challenges:** Businesses face challenges in navigating diverse regulatory environments, which can lead to increased compliance costs and complexities. Adapting to varying regulations requires a strategic approach to manage cross-border operations effectively.
3. **Best Practices:** Effective governance practices often emerge from countries with stringent regulatory standards and robust enforcement mechanisms. These practices include rigorous disclosure requirements, independent board oversight, and stakeholder engagement.
4. **Implications for Stakeholders:** Policymakers, businesses, and investors must consider the impact of regulatory variations on corporate practices and investor confidence. Policymakers should aim for balanced regulations that promote transparency while minimizing compliance burdens. Businesses need to develop adaptable strategies to comply with diverse regulations, and investors should be aware of the regulatory environment when making investment decisions.

In conclusion, the cross-country comparative analysis underscores the dynamic nature of corporate governance regulations and their significant implications for businesses and investors worldwide. By understanding regulatory variations and their impacts, stakeholders can navigate diverse regulatory landscapes more effectively and make informed decisions in a globalized economy.

4. ADVANCING RISK MANAGEMENT PRACTICES IN GREECE: A CASE STUDY APPROACH

Effective risk management is crucial for ensuring the resilience and sustainability of businesses, and in Greece, integrating robust risk management practices into corporate governance is becoming increasingly significant. This section presents a case study of risk management practices in Greece to illustrate and build upon the insights and recommendations discussed in previous sections. The focus will be on the Hellenic Corporate Governance Code and the practices adopted by leading companies in both the banking and non-banking sectors, drawing on the example of Coca-Cola HBC to propose actionable recommendations for enhancing risk management practices and improving transparency in risk disclosures.

4.1 The Regulatory Landscape and Voluntary Codes: A Case Study

The Hellenic Corporate Governance Code provides a framework for integrating risk management into corporate governance through a 'comply and explain' approach. The regulatory landscape in Greece is influenced by the Hellenic Corporate Governance Code. This allows businesses to adapt risk management practices to their specific industry conditions while encouraging the implementation of best practices. Our case study illustrates the following aspects:

1. **Standardization of risk reporting:** while the Code offers flexibility, there is a notable absence of standardized risk reporting practices. This case study highlights the variability in how companies report risks and how this impacts stakeholders' ability to assess and compare risk management practices. Standardizing risk reporting could enhance comparability and transparency.
2. **Integration with Sustainability Reporting:** The case study reveals a gap between risk management and sustainability reporting. Many companies treat these as separate processes, leading to incomplete disclosures. The integration of these reporting mechanisms is essential for providing a holistic view of risks and their long-term impacts.

4.2 Risk Management in The Greek Banking Sector: Insights From Practice

The Greek banking sector, including major institutions like Piraeus Bank, Alpha Bank, and Eurobank, operates under rigorous regulatory frameworks that mandate extensive risk disclosures. This case study sheds light on:

1. **Integrated approach to sustainability reporting:** Despite comprehensive risk reporting, Greek banks often struggle to integrate these reports with sustainability disclosures. This case study suggests adopting global frameworks such as COSO xor ISO 31000 to enhance the consistency and robustness of risk disclosures and align them with sustainability reporting. Adopting global frameworks such as ISO 31000 can enhance the consistency and robustness of risk disclosures (ISO, 2018).

2. **Enhanced reporting standards:** The case study demonstrates the need for improved alignment with international best practices. Developing standardized guidelines could address discrepancies in risk reporting and improve stakeholder understanding.

4.3 Challenges and Opportunities for Non-Banking Greek Companies: Analyzing Practice Gaps

In contrast to the banking sector, non-banking companies in Greece, such as Hellenic Petroleum and Aegean Airlines, face challenges in adopting effective risk management practices. The case study highlights:

1. **Fragmented Shareholder Communication:** These companies often provide limited quantitative risk disclosures, leaving shareholders with insufficient information about risk exposure and mitigation strategies. The case study underscores the need for more detailed and transparent reporting.

2. **Emulating Best Practices:** Non-banking companies can benefit from adopting the comprehensive risk management practices of leading firms. The case study illustrates how integrating structured risk management frameworks can enhance transparency and stakeholder confidence.

4.4 Exemplary Practices at Coca-Cola HBC (Coca-Cola Hellenic Bottling Company): A Model for Success

Coca-Cola HBC exemplifies high standards in risk management, aligning with COSO and ISO 31000 frameworks. This case study reveals:

1. **Holistic risk management:** Coca-Cola HBC's 'Smart Risk' approach encompasses economic, social, and environmental risks, demonstrating how a comprehensive strategy integrates risk management into all aspects of the business.
2. **Integrated reporting:** The company's integration of risk disclosures into both financial and non-financial reports, combined with regular risk reviews at multiple levels, provides a model for effective risk management.

5. PRECEPTS AND RECOMMENDATIONS FOR ENHANCING RISK MANAGEMENT AND CORPORATE RESPONSIBILITY

Drawing insights from a range of exemplary practices and the analysis of risk management challenges in Greece, this section outlines key precepts and recommendations aimed at advancing risk management practices and aligning with evolving expectations of corporate responsibility. These recommendations address critical aspects of risk management and corporate governance, including responsibility dilution, risk ownership, and social corporate responsibility.

5.1 Recommendations for Enhancing Risk Management Practices

1. **Standardize risk reporting:** Develop and promote standardized risk reporting frameworks across industries to improve comparability and transparency. Industry-specific guidelines aligned with international standards can help achieve consistency in reporting practices.
   Standardized reporting enhances stakeholders' ability to make informed comparisons and decisions based on uniform risk information, fostering greater transparency.
2. **Integrate risk and sustainability reporting:** Ensure that risk management and sustainability reporting are seamlessly integrated. This will provide stakeholders with a comprehensive view of risks and their long-term implications for sustainability.

Integrated reporting aligns risk management with broader sustainability goals, improving the quality of disclosures and offering a holistic view of the organization's risk landscape.

3. **Encourage best practices:** Promote the adoption of best practices in risk management by encouraging companies to follow successful models. Emphasize the importance of aligning risk management strategies with corporate objectives and industry standards.

Emulating best practices leads to improved risk management outcomes and strengthens stakeholder confidence by demonstrating adherence to proven methodologies.

4. **Enhance Stakeholder Communication:** Improve communication with shareholders by providing detailed, quantitative disclosures of risks and mitigation strategies. Regular updates in annual reports and other communications can enhance transparency.

Clear and detailed disclosures build trust and support informed decision-making by stakeholders, ensuring they are well-informed about the company's risk profile and management strategies.

5. **Strengthen board oversight:** Empower Board-level Risk Committees with the resources and authority needed to oversee risk management practices effectively. Ensure that these committees are aligned with corporate objectives and have a well-defined mandate.

Effective board oversight ensures that risk management practices are rigorously monitored and aligned with strategic goals, improving governance and risk management effectiveness.

6. **Invest in Risk Awareness:** Increase risk awareness among stakeholders through targeted education and training programs. Highlight the importance of transparency and accountability in risk management.

Educating stakeholders fosters a culture of risk awareness and accountability, which is crucial for effective risk management and organizational resilience.

5.2 Addressing Responsibility Dilution and Risk Ownership

1. Combat Responsibility Dilution:
   - **Recommendation**: Establish clear frameworks that delineate roles, responsibilities, and accountability mechanisms within the organization. Define the specific duties of board members and oversight committees to prevent gaps in accountability.

- **Rationale**: Clear delineation of responsibilities helps prevent oversight gaps and enhances decision-making processes, ensuring comprehensive accountability across all organizational levels.
- **Challenges**: The primary challenge lies in the complexity of defining specific roles within diverse and dynamic corporate structures. Achieving clarity and consensus among stakeholders can be difficult.
- **Achievements**: Developed a robust framework that successfully delineates roles and responsibilities, improving accountability and decision-making processes within participating organizations.

2. Promote Decentralized Risk Ownership:
- **Recommendation**: Encourage a decentralized approach to risk ownership by empowering employees at all levels to identify and address risks. Foster a culture where risk management is seen as a collective responsibility.
- **Rationale**: Decentralized risk ownership improves agility and responsiveness, leading to better risk management and organizational resilience. Empowering employees at all levels helps in identifying and managing risks more effectively.
- **Challenges**: Promoting a decentralized risk ownership culture requires significant cultural and structural changes within organizations. Resistance to change and lack of appropriate training can impede progress.
- **Achievements**: Successfully fostered a culture of decentralized risk ownership in several case studies, leading to enhanced agility and more effective risk management.

5.3 Embracing Social Corporate Responsibility (CSR)

1. Integrate Social and Environmental Considerations:
- **Recommendation**: Integrate social and environmental considerations into business strategies and operations. Adopt initiatives such as ethical sourcing, diversity programs, and community engagement.
- **Rationale**: Embracing social corporate responsibility enhances reputation, mitigates reputational risks, and supports long-term sustainable growth. Companies that address broader societal issues strengthen their social license to operate and appeal to a wider stakeholder base.
- **Challenges**: Integrating social and environmental considerations into core business strategies can be challenging due to potential conflicts with short-term profit goals and existing operational processes.

- **Achievements**: Developed and implemented initiatives that significantly improved companies' reputations and supported sustainable growth, evidenced by positive stakeholder feedback and improved public perception.
2. Enhance Corporate Responsibility Initiatives:
   - **Recommendation**: Develop and implement robust corporate responsibility programs that align with stakeholder expectations and regulatory pressures. Regularly assess and report on the impact of these initiatives.
   - **Rationale**: Effective corporate responsibility programs demonstrate commitment to broader societal goals and contribute to a positive corporate reputation. Regular assessment and reporting ensure that initiatives remain relevant and impactful.
   - **Challenges**: Ensuring that corporate responsibility initiatives align with both stakeholder expectations and regulatory requirements can be complex and resource intensive.
   - **Achievements**: Created comprehensive corporate responsibility programs that not only aligned with stakeholder expectations but also met regulatory standards, resulting in enhanced corporate reputations and increased stakeholder engagement.
3. Contributions and Insights
   Major Difficulties and Challenges
   1. **Data Availability**: Access to comprehensive and reliable data was a significant challenge, particularly when assessing the effectiveness of ERM frameworks across different industries and geographical regions.
   2. **Regulatory Differences**: Navigating the varying regulatory landscapes across countries posed challenges in creating a universally applicable framework.
   Achievements
   1. **Comprehensive Framework Development:** Successfully developed a comprehensive framework for assessing ERM effectiveness, tailored to address the unique challenges and requirements of different industries.
   2. **Enhanced Corporate Governance:** Improved corporate governance practices through the clear delineation of roles and responsibilities, fostering a culture of decentralized risk ownership.
   3. **Sustainable Growth Initiatives:** Facilitated the integration of social and environmental considerations into business strategies, promoting long-term sustainable growth and enhancing corporate reputations.

By adopting these recommendations, organizations can advance their risk management practices and align with evolving expectations of corporate responsibility. The insights drawn from various successful practices and identified challenges provide a valuable foundation for improving risk management and enhancing overall corporate governance. Embracing a proactive and comprehensive approach to risk management is essential for navigating uncertainties and achieving long-term success.

7. DISCUSSION AND CONCLUSION

Key Developments

The transformation of corporate governance and risk management practices has been significantly influenced by societal changes, evolving government regulations, and emerging business trends. This study highlights several key developments:

1. **Regulatory Measures**: The Sarbanes-Oxley Act and the COSO ERM framework have reshaped how businesses approach governance, mandating more comprehensive risk management practices and greater transparency.
2. **Global Variations**: The study explores the global variations in corporate governance and risk management approaches. While there is a universal recognition of the importance of board-level oversight and transparent risk reporting, the methods and rigor of implementation differ across regions. This diversity is driven by varying legal and cultural contexts, which influence how companies perceive and manage risks.
3. **Technological Integration**: The role of technology in modern governance practices cannot be overstated. The integration of data analytics, artificial intelligence, and cybersecurity measures is revolutionizing risk management, providing organizations with new tools to anticipate and mitigate risks. This technological integration is critical for enhancing transparency and accountability, which are essential for building stakeholder trust.
4. **Social Corporate Responsibility**: The study emphasizes the growing importance of social corporate responsibility. By incorporating ethical considerations into business strategies, organizations can strengthen their reputation and gain the trust of stakeholders, which is increasingly vital in today's socially conscious market.

The integration of risk management into corporate governance frameworks is essential for building resilient and sustainable businesses. The study underscores the importance of regulatory measures like the Sarbanes-Oxley Act in enforcing these practices, while also highlighting the global differences in governance approaches.

Findings

- Organizations must continue to prioritize clear accountability, empower employees to manage risks proactively, and incorporate social responsibility into their strategies.
- Transparency in risk disclosure and the adoption of advanced technological tools are crucial for enhancing corporate resilience and stakeholder confidence.

Future Research Directions

- Future research should focus on evaluating the effectiveness of ERM frameworks and exploring the impact of emerging technologies on corporate governance.
- As businesses navigate an increasingly complex and uncertain environment, adopting a proactive and integrated approach to risk management and governance will be key to achieving long-term success.

By addressing these areas, organizations can better align with the evolving landscape of corporate governance and risk management, ensuring sustained success and resilience in the face of future challenges.

REFERENCES

British Business Bank. (2023). *Annual report and accounts 2023*. Retrieved from https://www.british-business-bank.co.uk/about/research-and-publications/annual-report-and-accounts-2023

Committee of Sponsoring Organizations of the Treadway Commission (COSO). (2017). Retrieved from https://www.coso.org/_files/ugd/3059fc_61ea5985b03c4293960642fdce408eaa.pdf

Deloitte. (2014). *Enterprise risk management*. Retrieved from https://www2.deloitte.com/gr/en/misc/litetopicpage.global-topic-tags.enterpriseriskmanagement.html

European Commission. (2018). *Streamlining and strengthening corporate governance within the European Commission*. Retrieved from https://commission.europa.eu/system/files/2018-11/streamlining-strengthening-corporate-governance-european-commission_en.pdf

Financial Reporting Council. (2014). *Guidance on risk management, internal control and related financial and business reporting* (1st ed.). The Financial Reporting Council Limited. Retrieved from https://www.frc.org.uk/news-and-events/news/2014/09/frc-updates-uk-corporate-governance-code/

Financial Reporting Council. (2018). *Guidance on risk management, internal control and related financial and business reporting*. Retrieved from https://www.frc.org.uk/getattachment/d672c107-b1fb-4051-84b0-f5b83a1b93f6/Guidance-on-Risk-Management-Internal-Control-and-Related-Reporting.pdf

Financial Reporting Council. (2020). *Company guidance (Updated 20 May 2020) (COVID-19)*. Retrieved from https://www.frc.org.uk/news-and-events/news/2020/05/covid-19-update-7-may-2020/

Hellenic Corporate Governance Council. (2021). Code of corporate governance for listed companies. Retrieved from https://www.esed.org.gr/en/code-listed

ISO. (2018). *ISO 31000*. Retrieved from https://www.iso.org/obp/ui#iso:std:iso:31000:ed-2:v1:en

McKinsey & Company. (2020). *Investors remind business leaders: Governance matters*. Retrieved from https://www.mckinsey.com/business-functions/strategy-and-corporate-finance/our-insights/investors-remind-business-leaders-governance-matters

OECD. (2015). *G20/OECD principles of corporate governance*. OECD Publishing., DOI: 10.1787/9789264236882-

OECD. (2019). *OECD corporate governance factbook 2019*. OECD Publishing. Retrieved from https://www.oecd.org/corporate/Corporate-Governance-Factbook.pdf

OECD. (2020). Executive summary. In *Implementing the OECD guidelines on corporate governance of state-owned enterprises: Review of recent developments*. OECD Publishing. DOI: 10.1787/deac8436-

Sarbanes-Oxley Act of 2002: Conference report (to accompany H.R. 3763). (2002). U.S. G.P.O.

SpencerStuart. (2019). *Corporate governance in the UK*. Retrieved from https://www.spencerstuart.com/-/media/2019/ukbi-2019/uk_board_index_2019_final_version.pdf

KEY TERMS AND DEFINITIONS

Accountability: The obligation to take responsibility for actions, report on outcomes, and be answerable to stakeholders.

Committee of Sponsoring Organisations (COSO): An organisation providing frameworks for internal control, risk management, and fraud deterrence, widely adopted by businesses for governance practices.

Corporate Governance: The system by which companies are directed and controlled, ensuring transparency, accountability, and fairness in balancing the interests of stakeholders.

Cybersecurity: The protection of systems, networks, and data from digital threats, ensuring their confidentiality, integrity, and availability.

Data Analytics: The analysis of raw data to uncover patterns and insights, informing decision-making.

Enterprise Risk Management (ERM): A comprehensive approach to managing risks across an organisation, aligning them with its strategic goals.

Risk Management: The process of identifying, assessing, and mitigating potential threats to an organisation's objectives and assets.

Sarbanes-Oxley Act: A 2002 US law enacted to enhance corporate financial transparency and prevent accounting fraud, introducing strict regulations for corporate governance.

Social Responsibility: An organisation's ethical obligation to contribute positively to society, often extending beyond legal requirements to address social, environmental, and economic issues.

Transparency: The practice of openly and clearly sharing accurate information about a company's operations and decisions with stakeholders.

Chapter 6
Extrapolating the Influence of Risk Assessment Tools on Organizational Effectiveness Within the Automobile Industry:
An Empirical Study

K. Madhu Kishore Raghunath
https://orcid.org/0000-0002-8134-5718
GITAM University, Visakhapatnam, India

S. L. Tulasi Devi
https://orcid.org/0000-0002-1285-4447
National Institute of Technology, Warangal, India

P. Sheela
https://orcid.org/0000-0003-3689-1530
GITAM University, Visakhapatnam, India

EXECUTIVE SUMMARY

Risk assessment as the need of the hour is what managers agree upon unanimously in today's competitive environment. The main objective of this research study is to examine the aspects of risk and risk assessment in organizational setup and further analyze the relationship between risk assessment tools and organizational effectiveness in the Indian automobile industry. The study will give managers a

DOI: 10.4018/979-8-3693-2675-6.ch006

perspective of how risk assessment tools are different from one another in terms of their perceived benefits as managers have plenty of risk assessment tools to choose from within an industry and the contributions of this study will render great insight to risk managers and future entrepreneurs in managing risk innovatively. The present study is among the first few to identify and explore the impact of risk assessment tools on organizational effectiveness via perceived benefits. These findings advance the understanding of risk assessment tools upon organizational effectiveness and help risk managers assess and control risk in a better way.

1. INTRODUCTION

The term risk and the aspects of risk assessment are age-old for our generation, but their application is very much relevant and necessary for the survival of organizations to the present date also. The risk-taking mindset of organizations makes risk assessment a prerequisite while performing their usual business operations or while they test the uncharted waters of new businesses. Application of risk assessment is facilitated via various risk assessment tools in every organization and the evolution of research on risk assessment tools can be attributed to National Research Council's report *Risk assessment in the federal government: Managing the process*, popular known as "The Red Book", where it addressed the standard terminology and concepts for risk assessments.

The concepts of risk assessment have evolved and ventured into various dimensions ranging from industry to industry with various risk assessment tools at the helm of the organizational risk-based decision-making process. Risk assessment tools are predominantly various methodologies used to treat or manage risk in an organizational setup. Jacxsens et al (2016); Raghunath et al (2017) posited that risk assessment processes are generally performed qualitatively or quantitatively based on their decisions to be made.

Risk assessment models are key contributors in risk control at many platforms namely community issues management, synergy risk management and sustainability parameters (Eydeland & Wolyniec, 2003; Weber et al, 2010) in curtailing risk in everyday decisions. These tools emphasise the prerequisite for effective root cause analysis in identifying and mitigating risk factors to achieve their organisational goals. Arias & Stern (2011) also observed that the key for better efficiency and success among organisations is highly attributed by risk management tools and techniques.

The term risk assessment has been explained in the past and will be redefined in the future with changing organizational procedures. Still, there is a lot to explore given the vast area of study in risk analysis and assessment. Studies also are emphasised on correlations between risk and the latent concepts of perceived benefit within various streams. Renn (2017) & Slovic (2016) observed that instances where perceived benefits are higher, the risk exposure seems to be less. The existing literature motivates and acts as a precursor to test the psychological benefits present among risk assessment tools to assess inverse relationship and large inequality among risks and benefits (Kochan & Nowicki, 2018; Ali & Golgeci, 2019).

1.1 Risk Assessment and Automobile Industry

The Indian automotive industry is supposed to reach a valuation of 251.4-282.8 billion US dollars by 2027 (IBEF, 2023) and automotive industry constituting 7.1% of India's GDP, India is the largest producer of 2W & 3W and 3rd largest manufacturer of passenger cars in the world of commercial vehicles worldwide (IBEF, 2024). Further, the auto-component sector is also a significant boost to Indian economy. In line with significant changes happening in the automobile industry and with an inherent plague of risks affecting automobile manufacturing and assembling operations, manufacturers within the industry are also subjected to constant demand fluctuation, further deteriorating the situation (IBEF, 2024).

A statistical survey by India risk survey identified that all the categories within the automobile industry have seen a slowdown, which has negatively affected automobile dealers all over the country in recent times, attributing to utmost stagnation in operations of about 300 dealers (ACMA, 2022). This situation when analyzed further has led to the finding that automobile manufacturers' and dealers' risk assessment tactics and tools used for analyzing risk were not sufficient and significant (SIAM, Society of Indian Automobile Manufacturers, 2022).

With these existing challenges and the future, automotive industry needs constant risk assessment via risk assessment tools and methodologies. Aneziris et al (2008) expressed risk assessment as a core element of risk management and a platform to provide enhanced safety management. It is also a contemplating phenomenon that facilitates the management of establishing priorities and apportioning resources in a way to eliminate risks and eventually ensure health and safety at work. Jeong et al (2018) followed it by positing that in case the projected risk for the entire operation is very high, the overall risk should be reassessed with the help of new measures till it becomes tolerable.

The present study will examine how perceived benefits of various tools will impact the automobile industry's organizational effectiveness leading to the research question.

RQ1. What is the impact of risk assessment tools on Organizational effectiveness within the Automobile industry?

The objective of present article is to assess the influence of Risk tools within the Automobile industry and strengthen risk-based decision-making process within business managers and decision makers. This phenomenon has been extensively underpinned by several studies to study the respondent's perceptions towards an outcome in Finance (Sharif et al., 2021 & Maryam et al., 2021), Marketing (Kumar et al., 2022 & Ahadiat et al., 2021), Hospitality (Tajeddini et al., 2021 & Pahrudin et al., 2021), Supply chain (Carfora et al., 2021 & Centobelli et al., 2021) and Sustainability (Muler et al., 2021). Further the manuscript is structured as mentioned; Section 2 will examine the past studies and provide the hypotheses. Section 3 put forth the methodology part, section 4 will deal with the outcomes and discussions and finally Section 5 will provide the conclusion.

2. LITERATURE REVIEW AND DEVELOPMENT OF HYPOTHESES

2.1 Risk Assessment and Organizational Effectiveness

Callahan & Soileau (2017); CGMA (2016) expressed that risk assessment controls are built to fortify the attainment of organisational objective and firms which are highly centralised with risk strategies showcase higher operating performance. Further Raghunath & Devi (2018); Junior & Carvalho (2013) articulated that synchronization of risk assessment tools enhance better implementation of decisions and helps achieving higher operating performances, which leads to better safety and organizational success.

Dallat et al (2017) in their research observed that to mitigate risk in organizations; managers are in need of a dynamic change and synergy that only risk assessment tools can provide. Aven (2011) observed that engineering risk assessments must be supported by a broader risk perspective in addition to existing probability and alternate approaches to make risk assessment an efficient process in dealing with ubiquitous risk scenarios which jeopardize organizational effectiveness.

Rausand (2013) & Manuele (2016) posited that assessment of risk factors is a precursor for determining possible mishaps along with their likelihood and consequences along with tolerance strategies to be put in place. Risk assessment in most organizations is performed with the help of qualitative, quantitative, and hybrid tools. Risk assessment is an intrinsic part of broader risk management strategy which has become the key to controlling business and operational risks within a pandemic situation (Global Risk Survey, 2022). Ostrom& Wilhelmsen (2012) pointed out that risk assessment has evolved from being a limited science discipline to a multidisciplinary engineering requirement that is complimented by risk assessment tools

& techniques to identify and analyze potential threats within the environment. It is also emphasized that the absence of risk assessment within an organization will jeopardize organizational efficiency & effectiveness. Jacxsens et al., (2016); Lima et al ., (2020) & Chlodnicka & Zimon (2020) also posited that risk assessment facilitates overall complete evaluation of hazards in business activities which when ignored, leads to side effects such as companies insolvency and liquidation.

2.1.1 Risk Assessment Tools Used for the Study

From the initial studies carried out in the automobile industry, it was observed that the risk assessment procedure implemented in this industry was similar to other industries and most of the risk assessment tools fall in common category for risk assessment in every industry.

Figure 1 showcases the various tools under risk assessment (Marhavilas et al., 2011) operational in various spheres of automobile industry to achieve its risk mitigations objectives.

Figure 1. Risk assessment tools used for the study

Qualitative Risk Assessment Tools
What if Analysis
Delphi Technique
Sequential Timed Event Plotting
Hazard & Operability Study
Scenario Analysis

Quantitative Risk Assessment Tools
Decision Matrix Risk Analysis
Monte Carlo Simulation
Weighted Risk Analysis
Domino Effect
Proportional Risk Assessment Technique

Hybrid Risk Assessment Tools
Human Error Analysis Technique
Failure Mode Effect Analysis
Fault Tree Analysis
Event Tree Analysis

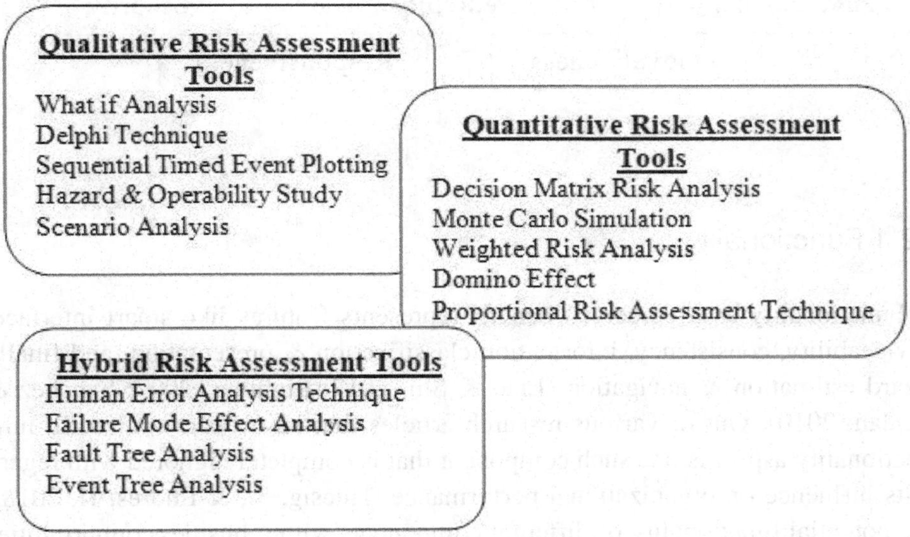

2.2 Perceived Benefits

K. M. K., & Devi, S. T. (2022) articulated that risk assessment tools are renowned for providing efficient solutions for procrastinating disastrous scenarios. Raghunath & Devi (2018) also illustrated that efficiency of risk-based decision-making relies upon use of assessment tools and further contemplation on their latent perceived benefits reinvigorates organizational effectiveness.

Perceived benefits in general are allied with the cognitive and behavioural intent and both variables are positively related (Yoon and Chung, 2018). In the words of Chandon et al (2000) the concept of "Perceived benefits are philosophy of constructive results allied with performance to a existing threat". Leung, Y. (2013) also acknowledged perceived benefits for "The perception of the positive result from a specific action". It is also observed that many managers in their fields of operations try to analyse positive perceptions as individual motives are driven by their cognitive abilities. Figure 2 explores the benefits of tools.

Figure 2. Perceived benefits

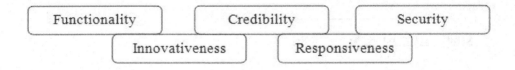

2.2.1 Functionality

Functionality as a perceived benefit represents features like smart interface, serviceability, consistency, information classification & presentation, and finally hazard estimation & navigation (Liao & Shi, 2017; Lightner, 2007; Sanchez & Rondan, 2010). Out of various research articles that have been written till now functionality aspect is one such component that is completely ignored with regard to its influence on organizational performance (Huesig, S., & Endres, H. 2018). The potential functionality of different components within business opportunities is very important for organizational effectiveness (Yoo et al. 2012).

Functionality also envisages capability, suitability, and the range of operations that can be pursued with the help of a tool in conformance with the requirements specified. When it comes to organizational setup, the functionality of risk assessment tools represents its performance execution capability to identify and manage different risk scenarios in various business activities. Raghunath et al., (2021) in their study pointed out that functionality is positively significant with qualitative and hybrid risk tools whereas the impact was not significant for quantitative risk assessment tools in the construction business. They further illustrated that when it comes to information technology industry, the aspect of functionality within hybrid and qualitative risk assessment tools are not positively significant contrary to quantitative risk assessment tools which are positively significant.

H1. Functionality aspect under risk assessment tools have a positive impact on the Organizational Effectiveness of the Automobile Industry.

2.2.2 Innovativeness

Nasierowski & Arcelus (2012) posited in their research that innovation in an enterprise denotes an economic resolution to attain benefit of the system in an inventive and resourceful way to avert uncertainties from becoming a reality. Innovativeness is strategy which provides significant advantage for the company in all aspects. The innovativeness of risk assessment tools within an organization provides the ability to capture risk scenarios through a variety of methods and allows businesses to work with a lot more efficiency. Innovativeness provides a quick and easy way to mitigate or sort through risk scenarios and prevent risk factors from slipping through the cracks where the root causes of these risk factors are identified regularly. Nambisan et al., (2017) opined innovativeness to be the substantial takeaway from the organizational process and tools for enhancing organizational effectiveness. Huesig, S., & Endres, H. (2018) also posited that innovativeness within organizational tools should be finely nuanced for better performance and output. Though innovativeness in risk assessment is a prerequisite, it is the opposite as Raghunath, K. M. K., & Devi, S. T. (2022) observed that the innovativeness aspect in the construction industry & information technology was completely insignificant.

H2: Innovativeness aspect under risk assessment tools have a positive impact on the Organizational Effectiveness of the Automobile Industry.

2.2.3 Responsiveness

Responsiveness of a product or tool is one of the key perceived benefits for a customer to utilize that product or tool in the first place to perform the job efficiently. According to (Sweet, 2000), responsiveness signifies the capacity of a structure or system to comprehend and complete its tasks promptly. Responsiveness as a latent variable signifies the approach a tool responds speedily and successfully to a broad range of risk scenarios. Reis, H. T., & Clark, M. S. (2013) articulated that responsiveness should be an interpersonal process within organizational activities to ensure far-reaching results; hence, responsiveness is a prerequisite for perceived benefits from organizational processes. Raghunath, K. M. K., & Devi, S. T. (2022) expressed that the responsiveness of qualitative tools in IT industry is positively significant. In contrast, the responsiveness of quantitative and hybrid tools is not substantial. Responsiveness as a perceived benefit is consistently effective in making an appropriate and timely estimate of risk occurrences and it further forecasts short-range variability in normal conditions, which call for necessary amends in the overall business environment. Responsiveness renders the tools to not only react quickly but regularly monitor all the important accessible information to formulate the best possible solution/decision to mitigate the risk& drive both the consistency and value of business outcomes.

H3 Responsiveness aspect under risk assessment tools have a positive impact on the Organizational Effectiveness of the Automobile Industry.

2.2.4 Credibility

The term Credibility is equivalent to ability and dependability. A credible tool in general represents the mentioned features a) Competence in recognizing uncertainty b) Conviction to control diverse risk elements and to mitigate risk factors in organisation (Bentele & Nothaft, 2011). Credibility aspects in terms of qualitative and hybrid tools are positively significant, while quantitative tools are insignificant in the IT industry (Raghunath, K. M. K., & Devi, S. T., 2022). Credibility is a multidimensional perception construct that contributes a lot to any business activity and eliminates unexpected sensitive behavior with regard to risk factors and puts forward strategies to create value. The risk management process becomes effortless and effective from the viewpoint of risk managers and employees when the tools are trusted and believed to eradicate ubiquitous risk scenarios and create value for an organization (Jackob, 2008).

H4 Credibility aspect under risk assessment tools have a positive impact on the Organizational Effectiveness of the Automobile Industry.

2.2.5 Security

Perceived security can be defined as an attribute within a tool or component with which an individual feels protected against security threats (Compromised safety, financial losses and reputational harms) resulting from various risk scenarios in business activities. Security factor encompasses a range of tactics that avert, threats pertinent within a situation. It additionally involves protecting human resources, systems and data from intrusions, and other vulnerabilities that could jeopardize an entity (Vasile & Croitoru, 2012). Security is a substantial parameter for organizations, all the tools are positively significant in the IT industry (Raghunath, K. M. K., & Devi, S. T., 2022). Lee, M. C. (2009) illustrated that the overall implications of perceived benefits on organizational effectiveness are necessary, but a tool's security aspect is substantially important. Security as a feature within risk assessment tools is a prerequisite to protect organizations against job hazards and different risk scenarios and envisage future business opportunities (Alli, 2008). Security as a perceived benefit is decisive for enterprises of all shapes and sizes to function effectively under the shadow of potential risks. Security factor eventually provides integrity, and confidentiality towards business information and tools which are critical success factors. (Hartono et al., 2014).

H5 Security aspect under risk assessment tools have a positive impact on the Organizational Effectiveness of the Automobile Industry.

Furthermore, the phenomenon of perceived benefits and risk assessment in regard to organizational success has never been articulated directly, which has led to this research, where readers can witness a novel way of approaching risk assessment concept for attaining success.

2.3 Research Framework

The research framework shown in Figure 3, presents an underlying structure or model to support the author's collective research efforts, where the framework articulates the different variables within the study, which serve the purpose of justifying the hypotheses framed within the study regarding the Independent and dependent variables.

Figure 3. Research framework

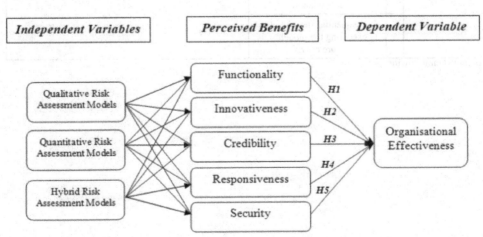

3. RESEARCH METHODOLOGY

Determinants of the study i.e., the constructs and the associating variables were categorised grounded on an exhaustive literature study and the questions were sent to academicians for verification. Based on the comments and suggestions received from the academician, further changes were incorporated, this helped the questionnaire in achieving content validity (Nagariya et al., 2020). The survey further was divided into two divisions. Part 1 consisted of questions related to Industry type, designation, type of firm, and total workforce in the firm, whereas Part 2 consisted of questions relating to the respondent's insight of the five latent constructs. A five-point Likert scale- Strongly Agree (5) to Strongly Disagree (1) was selected for the study (Nemoto & Beglar., 2014). Further, SPSS 20.0 and AMOS 22.0 were used for study. Table 1 further shows the measurement instrument.

Table 1. Measurement instrument

Latent Construct		Description of Question	Adapted Source
Functionality (FUNC)	1	Risk assessment tools are reliable and result oriented.	Huesig, S., & Endres, H. (2018), Yoo et al., (2012), Raghunath, K. M. K., Devi, S. T., Anuradha, K., &Veni, K. V. S. K. (2021) &Raghunath, K. M. K., & Devi, S. T. (2022).
	2	Risk assessment tool covers all the probable variables of risk.	
	3	Risk assessment models enhance departmental functionality	
	4	Risk assessment models help in the effective mapping of uncertainty present in an organization.	
	5	The sequential steps involved in executing the model/tools are easy.	

continued on following page

Table 1. Continued

Latent Construct		Description of Question	Adapted Source
Innovativeness (INNO)	1	Risk tools facilitate the critical evaluation of several risk scenarios.	Fichman et al., (2014), Huesig, S., & Endres, H. (2018), Raghunath, K. M. K., & Devi, S. T. (2022)&Nambisan et al., (2017)
	2	Scope for creative problem solving is high with risk tools	
	3	Risk tools have a user-friendly Interface	
	4	Innovation is a predominant aspect with this tool	
	5	Risk assessment tools are useful in predicting futuristic risk scenarios.	
Responsiveness (RESP)	1	Level of control provided by tools over risk scenarios is ideal.	Reis, H. T., & Clark, M. S. (2013), Raghunath, K. M. K., & Devi, S. T. (2022), Husted, J. A., Cook, R. J., Farewell, V. T., & Gladman, D. D. (2000).
	2	Organizations depend highly on risk assessment tools to assess and mitigate uncertainty.	
	3	Risk assessment tools are quick to identify and assess risk at work sites.	
	4	Risk assessment tools are dynamic enough for all risk scenarios.	
	5	Risk models are highly responsive each and every time	
Credibility (CRED)	1	Risk tools attribute to the credibility of every organization.	Gaziano, C., & McGrath, K. (1986), Liu, B. (2006), Self , C. C. (2014) & Raghunath, K. M. K., & Devi, S. T. (2022).
	2	Risk tools are cost-effective.	
	3	Risk tools boost up the success rate under severe circumstances.	
	4	Risk tools are highly preferred for your organization.	
	5	Organizations often underestimate the credibility of risk assessment tools in decision making.	

continued on following page

Table 1. Continued

Latent Construct		Description of Question	Adapted Source
Security (SECU)	1	Possibility of tool inefficiencies while operating are minimum.	Lee, M. C. (2009), Pei, Y., Wang, S., Fan, J., & Zhang, M. (2015) & Raghunath, K. M. K., & Devi, S. T. (2022)
	2	Risk tools provide certainty of safety in decision making.	
	3	Risk assessment tools provide real-time information regarding risk scenarios.	
	4	Levels of security by risk tools are effective & reliable.	
	5	Models Provide an complete analysis of different risk scenarios.	
Organizational Effectiveness (OE)	1	Risk assessment tools provide synergy & stability to various functional departments.	Holzmann& Jorgensen (1999), Eydeland&Wolyniec (2003), Weber et al, (2010), Callahan& Soileau (2017), Raghunath & Devi 2018) &Jacxsens et al (2016) &Raghunath, K. M. K., & Devi, S. T. (2022)
	2	Risk assessment tools facilitate enhanced risk-based decision making.	
	3	Results provided by risk assessment tools do influence the Profitability Index.	
	4	Risk assessment tools result in improved performance management.	
	5	Quality of strategic planning is enhanced through risk assessment models	
	6	Operational efficiency is enhanced by using risk tools	
	7	Organizational productivity and efficiency are optimised by risk assessment tools.	

3.1 Data and Sample

Data used under primary study was gathered via an online survey, where a preset questionnaire was sent through email to employees at various levels. The potential list of respondents was finalised via websites of multiple Automobile original equipment manufacturers and automobile parts manufacturers in India.

The survey was thoroughly discussed among employees and responses were segregated. In total 324 responses were received out of 500 respondents contacted via online and personal interaction. Finally, after screening, 150 complete responses were finalized for the study. A simple random sampling method was implemented to accumulate data (Hair et al., 2010). Common bias test within the data was using Harman's single-factor test. The result of maximum variance factor was within the level of 50% (Podsakoff, 2003).

3.3 Demographics of the Respondents

The data was collected from more than 50 companies, with organizations ranging from 50 to 250 employees. The respondents mainly constituted Risk management directors (6%), chief risk officers (11%), risk managers (19%), risk management teams (24%), risk supervisors (21%), and other employees (19%). Table 2 further shows the categorization of respondents in a detailed way.

Table 2. Respondents profile

Designation	Automobile Industry	
	Frequency	%
Risk Management Director	9	6
Chief Risk Officers	16	11
Risk Managers	28	19
Risk Management Teams	36	24
Risk Supervisors	32	21
Other Employees	29	19
	150	100

4. RESULTS

The final output of the current study will be discussed and analysed step by step with the support of three structural equation model, which has achieved all ideal model fit indices. Assessment of the structural models will be further strengthened by evaluating the Reliability indices, Validity indices and finally model fit indices.

4.1 Harman's Single Factor Test

This test was executed to evaluate common bias among responses and the results indicate that, first factor explains maximum variance. For the qualitative risk assessment tools, the value is 28.87%; for quantitative risk assessment tools the value is 30.33%; and hybrid risk assessment tools is 33.45% which is within the limit of 50% (Podsakoff, et al., 2003).

4.2 Cronbach Alpha (α)

All factor values within the model should be higher than 0.70 (Nunnally and Bernstein, 1994; Lin et al., 2010) and as depicted through table 3, all factor values are above .70.

4.3 Exploratory Factor Analysis (EFA)

The foremost step in model building is to identify the factors and then perform EFA. Where Kaiser-Meyer-Olkin (KMO) value stood at 0.738 for qualitative risk assessment tools, 0.769 for Hybrid risk assessment tools and 0.772 for quantitative risk assessment tools, all factors had values beyond 0.60 level (Hair et al., 2010). Principal component analysis was conducted with varimax rotation as an extraction method. Total variance represented by all five components of qualitative risk tools was 68.534, quantitative risk tools were 63.696 and hybrid risk tools were 62.073, which in all cases is above 60%. CFA is illustrated in the next step where SEM was used to test the model fit.

4.4 Confirmatory Factor Analysis (CFA)

As a part of CFA, the following results were obtained under qualitative risk assessment tools in AMOS 22.0. The model fit parameters were tested as $\chi2/df$ (CMIN/DF) was 1.273, RMSEA was 0.068, CFI was 0.921, TLI was 0.926, and GFI = 0.890, PCFI = 0.853 and PNFI = 0.759, all the values were below the cutoff values mentioned by (Hu et al., 2009; Becker et al.,2012; Byrne, 2013). For the quantitative risk assessment tools, the following are the CFA outputs obtained in AMOS 22.0. The model fit parameters were tested through some measures of fit as mentioned further, $\chi2/df$ (CMIN/DF)=1.219, RMSEA= 0.065, CFI = 0.974, TLI = 0.961, and GFI = 0.854, PCFI = 0.713 and PNFI = 0.798, all the values were within the cutoff values mentioned by (Hu et al., 2009; Becker et al.,2012; Byrne, 2013). For the hybrid risk assessment tools, the following are the CFA outputs obtained in AMOS 22.0. The model fit parameters were estimated as $\chi2/df$ (CMIN/DF) =1.376,

RMSEA= 0.079, CFI = 0.937, TLI = 0.956, and GFI = 0.923, PCFI = 0.793 and PNFI = 0.751, all the values are within cutoff mentioned (Hu et al., 2009; Becker et al., 2012; Byrne, 2013).

4.4.1 Composite Reliability (CR)

It measures the consistency & reliability of all factors (Henseleret al., 2009) and all factors of perceived benefits are within the threshold as all constructs have values > 0.7. Table 3 shows composite reliability results.

4.4.2 Convergent Validity (CV)

Convergent validity of risk assessment tools is visualized through Average Variance Extracted (AVE) values (Fornell & Larcher, 1981; Koufteros, 1999) and all the constructs have value above 0.50 which means the variance is highly shared and the value is within the cutoff level (Fornell and Larcker, 1981). Table 3 shows the AVE values.

Table 3. Results of factor loadings, AVE, CR, and Cronbach's alpha

Construct	Code	Qualitative Risk Assessment Tools				Quantitative Risk Assessment Tools				Hybrid Risk Assessment Tools			
		Factor Loadings	AVE	CR	Cronbach Alpha	Factor Loadings	AVE	CR	Cronbach Alpha	Factor Loadings	AVE	CR	Cronbach Alpha
Functionality	Fun_Qlty1	--				0.8				--			
	Fun_Qlty2	0.854				0.854				0.903			
	Fun_Qlty3	0.907	0.58	0.84	0.92	0.891	0.6	0.89	0.93	0.828	0.62	0.89	0.9
	Fun_Qlty4	0.867				0.85				0.861			
	Fun_Qlty5	0.85				0.845				0.752			
Innovativeness	Inno_Qlty1	0.723				0.781				0.819			
	Inno_Qlty2	--				0.894				0.971			
	Inno_Qlty3	0.935	0.61	0.87	0.9	0.878	0.6	0.88	0.91	0.827	0.59	0.87	0.91
	Inno_Qlty4	0.953				0.868				--			
	Inno_Qlty5	0.689				--				0.767			

continued on following page

Table 3. Continued

Construct	Code	Qualitative Risk Assessment Tools				Quantitative Risk Assessment Tools				Hybrid Risk Assessment Tools			
		Factor Loadings	AVE	CR	Cronbach Alpha	Factor Loadings	AVE	CR	Cronbach Alpha	Factor Loadings	AVE	CR	Cronbach Alpha
Responsiveness	Resp_Qlty1	0.693	0.56	0.83	0.8	0.706	0.50	0.7	0.76	--	0.58	0.86	0.73
	Resp_Qlty2	0.792				0.761				--			
	Resp_Qlty3	0.706				--				0.613			
	Resp_Qlty4	0.691				0.679				0.934			
Credibility	Cred_Qlty1	--	0.52	0.83	0.88	0.815	0.56	0.8	0.91	0.832	0.51	0.71	0.93
	Cred_Qlty2	--				0.978				0.852			
	Cred_Qlty3	0.848				--				0.907			
	Cred_Qlty4	0.91				0.795				0.828			
	Cred_Qlty5	0.789								0.88			
Security	Secu_Qlty1	0.744	0.51	0.77	0.87	0.87	0.52	0.82	0.87	0.812	0.51	0.81	0.87
	Secu_Qlty2	0.76				0.92				0.971			
	Secu_Qlty3	0.748				0.65				0.601			
	Secu_Qlty4	0.848				0.746				0.721			
	Secu_Qlty5	0.668				--				--			
Organizational Effectiveness	OE_Qlty1	0.64	0.53	0.9	0.88	0.799	0.50	0.87	0.86	0.752	0.55	0.8	0.88
	OE_Qlty2	--				0.868							
	OE_Qlty3	--				0.756				0.789			
	OE_Qlty4	0.856				--				0.812			
	OE_Qlty5	0.768				--				0.646			
	OE_Qlty6	0.775				0.724				--			
	OE_Qlty7	0.77				--				--			

4.4.3 Discriminant Validity

Table 4 illustrates the discriminant validity matrix for the overall risk assessment tools used in the current study to analyse the distinctness of the variables from different proposed models. To justify the validity, square roots of the AVEs are compared with the correlation of latent variables (Fornell and Larcker, 1981).

Table 4. Discriminant validity correlation matrix for risk assessment tools

		FUNC	INNO	RESP	CRED	SECU
Qualitative Risk Assessment tools	FUNC	0.78				
	INNO	0.261	0.749			
	RESP	0.375	0.244	0.653		
	CRED	0.327	0.533	0.388	0.761	
	SECU	0.211	0.548	0.135	0.492	0.693
Quantitative Risk Assessment tools	FUNC	0.776				
	INNO	0.375	0.779			
	RESP	0.404	0.297	0.63		
	CRED	0.362	0.454	0.339	0.751	
	SECU	0.24	0.343	0.09	0.568	0.721
Hybrid Risk Assessment tools	FUNC	0.768				
	INNO	0.401	0.764			
	RESP	0.218	0.202	0.659		
	CRED	0.296	0.307	0.451	0.758	
	SECU	0.272	0.488	0.175	0.215	0.713

4.5 Structural Equation Modelling

The study is articulated meaningfully by using three structural models. The model fit parameters for all three structural models are displayed in Table 5, which are all within the cut-off levels (Byrne, 2013). For qualitative risk assessment tools $\chi2/$df (CMIN/DF) = 1.181, RMSEA= 0.03, Comparative Fit Index (CFI) was 0.985, Tucker–Lewis index (TLI) was 0.983, and Goodness of Fit Index (GFI) stood at 0.901, Parsimony Comparative Fix Index (PCFI) was 0.701 and Parsimony Normed Fixed Index (PNFI) was 0.776; for quantitative risk assessment tools, the model fit parameters were tested as $\chi2/$df (CMIN/DF) = 1.139, RMSEA= 0.051, CFI was 0.963, TLI was 0.956, and Goodness of Fit Index (GFI) stood at 0.924, Parsimony Comparative Fix Index (PCFI) was 0.654 and PNFI was 0.733; for hybrid risk assessment tools, the model fit parameters were tested as $\chi2/$df (CMIN/DF) = 1.539,

RMSEA= 0.06, CFI = 0.950, TLI = 0.941, and GFI = 0.901, PCFI = 0.626 and PNFI = 0.733, all the above fit indices were under the cut-off values (Hu et al., 2009; Becker et al., 2012; Byrne, 2013). The test result illustrate that all seven hypotheses are accepted (Hair et al., 2012). The first structural model in Figure 4, explains 41% of the variance; the second structural model in Figure 5, explains 37% of the variance; and the third structural model in Figure 6, explains 42% of the variance.

Hypothesis 4, credibility ($\beta = 0.384$), and hypothesis 5, security ($\beta = 0.168$) are significant contributors toward organizational effectiveness under qualitative risk assessment tools. Hypothesis 2, innovativeness ($\beta = 0.317$), hypothesis 3 ($\beta = 0.226$) responsiveness are significant contributors towards organizational effectiveness under quantitative risk assessment tools. Hypothesis 1 functionality and hypothesis 3 responsiveness are significant contributors towards organizational effectiveness under hybrid risk assessment tools.

Figure 4. Structural model for quantitative risk assessment tools

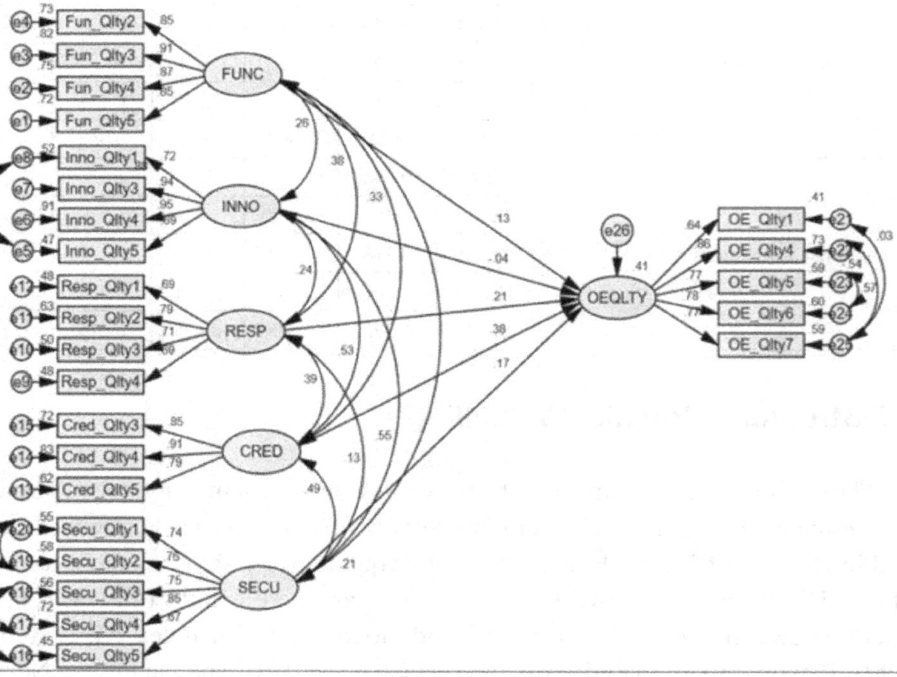

Figure 5. Structural model for quantitative risk assessment tools

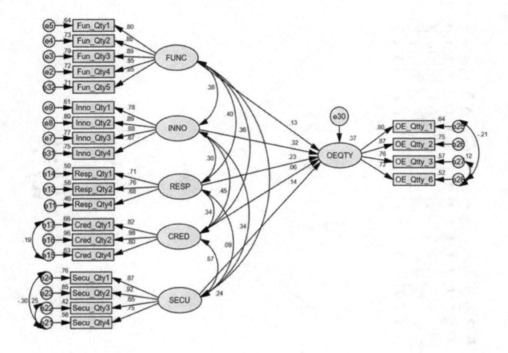

Figure 6. Structural model for hybrid risk assessment tools

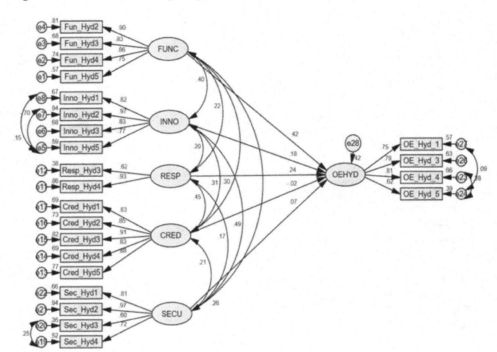

Table 5 displays the model fit indices for the risk assessment tools used in the study. From the output table 5, it can be interpreted that all the indices in all three structural model indices are within the recommended level.

Table 5. Model fit indices for hybrid risk assessment tools

Measure of Fit		Cut-Off Value	Actual Fit Value		
			Qualitative Tools	Quantitative Tools	Hybrid Tools
Absolute Fit Indices	CMIN/df	≤ 3.0	1.181	1.394	1.539
	RMSEA	≤ 0.08	0.03	0.051	0.06
	GFI	≥ .90	0.859	0.869	0.901
Incremental Fit Indices	CFI	≥ .90	0.985	0.963	0.95
	TFI		0.983	0.956	0.941
	NFI		0.912	0.883	0.872
Parsimony Fit Indices	PCFI	≥ .50	0.701	0.654	0.626
	PNFI		0.776	0.733	0.733

Table 6 interprets the values of the path analysis for all three structural models. The results illustrate that seven hypotheses out of fifteen have been accepted and proved to be a significant contributor towards organizational effectiveness. limited studies have been recorded in past in regard to the perceived benefits of tools.

Table 6. Path analysis result of the structural models

	Path b/w Constructs			Estimate	S.E.	C.R.	P-value	Result
	OEQLTY	<- --	FUNC	0.135	0.047	1.887	0.059	Insignificant
	OEQLTY	<- --	INNO	-0.41	0.089	-0.499	0.618	Insignificant
Qualitative Risk Assessment tools	OEQLTY	<- --	RESP	0.215	0.065	2.648	0.008	Significant
	OEQLTY	<- --	CRED	0.384	0.067	4.011	***	Significant
	OEQLTY	<- --	SECU	0.168	0.085	1.971	0.045	Significant
	OEQTY	<- --	FUNC	0.128	0.087	1.406	0.16	Insignificant
	OEQTY	<- --	INNO	0.317	0.09	3.324	***	Significant
Quantitative Risk Assessment tools	OEQTY	<- --	RESP	0.226	0.103	2.202	0.028	Significant
	OEQTY	<- --	CRED	0.056	0.133	0.53	0.596	Insignificant
	OEQTY	<- --	SECU	0.136	0.14	1.378	0.168	Insignificant
	OEHYD	<- --	FUNC	0.422	0.088	4.606	***	Significant
	OEHYD	<- --	INNO	0.18	0.112	1.917	0.055	Insignificant
Hybrid Risk Assessment Tools	OEHYD	<- --	RESP	0.234	0.103	2.456	0.014	Significant
	OEHYD	<- --	CRED	-0.016	0.082	-0.167	0.867	Insignificant
	OEHYD	<- --	SECU	0.07	0.111	0.8	0.424	Insignificant

5. DISCUSSIONS

Research studies with regard to risk tools and their benefits are scarce as very few researchers have highlighted this particular combination, even those who highlighted have explored perceived benefits in other areas. The study by Alhakami & Slovic (1994) was the starting point where the need for analysis of risk and perceived benefits was emphasized. The present papers have reinvigorated the connection between the perceived benefits of risk assessment tools and organizational effectiveness in the automobile industry with significant outcomes.

In response to the claimed hypotheses H1, the present study has shown that the functionality aspect of perceived benefits is insignificant under qualitative and quantitative risk assessment tools, but is indeed significant under hybrid tools whereas a similar study by Raghunath, K. M. K., & Devi, S. T. (2022) in construction industry posited that functionality aspect under qualitative and hybrid tools have a favourable impact whereas quantitative tools are insignificant towards organisational effectiveness. Another study in IT industry by Raghunath et al., (2021) articulated that functionality under qualitative and hybrid tools is insignificant whereas quantitative tools are significant on organizational effectiveness. The reason for the variability in the performance of qualitative and quantitative tools in terms of functionality can be attributed to the industry-specific risk scenarios and the insufficient threat forecasting and navigation phenomenon within these tools. Qualitative and quantitative tools are efficient, but they still lack the threat forecasting and navigation phenomenon provided by probabilistic and stochastic risk assessment tools in the case of automobile industries.

In response to Hypotheses H2, the present study states that the Innovativeness aspect under qualitative and hybrid risk tools is insignificant and that of Quantitative tools is significant, which is almost in line with what K. M. K., & Devi, S. T. (2022); Raghunath et al (2021) statement when they articulated that innovativeness aspect is insignificant with all the risk assessment tools in construction and information technology industry. According to automotive industry experts, the reason for this invariability of performance in the automobile industry can be associated with the issue qualitative and hybrid tools have in terms of capturing evolving new risk scenarios on different occasions with manufacturing and production processes. They also suggested that the use of probabilistic and stochastic risk assessment tools will strengthen the risk assessment by increasing the validity and interpretability of perceived benefits.

Hypotheses H3 claims the significance of responsiveness in the automobile industry. The responsiveness aspect is significant all the 3 risk assessment categories which is similar to the analysis made by Raghunath et al., (2021) in the construction industry. Another study conducted by K. M. K., & Devi, S. T. (2022) in the IT industry states that the responsiveness aspect of qualitative tools is significant but the same is quite insignificant with hybrid and quantitative risk tools in automobile industry.

For hypothesis H4, the present study shows that the Credibility aspect of the qualitative tools is significant whereas it is insignificant under hybrid and quantitative risk tools, the similar results were obtained by K. M. K., & Devi, S. T. (2022) under the information technology industry. The same study had different results in the construction industry as the credibility aspect was significant with qualitative and hybrid risk tools and was insignificant with quantitative risk tools. The reason for the insignificance of credibility aspect within automobile industry can be attributed to insignificant results obtained in the functionality aspect and Innovativeness aspects with quantitative tools and hybrid tools.

For Hypotheses H5, the study articulates that the security aspect of only qualitative risk tools is significant whereas the security aspect under hybrid and quantitative risk tools is insignificant. A common study of the same kind in the construction and information technology industry by K. M. K., & Devi, S. T. (2022); Raghunath et al (2021) depicted that the security aspect of qualitative risk tools was insignificant, but the same aspect was significant with quantitative and hybrid tools. Though hybrid and quantitative tools are effective, insignificant results with security aspects can be attributed to the tool's inability to recognize the random probabilistic risk occurrence, which is difficult to identify unless organisations have probabilistic and stochastic risk tools.

5.1 Managerial Implications

The current study primarily provides suggestions to enhance organizational effectiveness through risk assessment tools as they will provide a great synergy to decisions makers and managers for critical decision-making, the specific findings are as follows: Functionality as one of the perceived benefits, HAZOP study, Monte-Carlo analysis and FMEA under were highly preferred to analyse risk. With regard to managing risk innovatively Scenario analysis, PRAT and Event Tree Analysis were mostly preferred for analysing risk. Speaking of the responsiveness aspect within tools, What if analysis, Monte Carlo, and FMEA were highly recommended. For achieving credibility HAZOP study, Domino effects, and FMEA were highly recommended. Scenario analysis, DMRA and HEAT techniques were highly preferred under security aspect.

Risk experts further have acknowledged some suggestions to guarantee better risk assessment in the automobile industry.

i. Techniques like what-if analysis- Fault Tree Analysis and Event Tree Analysis can be incorporated together for better results.

ii. Assessment of credible domino scenarios should be enhanced.

iii. Scenario analysis and HAZOP study should be combined for efficient risk forecasting.

iv. A hybrid technical framework for optimizing hazards analysis could be developed by combining HAZOP analysis, what-if analysis, and DMRA in one framework

6. CONCLUSION

Risk is imminent in every activity, and for business organizations, managing risk is their inherent motive. As people believe "prevention is better than cure", risk management and risk assessment operate as a recognized area of knowledge in providing significant insights while promising effective results within organizations. The models built as a part of this study will provide significant insights into enterprise risk knowledge. Further, the present study will strengthen the motives of managers and leaders in ensuring timely decisions.

As for the future risk scenarios being unknown, the contemporary assessment tools would put up a robust risk evaluation platform for employees, employers, future leaders, and other parties, which will enable organizations to manage risk with a better prediction and forecasting to help the businesses overcome uncertainties underlying business opportunities.

6.1 Limitations and Future Scope

The study is limited to only one industry within metropolitan cities of our country which should be further extended to various industries. The study is completely focused on qualitative, quantitative, and hybrid risk assessment tools, further advancement can be done by exploring probabilistic and stochastic risk tools within industries that were highly recommended by managers. Lastly, the existing study has been focused only on metropolitan towns in India. In future, the implications can be generalized by extending the study to other international areas to enhance strategic risk assessment. Eventually, as risk signifies uncertainty and variability of outcome, an efficient risk assessment framework is need of the hour to handle risk scenarios in future and to envisage dynamic of risk factors.

CONFLICTS OF INTEREST

The authors have no conflicts of interest to declare. All co-authors have seen and agree with the contents of the manuscript and there is no financial interest to report. We certify that the submission is original work and is not under review at any other publication.

REFERENCES

Abbasi, K., Alam, A., Brohi, N. A., Brohi, I. A., & Nasim, S. (2021). P2P lending Fintechs and SMEs' access to finance. *Economics Letters*, 204, 109890. DOI: 10.1016/j.econlet.2021.109890

ACMA. (2020). Automotive Components Manufacturers Association of India. Retrieved from https://www.acma.in/annual-report.php

Ahadiat, A., Ribhan, R., Maydiantoro, A., & Dwi Kesumah, F. S. (2021). The theory of planned behavior and marketing ethics theory in predicting digital piracy intentions. *WSEAS Transactions on Business and Economics*, 18, 679–702. DOI: 10.37394/23207.2021.18.68

Ajzen, I. (1991). The theory of planned behavior. *Organizational Behavior and Human Decision Processes*, 50(2), 179–211. DOI: 10.1016/0749-5978(91)90020-T

Alhakami, A. S., & Slovic, P. (1994). A psychological study of the inverse relationship between perceived risk and perceived benefit. *Risk Analysis*, 1(6), 1085–1096. DOI: 10.1111/j.1539-6924.1994.tb00080.x PMID: 7846317

Ali, I., & Gölgeci, I. (2019). Where is supply chain resilience research heading? A systematic and co-occurrence analysis. *International Journal of Physical Distribution & Logistics Management*, 49(8), 793–815. DOI: 10.1108/IJPDLM-02-2019-0038

Alli, B. O. (2008). Fundamental principles of occupational health and safety (2nd ed.). International Labour Organization.

Aneziris, O. N., Papazoglou, I. A., Mud, M. L., Damen, M., Kuiper, J., Baksteen, H., Ale, B. J., Bellamy, L. J., Hale, A. R., Bloemhoff, A., Post, J. G., & Oh, J. (2008). Towards risk assessment for crane activities. *Safety Science*, 46(6), 872–884. DOI: 10.1016/j.ssci.2007.11.012

Arias, J. C., & Stern, R. (2011). Review of risk management methods. *Business Intelligence Journal*, 4(1), 51–78.

Aven, T. (2011). On some recent definitions and analysis frameworks for risk, vulnerability, and resilience. *Risk Analysis*, 31(4), 515–522. DOI: 10.1111/j.1539-6924.2010.01528.x PMID: 21077926

Belanche, D., Casaló, L. V., & Flavián, C. (2014). The role of place identity in smart card adoption. *Public Management Review*, 16(8), 1205–1228. DOI: 10.1080/14719037.2013.792385

Bentele, G., & Nothaft, H. (2011). Trust and credibility as the basis of corporate social responsibility. The handbook of communication and corporate social responsibility, 208-230. DOI: 10.1002/9781118083246.ch11

Byrne, B. M. (2013). *Structural equation modeling with Mplus: Basic concepts, applications, and programming*. Routledge.

Callahan, C., & Soileau, J. (2017). Does enterprise risk management enhance operating performance? *Advances in Accounting*, 37, 122–139. DOI: 10.1016/j.adiac.2017.01.001

Carfora, V., Cavallo, C., Catellani, P., Del Giudice, T., & Cicia, G. (2021). Why do consumers intend to purchase natural food? Integrating theory of planned behavior, value-belief-norm theory, and trust. *Nutrients*, 13(6), 1904. DOI: 10.3390/nu13061904 PMID: 34205879

Centobelli, P., Cerchione, R., Esposito, E., Passaro, R., & Shashi, . (2021). Determinants of the transition towards circular economy in SMEs: A sustainable supply chain management perspective. *International Journal of Production Economics*, 242, 108297. DOI: 10.1016/j.ijpe.2021.108297

Chandon, P., Wansink, B., & Laurent, G. (2000). A benefit congruency framework of sales promotion effectiveness. *Journal of Marketing*, 64(4), 65–81. DOI: 10.1509/jmkg.64.4.65.18071

Chapman, R. J. (1998). The effectiveness of working group risk identification and assessment techniques. *International Journal of Project Management*, 16(6), 333–343. DOI: 10.1016/S0263-7863(98)00015-5

Chłodnicka, H., & Zimon, G. (2020). Bankruptcu risk assessment measures of polish SMEs. *WSEAS Transactions on Business and Economics*, 17(3), 14–20. DOI: 10.37394/23207.2020.17.3

Dallat, C., Salmon, P. M., & Goode, N. (2017). Risky systems versus risky people: To what extent do risk assessment methods consider the systems approach to accident causation? A review of the literature. *Safety Science*.

de Araújo Lima, P. F., Crema, M., & Verbano, C. (2020). Risk management in SMEs: A systematic literature review and future directions. *European Management Journal*, 38(1), 78–94. DOI: 10.1016/j.emj.2019.06.005

Eydeland, A., & Wolyniec, K. (2003). *Energy and power risk management: New developments in modeling, pricing, and hedging* (Vol. 206). John Wiley & Sons.

Fichman, R. G., Dos Santos, B. L., & Zheng, Z. (2014). Digital innovation as a fundamental and powerful concept in the information systems curriculum. *Management Information Systems Quarterly*, 38(2), 329–A15. DOI: 10.25300/MISQ/2014/38.2.01

Fishbein, M., & Ajzen, I. (1974). Attitudes towards Objectives as Predictors of Single and Multiple Behavorial Criteria. *Psychological Review*, 81, 1–59.

Fornell, C., & Larcher, D. F. (1981). Evaluating Structural Equation Models with Unobservable Variables and Measurement Error. *JMR, Journal of Marketing Research*, 25, 186–192.

Frankelius, P. (2009). Questioning two myths in innovation literature. *The Journal of High Technology Management Research*, 20(1), 40–51. DOI: 10.1016/j.hitech.2009.02.002

Gale, N. K., Heath, G., Cameron, E., Rashid, S., & Redwood, S. (2013). Using the framework method for the analysis of qualitative data in multi-disciplinary health research. *BMC Medical Research Methodology*, 13(1), 1–8. DOI: 10.1186/1471-2288-13-117 PMID: 24047204

Gaziano, C., & McGrath, K. (1986). Measuring the concept of credibility. *The Journalism Quarterly*, 63(3), 451–462. DOI: 10.1177/107769908606300301

Geller, E. S., Roberts, D. S., & Gilmore, M. R. (1996). Predicting Propensity to Actively Care for Occupational Safety. *Journal of Safety Research*, 27(1), 1–8. DOI: 10.1016/0022-4375(95)00024-0

Gligor, D., Bozkurt, S., Russo, I., & Omar, A. (2019). A look into the past and future: Theories within supply chain management, marketing, and management. *Supply Chain Management*, 24(1), 170–186. DOI: 10.1108/SCM-03-2018-0124

Graydon, P. J., & Holloway, C. M. (2017). An investigation of proposed techniques for quantifying confidence in assurance arguments. *Safety Science*, 92, 53–65. DOI: 10.1016/j.ssci.2016.09.014

Haimes, Y. Y. (2009). On the definition of resilience in systems. *Risk Analysis*, 29(4), 498–501. DOI: 10.1111/j.1539-6924.2009.01216.x PMID: 19335545

Hair, J., Hollingsworth, C. L., Randolph, A. B., & Chong, A. Y. L. (2017). An updated and expanded assessment of PLS-SEM in information systems research. *Industrial Management & Data Systems*, 117(3), 442–458. DOI: 10.1108/IMDS-04-2016-0130

Hartono, E., Holsapple, C. W., Kim, K. Y., Na, K. S., & Simpson, J. T. (2014). Measuring perceived security in B2C electronic commerce website usage: A respecification and validation. *Decision Support Systems*, 62, 11–21. DOI: 10.1016/j.dss.2014.02.006

Henseler, J., Ringle, C. M., & Sinkovics, R. R. (2009). The use of partial least squares path modeling in international marketing. In *New challenges to international marketing*. Emerald Group Publishing Limited. DOI: 10.1108/S1474-7979(2009)0000020014

Hillson, D. (2012). *Managing risk in projects*. Gower Publishing, Ltd.

Holmes-Smith, P. (2006). *School socio-economic density and its effect on school performance*. Mceetya.

Holzmann, R., & Jorgensen, S. (1999). *Social protection as social risk management*. The World Bank.

Huang, Y., McMurran, R., Dhadyalla, G., & Jones, R. P. (2008). Probability based vehicle fault diagnosis: Bayesian network method. *Journal of Intelligent Manufacturing*, 19(3), 301–311. DOI: 10.1007/s10845-008-0083-7

Huesig, S., & Endres, H. (2018). Exploring the digital innovation process: The role of functionality for the adoption of innovation management software by innovation managers. *European Journal of Innovation Management*, 22(2), 302–314. DOI: 10.1108/EJIM-02-2018-0051

Hull, T. (2010), April. A deterministic scenario approach to risk management. In *2010 Enterprise Risk Management Symposium* (pp. 1-7).

Husted, J. A., Cook, R. J., Farewell, V. T., & Gladman, D. D. (2000). Methods for assessing responsiveness: A critical review and recommendations. *Journal of Clinical Epidemiology*, 53(5), 459–468. DOI: 10.1016/S0895-4356(99)00206-1 PMID: 10812317

IBEF. (2021). Indian Brand Equity Foundation. https://www.ibef.org/economy/indian-economy-overview

IBEF. (2022). Indian Brand Equity Foundation. https://www.ibef.org/economy/economic-survey-2021-22

IBEF. (2024). Indian Brand Equity Foundation. https://www.ibef.org/industry/india-automobiles

Jackob, N. (2008). *Credibility effects*. The International Encyclopedia of Communication. DOI: 10.1002/9781405186407.wbiecc153

Jacxsens, L., Uyttendaele, M., & De Meulenaer, B. (2016). Challenges in risk assessment: Quantitative risk assessment. *Procedia Food Science*, 6, 23–30. DOI: 10.1016/j.profoo.2016.02.004

Jeong, C. B., Kang, H. M., Lee, Y. H., Kim, M. S., Lee, J. S., Seo, J. S., Wang, M., & Lee, J. S. (2018). Nanoplastic ingestion enhances toxicity of persistent organic pollutants (POPs) in the monogonont rotifer Brachionus koreanus via multixeno-biotic resistance (MXR) disruption. *Environmental Science & Technology*, 52(19), 11411–11418. DOI: 10.1021/acs.est.8b03211 PMID: 30192528

Junkes, M. B., Tereso, A. P., & Afonso, P. S. (2015). The importance of risk assessment in the context of investment project management: A case study. *Procedia Computer Science*, 64, 902–910. DOI: 10.1016/j.procs.2015.08.606

Kochan, C. G., & Nowicki, D. R. (2018). Supply chain resilience: A systematic literature review and typological framework. *International Journal of Physical Distribution & Logistics Management*, 48(8), 842–865. DOI: 10.1108/IJPDLM-02-2017-0099

Koufteros, X. A. (1999). Testing a model of pull production: A paradigm for manufacturing research using structural equation modeling. *Journal of Operations Management*, 17(4), 467–488. DOI: 10.1016/S0272-6963(99)00002-9

Kumar, P.S., Ravi, M. & Vijayakumar, K.C.K. (2016). Risk Assessment for Machinery Shop in Automobile Industry. *International Journal of Mathematical Sciences and Engineering, 5.*

Kumar, R., & Lightner, R. (2007). Games as an interactive classroom technique: Perceptions of corporate trainers, college instructors and students. *International Journal on Teaching and Learning in Higher Education*, 19(1), 53–63.

Kumar, S., Xiao, J. J., Pattnaik, D., Lim, W. M., & Rasul, T. (2022). Past, present and future of bank marketing: A bibliometric analysis of International Journal of Bank Marketing (1983–2020). *International Journal of Bank Marketing*, 40(2), 341–383. DOI: 10.1108/IJBM-07-2021-0351

Lee, M. C. (2009). Predicting and explaining the adoption of online trading: An empirical study in Taiwan. *Decision Support Systems*, 47(2), 133–142. DOI: 10.1016/j.dss.2009.02.003

Leung, Y. (2013). Perceived benefits. Encyclopedia of behavioral medicine, 1450-1451. DOI: 10.1007/978-1-4419-1005-9_1165

Liao, Z., & Shi, X. (2017). Web functionality, web content, information security, and online tourism service continuance. *Journal of Retailing and Consumer Services*, 39, 258–263. DOI: 10.1016/j.jretconser.2017.06.003

Lien, C. H., Hsu, M. K., Shang, J. Z., & Wang, S. W. (2021). Self-service technology adoption by air passengers: A case study of fast air travel services in Taiwan. *Service Industries Journal*, 41(9-10), 671–695. DOI: 10.1080/02642069.2019.1569634

Lim, M. K., Bahr, W., & Leung, S. C. (2013). RFID in the warehouse: A literature analysis (1995–2010) of its applications, benefits, challenges and future trends. *International Journal of Production Economics*, 145(1), 409–430. DOI: 10.1016/j.ijpe.2013.05.006

Lin, Y., Wang, Y., & Yu, C. (2010). Investigating the drivers of the innovation in channel integration and supply chain performance: A strategy orientated perspective. *International Journal of Production Economics*, 127(2), 320–332. DOI: 10.1016/j.ijpe.2009.08.009

Liu, B. (2006). A survey of credibility theory. *Fuzzy Optimization and Decision Making*, 5(4), 387–408. DOI: 10.1007/s10700-006-0016-x

Manuele, F. A. (2016). Root-Causal Factors: Uncovering the Hows & Whys of Incidents. *Professional Safety*, 61(05), 48–55.

Marhavilas, P. K., Koulouriotis, D., & Gemeni, V. (2011). Risk analysis and assessment methodologies in the worksites: On a review, classification and comparative study of the scientific literature of the period 2000–2009. *Journal of Loss Prevention in the Process Industries*, 24(5), 477–523. DOI: 10.1016/j.jlp.2011.03.004

Maryam, S. Z., Ahmad, A., Aslam, N., & Farooq, S. (2022). Reputation and cost benefits for attitude and adoption intention among potential customers using theory of planned behavior: An empirical evidence from Pakistan. *Journal of Islamic Marketing*, 13(10), 2090–2107. DOI: 10.1108/JIMA-03-2021-0059

Mueller, K. L., Lauvaux, T., Gurney, K. R., Roest, G., Ghosh, S., Gourdji, S. M., Karion, A., DeCola, P., & Whetstone, J. (2021). An emerging GHG estimation approach can help cities achieve their climate and sustainability goals. *Environmental Research Letters*, 16(8), 084003. DOI: 10.1088/1748-9326/ac0f25

Nagariya, R., Kumar, D., & Kumar, I. (2020). Service supply chain: From bibliometric analysis to content analysis, current research trends and future research directions. *Benchmarking*, 28(1), 333–369. DOI: 10.1108/BIJ-04-2020-0137

Nambisan, P. (2017). *An introduction to ethical, safety and intellectual property rights issues in biotechnology*. Academic Press.

Nasierowski, W., & Arcelus, F. J. (2012). What is innovativeness: literature review. *Foundations of Management, 4*(1), 63-74.

Nunnally, J. C. (1978). An overview of psychological measurement. *Clinical diagnosis of mental disorders: A handbook*, 97-146.

Ostrom, L. T., & Wilhelmsen, C. A. (2019). *Risk assessment: tools, techniques, and their applications*. John Wiley & Sons. DOI: 10.1002/9781119483342

Pahrudin, P., Chen, C. T., & Liu, L. W. (2021). A modified theory of planned behavioral: A case of tourist intention to visit a destination post pandemic Covid-19 in Indonesia. *Heliyon*, 7(10), e08230. DOI: 10.1016/j.heliyon.2021.e08230 PMID: 34708160

Pei, Y., Wang, S., Fan, J., & Zhang, M. (2015, August). An empirical study on the impact of perceived benefit, risk and trust on e-payment adoption: Comparing quick pay and union pay in China. In *2015 7th international conference on intelligent human-machine systems and cybernetics* (Vol. 2, pp. 198-202). IEEE.

Podsakoff, P. M., MacKenzie, S. B., Lee, J. Y., & Podsakoff, N. P. (2003). Common method biases in behavioral research: A critical review of the literature and recommended remedies. *The Journal of Applied Psychology*, 88(5), 879–903. DOI: 10.1037/0021-9010.88.5.879 PMID: 14516251

Raghunath, K. M. K., & Devi, S. L. T. (2018). Supply Chain Risk Management: An Invigorating Outlook. *International Journal of Information Systems and Supply Chain Management*, 11(3), 87–104. DOI: 10.4018/IJISSCM.2018070105

Raghunath, K. M. K., Devi, S. L. T., Anuradha, K., & Veni, K. V. S. K. (2021). Reinvigorating Organizational Effectiveness and Sustainability Through Risk Assessment Tools Within the Construction Industry. In *Remote work and sustainable change for the future of global business*. IGI Global. DOI: 10.4018/978-1-7998-7513-0.ch009

Raghunath, K. M. K., Devi, S. L. T., & Patro, C. S. (2017). An empirical take on qualitative and quantitative risk factors. *International Journal of Risk and Contingency Management*, 6(4), 1–15. DOI: 10.4018/IJRCM.2017100101

Raghunath, K. M. K., & Devi, S. T. (2021). Effectiveness of risk assessment models in business decisions: Reinforcing knowledge. In *Research Anthology on Small Business Strategies for Success and Survival* (pp. 1076–1096). IGI Global. DOI: 10.4018/978-1-7998-9155-0.ch053

Raghunath, K. M. K., & Devi, S. T. (2022). Risk Assessment in the Information Technology Industry: An Imperative Phenomenon. In *Global Risk and Contingency Management Research in Times of Crisis* (pp. 122-141). IGI Global.

Raghunath, K. M. K., Devi, S. T., & Patro, C. S. (2018). Impact of Risk Assessment Models on Risk Factors: A Holistic Outlook. In *Research, Practices, and Innovations in Global Risk and Contingency Management* (pp. 134-153). IGI Global DOI: 10.4018/978-1-5225-4754-9.ch008

Raghunath, K. M. K., Patro, C. S., & Sirisha, K. (2019). Paraphernalias of Entrepreneurship–A Contemplating Outlook. *International Journal of E-Entrepreneurship and Innovation*, 9(1), 47–62. DOI: 10.4018/IJEEI.2019010105

Rausand, M. (2013). *Risk assessment: theory, methods, and applications* (Vol. 115). John Wiley & Sons.

Renn, O. (2017). *Risk governance: coping with uncertainty in a complex world.* Routledge. DOI: 10.4324/9781849772440

Sanchez-Franco, M. J., & Rondan-Cataluña, F. J. (2010). Virtual travel communities and customer loyalty: Customer purchase involvement and web site design. *Electronic Commerce Research and Applications*, 9(2), 171–182. DOI: 10.1016/j.elerap.2009.05.004

Self, C. C. (2014). Credibility. In *An integrated approach to communication theory and research* (pp. 449–470). Routledge.

SIAM. (2020). Society of Indian Automobile Manufacturers. Retrieved from https://www.siam.in/uploads/filemanager/319SIAMAnnualReport2020-21.pdf

Slovic, P. (2016). Understanding perceived risk: 1978–2015. *Environment*, 58(1), 25–29. DOI: 10.1080/00139157.2016.1112169

Sweet, A. S. (2000). *Governing with judges: constitutional politics in Europe.* OUP Oxford. DOI: 10.1093/0198297718.001.0001

Tajeddini, K., Rasoolimanesh, S. M., Gamage, T. C., & Martin, E. (2021). Exploring the visitors' decision-making process for Airbnb and hotel accommodations using value-attitude-behavior and theory of planned behavior. *International Journal of Hospitality Management*, 96, 102950. DOI: 10.1016/j.ijhm.2021.102950

Vasile, E., & Croitoru, I. (2012). Integrated risk management system–key factor of the management system of the organization. Risk management-Current issues and challenges. InTech.

Vinodkumar, M. N., & Bhasi, M. (2010). Safety Management Practices and Safety Behaviour: Assessing the Mediating Role of Safety Knowledge and Motivation. *Accident; Analysis and Prevention*, 42(6), 2082–2093. DOI: 10.1016/j.aap.2010.06.021 PMID: 20728666

Weber, O., Scholz, R. W., & Michalik, G. (2010). Incorporating sustainability criteria into credit risk management. *Business Strategy and the Environment*, 19(1), 39–50. DOI: 10.1002/bse.636

Yoo, Y., Boland, R. J.Jr, Lyytinen, K., & Majchrzak, A. (2012). Organizing for innovation in the digitized world. *Organization Science*, 23(5), 1398–1408. DOI: 10.1287/orsc.1120.0771

Yoon, B., & Chung, Y. (2018). The effects of corporate social responsibility on firm performance: A stakeholder approach. *Journal of Hospitality and Tourism Management*, 37, 89–96. DOI: 10.1016/j.jhtm.2018.10.005

Zailani, S., Iranmanesh, M., Masron, T. A., & Chan, T. H. (2016). Is the intention to use public transport for different travel purposes determined by different factors? *Transportation Research Part D, Transport and Environment*, 49, 18–24. DOI: 10.1016/j.trd.2016.08.038

KEY TERMS AND DEFINITIONS

Organisational Effectiveness: Organisations ability to produce desired results as per the established parameter of performance.

Perceived Benefits: These are the perception of positive consequences that an organisation expects as the outcome of its actions.

Risk: The possibility of unexpected variation in the expected results is called risk.

Risk Assessment: The process of evaluating and appraising existing measures of security and controls by assessing their adequacy in response to the impending threats faced by the organization, so as to identify, evaluate, and report them periodically.

Risk Assessment Tools: Tools developed to assess risk for particular outcomes that help in evaluating and appraising the efficiency of risk assessment.

Risk Factors: Variables/components that lead to unexpected variation in results.

Risk Management: The process of assessing and evaluating the various internal and external threats within organisation, so to mitigate them and bring stability within organizations.

Risk Scenarios: Risk scenarios are probable situations in an organization that describes the potential uncertain event that may lead to adverse outcomes.

Risk-Based Decision Making: It is the process of making decisions in an organization by considering ubiquitous possible risks associated with different options and choosing the best one by balancing benefits and risks to achieve organisational objective.

Chapter 7
Fractally Organized Humanitarian Units May Increase Their Effectiveness in Protracted Crises

Danuta Kaźmierczak

(iD) https://orcid.org/0000-0003-2513-2942

University of the National Education Commission, Poland

Stanisław Kowalkowski

War Studies University, Poland

Marek Wrzosek

War Studies University, Poland

EXECUTIVE SUMMARY

Although every protracted crisis is unique, they often share several characteristics: long duration, conflict, weak governance or public administration structures, unsustainable livelihood systems, poor food security outcomes, and breakdown of local institutions. The Directorate-General for European Civil Protection and Humanitarian Aid Operations reports difficulties in cooperating with national and local authorities and the existence of double coordination structures. This chapter discusses the need for humanitarian units in national DRM structures, consisting of the representatives of all sectors providing security to citizens—police, social services, healthcare, border guards, fire service, armed forces, NGOs, local governors, and fellow citizens—would ensure higher effectiveness due to their fractal

DOI: 10.4018/979-8-3693-2675-6.ch007

structures. Advantages include accurate decision-making, assigning tasks and assets to proper personnel, supporting multi-actor teams in action, communicating with international organizations and avoiding task duplication, and interoperability across teams and flexible response.

INTRODUCTION

According to the Sendai Framework for Disaster Risk Reduction 2015–2030, an international accord adopted by the United Nations, "Disaster risk management needs to be based on an understanding of disaster risk in all its dimensions of vulnerability, capacity, exposure of persons and assets, hazard characteristics and the environment." The importance of this message continues to grow as conflicts, shocks and crises have become more and more complex and protracted worldwide.

In this paper, we hypothesize that addressing the effects of reoccurring, complex hazards requires linking disaster risk management and humanitarian action with social protection on national and international levels. Such comprehensive assistance could be executed effectively by multi-actor, cross-sectoral humanitarian units organized fractally within the disaster risk management (DRM) system structures. However, the model of fractal humanitarian units first requires hands-on testing in the field for efficiency and interoperability with other units within the DRM system and international humanitarian units; this testing should be conducted using empirical studies.

We have formulated the hypothesis based on analyses, findings and recommendations outlined in reports by international entities such as the United Nations, the European Union, and World Bank, as well as media sources and the published statements and experiences of experts engaged in humanitarian actions. The material analyzed deals with the coordination challenges that occur when assistance is delivered by multiple actors, looking at a variety of regions and types of crises, including war, conflicts, natural disasters and social instability. All of the places examined are affected by compound and protracted crises, never a single one. The discussion will focus mainly on optimizing humanitarian aid delivery from the perspective of fractal organization theory.

PROTRACTED CRISES

Humanitarian Coalition, a Canadian aid organization, states on its website, "Protracted crises refer to situations in which a significant portion of a population is facing a heightened risk of death, disease, and breakdown of their livelihoods." These circumstances are often linked to recurrent natural disasters or conflicts. According to the Food and Agriculture Organization of the United Nations, in 2010 there were 22 countries, and over 160 million undernourished people, facing protracted crises. While every protracted crisis is unique, they often share the following characteristics: long duration, conflict, weak governance or public administration structures, unsustainable livelihood systems, poor food security outcomes and breakdown of local institutions (Humanitarian Coalition, n.d.). In many cases, there is a direct relationship between unsustainable livelihoods, inefficient governance and protracted crises in which any one condition can cause the other.

As Figure 1 illustrates, protracted crises may be generated by aggregate, cascading or compound hazards that cover a broad spectrum of events (Maguire & Hagan 2007).

Figure 1. Types of hazards (Adapted from Maguire & Hagan 2007; Zaitchik et.al. 2021)

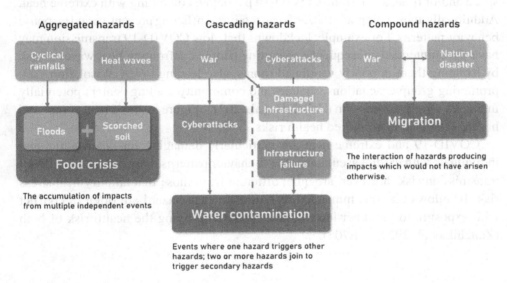

The aggregated multi-hazard situation results from the accumulation of impacts from multiple independent events. Such events may be unrelated but occurring sequentially at the same location (e.g., heavy rainfalls each year and locust plagues in Chad; waves of missile and drone attacks in Ukraine in 2023), or simultaneously in various locations but with parallel impacts, such as complex coordinated terrorist attacks in Sri Lanka in 2019 (US Department of Homeland Security 2019).

Cascading hazards occur when one danger triggers another. They can be natural, natural-technological or human-driven natural-technological hazards. For example, Europe is facing regular drought conditions that impact agriculture, energy and water resources, and a new drought is advancing around the Baltic Sea, Scandinavia, the UK, Ireland and Germany, creating serious concerns about crop yields (European Commission 14 July 2023). Cascading effects can also occur as a result of slow-onset events like rising sea levels, warming oceans and increasing lack of fresh water. At each stage, or node, of the cascade there is a possibility to interrupt the stream by stopping it outright or mitigating its effects. However, each node has the potential to aggravate impacts or create new, unexpected consequences, intensifying the cascade effect. Therefore, at each node, it is crucial to make decisions and take actions that protect individuals and communities from impending hazards. These responsibilities should be shared among governments, local authorities and any social agencies that have the potential to respond effectively (Below, 2019).

Compound hazards can include single extreme events, multiple coinciding events and sequential events. They have different origins but are correlated and interact in space and/or time, such as the COVID-19 pandemic coinciding with extreme heat. Additionally, these compound hazards can require conflicting preventive and response behavior patterns. For example, lockdowns that slow COVID-19 transmission may have the unintended consequence of putting people confronting heat waves at risk by isolating them in poorly ventilated rooms, also leading to social isolation. Yet, promoting group evacuations, shelters and community cooling centers potentially increases virus transmission (Zaitchik et al., 2021). Figure 2 shows how compound hazards can lead to amplified health risks.

COVID-19 and extreme heat are particularly damaging for older adults and individuals with cardiovascular disease. Behavior patterns that amplify COVID-19 transmission risk, however, are quite different from those that amplify heat stress risk. It follows that recommended responses to each hazard are often in conflict with exposure to the other hazard, potentially amplifying the health risk of both (Zaitchik et al. 2022, p. E705).

Figure 2. Compound hazards increase health risks (American Meteorological Society. Quoted in: Zaitchik et al. 2022.)

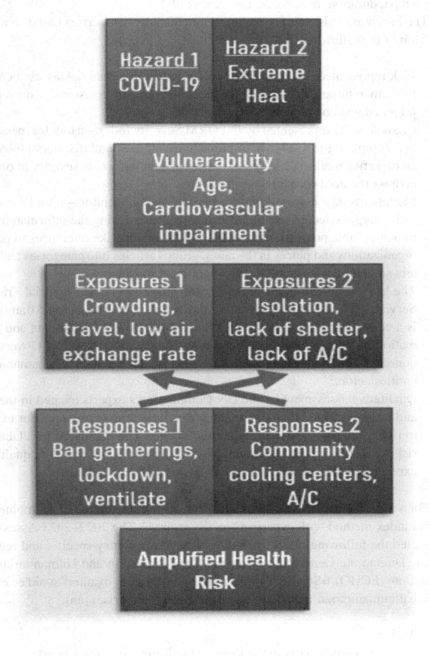

Protracted crises cover a broad spectrum of disasters that can be defined in terms of their agent (natural or human-caused), proximity, impact (visible or invisible), size, scope, duration, magnitude, and death toll.

The Forgotten Crises Assessment is a tool that identifies crises based on a combination of the following factors:

- Risk represented by the INFORM Risk Index - a global risk assessment tool for humanitarian crises and disasters; it may support decisions on prevention, preparedness and response.
- Crisis severity represented by INFORM Severity Index – a tool for measuring and comparing the severity of humanitarian crises and disasters globally in an objective manner; it provides deeper insight into crisis severity in order to address the needs of all those affected.
- Media coverage assessed via the Europe Media Monitor – a tool for monitoring large, selected sets of electronic media, reducing the information flow to manageable proportions; it extracts information, like references to people, organizations and places in the news, groups articles into categories and clusters similar articles, applying also sentiment/tonality.
- The level of humanitarian aid per capita assessed via the Financial Tracking Service (FTS) (UN Office for the Coordination of Humanitarian Affairs). FTS is a centralized source of selected and continuously updated data and information on humanitarian funding flows. The data are shared by Government donors, UN-administered funds, UN agencies, NGOs and other humanitarian entities/actors.
- Qualitative assessment by the UN Commission's experts located in the field and headquarters. All risk assessments include an expert judgement in order to make effective decisions under uncertainty. The likelihood for elaborated risk scenarios is assessed quantitatively, if possible, but based on qualitative expert judgement where there is no data or evidence available.

For a more comprehensive and informative measurement, the EU combines this global index method with expertise "on the ground." The 2022–2023 Assessment identified the following crises, including a range of country-specific and regional crises (Directorate-General for European Civil Protection and Humanitarian Aid Operations (ECHO), 6 Sept 2023) https://civil-protection-humanitarian-aid.ec.europa.eu/what/humanitarian-aid/needs-assessment/forgotten-crises_en):

- **Africa:**
    - Complex crisis in the Democratic Republic of the Congo
    - Complex crisis in Cameroon

- Complex crisis in Burundi
- Complex crisis in South Sudan
- Violence in West Darfur
- Complex crisis in the Central African Republic (CAR)
- Refugee crisis in Sudan
- CAR refugees in Chad
- Banditry in Northwest Nigeria
■ **Middle East and Northern Africa**
- Socioeconomic crisis in Lebanon
- Saharawi crisis in Algeria
■ **Asia**
- Rohingya refugee crisis in Bangladesh
■ **Latin America and the Caribbean**
- Displacements of Venezuelans in Ecuador
- Displacement of Venezuelans in Peru
- Complex crisis in Colombia

The UN Office for the Coordination of Humanitarian Affairs' 2023 Global Humanitarian Overview outlines the most serious humanitarian crises in 2023. They are triggered by protracted conflicts, accompanied by climate change, and have cascading or compound impacts on the local people.

IMPACT

The consequences of these crises include food insecurity; a tripled rate of undernourishment and livelihood disruption resulting from people's inability to support themselves due to displacement; loss of resources and economic decline; inequality; toxic social norms; and political polarization. Additionally, women suffer from higher risks of sexual abuse and gender-based violence and are more significantly affected by reduced access to health and education services. Moreover, women shoulder increased responsibility for the household when men migrate for job opportunities or to engage in fighting.

Migration has become a challenge for countries on all continents. However, the Report on The Impact of Climate Change on Migration (The White House, 2021) indicates a strong correlation between countries and regions that are most vulnerable to climate change and those that are damaged by a long war. Climate-related shocks may further increase a crisis situation in these countries and trigger forced displacement, if prevention efforts are ineffective. There are various types of migrants: voluntary and involuntary, internal and international, legal or illegal, environmental, and victims of human trafficking (Suárez-Orozco, 2019). People migrate for numerous reasons, including finding a promising job, strengthening family ties, engaging in new cultural opportunities, or due to emergencies like poverty or a lack of economic prospects, war or persecution, and long-term climate change–related disasters (The RAND Corporation 2021). However, the patterns of migration flow can fluctuate. In 2014, more than 2.8 million people born in El Salvador, Honduras, and Guatemala (the Northern Triangle of Central America) were living in the United States, having migrated to the United States over decades. The Center for Immigration Studies reports that over three million new documented and undocumented immigrants settled in the United States in 2014 and 2015 and were predominately women and children (Camarota, 2016). The European Commission indicates that due to the Russian-Ukrainian conflict, by December 2022 between 3.6 and 5.4 million people were internally displaced in Ukraine, while at least 7 million had moved outside of Ukraine. Overall, between 25% and 30% of the total Ukrainian population have been displaced. The EU has received the highest share of the people fleeing Ukraine (Knowledge Centre on Migration and Demography Data Portal, n.d.).

MANAGING A HUMANITARIAN CRISIS

Managing a humanitarian crisis in an area affected by conflict or natural disaster, as well as in the neighboring locations, requires various approaches applied in a coordinated manner. Actions related to disaster risk management usually occur in four consecutive phases: preparedness, planning, response, and recovery (Alexander, 2002). However, a protracted crisis with cascading and compound hazards creates a situation where phases coexist and overlap (The South Africa Green Paper on Disaster Management, South Africa 1998; Bosher, Chmutina, Niekerk 2021), making the coordination of action even more complicated.

Humanitarian agencies engage in three types of actions in response to protracted crises:

- livelihood provisioning—to meet immediate basic needs and protect people's lives,
- livelihood protection—to protect people's assets and to prevent the sale or destruction of productive assets, and
- livelihood promotion—to support livelihood assets, policies and institutions that can improve people's livelihoods (Humanitarian Coalition).

Addressing basic needs requires a prompt, comprehensive and coordinated approach. such as that offered by the EU Civil Protection Mechanism, for example. The Mechanism can be solicited by countries, the United Nations and international organizations needing assistance. In 2022, the Mechanism was activated 106 times to respond to war in Ukraine, wildfires in Europe, COVID-19 in Europe and worldwide, and floods in Pakistan. The Mechanism can be also activated for consular support such as evacuation operations (European Commission, EU Civil Protection Mechanism, n.d.).

Moreover, specific tools have been developed for addressing the fragility, conflict, and violence nexus (FCV) in the Middle East and North Africa, including integrated DRM-FCV approaches, analytical frameworks and targeted solutions (World Bank, 2022, p. 67-69). The global DRM-FCV program, created by the Global Facility for Disaster Reduction and Recovery, provides support to low- and middle-income countries and fosters an understanding of the interplay between disasters and conflict/fragility and higher operational costs in these areas.

Nevertheless, the collaboration of various entities at the operational level requires continuous improvement. Experts have identified the weaknesses in the coordination of activities between international and national humanitarian units. Below are examples of cases of DRM scenarios that lacked effective coordination, along with recommendations for change:

Natural disaster: Following the 2010 earthquake in Haiti, between 3000 and 10,000 aid organizations engaged in aid delivery, according to Kristoff and Panarelli (2010). However, Nolte (2018) points out the enormous challenges that resulted. Citing the 2013 report of the Center for Economic and Policy Research, Nolte observes,

Due to the constant influx of NGOs during the time of the earthquake response and due to the resulting complexity, there are no official statistics on the composition of aid during the Haiti earthquake response. At the time of the earthquake response, Haiti ranked 175 on the 182 scale of the corruption perceptions index and the lack of transparency and accountability of aid was highly criticized.

In humanitarian context accountability refers to transparent relations between people and institutions involved in a humanitarian action (government, international and national organizations, NGOs, and business) and the manner in which they use their power over populations affected by crisis. Accountability is a key element which determines to what extend the affected population can benefit from humanitarian response and relief operations (Turunen, 2020).

Food insecurity: Of the Venezuelan crisis, the DG ECHO Report (2023) noted,

The coordination of the humanitarian response to the Venezuelan regional crisis was complex and evolved differently across LAC countries during 2017-2021. [...] Several factors influenced the implementation and impact of the response during the evaluation period. Operational factors arose from the limited international/

humanitarian experience in Venezuela and other countries (especially at the onset of the crisis), difficulties in cooperating with national and local authorities in some countries and regions and existence of double coordination structures in the region.

However, the relationship among aid agencies may be structured in various ways: in the

forms which are less formalized and less coercive limiting agency independence, or the

forms which require higher levels of formalization and entails a more "authoritative"

management style). There is strong and justified voice in the literature that having various aid-

coordination models mean the flexibility which allows for adaptation, contextualization and

customization of the aid provided. Being based in more than 130 countries worldwide,

the UN provides plenty of possibilities for the application of a variety of aid-coordination

models, optimal in the particular context. An "optimal" level of coordination is the level

at which the gains from coordination are maximized through a reduction and/or elimination of

overlap and inconsistencies, while the costs of coordination on the side of participating UN

agencies and the partner government are minimized. Coordination should not be a goal in

itself, and investments in it should add value as to consistency and coherency gains (Mahn

2013).

Economic crisis: The increasing complexity of implementing humanitarian policy, including challenges associated with climate change and the global economic crisis, further emphasizes the urgency of collaboration and partnerships for improving the speed, quality and effectiveness of humanitarian response (Janz et al., 2009). The humanitarian assistance is not sufficient for that most affected households. When their savings are exhausted, they do not have other sources of income to cover basic living expenses they will fall into debt spiral and follow negative coping mechanisms: de-schooling, early marriage or child labor, increasing the households poverty. For instance, in Lebanon, 88% of Syrian refugee households are indebted and 51% live below the survival minimum expenditure basket (SMEB) of $ 2.90 per day (OECD, 2019).

While addressing the diversity of needs of the affected (the provision of health, food, shelter), it is crucial to take into account accessibility (the ease with which all people can reach, understand and use services) and acceptability (the extent to which people consider the services to be appropriate, e.g. whether they respect social and cultural norms or are sensitive to gender, age and disability requirements) (Handbook for the UN Resident and Humanitarian Coordinator)

War migration: Numerous observers have noted that Poland demonstrated a lack of cross-sectoral coordination in delivering assistance to migrants from Ukraine. The influx of Ukrainian refugees to Poland caused congestion in rail transport, which was difficult for the state to manage on its own. Moreover, others have noted that the spontaneous gestures of support from Poles, along with support from state and local governments and the European Union could have been even more effective if all these efforts had been coordinated (Woźniak, 2022; The Website of The Republic of Poland, 2022; The Website of Dziennik Gazeta Prawna 2023).

Edith Shiro, a clinical psychologist defines the migrant crisis as "a *collective trauma*: when a community, a group of people, or a whole culture experiences chronic, ongoing injustice and suffering with no resources to navigate it" (Time, 24 Jan. 8). Venezuelans who immigrated to the U.S., in 2023, when interviewed by E. Shiro, feel that their culture, belief systems, and tradition —their very existence —don't matter. Women are experiencing a loss of their professional identity, their roles within their family structure, and they no longer know how to define themselves and their purpose in life. Collective trauma requires collective healing, which can only happen when the country of origin and the host culture—the new community— acknowledges, recognizes, and validates the trauma of the immigrants' experience and provides a sense of safety (Shiro, Time, 24 Jan. 8).

Climate change: The DRM approaches in the United States have been criticized for their reactionary security measures, such as the "walls and bombs" responses at the Texas and Mexico border, which attack symptoms instead of causes. Additionally, top-down prescriptions are considered inefficient, since they have only fragmented knowledge about the capacity of the local communities and governments, e.g.: knowledge about the availability of resources for displaced families post-Hurricane Katrina in 2005. Therefore, it is advisable to involve the nation so that it could serve as a convener, collector, and collaborator that can support, enhance, and amplify action at every level from the local to the international. All over the world, local practitioners, leaders, civil society organizations, and institutions are doing the hard work of addressing the challenges of climate change and implementing them in creative ways to enable greater population adaptation for those most vulnerable (Haynie et al., 2021).

This issue of local knowledge may be discussed in broader international aid contexts. There is strict dependency of vulnerability of the affected people and the vulnerability of those who come with assistance. The representatives of aid organizations resist colonial history, racism, and social injustices, but on the other hand, they have limited knowledge of local culture and language, a lack of infrastructure and equipment to perform their tasks, and violent attacks such as kidnapping and rape (Zhukova, 2020).

Biological hazard: Speaking of the response to COVID-19 in Africa, Smith notes (2021),

When the humanitarian coordination system was activated during the COVID-19 response, this led to problems in Malawi and Zambia, for example, where it created confusion about where and by whom it should be coordinated. Lack of inclusion of social protection in the humanitarian response architecture also means there is no accountability for improving coordination of shock responses linked with social protection as there are no lines of responsibility defined.

In acute crisis situations, the collaboration might be restrained by the rule to follow the principles of neutrality, independence and impartiality to safeguard access to people in need. Whatever the context, collaboration must take place in a manner that brings together humanitarian principles and needs of the affected populations and safety of humanitarian workers (Handbook for the UN Resident and Humanitarian Coordinator).

Regardless of the kind of hazard DRM teams respond to, they tend to face the same limitation, namely, lack of comprehensive coordination of all actors delivering humanitarian aid. While there is unanimous agreement that robust coordination of humanitarian assistance is crucial, it remains challenging. On this topic, Smith (2021) notes,

The importance of strong coordination between actors preparing, designing and implementing shock responses is well accepted [...] So why is coordination so challenging? Put simply, it is difficult to bring together a multiplicity of actors, from different disciplines, and with different mandates, guiding principles, visions, and interests. [...] and these actors are siloed – physically, technically, and ideologically.

Breaking down silos involves building intersectoral collaborative networks and partnerships, which could benefit the affected communities and independent organizations themselves while also supporting security and DRM services. Pursuing joint goals creates the opportunity to exchange knowledge and effective practices, perform the tasks they do best during disaster response and address shared problems more efficiently (Nolte, 2018). Collaborative networks could also encourage linkage between humanitarian and social assistance, since at present, as Smith quips, "we are trying to drive a Ferrari with the engine of a Fiat." Smith (2021) further points out that there is no "social protection pillar" in the humanitarian response architecture, and thus no established locus for where, and by whom, a social protection response should be managed.

FRACTAL HUMANITARIAN UNITS

Linking humanitarian and social assistance would address the issue of responding to basic human needs in a comprehensive way. Scholars have defined basic human needs as falling into three categories (Benn & Peters 1959; Rosen, 1977): *biological needs* that ensure the functioning of an organism, such as oxygen, food, water and elimination; *basic needs*, including healthy food and properly heated and ventilated housing (sometimes basic and biological needs are used interchangeably); and *functional needs*, which are all those elements that allow people to perform their job.

Additionally, the United States Institute of Peace identifies the immediate survival needs of a population. These include clean water, food, shelter, proper sanitation, health services and protection from violence. Access to basic needs is, therefore, a condition in which the population can obtain water, food, shelter and health services in adequate quantity and quality to ensure survival and satisfy their right to "life with dignity".

Scholar Mary Kaldor (2014) emphasizes the importance of awareness of and empathy for human needs, observing,

Notions of "partnership," "local ownership" and participation are already key concepts in development policy, while soldiers often refer to the "ground truth" or to knowledge of the "human terrain." Decisions about the kind of security and development policies to be adopted [...] will only work if they take account of the most basic needs identified by the people who are affected by violence and insecurity. [...] People who live in the zones of insecurity are the only ones able to sustain long-term security. [...] Participation of teachers, doctors, tribal leaders, religious leaders and young people are all critical for both understanding and operationalizing human security (p. 72).

Therefore, based on the aforementioned review, we contend that fractal multi-actor humanitarian units would best serve the needs of those involved in conflict zones more effectively than current approaches.

MISSION OF HUMANITARIAN UNITS

The framework of humanitarian units allows for multiple actors to collaborate to foster livelihood promotion, livelihood protection and livelihood provision; meeting social needs can also be executed within the units, in alignment with the DRM phases of humanitarian assistance previously described. Moreover, humanitarian units are well suited to generate added value—positive relationships with and engagement of local communities (bottom-up initiative)—and achieve their goal of more effective, sustainable actions that engage the local citizens (Fig. 3). To improve interactions with local populations, humanitarian units may find it helpful to apply a methodology proposed by the consulting firm Gartner, specifically its customer experience pyramid (Gartner, 2018), adapted below:

- **Level 1: Communication**—Furnish civilians with the information they can use via the right channel at the right time.
- **Level 2: Responsive**—Solve the civilians' problems quickly and efficiently, using proper means and resources; consider civilians' problems as the concern of the humanitarian unit.
- **Level 3: Commitment**—Listen for, understand and resolve civilians' unique needs (a personalized approach).
- **Level 4: Proactive**—Provide experiences that resolve needs before civilians ask.
- **Level 5: Evolution**—Make civilians feel better, safer and more empowered.

The civilians' experience with humanitarian units reflects the quality of the humanitarian action, influencing its success in assisting people suffering from the atrocities of war and disasters to rebuild their communities and sustain them.

Figure 3. Perspectives of humanitarian actions (Own elaboration based on: Gart-ner (2018); Humanitarian Coalition; The South Africa Green Paper on Disaster Management, South Africa 1998)

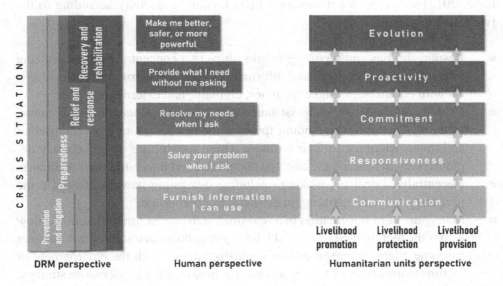

STRUCTURE OF HUMANITARIAN UNITS

The reality of countries plagued by war, natural disasters and other crises is complex, unpredictable, volatile and ambiguous. Responding to ongoing challenges requires adaptive tools, which fractal organization theory and fractal change management offer (Henderson & Boje, 2018). In 1975 Benoit Mandelbrot coined the term "fractal" (from the Latin *fractus*) to denote something that is irregular and fragmented, using it to describe the world: "[…] natural forms, and many man-made creations as well, are 'rough'" (NOVA, 2008). Mandelbrot showed the importance of outliers, nonlinear distributions and scalable repetition in limitless space (Henderson & Boje, 2018). Moreover, fractal theory has inspired scientists in many disciplines such as cosmology, medicine, engineering and genetics. With the contributions of Warnecke in 1993, fractal theory has been introduced to organizational management in different sectors, including manufacturing, financial, human resources and software development. Literature on fractal management even extends to public services, including health care, service-oriented organizations, military defense and the education sector (Peralta & Soltero, 2020). Thus, this approach is well suited to organize humanitarian units operating in unpredictable and complex environments.

Referring to the principle of fractal organization (Bhattacharya et al. 2022, Raye, 2013) we propose humanitarian units organized fractally according to the five following features:

- Responsibilities and reporting relationships that concentrate on maximizing interactions, connections, and information exchange across hierarchical levels with commanders and colleagues, civilians, and external partners.
- Value-creating delivery of assistance that leverages a network of dynamic, evolving capabilities, including those of the humanitarian units themselves and those belonging to their partners. These capabilities can be quickly deployed locally to reach the affected population and thus build their resilience.
- Decentralized decision-making, including delegating power to teams at the periphery who are operating in the field, as appropriate.
- Management of information in a real-time, transparent, multidirectional flow across the hierarchical levels and DRM system boundaries. Information flows from the edges, where front-line members interact with the environment of victims to the center of the organization, where core leaders focus on strategy, task delegation and resource allocation.
- Management of transactions occurs in a way that facilitates online transactions and information sharing by building digital platforms.

Furthermore, the humanitarian unit should be under the direction of the fire brigade commander and comprise representatives from all sectors responsible for providing security to citizens. These include the police; social services, labor office, welfare office, government housing, sanitary and epidemiological stations; health care providers such as doctors, nurses, rescuers and psychologists; border guards; fire service; armed forces; NGOs; local governors; and citizens. See Figure 4 for an overview of this structure. The composition of the unit (number of representatives) should be flexible, adjusted to the needs of the affected community, and the tasks delegated based on the responsibilities assigned to a given service in the country's DSM plans and extended to the specific functions of the humanitarian assistance.

Figure 4. Fractal structure of humanitarian units

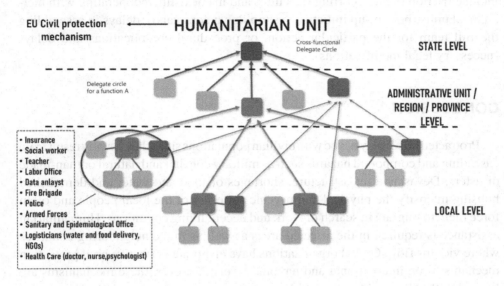

DISCUSSION

Organizing humanitarian assistance will foster addressing disaster risk in accord with aforementioned Sendai Framework for Disaster Risk Reduction 2015–2030. DRM multidimensional structure of humanitarian units would create an interactive and open operational environment. Multi-actor and multisectoral arrangement at international, national and local level would guarantee executing comprehensive assistance and linking disaster risk management and humanitarian action with social protection.

Moreover, the data suggest that humanitarian units with fractal structures would ensure higher effectiveness by the whole set of complementary features like enabling comprehensive assistance to the affected individuals and communities executed by supporting multi-actor teams in action, interoperability across teams and flexible response. Fractal structures would also enable faster and accurate communication with international organizations as well as reaching well-informed decisions through discussion and consensus based on real-time data analysis, expertise and experience. The next features like assigning tasks and assets to proper personnel and avoiding task duplication would further strengthen professional approach and efficient resource management (a catalyst for cost reduction).

However, the potential limitations of the fractally organized humanitarian unit include friction in the reporting structures and in coexisting/cooperating with hierarchical units (bottom-up initiatives vs top-down command), delays in assembling the full team for the particular action, or procedural complications and delays (necessary legal modifications).

CONCLUSION

Protracted crises play havoc with civilian populations since they usually result from cascading and compound hazards such as military conflict and natural or man-made disasters. Devastated infrastructure, shortages of food and water and demolished housing intensify the physical and psychic suffering of the local people and often force them to migrate in search of work and decent living conditions. Humanitarian assistance is required in the affected areas as well as in the neighboring countries where victims flow. Global organizations have elaborated effective civil protection mechanisms on international and national levels; however, these mechanisms are limited by the changeable nature of the security environment, especially the growing scale of crises, their prolonged duration and the need to sometimes apply contradicting and counterproductive measures.

Addressing the multiplicity of the civilian population's needs requires multiple actors engaged in cross-sectoral network collaboration—presenting a challenge for coordinating entities, especially in countries with unstable governance, which is often a feature of crisis situations. Humanitarian units represent a possibility to better respond to such situations. Ideally, they would consist of the representatives of all sectors responsible for providing security to civilians in disaster zones. Their fractal structure would ensure higher effectiveness by improving and streamlining administrative and communication tasks. Furthermore, theoretical models of fractally structured humanitarian units incorporated in DRM structures should meet the needs of people affected by present and future crises, as stated in the hypothesis. Therefore, it is recommended that fractal humanitarian units be tested and verified for efficiency and operational capability.

REFERENCES

Below, A. (2019). Climate change: The existential threat multiplier. In Understanding new security threats. Routledge.

Bhattacharya, A., Bürkner, H.P., Bailey, A., & Verma, S. (2022). The organization of the future is fractal. https://www.bcg.com/publications/2022/fractal-companies -are-the-organizations-of-the-future

Bosher, L., Chmutina, K., & van Niekerk, D. (2021). Stop going around in circles: Towards a reconceptualisation of disaster risk management phases. *Disaster Prevention and Management*, 30(4/5), 525–537. DOI: 10.1108/DPM-03-2021-0071

Bridge, J. (2023, Dec. 5). Warfare ruins the environment – and not just on the front lines. https://theconversation.com/warfare-ruins-the-environment-and-not-just-on -the-front-lines-218853

Camarota, S. A. (2016). New Data: Immigration Surged in 2014 and 2015. More than three million legal and illegal immigrants settled in the United States in the last two years. Center for Migration Studies. https://cis.org/Report/New-Data-Immigration -Surged-2014-and-2015

Clain, G. (2023, Apr. 14). What are compound climate risks and how might they impact companies? Ecoact. https://eco-act.com/blog/compound-risks-climate/

Cotroneo, A. & Triggiano, M. (2024, March 13). Exploring the intersection of armed conflict, climate risks and mobility: the ICRC's experience.

Haynie, B. (2021). *Climate Change Migration: Developing a Security Strategy for All*. RAND. (https://www.rand.org/well-being/portfolios/mass-migration.html)

Henderson, T., & Boje, D. M. (2018). *Organizational development and change theory managing fractal organizing processes*. Routledge.

Janz, M. R., Soi, N., Russell, R., & the World Vision International. (2009) Collaboration and partnership in humanitarian action. Humanitarian Practice Network, *45*(15). https://odihpn.org/publication/collaboration-and-partnership-in -humanitarian-action/

Kaldor, M. (2014). Human security: Political authority in a global era. In Martin, M., & Taylor, O. (Eds.), *Routledge Handbook of Human Security*. Routledge.

Kristoff, M., & Panarelli, L. (2010). Haiti: A republic of NGOs? In *Peace Brief*. United States Institute of Peace.

Mahn, T. (2013). *Country-Level Aid Coordination at the United Nations – Taking the ResidentCoordinator System Forward.* The German Development Institute.

Nolte, I. M. (2018). Interorganizational collaborations for humanitarian aid: An analysis of partnership, community, and single organization outcomes. *Public Performance & Management Review*, 41(3), 596–619. Advance online publication. DOI: 10.1080/15309576.2018.1462212

NOVA. (2008). A Radical Mind. https://www.pbs.org/wgbh/nova/article/mandelbrot -fractal/

OECD. (2019). *Lives in Crises: What Do People Tell Us About the Humanitarian Aid They Receive?* OECD Publishing. DOI: 10.1787/9d39623d-

Peralta, M.E.& Soltero, V.M. (2020). Analysis of fractal manufacturing systems framework towards industry 4.0. *Journal of Manufacturing Systems, 57*, 46–60.

Ranjan, R., & Karmakar, S. (2024). Compound hazard mapping for tropical cyclone-induced concurrent wind and rainfall extremes over India. *NPJ Natural Hazards*, 1(1), 15. DOI: 10.1038/s44304-024-00013-y

Raye, J. (2013). Fractal Organization Theory. *Proceedings of the 56th Annual Meeting of the ISSS - 2012, San Jose, CA, USA.* Retrieved from https://journals.isss.org/ index.php/proceedings56th/article/view/1796

Rosen, F. (1977). Basic needs and justice. *Mind*, 86(341), 88–94. DOI: 10.1093/ mind/LXXXVI.341.88

Shiro, E. (2024, Jan. 8). The Current Migrant Crisis Is a Collective Trauma. Time. https://time.com/6553088/venezuelan-migrant-crisis-collective-trauma-essay/

Simonovic, S. P., Kundzewicz, Z. W., & Wright, N. (2021). Floods and the COVID-19 pandemic-A new double hazard problem. *WIREs. Water*, 8(2), e1509. DOI: 10.1002/wat2.1509 PMID: 33786171

Smith, G. (2021). Overcoming barriers to coordinating across social protection and humanitarian assistance—building on promising practices.

Suárez-Orozco, M. M. (2019). Introduction: Catastrophic migrations. In Suárez-Orozco, M. M. (Ed.), *Humanitarianism and Mass Migration: Confronting the World Crisis* (1st ed., pp. 1–40). University of California Press. DOI: 10.2307/j.ctv9zchv9.5

The Directorate-General for European Civil Protection and Humanitarian Aid Operations (ECHO). (2023). Forgotten Crises. https://civil-protection-humanitarian -aid.ec.europa.eu/what/humanitarian-aid/needs-assessment/forgotten-crises_en

The Website of Dziennik Gazeta Prawna. (2023). Jak samorządy poradziły sobie z kryzysem uchodźczym i co jeszcze je czeka? (https://www.gazetaprawna.pl/perlysamorzadu/artykuly/8665348,jak-samorzady-poradzily-sobie-z-kryzysem-uchodzczym-i-co-jeszcze-je-czeka.html)

The Website of The Republic of Poland (2022). Support for Poland to help refugees from Ukraine.

The White House. (2021). Report on The Impact of Climate Change on Migration.

Thomas, M. A., Michaelis, A. C., Oakley, N. S., Kean, J. W., Gensini, V. A., & Ashley, W. S. (2024). Rainfall intensification amplifies exposure of American Southwest to conditions that trigger postfire debris flows. *npj. Npj Natural Hazards*, 1(1), 14. DOI: 10.1038/s44304-024-00017-8

Turunen, S. (2020). Accountability. In de Lauri, A. (Ed.), *Humanitarianism*. Brill.

UNISDR. (2017). C. Cross-Sectoral and Multi-Risk Approach to Cascading Disasters.

US Department of Homeland Security. (n.d.). Complex coordinated attacks. https://www.cisa.gov/sites/default/files/2022-11/Action%20Guide%20CCA%20508%20FINAL%2020190905.pdf)

World Bank. (n.d.). *GFDRR Annual Report2022: Bringing Resilience to Scale (English)*. World Bank Group. https://documents.worldbank.org/curated/en/099904102272326411/IDU0242fa9a607c8804e9a0b0d404a431f9a65a9

Woźniak, A. (2022). Fala uchodźców zaczyna już paraliżować polskie dworce. The Website of Rzeczposoplita Newspaper. https://www.rp.pl/transport/art35835921-fala-uchodzcow-zaczyna-juz-paralizowac-polskie-dworce

Zaitchik, B. F., Omumbo, J., Lowe, R., van Aalst, M., Anderson, L. O., Fischer, E., Norman, C., Robbins, J., Barciela, R., Trtanj, J., von Borries, R., & Luterbacher, J. (2022). Planning for compound hazards during the COVID-19 pandemic. *Bulletin of the American Meteorological Society*, 103(3), E704–E709. DOI: 10.1175/BAMS-D-21-0215.1

Zhukova, E. (2020). Vulnerability. In de Lauri, A. (Ed.), *Humanitarianism*. Brill.

KEY TERMS AND DEFINITIONS

Cascading Hazard: Occurs when one danger triggers another. They can be natural, natural-technological or human-driven natural-technological hazards. They can also occur as a result of slow-onset events like rising sea levels, warming oceans and increasing lack of fresh water. At each stage, or node, of the cascade there is a possibility to interrupt the stream by stopping it outright or mitigating its effects. However, each node has the potential to aggravate impacts or create new, unexpected consequences, intensifying the cascade effect (Below 2019).

Civil Protection: Is about addressing basic needs requires a prompt, comprehensive and coordinated approach. such as that offered by the EU Civil Protection Mechanism, for example. The Mechanism can be solicited by countries, the United Nations and international organizations needing assistance. In 2022, the Mechanism was activated 106 times to respond to war in Ukraine, wildfires in Europe, COVID-19 in Europe and worldwide, and floods in Pakistan. The Mechanism can be also activated for consular support such as evacuation operations (Below 2019).

Compound Hazard: Can include single extreme events, multiple coinciding events and sequential events. They have different origins but are correlated and interact in space and/or time, such as the COVID-19 pandemic coinciding with extreme heat. Additionally, these compound hazards can require conflicting preventive and response behavior patterns, e.g., lockdowns that slow COVID-19 transmission may have the unintended consequence of putting people confronting heat waves at risk by isolating them in poorly ventilated rooms, also leading to social isolation (Zaitchik et al. 2022).

Disaster Risk Management (DRM): Managing a humanitarian crisis in an area affected by conflict or natural disaster, as well as in the neighboring locations. Disaster risk management occurs in four consecutive phases: preparedness, planning, response, and recovery. However, a protracted crisis with cascading and compound hazards creates a situation where phases coexist and overlap making the coordination of action even more complicated. Specific tools have been developed for addressing the fragility, conflict, and violence nexus (FCV) in the Middle East and North Africa, including integrated DRM-FCV approaches, analytical frameworks and targeted solutions.

Fractal (Theory): In 1975 Benoit Mandelbrot coined the term "fractal" (from the Latin fractus) to denote something that is irregular and fragmented, using it to describe the world. He showed the importance of outliers, nonlinear distributions and scalable repetition in limitless space. With the contributions of Warnecke in 1993, fractal theory has been introduced to organizational management in different sectors, including manufacturing, financial, human resources and software development, public services, including health care military defense and the education sector. A fractal organizational structure: breaks centralized operations and creates individual teams empowered to respond to opportunities from outside the core; designs a delivery model around a network of evolving capabilities; enables the real-time, transparent, multidirectional flow of data; focuses less on hierarchy and more on maximizing interactions, connections among all entities involved (Bhattacharya et.al. 2022).

Humanitarian Crisis: Is triggered by protracted conflicts, accompanied by climate change, and have cascading or compound impacts on the local people. The consequences include food insecurity; a tripled rate of undernourishment and livelihood disruption resulting from people's inability to support themselves due to displacement; loss of resources and economic decline; inequality; toxic social norms; and political polarization (UNOCHA 2023).

Humanitarian Unit/Assistance: Humanitarian agencies engage in three types of actions in response to protracted crises: livelihood provisioning to meet immediate basic needs and protect people's lives; livelihood protection of people's assets and to prevent the sale or destruction of productive assets, and livelihood promotion to support livelihood assets, policies and institutions that can improve people's livelihoods (Humanitarian Coalition).

Protracted Crisis: The situations in which a large number of a population is experiencing a heightened risk of death, disease, and breakdown of their livelihoods. While every protracted crisis is unique, they often share the following characteristics: long duration, conflict, weak governance or public administration structures, unsustainable livelihood systems, poor food security outcomes and breakdown of local institutions (Humanitarian Coalition).

Chapter 8
Projects Selection and Prioritization in the Portuguese Navy

Jorge Vareda Gomes
https://orcid.org/0000-0003-0656-9284
Universidade Lusófona, Portugal

Mário Romão
https://orcid.org/0000-0003-4564-1883
ISEG, Universidade de Lisboa, Portugal

Ricardo Simplício
ISEG, Universidade de Lisboa, Portugal

EXECUTIVE SUMMARY

In times of major technological changes with ever shorter production cycles, subject to strong global competition, it is vital for organizations to optimize resources and benefit from their investments to achieve the expected successes. One of the main difficulties that organizations face is the high number of projects in their portfolio. Selecting and prioritizing projects is essential to ensure the maximum return on investment and the sustainability of the organization. The analysis and selection of projects is carried out using different approaches, each with advantages and disadvantages that need to be considered. The selection and prioritization of projects depends largely on the nature and profile of managers, organizational culture, and techniques that best fit the organization's environment. This study intends to confront the pilot model of selection and prioritization developed by the Portuguese Navy and establish a bridge with the academic literature.

DOI: 10.4018/979-8-3693-2675-6.ch008

INTRODUCTION

In recent decades, dramatic changes in the business world, driven by technology and globalization, have led organizations to adopt more flexible and cost-effective structures to seize innovation opportunities (Gemünden et al., 2018; Brynjolfsson & McAfee, 2014). Projects have become increasingly vital for organizational success and are essential for effective management of business processes (Plattfaut, 2022; Kerzner, 2023), especially those related to innovation and technology (Yohannes and Mauritsius, 2022; Díaz-Díaz & Pérez-Bustamante, 2020).

A major challenge for organizations today is managing the large number of competing projects in their portfolios. Limited budgets and resources often lead to conflicts among projects, potentially compromising an organization's strategic goals. Therefore, the ability to effectively select and prioritize projects is crucial for maximizing return on investment (Archer & Ghasemzadeh, 1999; Cooper & Edgett, 2009). While some organizations rely solely on financial indicators like ROI, NPV, or Payback for project selection, research shows that this approach often results in poorer portfolio performance (Cooper & Edgett, 2009; Killen et al., 2008). Aligning projects with organizational strategy is a key factor in achieving success (Cooper, 2008; Petro & Gardiner, 2015; Morris & Jamieson, 2005). Moreover, incorporating strategic considerations and qualitative assessments alongside financial metrics can enhance decision-making and project outcomes (Martinsuo & Lehtonen, 2007; Shenhar et al., 2001).

Companies strive to identify the optimal set of projects that align with strategic goals while adhering to essential constraints (Bai et al., 2021). Project Portfolio Management (PPM) has emerged as a crucial method for the coordinated management of multiple projects within an organization. PPM facilitates strategic project management by efficiently allocating scarce resources and guiding portfolios to achieve strategic benefits (Clegg et al., 2018; Müller et al., 2008). By integrating project selection with organizational objectives, PPM ensures that projects deliver maximum value and contribute to long-term success (Kester et al., 2011; Jonas, 2010). Effective PPM involves balancing project risk, resource availability, and strategic alignment to enhance overall organizational performance (Kester et al., 2009; Meskendahl, 2010).

While there is no one-size-fits-all approach to project selection, effective portfolio management should strive to deliver optimal results by carefully selecting and prioritizing projects that align with strategic objectives (Cooper & Edgett, 2009; Teller et al., 2012). This case study examines the Portuguese Armed Forces (PAF), specifically the Portuguese Navy, with a focus on building a project portfolio as PAF's primary investment tool. As in other sectors, project selection and prioritization are critical to organizational success. The goal is to build and maintain the necessary resources for PAF missions, which is vital to both the organization and the nation (Martinsuo, 2013). By aligning projects with strategic goals, the PAF can ensure that its investments contribute effectively to national defense and organizational efficiency (Petit & Hobbs, 2010; Blomquist & Müller, 2006).

Following an analysis of the PAF's strengths and weaknesses, projects are identified to address identified deficiencies, impacting PAF missions and contributing to national defense policy. Prioritization is initially determined through multicriteria analysis, considering risk assessments for each identified gap. A subsequent cost-benefit and sensitivity analysis considers constraints such as available financial resources.

The study aims to identify theoretical models from academic literature and validate the PAF pilot model within the military context, supported by these theoretical frameworks.

LITERATURE REVIEW

Project Portfolio

A project portfolio consists of various components, including projects, programs, and tasks such as maintenance and ongoing operations. These elements are grouped together to facilitate the coordinated management of efforts toward achieving strategic objectives (Mohagheghi et al., 2019). A portfolio encompasses projects, programs, sub-portfolios, and operations that are managed collectively to meet strategic goals, all while sharing and competing for limited resources (PMI, 2017).

Within a portfolio, the components do not necessarily have to be interdependent or share common objectives, but they must be quantifiable, classified, and prioritized individually. A project portfolio is a collection of projects that compete for scarce resources and are conducted under the sponsorship or management of a specific organization (Archer & Ghasemzadeh, 1999; Shenhar et al., 2001; Elonen & Artto, 2003; Martinsuo & Lehtonen, 2007; PMI, 2017).

Keskin (2020) expands on the classic definition of project portfolio selection by Archer and Ghasemzadeh (1999), describing it as the creation of a portfolio from a set of proposed projects that must consider all dimensions of the organizational strategy, the interactions between projects, resource needs, and the shared resources among them. Keskin's definition highlights key dimensions to consider in project portfolio selection:

● Importance of Organizational Strategy: Ensuring that the portfolio aligns with the broader strategic goals of the organization.

- Interdependencies Between Projects: Recognizing how projects within the portfolio influence and relate to each other.
- Multiple Objectives: Balancing diverse objectives that the organization seeks to achieve through its portfolio.
- Resource Constraints: Managing the limitations in available resources that affect project execution.

Portfolio management aims to achieve three primary objectives (Elonen & Artto, 2003; Cooper et al., 2002; Meskendahl, 2010; Ahonen et al., 2020):

- Maximization of Portfolio Value: Ensuring that the portfolio generates the highest possible value.
- Linkage of the Portfolio to Strategy: Ensuring that the portfolio aligns with and supports the organization's strategic goals.
- Balancing the Portfolio: Maintaining a balanced portfolio that considers risks, rewards, and strategic alignment.

According to the literature, project portfolio success encompasses several dimensions (Martinsuo & Lehtonen, 2007; Cooper, Dewe, & O'Driscoll, 2001; Meskendahl, 2010; Müller, Martinsuo, & Blomquist, 2008):

- Average Project Success: This includes traditional success criteria such as adherence to budget, schedule, and quality, as well as customer satisfaction across all projects within the portfolio (Shenhar et al., 2001; Martinsuo & Lehtonen, 2007; Turner & Müller, 2005).
- Use of Synergies: Measures the extent to which projects in the portfolio leverage technical and market skills among themselves to create additional value (Shenhar et al., 2001; Martinsuo & Lehtonen, 2007; Jonsson & Mårtensson, 2018).
- Strategic Fit: Assesses how well the projects align with and reflect the corporate business strategy (Dietrich & Lehtonen, 2005; Rego et al., 2018).
- Portfolio Balance: Refers to the balance within the portfolio concerning risks and expected benefits, ensuring a diversified and manageable risk profile (Archer & Ghasemzadeh, 1999; Verma & Sinha, 2018).
- Preparing for the Future: Focuses on the long-term aspects and the organization's ability to capitalize on future opportunities after project completion (Shenhar et al., 2001; Müller, & Turner, 2013).
- Economic Success: Addresses short-term economic impacts at the corporate level, including market performance and commercial success of the organiza-

tion or business unit (Shenhar et al., 2001; Meskendahl, 2010; Ahonen et al., 2020).

An organizational focus on project portfolio management indicates that effective management of individual projects can significantly enhance overall business efficiency and help achieve strategic objectives (Ershadi et al., 2020; Patanakul, 2015; Petro & Gardiner, 2015). Project portfolio management is viewed as a dynamic decision-making process that is continually updated and revised (Cooper, Edgett, & Kleinschmidt, 2001). In this process, new projects are evaluated, selected, and prioritized; existing projects may be accelerated, abandoned, or de-prioritized, and resources are allocated and reallocated accordingly (Cooper et al., 2001; Pajares & López, 2014; Nowak, 2013; Kester et al., 2011).

Many scholars and practitioners emphasize that decision-making, prioritization and reprioritization, strategic alignment and realignment, as well as resource allocation and reallocation, are integral to the ongoing processes of project portfolio management (Cooper, Dewe, & O'Driscoll, 2001; Kester et al., 2011; Teller, 2013). Project selection is a strategic decision and must align with the organization's business strategy to maximize the return on the selected portfolio (Archer & Ghasemzadeh, 1999; Petro & Gardiner, 2015; Meskendahl, 2010; Pajares & López, 2014; Nowak, 2013; Dutra et al., 2014; Teller, 2013; Ahonen et al., 2020).

The process of selecting and prioritizing projects among numerous alternatives is complex and requires clear and well-defined criteria (Khalili-Damghani & Tavana, 2014; Padovani, 2008; Faramarzi et al., 2020). Conflicts may arise during the selection and prioritization process due to discrepancies in qualitative or quantitative profiles, alignment with organizational strategic objectives, and balancing gains against costs and resource limitations (Khalili-Damghani & Tavana, 2014; Kock & Gemünden, 2016; Orosz et al., 2021). Although numerous methods are available for analyzing and selecting projects, there is no universal agreement on the best methodologies since each method has its own advantages and disadvantages. The choice of method often depends on the specific context of the organization and the preferences of the decision-makers (Dutra et al., 2014; Iamratanakul et al., 2008; Ahonen et al., 2020; Kizito et al., 2021).

Projects within a portfolio should be prioritized based on the benefits they provide to the organization, which can be quantified through metrics such as Return on Investment (ROI), strategic alignment, and other performance measures (Petro & Gardiner, 2015; Müller & Turner, 2013; Baidoo et al., 2021).

Archer and Ghasemzadeh (1999) proposed an integrated framework for project portfolio selection, which highlights the use of various tools and techniques to support decision-making. This framework includes three main phases:

- Strategic Evaluation: This phase involves assessing both internal (strengths and weaknesses) and external (marketplace) factors to develop a competitive advantage and inform strategy development (Archer & Ghasemzadeh, 1999; Meskendahl, 2010; Zhang et al., 2021).
- Individual Project Evaluation: Focuses on measuring the benefits and value that each project contributes to achieving the portfolio's objectives (Archer & Ghasemzadeh, 1999; Rego et al., 2018; Balatbat et al., 2022).
- Portfolio Selection: Involves comparing multiple projects simultaneously, ranking them, and selecting projects for inclusion in the portfolio based on predefined criteria and available resources (Archer & Ghasemzadeh, 1999; Cooper et al., 2001; Zopounidis & Doumpos, 2021).

Cooper (2005) proposed a selection framework comprising two levels. The first level, termed 'strategic portfolio decisions' (strategic buckets), is crucial for organizations aiming to categorize projects into distinct subsets or categories. The second level, known as 'tactical portfolio decisions,' focuses on the project selection process itself, employing various techniques and tools to choose the appropriate projects for each strategic bucket.

Meskendahl (2010) introduced a reference model emphasizing the alignment of organizational strategy with portfolio structure and success. The model suggests that strategic orientation's impact is mediated through the portfolio's structure, influencing overall success.

Khalili-Damghani and Tavana (2014) developed a framework designed to align organizational strategy—including mission, vision, and values—with tactical and operational considerations, creating a sustainable strategy for project selection.

Brooke and Pagnanelli (2014) proposed a five-step framework for integrating sustainability into the innovation project portfolio management process, particularly in product development. This framework is applicable to managing portfolios comprising breakthrough projects, platform projects, and derivative projects.

Kudratova et al. (2018) introduced a novel approach to sustainable project selection that incorporates sustainability and reinvestment strategies. Their method aims to balance environmental protection with efficient budget allocation, maximizing investor returns.

Schipper and Silvius (2018) developed an open intra-organizational model that connects stakeholders with economic, environmental, and social interests to the strategy planning and Project Portfolio Management (PPM) process through a sense-making approach. This framework allows for the integration of emerging sustainability strategies throughout project execution.

Mohammad and Pan (2021) argue that Project Portfolio Management should evolve beyond project selection and management to include processes related to corporate social responsibility (CSR) reporting. This expansion supports the development of best practices that enhance project management and deliver sustainable outcomes.

Zarjou and Khalilzadeh (2021) created a model for project portfolio selection that considers organizational goals such as budgets, sustainability, cash flow, and reinvestment strategies in uncertain environments. Their study focuses on the implications of investment quantities and the costs associated with sustainable projects.

Kim and Park (2021) introduced a hybrid approach for sustainable project portfolio management, integrating machine learning and multi-criteria decision-making to address modern challenges.

Liu, Wang, and Zhao (2022) provided a systematic review and future research agenda on dynamic project portfolio management, highlighting new perspectives in sustainability.

Silvius and Marnewick (2022) presented a conceptual framework highlighting the interconnections between integrating sustainability into organizational strategy, project portfolio management, and project management practices.

Hadjinicolaou et al. (2022) explored how firms can leverage Project Portfolio Management tools to foster innovation and absorb innovative developments. Their study specifically examines small- and medium-sized enterprises with mid-range planning horizons that must innovate strategically to maintain competitiveness and capitalize on new opportunities.

Smith and Johnson (2023) explored how to align project portfolio management with organizational sustainability, offering new perspectives and approaches for integration (Smith & Johnson, 2023).

Aghajani, Ruge, and Jugdev (2023) conducted a structured literature review from 2000 to 2021, developing an integrative framework that presents a holistic view of sustainability in project portfolios. Their framework emphasizes three core research themes: sustainability mindset, sustainability assessment, and sustainability integration in project portfolio processes.

Fagarasan et al. (2023) proposed a data-driven scoring model for software firms to incorporate sustainability metrics into their project and portfolio performance assessments. This model is designed to enhance delivery performance while reinforcing the sustainability of the software development lifecycle.

Several challenges complicate the selection of an appropriate project portfolio framework:

- Limited Resource Availability: Constraints in budget, personnel, and technology can restrict the number of projects an organization can undertake simultaneously (Archer & Ghasemzadeh, 1999; Zhang et al., 2022).

- Strategic Alignment: Ensuring that selected projects align with the organization's overall strategic goals and objectives remains a persistent challenge (Cooper, Edgett, & Kleinschmidt, 2000; Fong et al., 2023).
- Human Biases: Project portfolio selection can be influenced by human biases, such as lobbying and favoritism, which can undermine rational decision-making (Yelin, 2005; Van der Meer-Kooistra & Vosselman, 2023).
- Information Deficiencies: Inadequate or unreliable information regarding project costs, timelines, resource availability, and expected benefits can complicate the selection process (Cooper, Dewe, & O'Driscoll, 2001; Rădulescu & Rădulescu, 2001; Ali & Hsu, 2023).
- Annual Planning Reviews: The review process of annual plans can eliminate opportunities for new project proposals, limiting the flexibility of project selection (Kendall & Rollins, 2003; Smith & Johnson, 2023).
- Risk-Reward Balance: Projects with high potential rewards often come with significant risks, and managing this risk-reward balance is complex (Chapman & Ward, 2003; Zhang & Yang, 2022).
- Continuous Monitoring: Ongoing monitoring and feedback are essential to ensure projects remain aligned with strategic goals and deliver anticipated benefits (Levine, 2005; Liu & Xu, 2023).
- Dynamic Change: Large organizations must develop dynamic capabilities to adapt to changes and outperform competitors, which can be challenging (Bolman & Deal, 2017; Bechtel & Squires, 2001; Chrusciel & Field, 2006; Walker et al., 2007; Rao et al., 2023).
- Market and Technological Changes: Evolving market conditions, technological advancements, and regulatory changes can affect the feasibility and desirability of projects (Olsson, 2006; Smith & Jones, 2023).
- Stakeholder Interests: Different stakeholders often have conflicting priorities and interests, complicating project selection (Jepsen & Eskerod, 2009; Thompson & Smith, 2022).
- Evaluation Criteria: Establishing clear, consistent, and measurable criteria for project evaluation and selection can be challenging (Meskendahl, 2010; Zhao & Wang, 2023).
- Integration with Tools: Integrating project selection frameworks with existing project management and business intelligence tools can be problematic, particularly in organizations with legacy systems (Ward & Daniel, 2012; Green & Harris, 2023).
- Data Reliability: Reliable data is crucial for informed decision-making. Poor quality or insufficient data can undermine the project selection process (Davis, 2014; Patel & Kumar, 2022).

- Forecasting Benefits: Accurately forecasting the potential benefits and returns from each project can be difficult (Bradley, 2016; Zhao et al., 2023).

CASE STUDY

The Organization

Project prioritization and selection are critical not only in private companies but also within public sector organizations, such as the Ministry of National Defense representing the Portuguese Government. The nature of project selection in the public sector differs significantly from that in the private sector, given its collective and national importance. Projects in this domain are crucial for national defense and for affirming Portugal's sovereignty. Due to the unique characteristics of the organization, the context of the subject matter, and challenges in data collection, this study adopts a single-case study approach (Yin, 2018).

The research is grounded in the structural documentation related to the military context of national defense. These documents underpin the country's military strategic objectives, guide military actions, and outline the necessary capabilities for operational success.

As part of the triangulation process, the study included interviews with several key individuals involved in the project portfolio management process. These interviews featured the model creator, the developer, and other essential personnel engaged in managing the portfolio, providing diverse perspectives on the subject.

Model of Prioritization and Selection of Projects

The current model is designed using risk and portfolio analysis methodologies to aid in the evaluation and prioritization of gaps identified from comparing the planned resources and capabilities for 2018 with the Portuguese Armed Forces' (PAF) missions. Unlike other prioritization and selection models where only selected projects are considered, in this model, all proposed projects compete for inclusion in the portfolio. The process begins with the prioritization of all projects, followed by their integration into the portfolio through a multi-criteria and cost-benefit analysis.

This model provides a structured approach to define criteria for evaluating and selecting initiatives related to military equipment, modernization, and operationalization of the forces. It focuses on addressing gaps and assessing their significance. The relevance of each gap influences the value of a project, based on the importance of the gap it aims to address. The degree of gap closure measures how effectively a project mitigates the identified gap. Once projects are approved, they are incorporated into the PAF's portfolio. The model consists of four main modules (Table 1).

Table 1. Modules of PAF model

Module	Description
Strategic	— Qualitative Assessments of the PAF's Structural Documentation: This module involves a detailed qualitative analysis of the PAF's structural documents to assess and quantify the relative value of each resource type required for fulfilling the PAF's missions. This involves a systematic approach to evaluate how well different resources contribute to meeting the strategic objectives. — Numeric Value Attribution: This module focuses on assigning a numeric value ranging from 1 to 6 to different resources. This scoring system helps in quantifying the importance and effectiveness of each resource type in various operational scenarios, enabling a more objective comparison. — Scoring Based on Specificities and Performance Scenarios: Resources are scored according to their specific characteristics and performance in different scenarios. This assessment considers how each type of resource performs under varying conditions and its relevance to achieving mission objectives.
Operational	— Translation of Needs into Projects for a Sustainable System: This module focuses on translating identified needs into actionable projects by evaluating how each proposed project contributes to addressing specific gaps. It emphasizes integrating sustainability considerations into the project selection process, ensuring that each project contributes effectively to building a robust and sustainable system. — Impact Assessment of Absence: This step involves assessing the impact or degradation resulting from the absence of a specific resource or capability. It estimates the potential consequences of not addressing a particular gap, providing insights into the urgency and importance of filling this gap. — Project and Program Proposals: Based on the identified shortcomings and their impact, this module involves formulating and proposing projects and programs aimed at addressing these gaps. These proposals are designed to bridge the identified deficiencies, ensuring that the PAF's capabilities and resources are aligned with its strategic goals.
Analysis	— Portfolio Analysis for Project Adjustment: This module involves a comprehensive portfolio analysis to refine the initial project evaluations. It takes into account cost-benefit constraints and the initial assumptions, aiming to select the optimal combination of projects that best aligns with organizational objectives. This process ensures that projects are evaluated and adjusted based on their overall strategic and financial contributions. — Prioritization and Selection for Execution: This phase focuses on prioritizing and selecting projects that will advance to the execution stage. It utilizes the portfolio analysis capabilities of the Enterprise Project Management (EPM) tools, such as Microsoft Project Server. This tool facilitates multi-criteria analysis followed by a detailed cost-benefit analysis, ensuring that only the most valuable projects proceed to execution. — Optimizing Strategic Value and Financial Efficiency: This module ensures the selection of the ideal project combination that maximizes strategic value while minimizing financial costs. The goal is to achieve the best value for money by balancing the strategic benefits with financial expenditure, thus optimizing overall portfolio performance.

continued on following page

Table 1. Continued

Module	Description
Portfolio Project Management	— Project Management and Adjustment: This module manages the set of approved projects to accommodate any changes, such as the addition of new projects or alterations in cost restrictions that might affect the originally approved project selection. Each project is monitored individually to detect and address any deviations in terms of time and cost early, ensuring timely corrective actions. — Strategic and Financial Maintenance: This component focuses on preserving both the strategic value and the initial financial cost of the project portfolio. Activities are geared towards maintaining alignment with strategic goals and controlling costs throughout the lifecycle of the projects. — Optimization and Opportunity Management: This module aims to optimize the portfolio by leveraging new opportunities, such as additional financial resources or the introduction of new projects. It also addresses the mitigation of negative impacts resulting from budgetary cuts or reductions in human resources. The goal is to enhance the overall value and effectiveness of the project portfolio while managing risks and seizing available opportunities.

Comparison

A comparison table (Table 2) was built to map the different contributions of the academic literature and the PAF model.

Table 2. Mapping the PAF model with the different academic approaches

Approach	Method	Measure	PAF Model	Reference
Qualitative	Strategic Method	Balanced Scorecard; Bucket Approach		Cooper & Edgett, 2009; Cooper & Sommer, 2023; Chao & Kavadias, 2008; Eilat et al., 2006; Grigoroudis et al., 2012; Kaplan & Norton, 1992; Mills & Merchen, 2004; Ittner & Larcker, 2021
	Delphi Method			Dutra et al., 2014; Lee & Kim, 2000; Linstone & Turoff, 2002; Skulmoski & Hartman, 2007; Vidal & Bocquet, 2011; Tavana et al., 2018
	Hybrid multiple-criteria decision-making			Jyh et al., 2015; Pitsis et al., 2004; Wang et al., 2018; Sahoo & Goswami, 2023; Khalili-Damghani & Tavana, 2022
	Bubble Chart			Basu, 2015; Cooper & Edgett, 2009; Cooper et al., 2000; Zhan et al., 2021
	Scoring models		Scoring models	Cooper & Edgett, 2009; Iamratanakul et al., 2008; Cooper et al., 2000; De la Torre et al., 2020
	Fuzzy logic			Iamratanakul et al., 2008; Chen & Cheng, 2009; Lin & Chen, 2004; Giacomin et al., 2021

continued on following page

Table 2. Continued

Approach	Method	Measure	PAF Model	Reference
Quantitative	Financial	ROI; TIR; VAL; Payback; Cost analysis	Best Value for Money	Archer & Ghasemzadeh, 1999; PMI, 2013; Cooper et al., 2000; Halawa et al., 2013; Hasu et al., 2015; Kerzner, 2023; Lappe & Spang, 2014; Myers et al., 2014; Saaty, 2008; Weber, 2014; Neely et al., 2021
Qualitative/ Quantitative	Decision tree			Iamratanakul et al., 2008; López-Cha et al., 2013; Sok et al., 2015; Liu et al., 2022
	Analytic hierarchy process		Multi-criteria analysis	Iamratanakul et al., 2008; Saaty, 2008; Ho, 2008; Bai & Sarkis, 2022
	Analytic network process			Lee & Kim, 2000; Subramanian & Ramanathan, 2022
Others	Risk		Risk analysis	Archer & Ghasemzadeh, 1999; PMI, 2013; Teller, 2013; Martinsuo et al., 2014; Teller & Kock, 2013; Zhang et al., 2021

DISCUSSION

The evaluation process for the FAP's (Forças Armadas Portuguesas) missions begins with a detailed analysis based on specific pre-defined priorities and guidelines. These missions are aggregated according to their nature and then subdivided into sub-scenarios, such as the security and defense of the national territory and its citizens. For the quantification process, various attributes are considered, and metrics are determined by a panel of experts from the Military Strategic Council (CMS). These experts assess each sub-scenario and integrate contributions from different Capacity Areas, which determine the importance level of each mission. The aggregated contributions are converted into numerical values, and the average is calculated for each mission.

The evaluation of means involves quantifying their suitability for executing the FAP's missions. This process considers the relative strategic-military value of each typology based on the importance of the mission. Gaps are assessed by evaluating the impact of their absence or degradation on mission performance, allowing for the estimation of the consequences of using current means. Identifying and characterizing these gaps, including determining their weight, involves several analysis sessions with specialists from various technical and operational areas.

Proposed projects and programs, designed to address the identified gaps, aim to fill these gaps as effectively as possible. The valuation of these proposals is based on their percentage rate of gap completion and the value of the corresponding means. A higher percentage of gap-filling and higher value of the typology result in a higher overall value for the proposed forces.

Once the gaps and proposals are evaluated and prioritized, the portfolio analysis module from the Enterprise Project Management (EPM) system, specifically Microsoft Project Server, is utilized. Through multi-criteria and cost analysis, projects are selected for inclusion in the portfolio. This involves defining strategic criteria for project selection and assigning weights to these criteria, which is a crucial step to ensure alignment with the initially defined strategic objectives.

The defined criteria are the following: (1) Gap value; (2) Degree of completion; (3) Level of political ambition, and (4) Political priority (Table 3).

Table 3. Prioritization criteria

Criteria	Description
Gap value	This criterion evaluates projects based on the importance and value of the gap they are intended to address. The gap value reflects how critical the identified shortfall is in achieving the strategic objectives of the FAP. Projects are assessed on their potential to fill significant gaps, with higher values assigned to those addressing more critical or high-impact deficiencies (Khalili-Damghani & Tavana, 2022; Lee & Kim, 2000).
Degree of completion	This criterion measures how effectively each project addresses and mitigates the identified gap. It assesses the extent to which a project fulfills its intended purpose of closing the gap, with higher ratings given to projects that achieve greater levels of gap closure (Giacomin et al., 2021; Silvius & Marnewick, 2022).
Level of political ambition	Projects are evaluated based on their alignment with the established political and strategic ambitions. This criterion considers how well each project supports the broader political goals and aspirations set by decision-makers. It reflects the strategic alignment of the projects with national defense and security priorities (Bechtel & Squires, 2001; Grigoroudis & Siskos, 2012)
Political priority	This criterion assesses projects according to their contribution to priority scenarios identified by political and defense authorities. It evaluates the impact of projects on building essential capabilities that align with the highest political and strategic priorities, ensuring that resources are directed towards the most critical and prioritized scenarios (Bai & Sarkis, 2022; Pitsis & Langer, 2004).

The method used in the PAF model enables the prioritization of all projects intended to address the identified gaps. Initially, projects are ranked based on their strategic value. Following this, a cost analysis is conducted, considering the annual budget, to optimize the project list. This approach allows for the selection of projects that offer the highest strategic value at the lowest cost, aligning with the principle of "Best Value for Money."

In terms of portfolio management, the Portuguese Navy undertakes several critical actions:

● Individual Tracking: Each project is monitored for time and cost to identify deviations early and implement corrective actions to mitigate their impact.

- Portfolio Management Activities: Various activities are conducted to preserve the strategic value and initial financial cost of the portfolio, including optimizing it by leveraging emerging opportunities.

The PAF model employs a range of methodologies and approaches, integrating qualitative, quantitative, and risk-based methods. This multifaceted approach distinguishes the model and enhances the project selection and prioritization process. By applying multiple perspectives, the model identifies which projects are most relevant and require focused attention in alignment with the PAF's missions.

Methodological Approaches in the PAF Model:

- Multi-Criteria Analysis (Qualitative/Quantitative Approach): This method evaluates projects from various criteria, both qualitative and quantitative, to assess their overall fit and importance (Meskendahl, 2010; Khalili-Damghani & Tavana, 2022).
- Cost Analysis (Quantitative Approach): This involves a detailed financial assessment to ensure that the selected projects deliver the best strategic value at the minimal cost, adhering to budgetary constraints (Archer & Ghasemzadeh, 1999; PMI, 2013).
- Scoring Models (Qualitative Approach): Scoring models are used for the strategic module, which prioritizes PAF missions based on their strategic significance (Cooper & Edgett, 2009; Iamratanakul et al., 2008).
- Risk Assessment: The model incorporates a risk management approach throughout, identifying and mitigating potential risks associated with project execution (Teller, 2013; Martinsuo et al., 2014).

The PAF model's strategic orientation aligns with the frameworks proposed by other scholars, emphasizing the integration of strategic focus in project portfolio management (Archer & Ghasemzadeh, 1999; Meskendahl, 2010; Khalili-Damghani & Tavana, 2022).

This holistic approach ensures a well-rounded evaluation, enabling the Portuguese Navy to effectively address its strategic defense and operational needs.

CONTRIBUTIONS, LIMITATIONS AND FUTURE RESEARCH

Given the extensive research on project portfolio prioritization and selection, this article explores a unique area where data access is typically restricted due to military confidentiality. The information available enables the characterization of a model currently undergoing testing across all branches of the Armed Forces, although it has not yet been fully implemented by the Navy.

Limitations of the Study

- Classified Information: The presence of classified and strategically sensitive documents limited the scope of data available for review, impacting the depth and comprehensiveness of the model analysis.
- Pilot Phase: The model is still in its pilot phase, which means that modifications made post-evaluation are not reflected in this study. Consequently, the current findings may not fully represent the model's final capabilities or effectiveness.
- Military Context: The study's military context presents inherent limitations. The specific characteristics and constraints of military settings may affect the generalizability of the findings to other sectors or contexts.

Future Research Directions

- Extended Evaluation: To ascertain the model's effectiveness and make necessary adjustments, further studies over a longer period are recommended. This will help determine the model's success and identify areas for improvement.
- Alignment with NATO Standards: Developing a model that aligns more closely with NATO's project prioritization and selection frameworks could facilitate a more seamless integration from strategic military to operational levels. This alignment would enhance compatibility and operational coherence within international defence contexts.

Overall, while the model presents promising advancements, ongoing evaluation and alignment with broader standards will be crucial for its successful implementation and adaptation across various branches of the Armed Forces.

CONCLUSION

Project management and project portfolio management are essential for enhancing organizational competitiveness by aligning with and supporting the implementation of organizational strategies (Ahlemann et al., 2024). Effective project portfolio management is crucial for decision-making and governance, ensuring that business objectives are met with the optimal set of projects (Levine, 2005). Both public and private organizations face the challenge of managing limited resources, which necessitates a precise selection of projects within their portfolios. This selection must align with the organization's strategic goals to ensure the achievement of objectives and the creation of value for stakeholders. This value may manifest as economic returns, sustainability achievements, market share growth, or social visibility.

The selection of projects within a portfolio is a critical activity that helps organizations define the most effective set of projects to meet their strategic objectives (Vieira et al., 2024). This study introduces a pilot model for project prioritization and selection, specifically designed to meet the missions outlined by the PAF. Given the unique context in which this model was developed, it required a thorough identification of attributes and factors related to reliability and sustainability.

The model's primary strength lies in its reliability and standardized processes. Projects were selected based on their relative strategic-military value, assessed through a rigorous evaluation of identified gaps to minimize any external influences on the decision-making process. The metrics used in the model were established by experts and are closely related to mission characterization. Moreover, the model ensures alignment with strategic guidelines through established correlations between capabilities, capacity areas, and missions. This approach aims to maintain a high level of accuracy and consistency in project selection and prioritization.

REFERENCES

Aghajani, M., Ruge, G., & Jugdev, K. (2023). An Integrative Review of Project Portfolio Management Literature: Thematic Findings on Sustainability Mindset, Assessment, and Integration. *Project Management Journal*, 54(6), 629–650. DOI: 10.1177/87569728231172668

Ahlemann, F., Bergan, P., Karger, E., Greulich, M., & Reining, S. (2024). Making Sense of Projects—Developing Project Portfolio Management Capabilities. *Schmalenbachs Zeitschrift fur Betriebswirtschaftliche Forschung = Schmalenbach Journal of Business Research*, 76(2), 293–325. DOI: 10.1007/s41471-023-00178-8

Ahonen, K., Seppänen, P., & Kallio, K. (2020). Project portfolio management in public sector organizations: Case studies in municipal organizations. *International Journal of Project Management*, 38(4), 237–251.

Ali, I., & Hsu, L. (2023). Decision-making challenges in project portfolio management: A comprehensive review. *Journal of Project Management*, 39(2), 112–126.

Archer, N., & Ghasemzadeh, F. (1999). An integrated framework for project portfolio selection. *International Journal of Project Management*, 17(4), 207–216. DOI: 10.1016/S0263-7863(98)00032-5

Bai, C., & Sarkis, J. (2022). Integration of sustainability in project portfolio management: A systematic review and research agenda. *Journal of Cleaner Production*, 350, 131453.

Bai, C., Sarkis, J., & Dou, Y. (2021). Corporate sustainability development in the context of China's institutional environment: An integration of institutional and stakeholder theories. *Journal of Cleaner Production*, 312, 127749.

Bai, L., Han, X., Wang, H., Zhang, K., & Sun, Y. (2021). A method of network robustness under strategic goals for project portfolio selection. *Computers & Industrial Engineering*, 161, 107658. DOI: 10.1016/j.cie.2021.107658

Baidoo, S., Donyina, J., & Alhassan, J. (2021). A review of project portfolio management methodologies: Trends and future directions. *Project Management Journal*, 52(1), 20–34.

Balatbat, M., Al-Saidi, M., & Adams, J. (2022). Evaluating project portfolios: A new approach based on decision-making frameworks. *International Journal of Project Management*, 40(1), 60–74.

Basu, R. (2015). *Managing Projects in Research and Development*. Gower Publishing Limited.

Bechtel, R., & Squires, J. (2001). Tools and Techniques to Facilitate Change. *Industrial and Commercial Training*, 33(7), 249–255. DOI: 10.1108/EUM0000000006001

Blomquist, T., & Müller, R. (2006). Practices, roles, and responsibilities of middle managers in program and portfolio management. *Project Management Journal*, 37(1), 52–66. DOI: 10.1177/875697280603700105

Bolman, L., & Deal, T. (2017). *Reframing Organizations* (6th ed.). Jossey-Bass. DOI: 10.1002/9781119281856

Bradley, G. (2016). *Benefit Realisation Management: A Practical Guide to Achieving Benefits Through Change*. Gower Publishing. DOI: 10.4324/9781315569055

Brooke, J., & Pagnanelli, F. (2014). Integrating sustainability into innovation project portfolio management – A strategic perspective. *Journal of Engineering and Technology Management*, 34, 46–62. DOI: 10.1016/j.jengtecman.2013.11.004

Brynjolfsson, E., & McAfee, A. (2014). *The Second Machine Age: Work, Progress, and Prosperity in a Time of Brilliant Technologies*. W. W. Norton & Company.

Chao, R., & Kavadias, S. (2008). A Theoretical Framework for Managing the New Product Development Portfolio: When and How to Use Strategic Buckets. *Management Science*, 54(5), 907–921. DOI: 10.1287/mnsc.1070.0828

Chapman, C., & Ward, S. (2003). *Project Risk Management: Processes, Techniques and Insights* (2nd ed.). John Wiley & Sons.

Chen, C., & Cheng, H. (2009). A comprehensive model for selecting information system project under fuzzy environment. *International Journal of Project Management*, 27(4), 389–399. DOI: 10.1016/j.ijproman.2008.04.001

Chrusciel, D., & Field, D. (2006). Success Factors in Dealing with Significant Change in an Organization. *Business Process Management Journal*, 12(4), 503–516. DOI: 10.1108/14637150610678096

Clegg, S., Killen, C., Biesenthal, C., & Sankaran, S. (2018). Practices, projects and portfolios: Current research trends and new directions. *International Journal of Project Management*, 36(5), 762–772. DOI: 10.1016/j.ijproman.2018.03.008

Cooper, C., Dewe, P., & O'Driscoll, M. (2001). *Organizational Stress: A review and critique of theory, research, and applications*. Sage. DOI: 10.4135/9781452231235

Cooper, R. (2005). Portfolio Management for Product Innovation. In Levine, H. A. (Ed.), *Project Portfolio Management: A Practical Guide to Selecting Projects, Managing Portfolios and Maximizing Benefit* (pp. 318–354). John Wiley and Sons.

Cooper, R. (2008). Perspective: The Stage-Gate® Idea-to-Launch Process—Update, What's New, and NexGen Systems. *Journal of Product Innovation Management*, 25(3), 213–232. DOI: 10.1111/j.1540-5885.2008.00296.x

Cooper, R., Edgett, S., & Kleinschmidt, E. (2000). New Problems, New Solutions: Making Portfolio Management More Effective. *Research Technology Management*, 16(2), 180–186. DOI: 10.1080/08956308.2000.11671338

Cooper, R., Edgett, S., & Kleinschmidt, E. (2000). New problems, new solutions: Making portfolio management more effective. *Research Technology Management*, 43(2), 18–33. DOI: 10.1080/08956308.2000.11671338

Cooper, R., Edgett, S., & Kleinschmidt, E. (2001). Portfolio Management in New Product Development: Results of an Industry Practices Study. *R & D Management*, 31(4), 361–381. DOI: 10.1111/1467-9310.00225

Cooper, R., Edgett, S., & Kleinschmidt, E. (2002). *Portfolio Management: fundamental for new product success*. Stage-Gate International and Product Development Institute Inc. Available at http://stage-gate.net/downloads/working_papers/wp_12.pdf

Cooper, R., Edgett, S., & Kleinschmidt, E. (2009). Portfolio Management for New Product Development: Results of an Industry Practices Study. *R & D Management*, 31(4), 361–380. DOI: 10.1111/1467-9310.00225

Cooper, R. G., & Sommer, A. F. (2023). Dynamic Portfolio Management for New Product Development. *Research Technology Management*, 66(3), 19–31. DOI: 10.1080/08956308.2023.2183004

Davis, K. (2014). Different stakeholder groups and their perceptions of project success. *International Journal of Project Management*, 32(2), 189–201. DOI: 10.1016/j.ijproman.2013.02.006

De la Torre, R., Hsu, K., & Chiang, H. (2020). Project portfolio management: A review and a new framework for balancing strategic value and risk. *Journal of Strategic and Performance Management*, 11(3), 55–72.

Díaz-Díaz, R., & Pérez-Bustamante, G. (2020). Digital innovation, ecosystem configurations, and the mediating role of absorptive capacity. *Journal of Business Research*, 120, 12–21.

Dietrich, P., & Lehtonen, P. (2005). Successful Management of Strategic Intentions through Multiple Projects – Reflections from Empirical Study. *International Journal of Project Management*, 23(5), 386–391. DOI: 10.1016/j.ijproman.2005.03.002

Dutra, C., Ribeiro, J., & Carvalho, M. (2014). An economic-probabilistic model for project selection and prioritization. *International Journal of Project Management*, 32(6), 1042–1055. DOI: 10.1016/j.ijproman.2013.12.004

Eilat, H., Golany, B., & Shtub, A. (2006). Constructing and evaluating balanced portfolios of R&D projects with interactions: A DEA based methodology. *European Journal of Operational Research*, 172(3), 1018–1039. DOI: 10.1016/j.ejor.2004.12.001

Elonen, S., & Artto, K. (2003). Problems in managing internal development projects in multi-project environments. *International Journal of Project Management*, 2(6), 395–402. DOI: 10.1016/S0263-7863(02)00097-2

Ershadi, M., Jefferies, M., Davis, P., & Mojtahedi, M. (2020). Towards successful establishment of a project portfolio management system: business process management approach. *Journal of Modern Project Management*, 23. .DOI: 10.19255/JMPM02302

Fagarasan, C., Cristea, C., Cristea, M., Popa, O., & Pisla, A. (2023). Integrating Sustainability Metrics into Project and Portfolio Performance Assessment in Agile Software Development: A Data-Driven Scoring Model. *Sustainability (Basel)*, 15(17), 13139. DOI: 10.3390/su151713139

Faramarzi, M., Azizi, M., & Zeynalzadeh, S. (2020). Multi-criteria decision-making approaches for project portfolio management: A systematic review. *Journal of Strategic and International Studies*, 15(2), 72–88.

Fong, P. S., Ng, C. K., & Ho, S. K. (2023). Strategic alignment in project portfolio management: Emerging trends and practices. *International Journal of Project Management*, 41(1), 54–67.

Gemünden, H.G., Lehner, P., & Kock, A. (2018). The project-oriented organization and its contribution to innovation. *International Journal of Project Management*, 36(1), 147–160. https://doi.org/.ijproman.2017.07.009.DOI: 10.1016/j

Giacomin, M., Wang, J., & Kuo, Y. (2021). Fuzzy logic applications in project portfolio management: A review and future directions. *International Journal of Project Management*, 39(6), 645–659.

Green, S., & Harris, M. (2023). Integrating project selection frameworks with business intelligence tools. *Journal of Information Technology*, 38(1), 89–104.

Grigoroudis, E., Orfanoudaki, E., & Zopounidis, C. (2012). Strategic performance measurement in a healthcare organisation: A multiple criteria approach based on balanced scorecard. *Omega*, 40(1), 104–119. DOI: 10.1016/j.omega.2011.04.001

Grigoroudis, E., & Siskos, Y. (2012). Decision Support Systems for the Selection of Projects: A Review of Multi-Criteria Methods. *European Journal of Operational Research*, 220(2), 305–317.

Hadjinicolaou, N., Kader, M., & Abdallah, I. (2022). Strategic Innovation, Foresight and the Deployment of Project Portfolio Management under Mid-Range Planning Conditions in Medium-Sized Firms. *Sustainability*, 14(80). Advance online publication. DOI: 10.3390/su14010

Halawa, W., Abdelalim, A., & Elrashed, I. (2013). Financial evaluation program for construction projects at the pre-investment phase in developing countries: A case study. *International Journal of Project Management*, 31(6), 912–923. DOI: 10.1016/j.ijproman.2012.11.001

Ho, W. (2008). Integrated analytic hierarchy process and its applications – A literature review. *European Journal of Operational Research*, 186(1), 211–228. DOI: 10.1016/j.ejor.2007.01.004

Hsu, S., Weng, K., Cui, Q., & Rand, W. (2015). Understanding the complexity of project team member selection through agent-based modeling. *International Journal of Project Management*, 34(1), 82–93. DOI: 10.1016/j.ijproman.2015.10.001

Hutchison-Krupat, J., & Kavadias, S. (2014). Strategic Resource Allocation: Top-Down, Bottom-Up, and the Value of Strategic Buckets. *Management Science*, (September), 391–412.

Iamratanakul, S., Patanakul, P., & Milosevic, D. (2008). Project portfolio selection: From past to present. *4th IEEE International Conference on Management of Innovation and Technology*.

Ittner, C. D., & Larcker, D. F. (2021). The audit committee's role in overseeing and ensuring effective risk management. *Journal of Accounting Research*, 59(2), 455–485. DOI: 10.1111/1475-679X.12350

Jepsen, A. L., & Eskerod, P. (2009). Stakeholder analysis in projects: Challenges in using current guidelines in the real world. *International Journal of Project Management*, 27(4), 335–343. DOI: 10.1016/j.ijproman.2008.04.002

Jonsson, P., & Mårtensson, M. (2018). Dynamic capabilities in project portfolio management: A conceptual framework. *International Journal of Project Management*, 36(4), 602–617.

Jyh, D. (2015). Strategic project portfolio selection for national research institutes. *Journal of Business Research*, 68(11), 2305–2311. DOI: 10.1016/j.jbusres.2015.06.016

Kaplan, R., & Norton, D. (1992). The balanced scorecard-measures that drive performance. *Harvard Business Review*, 70, 71–79. PMID: 10119714

Kendall, G., & Rollins, S. (2003). *Advanced Project Portfolio Management and the PMO, Multiplying ROI at Warp Speed*. J. Ross Publishing, Inc.

Kerzner, H. (2023). *Project Management: A Systems Approach to Planning, Scheduling, and Controlling*. Wiley.

Keskin, D. (2020). A two-stage fuzzy approach for Industry 4.0 project portfolio selection within criteria and project interdependencies context. *Journal of Multi-Criteria Decision Analysis*, 27(1–2), 65–83. DOI: 10.1002/mcda.1691

Kester, L., Griffin, A., Hultink, E. J., & Lauche, K. (2009). Portfolio decision-making genres: A case study. *Journal of Engineering and Technology Management*, 26(4), 327–341. DOI: 10.1016/j.jengtecman.2009.10.006

Khalili-Damghani, K., & Tavana, M. (2014). A comprehensive framework for sustainable project portfolio selection based on structural equation modelling. *Project Management Journal*, 45(2), 83–97. DOI: 10.1002/pmj.21404

Khalili-Damghani, K., & Tavana, M. (2022). Project portfolio management: A review and future research directions. *European Journal of Operational Research*, 299(3), 815–832. DOI: 10.1016/j.ejor.2021.07.023

Killen, C. P., Hunt, R. A., & Kleinschmidt, E. J. (2008). Project portfolio management for product innovation. *International Journal of Quality & Reliability Management*, 25(1), 24–38. DOI: 10.1108/02656710810843559

Kim, H., & Park, H. (2021). A Hybrid Approach for Sustainable Project Portfolio Management: Integration of Machine Learning and Multi-Criteria Decision-Making. *Journal of Cleaner Production*, 303, 127021.

Kizito, R., Abolhasani, M., & Cohen, J. (2021). Enhancing project portfolio management through a hybrid multi-criteria decision-making approach. *International Journal of Operations & Production Management*, 41(7), 1246–1272.

Kock, A., & Gemünden, H. G. (2016). The effects of project portfolio management on project success: A longitudinal study. *International Journal of Project Management*, 34(2), 119–133.

Kudratova, S., Huang, X., & Zhou, X. (2018). Sustainable project selection: Optimal project selection considering sustainability under reinvestment strategy. *Journal of Cleaner Production*, 203, 469–481. DOI: 10.1016/j.jclepro.2018.08.259

Lappe, M., & Spang, K. (2014). Investments in project management are profitable: A case study-based analysis of the relationship between the costs and benefits of project management. *International Journal of Project Management*, 32(4), 603–612. DOI: 10.1016/j.ijproman.2013.10.005

Lee, J., & Kim, S. (2000). An integrated approach for interdependent information system project selection. *International Journal of Project Management*, 2000(19), 111–118.

Levine, H. A. (2005). *Project portfolio management: A Practical Guide to Selecting Projects, Managing Portfolios, and Maximizing Benefits.* Pfeiffer Wiley.

Lin, C., & Chen, Y. (2004). Bid/no-bid decision-making - a fuzzy linguistic approach. *International Journal of Project Management*, 22(7), 585–593. DOI: 10.1016/j.ijproman.2004.01.005

Linstone, H., & Turoff, M. (2002). *The Delphi Method - Techniques and applications. The delphi method - Techniques and applications.* Adison Wesley.

Liu, Q., & Xu, J. (2023). Continuous monitoring in project portfolio management: Strategies and best practices. *International Journal of Operations & Production Management*, 43(1), 32–48.

Liu, W., Wang, X., & Zhao, Y. (2022). Dynamic Project Portfolio Management in the Age of Sustainability: A Systematic Review and Future Research Agenda. *International Journal of Project Management*, 40(3), 153–170.

López-Chaua, A., Cervantes, J., López-García, L., & Lamont, F. (2013). Fisher's decision tree. *Expert Systems with Applications*, 40(16), 6283–6291. DOI: 10.1016/j.eswa.2013.05.044

Martinsuo, M. (2013). Project portfolio management in practice and in context. *International Journal of Project Management*, 31(6), 794–803. DOI: 10.1016/j.ijproman.2012.10.013

Martinsuo, M., Korhonen, T., & Laine, T. (2014). Identifying, framing and managing uncertainties in project portfolios. *International Journal of Project Management*, 32(5), 732–746. DOI: 10.1016/j.ijproman.2014.01.014

Martinsuo, M., & Lehtonen, P. (2007). Role of single-project management in achieving portfolio management efficiency. *International Journal of Project Management*, 25(1), 56–65. DOI: 10.1016/j.ijproman.2006.04.002

Meskendahl, S. (2010). The influence of business strategy on project portfolio management and its success - A conceptual framework. *International Journal of Project Management*, 28(8), 807–817. DOI: 10.1016/j.ijproman.2010.06.007

Milis, K., & Mercken, R. (2004). The use of the balanced scorecard for the evaluation of Information and Communication Technology projects. *International Journal of Project Management*, 22(2), 87–97. DOI: 10.1016/S0263-7863(03)00060-7

Mohagheghi, V., Mousavi, S., Antucheviciene, J., & Mojtahedi, M. (2019). Project portfolio selection problems: A review of models, uncertainty approaches, solution techniques, and case studies. *Technological and Economic Development of Economy*, 25(6), 1380–1412. DOI: 10.3846/tede.2019.11410

Mohammad, J., & Pan, Y. (2021). Sustainability, the Fourth Pillar of Project Portfolio Management: A Holistic Approach. *Journal of Modern Project Management*, 27(9), 199-215. DOI: DOI: 10.19255/JMPM02714

Morris, P. W. G., & Jamieson, A. (2005). *Moving from corporate strategy to project strategy*. Project Management Institute. DOI: 10.1177/875697280503600402

Müller, R., Martinsuo, M., & Blomquist, T. (2008). Project portfolio control and portfolio management performance in different contexts. *Project Management Journal*, 39(3), 28–42. DOI: 10.1002/pmj.20053

Müller, R., & Turner, J. R. (2013). Leadership competency profiles of successful project managers. *International Journal of Project Management*, 31(1), 40–50.

Myers, S., Brealy, R., & Allen, F. (2014). Principles of Corporate Finance (10ᵃed.). New York: McGraw-Hill Irwin.

Neely, A., Gregory, M., & Platts, K. (2021). Performance Measurement System Design: A Literature Review and Research Agenda. *International Journal of Operations & Production Management*, 41(9), 88–112.

Nowak, M. (2013). Project portfolio selection using interactive approach. *Procedia Engineering*, 57, 814–822. DOI: 10.1016/j.proeng.2013.04.103

Olsson, R. (2006). Management of flexibility in projects. *International Journal of Project Management*, 24(1), 66–74. DOI: 10.1016/j.ijproman.2005.06.010

Orosz, G., Duran, A., & Merz, C. (2021). Managing project portfolio conflicts: A framework for handling discrepancies and alignment issues. *Journal of Strategic and International Studies*, 16(1), 33–45.

Padovani, M., Muscat, A., Camanho, R., & Carvalho, M. (2008). Looking for the right criteria to define projects portfolio: Multiple case study analysis. *Product: Management & Development*, 6(2), 127–134.

Pajares, J., & López, A. (2014). New Methodological Approaches to Project Portfolio Management: The Role of Interactions within Projects and Portfolios. *Procedia: Social and Behavioral Sciences*, 119, 645–652. DOI: 10.1016/j.sbspro.2014.03.072

Patanakul, P. (2015). Key attributes of effectiveness in managing project portfolio. *International Journal of Project Management*, 33(5), 1084–1097. DOI: 10.1016/j.ijproman.2015.01.004

Patel, S., & Kumar, R. (2022). Data reliability in project portfolio management: Current challenges and solutions. *Data and Information Management*, 6(4), 211–225.

Petit, Y., & Hobbs, B. (2010). Project portfolios in dynamic environments: Sources of uncertainty and sensing mechanisms. *Project Management Journal*, 41(4), 46–58. DOI: 10.1002/pmj.20201

Petro, Y., & Gardiner, P. (2015). An investigation of the influence of organizational design on project portfolio success, effectiveness and business efficiency for project-based organizations. *International Journal of Project Management*, 33(8), 1717–1729. DOI: 10.1016/j.ijproman.2015.08.004

Pitsis, T., Kornberger, M., & Clegg, S. (2004). The art of managing relationships in inter-organizational collaboration. *Management*, 7, 47–67.

Plattfaut, R. (2022). On the importance of project management capabilities for sustainable business process management. *Sustainability (Basel)*, 14(13), 7612. DOI: 10.3390/su14137612

PMI. (2013). A Guide to the project management body of knowledge, PMBoK Guide (5th ed.). Project Management Institute, Inc.

PMI. (2017). The Standard for Portfolio Management (4th ed.). Project Management Institute, Inc.

Rao, P., Mehta, R., & Zhang, J. (2023). Developing dynamic capabilities for competitive advantage in large organizations. *Journal of Business Research*, 143, 290–302.

Rego, P., Souto, C., & Oliveira, J. (2018). The relationship between project portfolio management and project success: A systematic review. *Journal of Strategic and International Studies*, 14(1), 92–110.

Saaty, T. (2008). Decision making with the analytic hierarchy process. *International Journal of Services Sciences*, 1(1), 83–98. DOI: 10.1504/IJSSCI.2008.017590

Sahoo, S., & Goswami, S. (2023). A Comprehensive Review of Multiple Criteria Decision-Making (MCDM) Methods: Advancements, Applications, and Future Directions. *Decision Making Advances*, 1(1), 25–48. DOI: 10.31181/dma1120237

Schipper, R., & Silvius, G. (2018). Towards a conceptual framework for sustainable project portfolio management. *International Journal of Project Organisation and Management*, 10(3), 191–221. DOI: 10.1504/IJPOM.2018.093977

Shenhar, A., Dvir, D., Levy, O., & Maltz, A. (2001). Project Success: A Multidimensional Strategic Concept. *Long Range Planning*, 34(6), 699–725. DOI: 10.1016/S0024-6301(01)00097-8

Silvius, G., & Marnewick, C. (2022). Interlinking Sustainability in Organizational Strategy, Project Portfolio Management and Project Management: A Conceptual Framework. *Procedia Computer Science*, 196, 938–947. DOI: 10.1016/j.procs.2021.12.095

Skulmoski, G., & Hartman, F. (2007). The Delphi Method for Graduate Research. *Journal of Information Technology Education*, 6, 1–21. DOI: 10.28945/199

Smith, J., & Johnson, R. (2023). Aligning Project Portfolio Management with Organizational Sustainability: New Perspectives and Approaches. *Sustainability*, 15(4), 2124.

Sok, H., Ooi, M., & Kuang, Y. (2015). Sparse alternating decision tree. *Pattern Recognition Letters*, 60-61, 57–64. DOI: 10.1016/j.patrec.2015.03.002

Subramanian, N., & Ramanathan, R. (2022). Analytic Network Process: A review of applications and methodology. *Omega*, 106, 102458.

Tavana, M., Santos-Arteaga, F. J., & Fadaei, M. (2018). Project portfolio selection: A review of methods and applications. *International Journal of Project Management*, 36(6), 775–787. DOI: 10.1016/j.ijproman.2018.04.004

Teller, J. (2013). Portfolio Risk Management and Its Contribution to Project Portfolio Success: An Investigation of Organization, Process, and Culture. *Project Management Journal*, 44(2), 36–51. DOI: 10.1002/pmj.21327

Teller, J., & Kock, A. (2013). An empirical investigation on how portfolio risk management influences project portfolio success. *International Journal of Project Management*, 31(6), 817–829. DOI: 10.1016/j.ijproman.2012.11.012

Teller, J., Unger, B. N., Kock, A., & Gemünden, H. G. (2012). Formalization of project portfolio management: The moderating role of project portfolio complexity. *International Journal of Project Management*, 30(5), 596–607. DOI: 10.1016/j.ijproman.2012.01.020

Thompson, L., & Smith, R. (2022). Managing stakeholder interests in project selection: A comprehensive review. *Project Management Journal*, 53(6), 101–115.

Van der Meer-Kooistra, J., & Vosselman, E. (2023). The impact of human biases on project selection: Evidence from recent studies. *Management Accounting Research*, 55, 123–135.

Verma, V., & Sinha, P. (2018). Managing project portfolio in a dynamic environment. *International Journal of Project Management*, 36(7), 995–1007.

Vidal, L., Marle, F., & Bocquet, J. (2011). Using a Delphi process and the Analytic Hierarchy Process (AHP) to evaluate the complexity of projects. *Expert Systems with Applications*, 38(5), 5388–5405. DOI: 10.1016/j.eswa.2010.10.016

Vieira, G., Oliveira, H., Almeida, J., & Belderrain, M. (2024). Project Portfolio Selection considering interdependencies: A review of terminology and approaches. *Project Leadership and Society*, 5, 100115. DOI: 10.1016/j.plas.2023.100115

Walker, H., Armenakis, A., & Bernerth, J. (2007). Factors influencing organizational change efforts: An integrative investigation of change content, context, process and individual differences. *Journal of Organizational Change Management*, 20(6), 761–773. DOI: 10.1108/09534810710831000

Wang, Y., Zhong, R. Y., & Xu, X. (2018). A decision support system for additive manufacturing process selection using a hybrid multiple criteria decision-making method. *Rapid Prototyping Journal*, 24(9), 1544–1553. DOI: 10.1108/RPJ-01-2018-0002

Ward, J., & Daniel, E. (2012). *Benefits Management: How to Increase the Business Value of Your IT Projects*. John Wiley & Sons. DOI: 10.1002/9781119208242

Weber, T. (2014). On the (non-) equivalence of IRR and NPV. *Journal of Mathematical Economics*, 52, 25–39. DOI: 10.1016/j.jmateco.2014.03.006

Yelin, K. (2005). Linking Strategy and Project Portfolio Management. In Levine, H. A. (Ed.), *Project Portfolio Management: A practical guide to selecting projects, managing portfolios and maximizing benefit* (pp. 137–145). Pfeiffer Wiley.

Yin, R. K. (2018). *Case Study Research and Applications: Design and Methods.* Sage Publications.

Yohannes, A., & Mauritsius, T. (2022). Critical success factors in information technology projects. *International Journal of Emerging Technology and Advanced Engineering*, 12(7), 45–67. DOI: 10.46338/ijetae0722_06

Zarjou, M., & Khalilzadeh, M. (2022). Optimal project portfolio selection with reinvestment strategy considering sustainability in an uncertain environment: A multi-objective optimization approach. *Kybernetes*, 51(8), 2437–2460. DOI: 10.1108/K-11-2020-0737

Zhang, J., Wang, M., & Chen, Y. (2021). Strategic alignment and portfolio management: A conceptual framework for successful project selection. *Project Management Journal*, 52(3), 47–61.

Zhang, Y., & Yang, X. (2022). Managing risk-reward balance in project portfolios: Recent advances and methodologies. *Risk Management*, 24(2), 99–114.

Zhao, H., Zhang, L., & Wang, X. (2023). Forecasting benefits in project portfolio management: Techniques and challenges. *Operations Research Perspectives*, 10, 100–112.

Zhao, X., & Wang, L. (2023). Challenges in establishing criteria for project evaluation and selection. *European Journal of Operational Research*, 295(3), 715–728.

Zopounidis, C., & Doumpos, M. (2021). Multi-criteria decision analysis in project portfolio management: Trends and developments. *European Journal of Operational Research*, 290(3), 827–839. DOI: 10.1016/j.ejor.2007.11.026

KEY TERMS AND DEFINITIONS

Best Value for Money: A balanced evaluation of costs, benefits, risks, and performance across various options. It involves making informed decisions that optimize resources and deliver maximum value over time.

Cost-Benefit Analysis: Helps in assessing the economic feasibility of a project by comparing its costs and benefits, thus aiding in informed decision-making.

Portfolio: Is a set of projects and/or programs that are managed together to achieve strategic objectives.

Project: Is a temporary endeavor undertaken to create a unique product, service, or result.

Project Management: Is the application of knowledge, skills, tools, and techniques to project activities to meet the project requirements.

Project Management Portfolio: Is a collection of projects, programs, sub-portfolios, and operations managed as a group to achieve strategic objectives.

Project Prioritization: Is the process of determining the relative importance and urgency of projects to ensure the effective allocation of resources to achieve the organization's strategic objectives.

Project Success: Can be measured by the degree to which project goals and objectives are achieved, the satisfaction of stakeholders, and the efficiency and effectiveness of the project execution process.

Risk Management: Is the systematic process of identifying, analyzing, and responding to project risk. It includes maximizing the probability and consequences of positive events and minimizing the probability and consequences of adverse events to project objectives.

Strategic Objectives: Are essential tools for organizations to articulate their long-term aspirations and provide a roadmap for achieving sustainable success.

Chapter 9
Strategic Management of Hospitality Security Under the Influence of Macro Trends

Lyudmila Bovsh
https://orcid.org/0000-0001-6044-3004
State University of Trade and Economics, Ukraine

Tetiana Tkachuk
https://orcid.org/0000-0001-8657-2621
Kyiv State University of Trade and Economics, Ukraine

Nataliia Zikii
https://orcid.org/0000-0001-9781-7479
Kyiv State University of Trade and Economics, Ukraine

Kamel Mouloudj
https://orcid.org/0000-0001-7617-8313
University of Medea, Algeria

Ahmed Chemseddine Bouarar
https://orcid.org/0000-0001-8300-9833
University of Medea, Algeria

EXECUTIVE SUMMARY

Hospitality entities face ongoing pressures at a macro level, necessitating effective strategic approaches to business security management. Therefore, the aim of this chapter was to explore the essential elements of strategic security management

DOI: 10.4018/979-8-3693-2675-6.ch009

in hospitality, influenced by macro trends. This involved examining the origins of risks and threats, as well as key components in developing a security management strategy, including metrics, key risk indicators (KRIs), objectives and key results (OKRs), and foresight capabilities. The analysis employs an analytical approach and underscores that effective security strategies not only mitigate risks but also foster a secure and trustworthy environment for guests and staff. Additionally, staying abreast of technological advancements and industry trends enables hospitality entities to adapt their security measures proactively. In conclusion, it is emphasized that implementing robust security protocols such as access control measures, surveillance systems, and emergency response plans is crucial for proactive risk management.

INTRODUCTION

The realm of digital literature has yielded valuable perspectives on the ways in which digital technology improves business outcomes. Bouarar et al. (2022) demonstrate through their study that effective digital transformation accelerates innovation, boosts productivity, enhances "customer experiences and satisfaction", minimizes costs, and ultimately enhances corporate outcomes. In the hospitality industry, the digitization represents a transformative shift in the way the industry operates (Bovsh et al., 2024a), leveraging technology to enhance guest experiences, streamline operations, and optimize business efficiency (Bouarar et al., 2023; Bovsh et al., 2024b; Shashwat & Rani, 2023). On the other hand, as new challenges and trends emerge, the security landscape undergoes constant evolution. The complete digitization of social and economic interactions has underscored the necessity to safeguard the cyber security of hospitality entities (HEs). Given that the hospitality sector's service provision involves direct physical interactions with customers (Bovsh et al., 2024c), it is particularly sensitive to changes during crises and is often the hardest hit in terms of financial losses (Bovsh et al., 2024a,b). This assertion finds support in the outcomes observed during the pandemic period and recent analyses detailing the repercussions of conflicts (see for example, Boyko et al., 2022; Bovsh et al., 2022; Bovsh et al., 2023; Kompanets, 2022; Kuzmenko, 2022; Markovska, 2022). In this context, Shabani and Munir (2020) illustrate that the methods presently employed by hotels to thwart cyber attacks are largely basic and obsolete. Moreover, they highlight that a significant portion of hotel personnel do not have the necessary knowledge and skills to effectively manage anticipated threats, rendering the hospitality sector increasingly susceptible to cyber threats and attacks. While efforts are made to enhance the overall physical security of hospitality establishments, the issue of environmental security linked to soil, water, and air pollution may concurrently escalate.

This situation sets unfavorable conditions for maintaining and revitalizing the capabilities of the national tourism infrastructure. It necessitates the development of a strategic outlook in managing business security, considering global challenges and macro trends. Furthermore, the impact of the global and macro environment strongly influences the emergence of crises within the national economy, leading to significant shifts in the strategic development priorities of business entities.

The primary challenges confronting Ukraine's hospitality industry in the present challenging environment include guaranteeing the physical safety of assets, staff, and guests, safeguarding the business's reputation and digital infrastructure, while also considering macro environmental trends. Failure to address these challenges could make the recovery of the hospitality sector in Ukraine exceedingly difficult and protracted. In particular, this applies to the affected hospitality entities, since some of the previously created potential is practically lost.

In this regard, it is essential to conceptualize strategic management directions for hospitality establishment security (Cró et al., 2020). Key elements of the security framework include assets, information systems and databases, personnel, and reputational capital. Analysis of scholarly literature and research reveals inadequate accessibility, and at times, a complete absence of essential information concerning the status and efficacy of security management processes. This greatly hampers the assessment of their effectiveness and the formulation of strategic management recommendations. Moreover, there is a lack of research into incorporating the influence of macro trends into business security strategy.

Therefore, the aim of this study was to pinpoint the primary facets of strategic safety management within Ukrainian hospitality enterprises and to establish models for its assurance amid macro trends' influence. To fulfill this objective, the following tasks were delineated: analyzing the theoretical dimensions of HE security management; delineating its principal determinants; investigating compliance control concerning the economic security of HE; and formulating theoretical and practical insights for adaptable management in the face of macro-level challenges.

General scientific methods such as comparison, analysis, synthesis, induction, were used to process information sources. Empirical methods—including historical data analysis, competitor observation, expert reviews, employee consultations, and testing and simulations—were used to identify potential threats, which inform the development of business security strategies. The logical modeling method was applied to create a model for strategic management of HE security and to develop a foresight-transformation mechanism for security. The results and conclusions are grounded in the research findings of scientists and online analytics..

The research findings are founded on a systematic exposition of theoretical propositions. This involved algorithmizing the principal stages of security management strategy within the HE, meticulously analyzing the primary determinants of security management, including fire safety, physical security, emergency preparedness, cyber security, and information protection. Additionally, a comprehensive examination of general cyber security threats was conducted. The crucial aspects of ensuring compliance with economic security standards within the HE were explored, drawing from pertinent macro- and micro-level security management standards. By organizing and synthesizing these concepts, a model for strategically managing security levels within the hospitality domain was formulated.

The novelty of this research lies in the advancement of the security foresight-transformation mechanism and the enhancement of the strategic management model for hospitality security. These developments aim to establish an efficient toolkit for addressing macro-level threats. However, limitations in the study stemmed from the scarcity of analytical and statistical data within the hospitality sector, particularly from official sources.

THEORETICAL INSIGHTS INTO STRATEGIC SECURITY MANAGEMENT OF A BUSINESS ENTITY

Strategic management relies on anticipating forthcoming threats, risks, and industry market trends. This aspect garners interest from both researchers, who develop theoretical frameworks and establish a priori models for strategic management in business entities, and practitioners, who provide practical insights. For instance, the work of Mazaraki and Bosovska (2013) delves into the theoretical and methodological underpinnings of forming integration strategies for enterprises. Helfat (2021) distinguishes between two fundamental types of theories: those developed within "strategic management", grounded in regularities and "economic logic", and those originating in economics but applied and "often evolved in new directions". The organizational view of strategic management is reflected in the work of Greve (2021), where attention is paid to the institutional theory and the theory of networks about the influence of the environment, as well as the theory of learning and the theory of resource dependence regarding organizational interaction with the environment. Additionally, Shaver (2021) investigates quantitative methods in strategic management using empirical data, while Graebner (2021) focuses on qualitative approaches, including theory building from many cases, "process analysis", "strategy as practice", "narrative", "discursive", "rhetorical approaches", and "deductive and illustrative case studies".

Regarding economic security, Zou and Sunindijo (2015) outline a strategic framework for safety management that encompasses both scientific and artistic elements. This framework identifies the key stages of safety management as "development, implementation, and evaluation". Stolzer et al. (2023) introduce a "model of safety risk management and safety assurance." Radaelli (2021) examines how European "Enterprise Risk Management" (ERM) practitioners mitigate potential risks. Ribeiro Ramos et al. (2022) present a theoretical model for assessing economic security in enterprises, including its methodology, functional structure, and level calculation based on an integral indicator. Piletska et al. (2021) further elaborate on the essence of economic security, methods for its assessment, and the development of a comprehensive evaluation model. Cró et al. (2020) highlight the importance of "safety and security" perceptions as strategic concerns for hospitality companies. The topic of digital and cyber security risks has also been explored by several researchers (e.g., Frigo, 2018; Jore et al., 2018; Mansour & Ben Salem, 2022; Trim & Lee, 2022; Tuna & Türkmendağ, 2022). Within the hospitality sector, research has predominantly focused on physical security (Korstanje, 2020; Soliman et al., 2023), particularly concerning terrorism and other "black swan" events (Enz, 2009), as well as occupational safety and health within safety management systems (Spencer & Tarlow, 2021) and cyber security (Verezomska et al., 2022).

In fact, the majority of scientific research, which predominantly addresses theoretical inquiries and individual recommendations, frequently overlooks the environmental challenges. Emphasis in scientific literature is mainly placed on the significance of strategic management and safety management models, leading to a research gap. Particularly, there is a lack of focus on how these concepts and models facilitate seamless progress in overall business management, which serves as the fundamental aspect of this investigation. Inadequate attention is paid to digital technologies in ensuring and managing security, resulting in an incomplete coverage of security issues and strategic planning omissions in security management within hospitality entities. Given the arguments outlined, developing a comprehensive model for strategic management and the evaluation of "economic security" in hospitality entities would be highly beneficial.

EMPIRICAL APPROACHES TO THE FORMATION OF HOSPITALITY ENTITIES' SECURITY STRATEGIES

Forecasting threats and preventing their impact on the safety of guests, employees and property are the main tasks of the HE security system management. In the conditions of dynamic transformations of macro environmental stressors and technical innovations, new challenges are created, which requires the analysis of both theoretical approaches and effective practices of strategic business security management, the focus of this study. Guided by the results of previous studies in this area (Boiko et al., 2022; Bovsh et al., 2021; Bovsh et al., 2022; Bovsh et al., 2023; Verezomska et al., 2022), we will rely on the interpretation of the management strategy the security of the hospitality entity as a comprehensive approach to the identification, analysis and management of risks related to business security, as well as the implementation of measures to ensure it. The main objects are the protection of clients (guests), employees, assets, information, and other resources from potential threats and unwanted events in the physical and digital plane. Business security strategies can be developed and improved using empirical methods, which are based on observation, analysis and experiments with real data (see Table 1).

Table 1. Empirical methods for developing security strategies in HE

Methods	Characteristics	Application results
Analysis of historical data	Examining previous security breaches or incidents within the hospitality sector, such as theft, assaults, fires, accidents, cyber attacks, data loss, internal fraud, and others, can offer valuable insights into typical threats and their potential impacts.	Through the analysis of such data, patterns, vulnerabilities, and areas of business risk can be identified, enabling the formulation of effective risk management strategies.
Observation and analysis of competitors	Studying the security practices (strategies, policies, and measures) adopted by competitors within the hospitality industry	This examination can assist in identifying security issues and vulnerabilities among competitors, as well as successful strategies. It can also offer insights and recommendations to enhance your own security strategy.

continued on following page

Table 1. Continued

Methods	Characteristics	Application results
Expert reviews and consultations	Engaging with security specialists and consultants brings invaluable expertise and insights into the latest industry trends, emerging threats, and best practices. These professionals can conduct thorough assessments of current security measures, identify potential vulnerabilities, and recommend tailored solutions to mitigate risks effectively.	By leveraging their knowledge and experience, hospitality entities can refine their security posture, enhance resilience against evolving threats, and ensure the protection of assets, personnel, and sensitive information.
Consultations with employees	Employees can have valuable experience and knowledge about potential risks and vulnerabilities in the facility	
Testing and simulations	Security audit involves evaluating the strategy's effectiveness through simulations of scenarios such as fires, evacuations, or attacks to assess the readiness and response capabilities of personnel.	It will help identify weaknesses and improve security plans and procedures

Source: Developed by the authors based on Denysov (2019); Moskalenko et al. (2018); KTK (2015); Zhivko et al, (2019).

As demonstrated in Table 1, employing empirical methods enables the identification of threats with the most significant impact on hospitality operations. This involves analyzing statistics and security threat reports, consulting with security specialists, monitoring trends, and drawing insights from past incidents. Subsequently, a tailored business security strategy can be formulated based on these findings and analyses. This strategy may encompass implementing security protocols, deploying technical safeguards, conducting training to foster a security-conscious workforce culture, and developing contingency plans for business recovery post-incident.

These actions should be carried out within a security management framework encompassing planning, implementation, validation, and adjustment. It is crucial to recognize that ensuring business security is a continuous endeavor, necessitating regular updates and adaptations to address evolving threats and circumstances. The key phases of the safety management strategy for HEs are delineated in Figure 1.

Figure 1. Algorithm for the key stages in the security management strategy of HE (Summarized by the authors from Frigo (2018); Graebner (2021); Moskalenko and Godlevsky (2018))

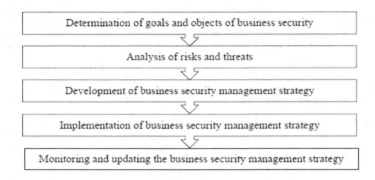

Let us describe some of the stages. Analysis of risks and threats includes identification of potential threats, assessment of their impact on business and determination of the level of risk acceptability. Simultaneously, it is crucial to consider both internal and external threats: terrorist acts, cyber attacks, natural disasters, financial risks, industrial safety risks, etc. When developing a strategy for managing the safety of the HE, it is necessary to take into account the peculiarities of the business entity and the legal framework to which the safety policy, standards, procedures, training of employees and other mechanisms should be adapted (Krasnomovets, 2023).

Thus, the security management strategy for each hospitality entity is tailored to its unique characteristics, business size, and other relevant factors. Implementing such a strategy not only mitigates risks but also enhances the business's resilience against potential threats.

MACRO-LEVEL PREDICATES OF THE STATE OF SECURITY MANAGEMENT OF HOSPITALITY ENTITIES

The key determinants of HE security management focus on the following aspects (Ghazi, 2016):

- Fire safety: HEs must comply with strict rules and regulations regarding fire safety, which includes the installation of fire alarm systems, fire protection systems, emergency lighting, smoke detectors and regular testing of their effectiveness. In addition, employees must be trained in fire evacuation and response procedures;

- Physical security: HEs must ensure the physical security of clients and their property (Krasnomovets, 2023). This includes installing access control systems, video surveillance, safes in hotel rooms, and training staff to recognize suspicious behavior or potential threats; insurance;
- Emergencies: HEs must have emergency plans, including evacuation of clients and response to natural disasters, terrorist threats or other emergency events. Employees must be prepared and trained in emergency response procedures;
- Cyber security: in the digital age, it is an important component of HE security, because it must protect personal data of customers, install security programs and encryption for secure information transmission. In addition, it is necessary to train staff on means of preventing phishing, viruses and other cyber threats;
- Information protection: HEs store a large amount of sensitive information about their regular customers and partners, in particular, such as passport data, bank details, etc. Safeguards must be used to prevent unauthorized access to this information: secure networks, data encryption, and restricted access rights.

We will analyze the relevance of the specified objects of strategic security management of the HE on the basis of analytics in the field of security.

Fire safety is a key aspect of strategic management of business physical security (Cró et al., 2020). Despite numerous fires in hotels and restaurants both before the full-scale war and during martial law, the situation remains critical (see Figure 2).

Figure 2. Number of fires in hotels and restaurants in Ukraine (not related to the consequences of military actions), 2018–2023 (State Emergency Service of Ukraine, 2023)

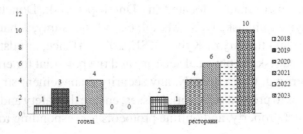

Fire statistics for hotels peaked in 2021, and for restaurants in 2023, which indicates the neglect of fire prevention management.

Issues of physical security and, in particular, emergency situations have become particularly acute since the beginning of the Ukrainian-Russian conflict.

Therefore, when assessing the security level of the environment, particularly for organizations in the hospitality sector, it is common to focus on the global terrorism index. The Global Terrorism Index is "a composite score" that gauges the "direct and indirect" effects of terrorism, including impacts on deaths, "injuries", "property damage", and "psychological consequences", with a range from "0 (no impact) to 10 (greatest impact)".

Losses in the field of hospitality also continue to grow: about 12 hotels with a total of almost 1,000 rooms were lost, as well as more than 1,000 food establishments (Sharitov, 2023). In general, losses from the conflict in the field of hospitality are estimated at the level of 2.2 billion dollars (see Figure 3). In this context, evaluating the losses to a country's cultural heritage is challenging not only due to its material value but also because of the difficulty in assessing its cultural and symbolic significance.

Figure 3. Number of hospitality sector objects damaged, 2022–2023 (compiled from KSE, 2023)

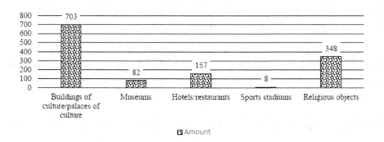

These facilities were mainly located in "Dnipropetrovsk, Donetsk, Zhytomyr, Zaporizhzhia, Kyiv, Luhansk, Lviv, Mykolaiv, Odesa, Sumy, Kharkiv, Kherson, Chernihiv regions and the city of Kyiv" (KSE, 2023). Hence, amidst ongoing conflict, the heightened risks to physical security and the potential for emergencies are profoundly concerning. Consequently, any security management strategy must incorporate measures to prevent substantial losses, ensure the safety and health of staff and visitors, protect property, and outline protocols for responding to emergencies.

In terms of cyber security, it's important to recognize that challenges are continuously evolving for both businesses and national security. The increasing digitalization of interactions and the adoption of artificial intelligence are transforming the socio-economic landscape. Consequently, cybercrimes are evolving and adapting to these new technologies. Statistical data illustrated in Figure 4 reveals that in 2022, the national market saw a significant rise in fraud through social engineering methods, with fraudulent transactions increasing by 26% compared to 2021.

Figure 4. The number of registered cybercrimes in Ukraine, 2013–2022 (compiled from Prasad, 2023)

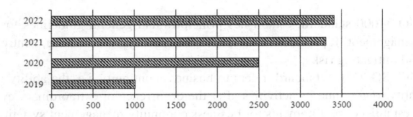

Internal risks also persist at a notable level, with approximately 25% of information leaks attributed to current or former employees, partners, and contractors (BDO USA, 2023). Nonetheless, hospitality entities may encounter several common cybersecurity threats:

- Phishing: attacks aimed at using social engineering to obtain confidential information such as passwords or financial data by misleading people;
- Decryption of passwords: hackers may attempt to crack passwords or use decrypted information to gain unauthorized access to the hospitality entity's systems or network;
- Viruses and malicious programs: infected files or programs can be used to access information systems or steal data;
- Ransom demand: distribution of malicious software (ransomware) can lead to the blocking of computer systems for the purpose of ransom demand;
- Access to wireless networks: Unsecured wireless networks can be a target for hackers trying to access private information of guests, business partners, etc.

Thus, the management of HE security must become a continuous process that requires internal organization, regular updating of policies and procedures, and training of security personnel. In this context, Andersen and Schrøder (2010) argued that "effective risk management" requires a combination of "centralized risk monitoring" and coordination processes, supported by "specialized risk functions", alongside the capability to address emerging risk events at the local level.

MANAGEMENT OF COMPLIANCE AND SECURITY OF HOSPITALITY ENTITIES

HEs must adhere to applicable legal norms and safety standards while striving for ongoing enhancement of its safety management strategy. Therefore, the compliance control of "economic security" within the HE is grounded in the following documents:

- ISO 31000 standard: establishes principles and general guidelines for risk management. It provides a framework for identifying, assessing, controlling and mitigating risks;
- The ISO 22301 standard: refers to business continuity, i.e. the ability of an entity to continue its activities after the occurrence of extraordinary events. It establishes requirements for business continuity management systems and recommendations for crisis planning and recovery;
- PCIDSS standard: to SGs that process payment cards. PCIDSS (Payment Card Industry Data Security Standard) defines the requirements for the protection of confidential information about payment cards, ensuring the security of card transactions and preventing data theft;
- Security standards of international hotel, restaurant chains, distribution systems (OTA, GDS), which develop their internal security standards and include requirements for physical, fire safety, access control, cyber security and other aspects of security.

Therefore, in challenging times, it is essential for hospitality establishments to rigorously adhere to safety and security standards to ensure the well-being of their guests and staff. Compliance with these standards not only helps protect against immediate threats but also fosters a sense of trust and reliability among patrons. During periods of heightened risk or uncertainty, such as during a public health crisis or increased security threats, maintaining strict safety protocols and security measures becomes even more crucial. By upholding these standards, hospitality establishments can mitigate potential risks, safeguard their operations, and demonstrate their commitment to creating a secure environment, thereby enhancing their resilience and reputation in the face of adversity.

STRATEGIC MANAGEMENT MODELING FOR ECONOMIC SECURITY OF HE WITHIN THE MACRO ENVIRONMENT ENVIRONMENT

The economic security of the HE is formed by predicting the threats and risks of the macro environment, as well as assessing the state of the internal security strategy of the business. Therefore, we suggest modeling strategic security management by levels (see Figure 5).

Figure 5. Model of strategic management for HE security (compiled by the Authors from Trim & Lee, 2023)

Based on the determined levels, we will form a foresight for the transformation of the security management strategies of hospitality entities in the context of instability. The mechanism of its implementation will be presented through the identification of objects and subjects of responsibility (see Figure 6).

Figure 6. Mechanism for foresight-transformation of security management strategies in HE (developed by the Authors)

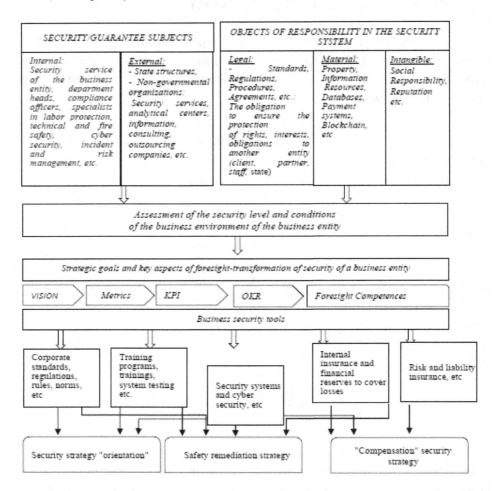

Thus, the development of a security management strategy, influenced by the vision and objectives of the HE as well as external conditions, may lead to the adoption of one of the following behavioral types: an orientation strategy (focused on eliminating or preventing security threats), a remediation strategy (aimed at mitigating damage from existing or potential threats), or a compensation strategy (designed to address and compensate for damage resulting from security threats).

The proposed security foresight-transformation mechanism makes it possible to shape future scenarios of events and the security management strategy of the HE thanks to flexible management and a clear definition of security guarantee subjects and objects of responsibility, regulations, strategic goals and key aspects of security (see Table 2).

Table 2. Objectives and key aspects of the security management strategy for HE

Aspect	Characteristics	Application results
Metrics	"Clean" data of the business entity, without relation to the plan, without comparison with other periods, with reference to the date: income, expenses, number of leads/new applications, state of processing of new leads, marketing indicators (number of conducted events/ published articles/comments for mass media/YouTube recordings (if any)/podcast recordings (if any)/posts/ stories in corps/persons FB or Inst/BD events, lead time, …etc.)	It simply shows numbers that give an assessment of the actual state of the object and what is happening with the company in strategic or short-term matters
KPI	Demonstrate business analytics on an operational dashboard reviewed weekly, monthly and at the end of the year, as well as trends formed by the dynamics of indicators over several years	Allows monitoring of work through the performance of a small number of indicators by each unit or employee
OKR (Objectives and Key Results)	A performance management system designed to establish, report and monitor organizational objectives and results; designed to form a transparent business management system and align the goals of the business, departments and individual employees of the hospitality entity	Replaces the "annual performance review process" with continuous performance monitoring, goal-setting, and feedback.
Foresight-competencies	Identifying markers of changes at the macro- and micro-levels, creating scenarios of probable and unlikely, dangerous for development and supporting development, events in the activity of the HE	Allows you to manage the development of events outside and inside the company, influencing the areas in which the order is broken or may be broken, which is signaled by certain "markers"

Source: Adapted from Ring (2019) and Riyako (2023)

Indicated in the Table 2 aspects with complex application, which is possible thanks to the "digitalization" of business, make it possible to:

- Quickly identify "strong", "weak", central and peripheral signals of changes in the business environment and in the company itself, investigate their consequences;
- To respond to unstable and disharmonious aspects of HE activity, leveling the negative impact on business security;
- Integrate individual markers of changes and events into integral alternative and complementary scenarios, improving the business security system;
- Structure chaotic information flows and deformalize routine business processes, use innovations, etc., to predict and minimize the negative impact on business, manage risks with the least reputational and financial losses, considering macro trends;

- Manage the development of events, transform the mission and organizational culture in accordance with trends and trends of the social and economic environment, etc.

Thus, the establishment and execution of strategic security management establish necessary conditions for the survival of businesses in physical as well as cyberspace. Consequently, leveraging proven expertise and regulations, along with utilizing the risk and threat management toolkit, notably the suggested approach for transforming security management strategies of HE, is highly recommended.

CONCLUSION

Hospitality security plays a crucial role in safeguarding customers, staff, and assets within hotels, resorts, restaurants, and event venues. It involves a comprehensive set of strategies aimed at preventing and addressing security risks such as theft, vandalism, terrorism, and natural disasters. Key components include "surveillance systems", "access control measures", "emergency response protocols", and "trained security personnel". Additionally, protecting digital systems and sensitive customer information from cyber threats is essential. Effective security practices not only improve the customer experience but also enhance the reputation and success of hospitality businesses. As the industry evolves, hospitality security must remain adaptable, continually responding to new threats and technological advancements.

On this basis, in the conditions of global challenges and macro trends, the formation of a security management strategy is a priority direction for every economic entity, because it ensures the implementation of a comprehensive approach aimed at forecasting threats and risks, minimizing or eliminating their impact on the activities of the HE, relying on foresight competencies and own resource. The identification of the key stages of the security management strategy demonstrated that business security is an ongoing process that demands systematic monitoring of changes in both "external and internal" factors. This continuous oversight necessitates regular adjustments to security development patterns. Specifically, the impact of the external environment, through macro trends, is evidenced by security indicators such as fire analytics and cyber attack data.

Taking into account global trends, there is a need to implement such security standards as ISO 31000, ISO 22301, PCI DSS and security standards of international hotel, restaurant chains, distribution systems in the activities of the HE, which is a necessary condition for ensuring economic security in global environment and society's perception of the national tourism system as reliable and responsible. Moreover, the focus of this study was to develop a foresight mechanism for the transformation of the security management strategies of HEs through scenarios of the development of events, a clear definition of security guarantee entities and objects of responsibility, regulations, strategic goals and key aspects of security. This made it possible to identify the following areas of the strategy for ensuring the security of the HE: "orientation" security strategy, security rehabilitation strategy, "compensation" security strategy.

In summary, future research in this field should focus on assessing the effectiveness of proposed security strategies by exploring various factors such as vision, metrics, Key Risk Indicators (KRIs), OKRs, and foresight competencies. It should also involve developing a safety threshold that enables hospitality establishments to better manage and reduce losses during unexpected events and global challenges.

REFERENCES

Andersen, T. J., & Schrøder, P. W. (2010). Strategic risk management. In *Strategic Risk Management Practice: How to Deal Effectively with Major Corporate Exposures* (pp. 200–224). Cambridge University Press. DOI: 10.1017/CBO9780511816017.010

BDO USA. (2023). TOP 10 business cyber security threats in 2023. Available at: https://surl.li/jaran

Boiko, M., Bovsh, L., & Okhrimenko, A. (2022). Crisis resilience of the tourism business in martial law. *The International Scientific-Practical Journal: Commodities and Markets*, 42(2), 31–47. DOI: 10.31617/2.2022(42)03

Bouarar, A. C., Mouloudj, S., & Mouloudj, K. (2022). Digital Transformation: Opportunities and Challenges. In Mansour, N., & Ben Salem, S. (Eds.), *COVID-19's Impact on the Cryptocurrency Market and the Digital Economy* (pp. 33–52). IGI Global. DOI: 10.4018/978-1-7998-9117-8.ch003

Bouarar, A. C., Stojczew, K., & Mouloudj, K. (2023). An Analytical Study on Digital Transformation in the Poland Hospitality Industry. In Fernandes, G., & Melo, A. (Eds.), *Handbook of Research on Innovation, Differentiation, and New Technologies in Tourism, Hotels, and Food Service* (pp. 32–50). IGI Global. DOI: 10.4018/978-1-6684-6985-9.ch002

Bovsh, L., Bosovska, M., & Okhrimenko, A. (2021). Compliance-strategizing of economic security of the business in digitalization conditions. *Herald of KNUTE.*, 6(6), 42–60. DOI: 10.31617/visnik.knute.2021(140)03

Bovsh, L., Hopkalo, L., & Rasulova, A. (2023). The concept of investment risk management by subjects of the hotel business in the conditions of martial law. In M. Sahaidak & T. Sobolieva (Eds.), Management: Challenges in global world (pp. 236-247). Kyiv National Economic University named after Vadym Hetman. http://doi.org/doi.org/10.35668/978-966-926-425-1

Bovsh, L., Hopkalo, L., Tonkonoh, I., Mouloudj, K., Bouarar, A. C., & Mechta, M. (2024a). Sustainable Competitive Edge in Rehabilitation Hospitality: Insights From Ukraine. In Rodrigues, P., Borges, A., Vieira, E., & Tavares, V. (Eds.), *Compelling Storytelling Narratives for Sustainable Branding* (pp. 343–365). IGI Global. DOI: 10.4018/979-8-3693-3326-6.ch018

Bovsh, L., Mouloudj, K., Bosovska, M., Alla, R., & Boiko, M. (2024b). Reputational Compliance in the Communicative Online Environment of a Hotel Entity. In Rouco, J., & Figueiredo, P. (Eds.), *Business Continuity Management and Resilience: Theories, Models, and Processes* (pp. 199–219). IGI Global. DOI: 10.4018/979-8-3693-1658-0.ch009

Bovsh, L., Mouloudj, K., Rasulova, A. M., & Tkachuk, T. M. (2024c). Viral Content in Event Management of Hospitality and Socio-Cultural Activities. In S. Kulshreshtha & C. Webster (Eds.), *New Technologies in Virtual and Hybrid Events* (pp. 228-257). IGI Global. DOI: 10.4018/979-8-3693-2272-7.ch012

Bovsh, L., Rasulova, A., & Muravyova, I. (2022). *The impact of the war on the tourism brand of Ukraine. Creative space of Ukraine and the world*. Collective Monograph. Available at https://www.newroute.org.ua/wp-content/uploads/2022/11/6.pdf

Chernikova, E. G., & Tarasyeva, L. V. (2010). The main directions of ensuring economic security of the enterprise. Problems of Ensuring Economic Security: Materials of the International Scientific and Practical Conference. Donetsk, DonNTU, 163-165.

Cró, S., Calisto, M. D., Martins, A. M., & Simões, J. M. (2020). Safety and Security Perception as Strategic Issues for Hospitality Companies. In Carvalho, L., Calisto, L., & Gustavo, N. (Eds.), *Strategic Business Models to Support Demand, Supply, and Destination Management in the Tourism and Hospitality Industry* (pp. 134–149). IGI Global. DOI: 10.4018/978-1-5225-9936-4.ch007

Denisov, O. E. (2019). Methods of ensuring the economic security of industries in the system of economic security of Ukraine. *State and Regions*, 6(111), 29–34. DOI: 10.32840/1814-1161/2019-6-6

Department of Technical Cybernetics(CPC). (2015). Electronic synopsis of lectures on the discipline "Empirical methods of software engineering". National Technical University of Ukraine "Kyiv Polytechnic Institute. Available at: https://surl.li/iwxjf

DSNS. (2023). Emergency events. https://dsns.gov.ua/news/nadzvicaini-podiyi

Enz, C. A. (2009). The physical safety and security features of U.S. hotels. *Cornell Hospitality Quarterly*, 50(4), 553–560. DOI: 10.1177/1938965509345963

Frigo, M. L. (2018). Strategic Risk Management. In Augier, M., & Teece, D. J. (Eds.), *The Palgrave Encyclopedia of Strategic Management*. Palgrave Macmillan. DOI: 10.1057/978-1-137-00772-8_522

Ghazi, K. (2016). Safety and security measures in Egyptian hotels. *Journal of Association of Arab Universities for Tourism and Hospitality*, 13(1), 165–190. DOI: 10.21608/jaauth.2016.49721

Graebner, M. E. (2021). Evolution of Qualitative Research Methods in Strategic Management. In Duhaime, I. M., Hitt, M. A., & Lyles, M. A. (Eds.), *Strategic Management: State of the Field and Its Future* (pp. 99–114). Academic. DOI: 10.1093/oso/9780190090883.003.0006

Greve, H. R. (2021). The Organizational View of Strategic Management. Strategic Management. In Duhaime, I. M., Hitt, M. A., & Lyles, M. A. (Eds.), *Strategic Management: State of the Field and Its Future* (pp. 43–60). Academic. DOI: 10.1093/oso/9780190090883.003.0003

Helfat, C. E. (2021). The Economic View of Strategic Management. In Duhaime, I. M., Hitt, M. A., & Lyles, M. A. (Eds.), *Strategic Management: State of the Field and Its Future* (pp. 61–80). Academic. DOI: 10.1093/oso/9780190090883.003.0004

Jore, S. H., Utland, I.-L. F., & Vatnamo, V. H. (2018). The contribution of foresight to improve long-term security planning. *Foresight*, 20(1), 68–83. DOI: 10.1108/FS-08-2017-0045

Kompanets, K., Antonyuk, I., & Medvedeva, A. (2022). Marketing techniques in the organization of the restaurant business of Ukraine during the war. *Science and Technology Today*, 5(5). Advance online publication. DOI: 10.52058/2786-6025-2022-5(5)-78-86

Korstanje, M. E. (2020). Tourism Security: A Critical Insight, Korstanje, M.E., & Seraphin, H. (Eds.) *Tourism, Terrorism and Security: Tourism Security-Safety and Post Conflict Destinations* (pp. 1-20). Emerald Publishing Limited, Leeds. DOI: 10.1108/978-1-83867-905-720201002

Krasnomovets, V. (2023). Theoretical foundations of hotel safety within the system of sustainable development. *Visegrad Journal on Bioeconomy and Sustainable Development*, 12(2), 54–59. DOI: 10.2478/vjbsd-2023-0011

KSE. (2023). A report on the direct damage to the infrastructure from the destruction caused by Russia's military aggression against Ukraine a year after the start of the full-scale invasion. https://kse.ua/wp-content/uploads/2023/03/UKR_Feb23_FINAL_Damages-Report.pdf

Kuzmenko, O., Makliuk, O., & Chernyshova, O. (2022). Business cybersecurity in a time of war. *Economy and Society*, 44. Advance online publication. DOI: 10.32782/2524-0072/2022-44-21

Kyiv School of Economics (KSE). (2023). Report on damages to infrastructure caused by Russia's war against Ukraine: One year after the start of the full-scale invasion. Available at: https://kse.ua/wp-content/uploads/2023/03/ENG_FINAL _Damages-Report_.pdf

Mansour, N., & Ben Salem, S. (Eds.). (2022). *COVID-19's Impact on the Cryptocurrency Market and the Digital Economy*. IGI Global. DOI: 10.4018/978-1-7998-9117-8

Markovska, A. V., & Zholobnyuk, D. O. (2023). Restaurant business during the war. *Black Sea Scientific Studies*, 65-67, 65–67. Advance online publication. DOI: 10.36059/978-966-397-300-5-18

Mazaraki, A. A., & Bosovska, M. V. (2013). Theoretical and methodological foundations of the formation of the integration strategy of enterprises. *Business Info*, 7, 299–308.

Moskalenko, V. V., & Godlevskyi, M. D. (2018). Modeli ta metody stratehichnoho upravlinnia rozvytkom pidpryiemstva [Models and methods of strategic management of enterprise development]. Ministry of Education and Science of Ukraine, National Technical University "Kharkiv Polytechnic Institute". Kharkiv: Tochka. http://library.kpi.kharkov.ua/en/node/8774

Piletska, S. T., Korytko, T. Yu., & Tkachenko, E. V. (2021). A model of integrated assessment of the enterprise economic security. *Economic Herald of Donbass*, 65(3), 56–66. DOI: 10.12958/1817-3772-2021-3(65)-56-65

Prasad, A. (2023). Google predicts an increase in Russian cyberattacks on Ukraine and NATO members in 2023. Forbes.ua. Available at: https://surl.li/jaqxk

Radaelli, P. (2021). Enterprise Risk Management in Practice: A European Perspective, Maffei, M. (Ed.) *Enterprise Risk Management in Europe* (pp. 261-278). Emerald Publishing Limited. DOI: 10.1108/978-1-83867-245-420211015

Ribeiro Ramos, O., Mironenko, E., Britchenko, I., Zhuk, O., & Patlachuk, V. (2022). Economic security as an element of corporate management. *Financial and Credit Activity: Problems of Theory and Practice*, 1(42), 304–312. DOI: 10.55643/fcaptp.1.42.2022.3698

Ring, D. (2019). Definition OKRs (Objectives and Key Results). Techtarget. Available at: https://www.techtarget.com/searchhrsoftware/definition/OKRs-Objectives -and-Key-Results (10/9/2023)

Riyako, E. (2023). Law Firm Metrics and KPIs: Management through Digital. Ligazakon.net. https://surl.li/jbiam

Shabani, N., & Munir, A. (2020). A review of cyber security issues in hospitality industry. In Arai, K., Kapoor, S., & Bhatia, R. (Eds.), *Intelligent Computing. SAI 2020. Advances in Intelligent Systems and Computing* (Vol. 1230, pp. 482–493). Springer. DOI: 10.1007/978-3-030-52243-8_35

Sharitov, O. (2023). Rockets instead of visitors. The war damaged more than 1,000 restaurants, cafes and hotels. How does business restore them and how can the state help. ForbesUkraine. https://surl.li/ixncp

Shashwat, K., & Rani, M. (2023). Technological Transformation in Hospitality Industry: An Overview. In Nadda, V., Tyagi, P., Moniz Vieira, R., & Tyagi, P. (Eds.), *Sustainable Development Goal Advancement Through Digital Innovation in the Service Sector* (pp. 133–151). IGI Global. DOI: 10.4018/979-8-3693-0650-5.ch009

Shaver, J. M. (2021). Evolution of Quantitative Research Methods in Strategic Management. In *Strategic Management: State of the Field and Its Future* (pp. 83-98). Oxford Academic. DOI: 10.1093/oso/9780190090883.003.0005

Soliman, M., Gulvady, S., Elbaz, A. M., Mosbah, M., & Wahba, M. S. (2023). Robot-delivered tourism and hospitality services: How to evaluate the impact of health and safety considerations on visitors' satisfaction and loyalty? *Tourism and Hospitality Research*, 24(3), 393–409. DOI: 10.1177/14673584231153367

Spencer, A., & Tarlow, P. (2021). *Tourism Security to Tourism Surety and Well-being, Tourism Safety and Security for the Caribbean (Tourism Security-Safety and Post Conflict Destinations).* Emerald Publishing Limited. DOI: 10.1108/978-1-80071-318-520211004

Stolzer, A. J., Sumwalt, R. L., & Goglia, J. J. (2023). *Safety Management Systems in Aviation* (3rd ed.). CRC Press. DOI: 10.1201/9781003286127

Trim, P., & Lee, Y.-I. (2022). *Strategic Cyber Security Management* (1st ed.). Routledge., DOI: 10.4324/9781003244295

Tuna, A. A., & Türkmendağ, Z. (2022). Cyber Business Management. In *Conflict Management in Digital Business* (pp. 281-301), Emerald Publishing Limited. DOI: 10.1108/978-1-80262-773-220221026

Ukrainian Truth. (2023). Everything you need to know about the Kakhovskaya HPP disaster. Available at: https://www.pravda.com.ua/articles/2023/06/6/7405590/

Verezomska, I., Bovsh, L., Prykhodko, K., & Baklan, H. (2022). Cyber protection of hotel brands. *Restaurant and hotel consulting.Innovation*, 5(2), 190–209. DOI: 10.31866/2616-7468.5.2.2022.270089

Zhivko, Z. B., Cherevko, O. V., Zachosova, N. V., Zhivko, M. O., Bavorovska, O. B., & Zanora, V. O. (2019). Organization and management of the economic security system of the enterprise: Educational and methodological manual. Yu. A. Chabanenko Publisher. https://surl.li/hmcbr

Zou, P. X., & Sunindijo, R. Y. (2015). *Strategic safety management in construction and engineering*. John Wiley & Sons. DOI: 10.1002/9781118839362

KEY TERMS AND DEFINITIONS

Hospitality Security: Refers to the practices and measures implemented to ensure the safety and security of guests, staff, facilities, and assets within the hospitality industry, which includes hotels, resorts, restaurants, event venues, and other hospitality establishments.

Safety Management: Refers to the systematic approach of identifying, assessing, and controlling risks to ensure the safety and well-being of individuals, assets, and environments within an organization or a specific context. It involves the implementation of policies, procedures, and practices aimed at preventing accidents, injuries, and other adverse events.

Strategic Management: Is the comprehensive process of formulating, implementing, and evaluating long-term objectives and initiatives to achieve organizational goals and sustain competitive advantage. It involves analyzing the internal and external environments, setting strategic direction, making decisions about resource allocation, and monitoring performance to ensure alignment with the organization's mission and vision.

Chapter 10
A Proposed Framework for Environmental Risk Assessment (ERA) in Airports

Elen Paraskevi Paraschi

https://orcid.org/0000-0002-7226-8239

University of Patras, Greece

EXECUTIVE SUMMARY

As environmental pressures increase globally, the need arises to understand and manage present and emerging environmental risks. The purpose of this chapter is to introduce a new Environmental Risk Assessment (ERA) approach to identify, assess, and report the level of environmental risks that can lead to significant interruptions, infrastructure damages, safety threats, and long-term effects on airport operations. ERA evaluates the quantitative and qualitative characteristics of environmental hazards, which involve physical, chemical, and biological factors that can imperil humans and infrastructure. The presented ERA framework is deployed in six phases, namely airport preparation, definition of the assessment scope and parameters, data collection and development of projection scenarios, risk assessment, mitigation and adaptation strategies, report, monitor, and review. In essence, the outlined ERA approach serves as a managerial tool to facilitate policy assessment and sustainable decision-making.

DOI: 10.4018/979-8-3693-2675-6.ch010

INTRODUCTION

Airports play a crucial role in air transport pipelines, facilitating global linkages and promoting economic growth. However, airport operations can result in significant burden on environment, including air and noise pollution, habitat deterioration, and the release of greenhouse gases (Paraschi & Poulaki, 2021). Conversely, natural elements such as intense rainfall, crosswinds, bird collisions, and volcano eruptions can lead to significant disturbances in airport activities (Distefano & Leonardi, 2014). The difficulties of environmental issues are often complex and wide-ranging: involving a variety of factors, affecting many ecological domains. The person who undertaking work in airport that bear loss of life and property as the result, public scrutiny, legal responsibilities or any other intricate functions performed in an airport must need to perform risk managements. An adaptive decision-making process must encompass these inter diferentes, and can you consider the uncertainty that goes with strategies within. Environmental Risk Assessment (ERA) is a key tool for the identification and consideration of environmental risks in the processes behind airport development, compliance with sustainability standards and protection of biodiversity.

Environmental hazards are defined as those factors that can threaten the natural balance and functioning of environmental systems and risks to human health and well-being resulting from alteration or degradation in environmental systems. Environmental dangers may be inimical to airport operations in that they may pose enormous threats to people as well as facilities. First, they are health threats because they can add up to pollutants, diseases, and epidemics. The covid-19 outbreak recently destroyed the air transport system all around the world (Rume & Islam, 2020). There are also some prominent economic consequences of environmental risk events that can damage the infrastructure, hinder trade and tourism, and result in rising poverty, inequality, and health expenditure (Chen et al. 2011; EUROCONTROL, 2018). Other factors that could impact air transportation operations from this perspective are environmental impacts such as reduced biodiversity, soil erosion, and changes in weather patterns (Paraschi, 2023).

Risk, in this context, pertains to the possibility of an adverse effect, either directly or indirectly, on the environment or human well-being. The concept encompasses both the probability of an event occurring and the possible severity of its negative consequences, particularly in relation to the ecosystem and human well-being (Bernard et al. 2000). A systematic approach should be employed to conduct an environmental risk assessment whenever a management action is found to have the potential to affect the state of the environment or the health and well-being of humans. Lopez (2016) defines risk assessment as a methodical procedure for delineating and measuring the risks linked to perilous substances, procedures, activities, or occurrences.

The field of risk assessment with a focus on the environment has received significant attention in the past twenty years due to the problems posed by climate change and the growing emphasis on sustainability. Increasingly frequent climate-induced extreme weather events can lead to substantial disruptions in airport services, resulting in considerable economic consequences. Typhoon Jebi struck Kansai International Airport in Japan on September 5, 2018, resulting in significant flooding that left approximately 3,000 travelers stranded at the terminal (BBC, 2018). In January 2024, a significant number of flights, totaling about 2,000, were canceled throughout the United States due to the presence of snow and ice caused by widespread storms (Irwin, 2024). According to Christodoulou and Demirel (2018), the closure of certain large airports can result in a cost exceeding 1 million dollars per hour. At the same time, airports worldwide are increasingly faced with the task of meeting new objectives and aims to enhance environmental performance, including actively lowering greenhouse gas (GHG) emissions and aiming for carbon neutrality. Recognizing the necessity to acknowledge and deal with these concerns, some airports have already put in place certain procedures to deal with environmental hazards. For example, the Amsterdam Airport Schiphol which has an altitude of four meters below sea level has developed a climate change emergency plan and the Oslo airports in Norway have conducted a risk assessment to deal with extreme precipitation events (De Vivo et al. 2023). European and global institutions show great awareness of environmental and sustainability issues, issuing numerous reports and guidelines to encourage organizations and especially critical infrastructures such as airports to carry out risk assessments to address the impacts of climate change and other environmental threats (EUROCONTROL, 2013; EU-CIRCLE, 2016; EEA 2016, 2017a, 2017b, 2019; ICAO, 2022).

Within this context, the purpose of this paper is to introduce a comprehensive Environmental Risk Assessment Framework (ERA) for airports to facilitate decision-making about the handling of environmental hazards. While the primary focus of an Airport Safety Management System is operational safety, integrating Environmental Risk Assessment (ERA) can provide a more holistic approach to managing risks. The ERA framework developed in the document can complement traditional safety risk assessments by addressing environmental hazards like climate change, which can indirectly affect airport operations. At this point, it needs to be clarified that there are two directions in the relationship between airports and environmental risks. On the one hand, there are anthropogenic (e.g., fire) and non-anthropogenic (e.g. earthquake) environmental hazards that affect the facilities and operation of airports, and on the other hand, there are anthropogenic environmental risks created by the operation of airports that have adverse impacts on the environment (e.g. air pollution). The ERA framework proposed in this paper can be used to diagnose and manage risks of both categories.

In the rest of the paper, first, the literature review is presented, then the ERA framework is explained and lastly, the managerial implications and the conclusions are discussed.

LITERATURE REVIEW

Safety Management System (SMS) and Risk Assessment Tools

Risk assessment in airports is most often associated with airside safety since most aircraft accidents and incidents are recorded at the movement area (apron, runway, and taxiways). Consequently, risk assessment is an integral part of the airports' Safety Management System (SMS) which involves identifying, evaluating, and addressing hazards or risks. The primary goal of SMS is to proactively manage potential hazards that could impact passengers, staff, aircraft, and infrastructure. The requirements for effective aviation safety management have been primarily set by the Annex 19 "Safety Management", issued in 2013 by the International Civil Aviation Organization (ICAO, 2013). This document is a reliable set of guidelines and recommended practices for safety management in aviation that must be obeyed by the aviation service providers such as air operators, maintenance organizations, and airports. Member states must set up a State Safety Program (SSP), that is the integration of SMS into a comprehensive national system. Annex 19 stresses the significance of safety data collection and analysis, safety performance indicators, hazard identification and risk management, safety assurance, and safety promotion. The ICAO Annex 19 is an international standard for safety management, in that it introduces safety management at early stages, incorporates safety practices in different sectors, and advances ongoing improvement. The usuel IP or subsete of the protocol with the round trip with the two contending devices is not enough to give a defined concurring protocol time index value that will signify it will not exhibit varying yet in the size depending on schedule of the best effort contract variable thesis multiplication there is a continuous independency under changing network characteristics.

IATA, the International Air Transport Association (IATA), the body that represents the global airlines, prudently emphasizes safety as its core value, therefore it lays down the rules and regulations that airline safety should follow by the way of its Safety Management System (SMS) which is an integral piece of IATA's air transport safety management tools. The IATA model consists of Safety Policy and Objectives, Safety Risk Management, Safety Assurance, and Safety Promotion. Hazard identification, risk assessment, and risk mitigation are the main components of IATA's SMS. For this IATA has come up with an IOSA, and the IATA Safety

Management System (SMS) Manual as well as the IATA Safety Risk Management (SRM) Toolkit which present a complete guide and useful tools for identification and mitigation of risk IATA, 2024).

EUROCONTROL is an intergovernmental organization specialized in developing, coordinating, and planning pan-European air traffic management initiatives. EUROCONTROL has at its disposal a set of risk analysis tools to support ATM and aviation safety management. These include the Air Navigation Service Provider Safety Risk Assessment Methodology, Integrated Risk Picture, Risk Analysis Tool, Human Error Analysis, Safety Assessment Methodology, Systemic Occurrence Analysis Methodology, Safety Framework Maturity Survey, and the Safety Improvement Sub-Group. The tools are used to help ANSPs in safety risk assessments, hazard identification, risk evaluation of the hazards, and mitigation measure recommendations. More specifically, IRP (Integrated Risk Picture) gives a full description of safety threats in the European ATM system, while RAT (Risk Analysis Tool) makes the measurement of risk severity in incidents and accidents equal. To accomplish this, the tools like Safety Library, Safety Management Toolkit, and European Co-ordination Center for Accident and Incident Reporting Systems (ECCAIRS) software have been developed which include those in European airspace, who render, in addition to that, information from a potentially disastrous happening, taking that all into account (EUROCONTROL, 2024).

Alongside international aviation organizations, researchers have created SMS tools and frameworks. Distefano & Leonardi (2014) came up with a risk assessment method for civil airports. This method has three steps: 1. To identify hazards (spotting bad or negative events that might cause danger and looking at how these events could happen and lead to harm) 2. To assess risks (figuring out how often something might happen and how bad the results could be) 3. To reduce risks (putting safety measures in place) In a related approach, Ketabdari et al. (2018) used a risk model to evaluate safety dangers linked to accidents involving runway excursions and undershoots. Their model had three parts that considered the chance (frequency), place, and results (severity) of such incidents. They also used sensitivity analysis to figure out how different input factors affected the chance of possible problems during aircraft operations.

Airport Environmental Risk Assessment

Environmental risk assessment, specifically Environmental Impact Assessment (EIA), is a commonly used method to evaluate the potential environmental effects of a planned project. Franssen et al. (2002) evaluated the effects of aircraft-related pollution on individuals in terms of the number of people impacted by aircraft noise irritation, odor annoyance, and hypertension caused by the expansion of the

Amsterdam Airport Schiphol with a fifth runway. The study findings suggest that being exposed to aircraft noise has a significant impact on the health of individuals residing near the airport. This impact manifests in terms of increased aggravation, sleep disruption, cardiovascular ailments, and diminished performance. Norton et al. (1992) devised a framework for ecological risk assessment encompassing three main stages: problem formulation, analysis, and risk characterization. This paradigm addresses risks related to ecological factors such as chemicals, physical elements, and biological agents. Chartres et al. (2019) delineated four stages in the process of environmental risk assessment: hazard identification, hazard characterization (probability estimation), exposure assessment (effect evaluation), and risk characterization as the amalgamation of both hazard characterization and exposure assessment.

The environmental issue that nowadays is monopolizing the environmental agenda across the world is climate change, therefore, airports and international aviation organizations have developed models and frameworks to evaluate its impact and plan their strategy. The International Civil Aviation Organization put forth a six-stage framework for aviation entities to follow when conducting a climate change risk assessment. These stages include (1) Preparing the organization for the assessment, (2) Specify the assessment's scope, (3) Gather climate data, encompassing the identification of climate stressors and scenarios, (4) Evaluate the impacts of climate change, (5) Finalize the evaluation in preparation for the development of a plan for adaptation, and (6) Supervise and evaluate the evaluation (ICAO (2022). In 2001, Jones developed a systematic approach for evaluating and controlling environmental hazards linked to climate change, consisting of seven sequential stages: (1) Identify the main climatic factors that affect the assessed exposure units, (2) Create scenarios or expected ranges for these important climatic factors, (3) Carry out a sensitivity analysis to understand the relationship between climate change and its effects, (4) Establish the impact thresholds that need to be examined for risk in collaboration with stakeholders, (5) Conduct a risk analysis, (6) Evaluate risks and identify potential adaptations that can be initiated internally through feedback mechanisms, and (7) Collaborate with stakeholders, analyze proposed adaptations, and recommend planned adaptive measures (Jones, 2001).

Lopez (2016) proposed a four-stage model for climate risk assessment. The first step is the estimation of a hazard release from a risk source, the second is the estimation of the exposure to this hazard, the third is the estimation of the consequences, and the final step is the risk estimation that integrates the estimations of the three previous steps. De Vivo et al. (2021) developed a theoretical framework to assess the potential dangers of climate change on Mediterranean airports. Their study specifically examined the impacts of excessive temperature, extreme precipitation, and rising sea levels. The definition of risk, based on the IPCC 2014 paradigm by Oppenheimer et al. (2015), incorporates the factors of hazard, exposure, and vulnerability. These factors are further divided into sensitivity and adaptive capacity. Subsequently, the study team utilized the aforementioned framework to assess the susceptibility of nine Italian airports (Malpensa, Bergamo, Linate, Fiumicino, Ciampino, Napoli, Catania, Palermo, and Cagliari) to the occurrence of severe precipitation events (De Vivo et al. 2023).

Vogiatzis et al. (2021) conducted a thorough evaluation of the potential dangers associated with climate change that could affect both the direct and indirect activities of Athens International Airport (AIA) in Greece. The researchers utilized a comprehensive seven-step ERA framework, which encompassed risk identification, appraisal of likelihood and severity, determination of risk priority, assessment of control rating, consideration of uncertainty in forecasts, and formulation of adaptation solutions. The risk assessment revealed a total of 27 risks in the short, medium, and long term, taking into account both the central and high climate scenarios. Most of the risks were associated with rising temperatures and humidity (e.g. increased firing risks), some were connected with storms (e.g., flooding risks), fog (e.g. low visibility risks), lighting (e.g. refueling risks) and wind (e.g. risks from foreign object debris-FODs that pose threats to aircraft and people).

Heathrow airport (LHR) in UK has identified climate change risks for short, medium, and long term, categorized into significant, moderate, and low risks. These risks are based on expert judgment, likelihood of exceeding critical thresholds, and the robustness of existing control measures. The risk assessment identified 34 risks in the short and medium to longer term, connected with temperature, precipitation, fog, lighting, wind and snow. Overall, the risk assessment concluded that Heathrow faces significant risks from climate change, including long-term temperature and precipitation extremes, and uncertainties in future wind conditions due to parallel runways and lack of cross-wind runway (LHR, 2011).

Changi Airport (CAG) in Singapore completed an environmental risk assessment to evaluate its resilience against the impacts of climate change, including rising sea levels and extreme weather events. The Changi's ERA revealed that there is a significant likelihood of flooding as a result of the increasing sea levels and intense precipitation. Additionally, extreme weather occurrences, such as typhoons and heatwaves, have the potential to cause disruptions to airport operations. The airport developed mitigation measures such as the implementation of a novel, elevated sea barrier and enhanced hydraulic infrastructure to avert inundation, the investment to renewable energy sources and energy-efficient technologies aiming to decrease the airport's carbon impact and the strengthening of infrastructure and the establishment of plans for responding to emergencies (Dolman & Vorage, 2020).

As pointed out by Chartres et al. (2019), the procedures and approaches employed by organizations conducting environmental Hazard Identification and Risk Assessment (HI/RA) for environmental hazards vary significantly. There is a demand for the adoption of empirically grounded tools and methodologies in the assessment, synthesis of evidence, and conclusion. This adoption should be consistent across all organizations engaged in ERA, aiming to enhance transparency, comparability, and the overall validity of assessments.

ERA FRAMEWORK

Multiple definitions exist in the literature to elucidate the concept of Environmental Risk Assessment. Bernard et al. (2000) define ERA as a method for assessing the probability of a negative outcome or event caused by human-induced pressures or alterations in environmental conditions. Galatchi (2006) defines Environmental Risk Assessment as the process of analyzing the quantitative and qualitative attributes of the environment in order to identify and assess the possible dangers to both the environment and human health resulting from the existence or utilization of particular contaminants. According to Jones (2001), Environmental Risk Management, usually referred to as risk assessment, involves the process of identifying, evaluating, selecting, and implementing methods to reduce the risk to human health and ecosystems.

Combining the above definitions with the most common risk assessment frameworks presented in the literature review, this paper proposes an Environmental Risk Assessment framework deployed in six key steps (Figure 1): (1) Get the organization ready for the assessment; (2) Define the assessment's scope and parameters; (3) Gather information (4) Identify and Evaluate of environmental hazards; (5) Develop response strategies; and (6) Report, take feedback and review.

Figure 1. Airport environmental risk assessment framework

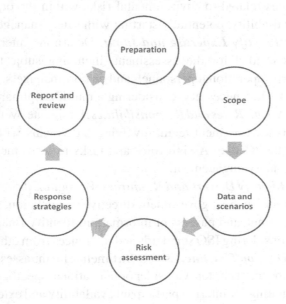

First step: Airport Preparation

This stage aims to pave the way for the evaluation and establish the structure for the assessment procedure (Jones, 2001; ICAO, 2022). An effective preparation phase will ensure that all airport stakeholders are informed and engaged and, that the work team has sufficient resources and a clear action plan to carry out its task. Therefore, the first step needs the following actions to be completed:

Action 1.1: Get Senior Leadership Commitment. Obtain commitment from senior leadership before initiating the assessment to legitimize the work and secure necessary human and financial resources. Communicate the assessment's objectives, expected goals, and target audience, and coordinate with external stakeholders.

Action 1.2: Inform Stakeholders. Provide information to stakeholders, especially those unfamiliar with environmental issues, ensuring their understanding and active participation. Familiarize them with environmental concepts and potential impacts through publications and briefings, acknowledging uncertainties.

Action 1.3: Identify Existing Governance. Check for existing frameworks or methodologies related to environmental risks within the organization, evaluating their usability, potentially starting with safety management systems.

Action 1.4: Identify Expertise and Input. Determine internal and external participants needed for the assessment, including subject-matter experts, safety experts, operational personnel, and airport managers. Engage external stakeholders when necessary, considering a multidisciplinary approach.

Action 1.5: Assign Roles and Responsibilities. Designate overall responsibility within the risk assessment team, involving individuals with key assets and operational knowledge. Assign roles and tasks to team members, fostering multi-disciplinary engagement.

Action 1.6: Identify Drivers and Resources. Recognize drivers for conducting the assessment, such as government directives, legislation, financial disclosure requirements, and past event information. Identify financial and human resources, considering ISO standards and references from other organizations.

Action 1.7: Develop Timeline. Establish a timeline for the assessment, allocating sufficient time for each step. Consider organizational specifics and assessment scope, accounting for internal participant availability and external stakeholder constraints. Align the timeline with regulatory deadlines or leadership requests.

Second step: Assessment Scope and Parameters

This step focuses on defining the geographical and organizational boundaries of the risk assessment, and determining what is included and excluded (Norton et al. 1992; Galatchi, 2006). There are three key actions in this step:

Action 2.1: Define Geographical Scope and Organizational Boundaries. Establishing the assessment's boundaries involves not only geographical considerations but also defining organizational boundaries. It is of utmost importance, particularly in situations when different companies have control over separate sections of an airport or when the infrastructure is simultaneously owned and leased. It is crucial to determine the accountable party for the evaluation and incorporate crucial components that are not under the airport's ownership. To guarantee a thorough scope that includes all possible effects on workers, passengers, equipment, and operations, it is important to involve asset operators, operational staff, facility managers, and decision-makers from the beginning of the process.

Action 2.2: Focus and Scope of Assessment. The assessment can range from a system-wide perspective to specific vulnerabilities in particular aspects. Clear documentation of the assessment's scope is vital, avoiding unforeseen repercussions such as overlooking key issues or impacts that may affect other components of the organization. The recommendation is to adopt a system approach for more comprehensive assessments, covering the entire airport infrastructure, operations, supply chain needs, and surface transportation, rather than focusing solely on specific elements and for instance, considering the broader impact of factors like noise on residents or sea-level rise affecting various airport stakeholders (operators, ground handlers, airlines, ANSP, fire services).

Action 2.3: Problem Formulation. This involves planning and scoping to connect regulatory or management goals with the risk assessment. The result is a conceptual model specifying environmental values to be protected, required data, and analysis methods. Problem formulation includes identifying and characterizing stressors, systems at risk, and ecological effects. It is an interactive process, with information gathering helping define airport sub-systems potentially at risk and stressor-system interactions relevant to exposure scenarios.
Third step: Data and scenarios

At this step, data will be collected for the environmental parameters decided in step 2. Afterwards, future scenarios about the change of these parameters across time should be formulated and decisions about tolerance levels should be made (Jones, 2001; Galatchi, 2006; Distefano & Leonardi, 2014). More specifically:

Action 3.1: Acquire Historical and Baseline Environmental Data. This action suggests obtaining historical environmental data, including reports of past incidents and impacts, to establish a baseline. This data can be provided through organizational reports, governmental records, or Meteorological Services (MET) for weather-related data.

Action 3.2: Acquire Environmental Change Projections. This action is specifically important for climate-related environmental risks, such as rising temperatures or sea level assessments. Considering geographical scale is crucial because organizations need to obtain climate change projections tailored to specific locations. Climate projections covering at least 30 years are advised, aligned with investment cycles for infrastructure, especially for airports and Air Navigation Service Providers (ANSP).

Action 3.3: Identify Stressor Confidence Levels and Scale of Change. This action involves determining confidence levels and the expected scale of change in environmental stressors, considering an organization's risk tolerance. The level of tolerance varies based on the type of operation or service offered, with major hub airports having a low tolerance for disruptions compared to smaller airports or those located in remote islands, where disruptions can have critical economic implications.

Fourth step: Risk Assessment

This step elaborates on the procedure of determining the potential environmental hazards and their effects on the airport and offers suggestions for creating a risk matrix and prioritizing risks accordingly (Norton et al. 1992; Jones, 2001; Galatchi, 2006; EUROCONTROL, 2013; Distefano & Leonardi, 2014; EU-CIRCLE, 2016; EEA, 2016, 2017a, 2017b, 2019; ICAO, 2022; Paraschi, 2023). There are five actions associated with this step:

Action 4.1: Risk Identification. According to Distefano & Leonardi (2014), a hazard is defined as any condition, object, action, or event that has the capability to cause injuries, damage to equipment or structures, loss of material, or a decrease in the ability to carry out a prescribed function. According to Chartres et al. (2019), dangers are substances or agents, whether natural or man-made, that might cause harmful health effects under certain conditions. These hazards can be in the form of chemicals, physical factors, or biological agents. Environmental dangers can be classified into multiple categories (Smith, 2013; Lopez, 2016): Geological hazards (earthquakes, volcanic eruptions, tsunamis, soil erosion, landslides, and avalanches), Physical hazards (reduced visibility, noise, light, wildfires), Biological hazards (pollution, bird strikes, infectious diseases and epidemics), Atmospheric hazards (convective storms, cyclones, tornadoes, extreme temperatures, hail, ice, snow, cross-winds), Hydrological hazards (sea-level rise, floods and droughts), Technological hazards (explosions, nuclear accidents, release of toxic or radioactive agents). Environmental hazards can occur naturally or may result from human constructions or activities, such as building collapses or injuries from mechanical equipment. Certain physical dangers, like explosions or radiation, might originate from either natural or human origins.

In the process of risk identification, it is crucial to refine the preliminary list of environmental hazards by selecting specific items. The selection criteria include assessing the significance of hazards based on their potential economic or social consequences, likelihood of increased risk, relationship to fundamental pressures, and feasibility for use in terms of data availability and assessment methodologies (Bernard et al. 2000). This step is vital for narrowing down and prioritizing the values for further evaluation in the Environmental Risk Assessment (ERA).

Therefore, it is necessary to assess the risk associated with each hazard by considering both the likelihood of its occurrence and the impact it would have on the airport (Jones, 2001).

Action 4.2: Estimation of risk probability. Depending on the type of available data, the risk probability (P) may be expressed in a qualitative or quantitative technique. Risk classes are utilized to delineate the spectrum of probability or possibility of an unfavorable result (Table 1).

Table 1. Risk probability

Risk probability class	Qualitative & Quantitative Definition	
Frequent (Very High)	Prone to frequent occurrence (has happened frequently) $P > 10^{-1}$	5
Occasional (High)	Prone to occasional occurrence (has happened infrequently) $10^{-2} < P < 10^{-1}$	4
Remote (Moderate)	Improbable but feasible (infrequently observed) $10^{-3} < P < 10^{-2}$	3
Improbable (Low)	Highly improbable (with no record of occurrence) $10^{-6} < P < 10^{-3}$	2
Extremely improbable (Very Low)	Highly unlikely that the event will happen $P < 10^{-6}$	1

Source: Adapted from Woodruff (2005) and Watson (2011).

Action 4.3: Estimation of risk severity. Risk severity (S) refers to the consequences caused by the environmental hazard to people and/or infrastructure. There are five severity classes described in Table 2.

Table 2. Risk severity

Risk severity class	Qualitative Definition and Monetary Value	
Catastrophic (Very High)	Deaths/permanent total disability/irreversible disastrous environmental damage Financial loss (>1,000,000 £)	5
Hazardous (High)	Major injuries/permanent partial disability/severe but reversible environmental damage, Financial loss (>100,000 £)	4
Major (Moderate)	Moderate injuries/mitigable environmental damage, Financial loss (>10,000 £)	3
Minor (Low)	Minor injuries & Environmental damage, Financial loss (>1,000 £)	2
Negligible (Very Low)	No injuries & Environmental damage, Financial loss (>100 £)	1

Source: Adapted from Woodruff (2005) and Watson (2011).

When estimating the severity of environmental hazards for airports, it is essential to identify the exposed samples or assets under threat. Airports are typically divided into landside and airside activities. Airside components include structures related to aircraft movement, while landside components involve public access areas (ICAO, 2022). Environmental risks can lead to direct impacts, causing damage to airport elements, and indirect impacts that affect interdependent resources, resulting in delays, cancellations, or economic losses. The interdependent nature of airport infrastructure implies that damage to a single component might result in significant problems in other operations. Instances such as excessive rainfall and the rise in sea level have the potential to undermine the ability of airports to effectively drain water, resulting in flooding, disruptions in services, and economic harm (De Vivo et al., 2021).

Action 4.4: Risk matrix. A risk matrix (Table 3) is a tool employed for risk assessment, evaluating the likelihood and impact of potential events. Each hazard is assigned a risk value (R) based on its probability (P) and severity (S) ratings (Woodruff, 2005).

Risk = Probability x Severity (*eq. 1*)

Table 3. Risk matrix

Probability (P)	Severity (S)				
	1	2	3	4	5
5	5	10	15	20	25
4	4	8	12	16	20
3	3	6	9	12	15
2	2	4	6	8	10
1	1	2	3	4	5

Source: Adapted from Woodruff (2005), Watson (2011), and ICAO (2022)

Potential risk values between 15 and 25 are considered high and are highlighted red, risk potential between 5-12 is considered medium and is highlighted yellow, and risk potential between 1-4 is considered low and is highlighted green. For instance, a rare but severe event like a one-in-500-year flood would be positioned in the upper-left of the matrix, indicating high consequences with low likelihood. Conversely, events with high probability but lower impact may be placed elsewhere based on organizational preparedness (ICAO, 2022). As different airports face varying impacts and probabilities, their risk matrices will differ accordingly.

Action 4.5: Estimation of Airport Vulnerability. Oppenheimer et al. (2015) and De Vivo et al. (2021) employ a methodology that calculates the level of risk by considering the factors of hazard, exposure, and vulnerability. The Vulnerability Index formula calculates the average of the sensitivity and adaptive capacity indices (equation 2).

Vulnerability = average (Sensitivity + Adaptive capacity) (*eq. 2*)

Sensitivity pertains to the extent to which an asset or system is influenced by exposure to environmental hazards, encompassing indicators that span from air traffic to geological and socio-economic issues. Adaptive capacity refers to the capability to adapt to environmental consequences, taking into account elements such as infrastructural improvements and operational preparedness.

The vulnerability and adaptive capacity assessment involves evaluating physical and social indicators, such as age and condition of structures, HVAC (heating, ventilation, and air conditioning) system readiness, alternative transport options during disruptions, multiple access roads, impervious surfaces, air traffic, and geological characteristics. Factors such as passenger numbers, flight frequency, and parking access are crucial for determining vulnerability. Busy airports face greater challenges in managing impacts from adverse weather events, and extreme temperatures can affect both outdoor and indoor workers. Physical aspects may also affect vulnerability, e.g. airport runways with elevation less than 5m are more susceptible to both recurring and permanent flooding occurrences brought on by mean sea level rise and more powerful storm surges. Specified indices such as the Coastal Vulnerability Index for assessing vulnerability to sea level rise could also be utilized (McLaughlin et al. 2010). ICAO (2022) emphasizes the importance of collecting both environmental and asset data, accounting for cascading effects, and conducting supplemental analyses for specific vulnerabilities. ICAO also advises identifying design and operational thresholds for each asset, Incorporating factors such as snow or wind loads for structures and high-temperature extremes for pavements in planned projects. Not all assets are affected by the same stressors, and underground utilities, for instance, may be more susceptible to flooding than wind.

Taking all the above into account, the final risk potential of the airport is calculated with the following formula (De Vivo et al. 2023):

Risk Potential = Risk x Vulnerability (*eq.* 3)

The relative risk potential can be utilized to prioritize essential measures for efficiently managing hazards based on the risk value specified in Table 4:

Table 4. Risk priority

Risk potential	Risk priority	Action
15-25	High	Urgent action is necessary
5-12	Medium	Continuous inspections and short-term planned approach for risk mitigation is necessary
1-4	Low	There is no need for immediate action, but regular inspections and attention are necessary to prevent future incidents related to attenuation

Source: Adapted from Di Bona et al. (2018)

Fifth step: Response Strategies

Response strategies should extend in four axes, namely mitigation, adaptation, collaboration, and education and awareness.

Action 5.1: Mitigation. Mitigation strategies involve efforts to reduce environmental impacts and conserve natural, technological, and human and resources. Specific mitigation measures taken by airports for environmental sustainability include reducing carbon footprint, improving air quality, managing noise, implementing green transportation, reducing waste, water management, and biodiversity protection (Paraschi & Poulaki, 2021; Paraschi et al. 2022).

Action 5.2: Adaptation. Adaptation involves constructing robust infrastructure and improving readiness for emergencies. It can be realized by tangible, societal, institutional, technological, and economic actions. The available solutions for adaptation can be classified into three categories: gray (technical), green (ecosystem-based), and soft (managerial, legal, political) measures (De Vivo et al. 2021). For example, adaptation measures to climate change could involve constructing flood barriers and higher runways, resurfacing structures with heat-resistant materials to cope with extreme temperatures, building longer runways in areas with higher temperatures, and installing vegetation on airport structures (De Vivo et al. 2021, 2022; Gratton et al. 2022; Paraschi, 2023). Potential opportunities emerging for changing environmental conditions should also be explored, such as an increase in tourism demand for some destinations or reduced de-icing requirements (ICAO, 2022).

Action 5.3: Collaboration. Collaboration among airport stakeholders is vital to address environmental risks. For example, incentives can be used by the airport operator, handling agents, airlines, ANSP, and/or the government to use adaptation practices. Consulting with airport stakeholders in analyzing and recommending adaptation options involves considering factors like planning horizon, stakeholder ability to adapt, knowledge of autonomous adaptations, experience in long-term planning, and perceptions of uncertainties and acceptability. The approval of adjustments for stakeholders is primarily influenced by a mix of economic, regulatory, and cultural variables that will vary depending on the unique scenario (Jones, 2001).

Action 5.4: Training and awareness. Finally, education and awareness must be offered both to airport employees and to the public, as well as to the numerous businesses operating in the airport. Furthermore, airport contingency plans should be updated in light of the risk assessment results, and emergency exercises for environmental hazards must be planned and executed at regular intervals.

Sixth step: Report and review

This step involves three actions, namely completing the risk assessment report, communicating the results, taking feedback, and reviewing.

Action 6.1: Final Report. The final risk assessment report should present the main findings such as environmental stressors and anticipated hazards along with their corresponding confidence levels, existing adaptation capabilities, and vulnerabilities. The report should be addressed to senior executives, who will need to decide the final level of risk acceptance and the minimum service levels to be maintained in the implementation methods.

Action 6.2: Communication Plan. In addition to the risk assessment report, it is necessary to create a communication plan to effectively convey the results of the risk assessment to stakeholders. Creating a communication strategy is essential for effectively communicating the results of a risk assessment, particularly when considering the possible harm, interruptions, and expenses resulting from environmental consequences. Jones (2001) acknowledges that while there is detailed information on communicating scenarios and climatic variables, the communication of risk, prioritization, and analysis of adaptation options is less clear. Experience from other areas of airport risk assessment where stakeholder participation and risk communication are better developed can also be utilized in environmental risk assessments.

Action 6.3: Monitor and review. This activity pertains to the development of a monitoring plan for the process of adaptation, which includes the schedule for execution and the evaluation of the measures that have been implemented. Regularly assessing both the Environmental Risk Assessment framework and the adaptation measures is crucial to confirm the effectiveness of implemented measures. If the desired results are not achieved, it enables the timely initiation of corrective actions. Periodic reviews of the risk assessment are also valuable for identifying emerging risks and facilitating the timely development and implementation of adaptation and resilience measures for those newly recognized challenges. Within the monitoring framework, there is a need to emphasize the necessity of reporting and communicating achievements, such as sustaining agreed-upon service levels during disruptions and potential cost savings from enhanced resilience. The ability to discern satisfactory or unsatisfactory progress and develop corrective actions is crucial for understanding successes. Additionally, it is essential to continuously assess the ERA implementation plan itself, questioning its validity and the need for updates. This monitoring endeavor highlights the integral relationship between ongoing assessment and adaptation efforts in response to evolving circumstances.

Table 5. Summarizes the six steps of the ERA framework and the corresponding actions.

Table 5. Steps and specific actions of the airport environmental risk assessment framework

ERA Steps	ERA Actions
1. Airport preparation	1.1. Get Senior Leadership Commitment 1.2. Inform Stakeholders 1.3. Identify Existing Governance 1.4. Identify Expertise and Input 1.5. Assign Roles and Responsibilities 1.6. Identify Drivers and Resources 1.7. Develop Timeline
2. Assessment scope and parameters	2.1. Define Geographical Scope and Organizational Boundaries 2.2. Focus and Scope of Assessment 2.3. Problem Formulation
3. Data and scenarios	3.1: Acquire Historical and Baseline Environmental Data 3.2: Acquire Environmental Change Projections 3.3: Identify Stressor Confidence Levels and Scale of Change
4. Risk assessment	4.1: Risk Identification 4.2: Estimation of risk probability 4.3: Estimation of risk severity 4.4: Risk matrix 4.5: Estimation of airport vulnerability
5. Response Strategies	5.1: Mitigation 5.2: Adaptation 5.3: Collaboration 5.4: Training and awareness
6. Report and Review	6.1: Final Report 6.2: Communication Plan 6.3: Monitor and review

MANAGERIAL IMPLICATIONS

This paper outlines a comprehensive risk assessment framework to deal with environmental hazards threatening airport operations. The proposed Environmental Risk Assessment approach serves as a tool to evaluate policies and make sustainable decisions. Its goal is to minimize or eliminate the negative effects of environmental risks on airports, airlines, and passengers. Airports may reduce their environmental effect, safeguard people, infrastructure, and natural resources, and enhance social welfare by employing a methodical approach to identify, evaluate, and tackle environmental issues. To achieve these sustainability goals, communication and collaboration among airport stakeholders is essential. As airports evolve to accommodate growing air travel needs, implementing comprehensive environmental risk assessment methods will be critical to ensure a sustainable aviation industry for future generations.

The primary objective of the airport ERA framework is to offer managers a decision-making context, enabling them to avoid unacceptable levels of risks, when the potential loss or harm, given its possibility and severity, exceeds the advantages that are anticipated, or when the potential loss or damage, given its possibility and severity, is so great that it cannot be mitigated or reversed (Bernard et al. 2000). ERA is a valuable tool for evaluating policies, land use planning, and resource management decision making. ERA also enables the transmission of expected hazards linked to actions, ensuring that stakeholders and the public are aware of the consequences for environmental values (Bernard et al. 2000). The ERA mandates the identification of environmental risks and necessitates the recognition of these risks both prior to and during decision-making processes. Increased awareness of risk promotes the dissemination of accountability and fosters a communal assumption of responsibility for risk management, ultimately resulting in decisions aimed at mitigating risk. The ERA methodology is methodical and may be utilized in a wide range of scenarios, spanning from situations with limited data and resources to ones with comprehensive inventories and intricate systems modeling. Additionally, it possesses adaptability and the ability to be utilized in intricate comprehensive examinations or in circumstances necessitating prompt and concise solutions.

CONCLUSIONS, LIMITATIONS, AND FUTURE DIRECTIONS

This paper introduces a risk assessment framework designed to evaluate environmental risks possibly faced by airports. As environmental issues, especially climate change, gain more and more attention due to repeated incidents causing serious disruptions in air transportation and because of increasing environmental regulation from national and international regulatory authorities, all airports must develop environmental management plans as an integral part of their operation manuals. This paper offers a comprehensive framework that could facilitate this requirement. By integrating risk assessment into the Airport Safety Management System and incorporating principles from the ERA framework, airports can enhance their ability to manage a wide range of risks, ensuring safer and more sustainable operations.

When dealing with environmental risk assessment and management, several challenges should be taken into account. Limited data availability regarding environmental parameters, random variation, complex interactions among environmental components, uncertainty of the prediction models, qualitative methodologies and inconsistencies in setting acceptable risk thresholds, multiple regulatory requirements, financial, geographical, and time constraints in applying adaptation measures, the dynamic nature of airport activities, conflicting interests among airport stakeholders are among them. To address the above limitations, Bernard et al. (2000) suggests engaging an "expert panel" to evaluate the risk analysis results and plan alternative management options. Expert opinions presented in an accessible manner hold greater value and are more likely to garner acceptance compared to intricate quantitative analyses that lack explicit assumptions or rationale support. Additionally, they assert that, as a rule, a high-quality qualitative evaluation is superior to a low-quality quantitative evaluation. Nevertheless, data triangulation, i.e., the combination of qualitative with quantitative data can be engaged whenever possible to enhance the results' robustness.

The research on environmental risk assessment and management is growing and airport environmental risk assessment methods have seen significant improvements as a consequence of research and technological advancements. These include the development of advanced modeling tools, decision support systems, sensor networks, and remote sensing techniques. In addition, there is a growing emphasis on incorporating ecosystem-based techniques, climate resilience, and sustainability concepts into ERA frameworks to encourage more thorough and cohesive assessments of environmental risks. To strengthen this research area, it is recommended that similar airports be selected as a sample group and examined in future research. For instance, Greek airports could serve this purpose. The Greek economy is highly dependent on tourism, which primarily arrives by plane. The majority of Greek airports are situated on islands at sea level, rendering them exceptionally susceptible to the adverse effects of climate change, including escalating temperatures and sea levels. These variables have the potential to significantly impede airport operations. Therefore, it is critical for Greece to conduct a detailed environmental risk assessment for its airports and share the findings with the public and the academic community.

REFERENCES

BBC. (2018). *Typhoon Jebi forced the closure of Kansai Airport, near Osaka in Japan*. Available online at https://www.bbc.com/news/world-asia-45417035

Bernard, M., Rankin, C., Griggs, J., & Utzig, G. (2000). *Environmental Risk Assessment (ERA): an Approach for Assessing and Reporting Environmental Conditions*. Habitat Branch, Ministry of Environment, Lands and Parks.

Chartres, N., Bero, L. A., & Norris, S. L. (2019). A review of methods used for hazard identification and risk assessment of environmental hazards. *Environment International*, 123, 231–239. DOI: 10.1016/j.envint.2018.11.060 PMID: 30537638

Chen, Z., Li, H., Ren, H., Xu, Q., & Hong, J. (2011). A total environmental risk assessment model for international hub airports. *International Journal of Project Management*, 29(7), 856–866. DOI: 10.1016/j.ijproman.2011.03.004

Christodoulou, A., & Demirel, H. (2018). *Impacts of climate change on transport. A Focus on Airports, Seaports and Inland Waterways*. European Union Publication Office. DOI: 10.2760/378464

De Vivo, C., Barbato, G., Ellena, M., Capozzi, V., Budillon, G., & Mercogliano, P. (2023). Climate-Risk Assessment Framework for Airports under Extreme Precipitation Events: Application to Selected Italian Case Studies. *Sustainability (Basel)*, 15(9), 7300. DOI: 10.3390/su15097300

De Vivo, C., Ellena, M., Capozzi, V., Budillon, G., & Mercogliano, P. (2021). Risk assessment framework for Mediterranean airports: A focus on extreme temperatures and precipitations and sea level rise. *Natural Hazards*, 1–20.

Di Bona, G., Silvestri, A., Forcina, A., & Petrillo, A. (2018). Total efficient risk priority number (TERPN): A new method for risk assessment. *Journal of Risk Research*, 21(11), 1384–1408. DOI: 10.1080/13669877.2017.1307260

Distefano, N., & Leonardi, S. (2014). Risk assessment procedure for civil airport. *IJTTE. International Journal for Traffic and Transport Engineering*, 4(1), 62–75. DOI: 10.7708/ijtte.2014.4(1).05

Dolman, N., & Vorage, P. (2020). Preparing Singapore Changi Airport for the effects of climate change. *Journal of Airport Management*, 14(1), 54–66. DOI: 10.69554/VETC9210

EEA (2016). *Map book urban vulnerability to climate change Factsheets*. European Environment Agency.

EEA. (2017a). *Climate change, impacts and vulnerability in Europe 2016. An indicator-based report*. European Environment Agency.

EEA (2017b). *Climate change adaptation and disaster risk reduction in Europe*. European Environment Agency.

EEA. (2019). European Aviation. European Environment Agency.

EU-CIRCLE. (2016). Impacts of climate change and extreme weather events on critical infrastructure state of the art review and taxonomy of existing knowledge. http:// www. eu- circle. eu/ for.

EUROCONTROL. (2013). *Challenges of growth 2013 - Task 8: Climate Change Risk and Resilience*.

EUROCONTROL. (2018). *European aviation in 2040. Challenges of Growth.*

EUROCONTROL. (2024). *Safety*. Available online at: https://www.EUROCONTROL .int/safety

Franssen, E. A., Staatsen, B. A., & Lebret, E. (2002). Assessing health consequences in an environmental impact assessment: The case of Amsterdam Airport Schiphol. *Environmental Impact Assessment Review*, 22(6), 633–653. DOI: 10.1016/S0195-9255(02)00015-X

Galatchi, L. D. (2006). Environmental risk assessment. *Chemicals as intentional and accidental global environmental threats*, 1-6.

IATA. (2024). *Safety*. Available online at: https://www.iata.org/en/programs/safety/

ICAO. (2013). *Annex 19 - Safety Management*. International Civil Aviation Organization.

ICAO. (2022). *Key Steps for Aviation Organisation Climate Change Risk Assessment and Adaptation Planning: Key Steps for Aviation Organisation Climate Change Risk Assessment and Adaptation Planning*. International Civil Aviation Organization.

Irwin, L. (2024, January 16). *Almost 2,000 flights canceled as airports deal with snow, ice*. The Hill. Available online at https://thehill.com/policy/transportation/4411649-winter-storm-flights-canceled-la-guardia-reagan/

Jones, R. N. (2001). An environmental risk assessment/management framework for climate change impact assessments. *Natural Hazards*, 23(2-3), 197–230. DOI: 10.1023/A:1011148019213

Ketabdari, M., Giustozzi, F., & Crispino, M. (2018). Sensitivity analysis of influencing factors in probabilistic risk assessment for airports. *Safety Science*, 107, 173–187. DOI: 10.1016/j.ssci.2017.07.005

LHR. (2011). *HAL final report*. Heathrow Airport Limited.

Lopez, A. (2016). Vulnerability of airports on climate change: An assessment methodology. *Transportation Research Procedia*, 14, 24–31. DOI: 10.1016/j.trpro.2016.05.037

Mclaughlin, S., & Cooper, J. A. G. (2010). A multi-scale coastal vulnerability index: A tool for coastal managers? *Environmental Hazards*, 9(3), 233–248. DOI: 10.3763/ehaz.2010.0052

Norton, S. B., Rodier, D. J., van der Schalie, W. H., Wood, W. P., Slimak, M. W., & Gentile, J. H. (1992). A framework for ecological risk assessment at the EPA. *Environmental Toxicology and Chemistry*, 11(12), 1663–1672. DOI: 10.1002/etc.5620111202

Oppenheimer, M., Campos, M., Warren, R., Birkmann, J., Luber, G., O'Neill, B., & Hsiang, S. (2015). Emergent risks and key vulnerabilities. In *Climate change 2014 impacts, adaptation and vulnerability: part a: global and sectoral aspects* (pp. 1039–1100). Cambridge University Press.

Paraschi, E. P. (2022). Current Aviation challenges and opportunities. *Journal of Airline Operations and Aviation Management*, 1(2), 7–14. DOI: 10.56801/jaoam.v1i2.6

Paraschi, E. P. (2023). Aviation and Climate change: Challenges and the way forward. *Journal of Airline Operations and Aviation Management*, 2(2), 86–95. DOI: 10.56801/jaoam.v2i1.5

Paraschi, E. P., & Poulaki, I. (2021). An overview on Environmental Management in Aviation. In *Challenging Issues on Environment and Earth Science*. International Book Publishing. DOI: 10.9734/bpi/ciees/v7/11732D

Paraschi, E.P., Poulaki, I., Papageorgiou, A. (2022). From Environmental Management Systems to Airport Environmental Performance: A Model Assessment. *Journal of Environmental Management and Tourism, (Volume XIII*, Summer), 3(59): 831- 852. https://doi.org/DOI: 10.14505/jemt.v13.3(59).22

Rume, T., & Islam, S. D. U. (2020). Environmental effects of COVID-19 pandemic and potential strategies of sustainability. *Heliyon*, 6(9), e04965. DOI: 10.1016/j.heliyon.2020.e04965 PMID: 32964165

Smith, K. (2013). *Environmental hazards: assessing risk and reducing disaster.* Routledge. DOI: 10.4324/9780203805305

Vogiatzis, K., Kassomenos, P., Gerolymatou, G., Valamvanos, P., & Anamaterou, E. (2021). Climate Change Adaptation Studies as a tool to ensure airport's sustainability: The case of Athens International Airport (AIA). *The Science of the Total Environment*, 754, 142153. DOI: 10.1016/j.scitotenv.2020.142153 PMID: 33254882

Watson, C. C. (2011, August). Risk assessment using the three dimensions of probability (likelihood), severity, and level of control. In *29th International Systems Safety Conference* (No. M11-0220).

Woodruff, J. M. (2005). Consequence and likelihood in risk estimation: A matter of balance in UK health and safety risk assessment practice. *Safety Science*, 43(5-6), 345–353. DOI: 10.1016/j.ssci.2005.07.003

KEY TERMS AND DEFINITIONS

Environmental Hazards: Variables that pose a threat to the natural balance and functionality of environmental systems, as well as risks to human health and well-being resulting from alterations or declines in environmental systems.

Environmental Risk Assessment: A process for estimating the likelihood or probability and the severity of an adverse outcome or event due to pressures or changes in environmental conditions resulting from natural or human activities.

Risk Mitigation: Efforts to reduce environmental impacts and conserve natural, technological and human and resources.

Risk Severity: The consequences caused by the environmental hazard to people and/or infrastructure.

Safety Management System (SMS): A comprehensive system which involves identifying, evaluating, and addressing hazards or risks.

Chapter 11
Sustainability Reporting on Istanbul Airport:
Analyzing Risks and Best Practices

Seda Ceken
https://orcid.org/0000-0002-5870-2246
Istanbul University, Turkey

EXECUTIVE SUMMARY

Sustainability practices at airports encompass a spectrum of environmental impacts stemming from airport operations and assets, as well as digital, social, and economic factors. The significance of sustainability practices, particularly within airport operations, is underscored by the intrinsic connection between sustainability and aviation. This significance arises from both international regulations and the demands of investors and stakeholders within the industry. This study employed a longitudinal case study approach to examine Istanbul Airport in Turkiye. The study aims to examine the quantity and quality of sustainability reporting by the Istanbul Airport through its sustainability report. It uses content analysis to examine the use of the Global Reporting Initiative (GRI) standards, and United Nations (UN) Sustainable Development (SD) goals. Furthermore, GRI reporting principles were used as the basis for the analysis of the quality of the sustainability report in the research. The findings were reported and discussed.

INTRODUCTION

The commercial air transportation sector has experienced remarkable growth in recent years and is expected to continue to do so in the future. Estimates show that the value of the sector will increase from $195.84 billion in 2023 to $248.11 billion

DOI: 10.4018/979-8-3693-2675-6.ch011

in 2024, with a compound annual growth rate (CAGR) of 26.7% (thebusinessresearchcompany.com, 2024). Furthermore, the sector is expected to grow strongly in the coming years, with the sector value expected to reach $308.24 billion by 2028, exhibiting a CAGR of 5.6%. This expected growth is attributed to several factors, including the increasing importance of sustainable aviation practices, the emergence of urban air mobility initiatives, strengthening global connectivity, prioritization of health and safety measures, and increased investments from governments (The Business Research Company, 2024). According to IATA Global Air Travel Demand data, total air traffic in 2023 increased by 36.9% compared to 2022, international traffic increased by 41.6% compared to 2022, and domestic traffic increased by 30.4% compared to the previous year. Although the strong post-pandemic (COVID-19) recovery has continued into 2023, governments need to take a strategic approach to maximize the benefits of air travel in a post-pandemic world (IATA, 2024). In the report titled 'Airport Environmental Sustainability' published by IATA (International Air Transport Association) in 2022, it was stated that there were decreases in carbon emission intensity and improvements in aircraft and engines in the aviation industry. As examples of these improvements, each new generation of aircraft has achieved double-digit fuel efficiency compared to the previous one, and CO_2 production per seat on aircraft has decreased (IATA, 2022). IATA members aim to achieve net zero carbon by 2050. Achieving the determined sustainability targets will be possible with supportive government policies and cooperation with the aviation industry (IATA, 2022). This means providing cost-effective infrastructure to meet demand, promoting the production of Sustainable Aviation Fuel (SAF) to achieve the target of net zero carbon emissions by 2050, and adopting regulations that provide a clear cost advantage. Completing the recovery should not be an excuse for governments to forget aviation's critical role in improving the well-being of people and businesses around the world. Rapid growth affects airport stakeholders with their economic, social, and environmental dimensions (Koc & Durmaz, 2015). Rapid growth negatively affects the environment, increases energy and fuel consumption, leads to the emission of greenhouse gases that cause climate change, the generation of significant amounts of solid and water waste, and increased air and noise pollution (Burleson & Maurice, 2003; Koc & Durmaz, 2015; Paraschi & Poulaki, 2021). When rapidly growing airports cannot develop their infrastructure at the same pace, they may encounter problems such as flight delays, incorrect baggage delivery, low service quality, and customer dissatisfaction. Due to these socio-economic and environmental impacts, airports around the world are increasingly managed within the framework of sustainable development principles and take measures as a result of pressure from various stakeholders (Koc & Durmaz, 2015).

The importance of sustainability practices in airport operations is emphasized due to the direct link between sustainability and aviation. This importance stems from both international regulations and the demands of investors and stakeholders within the sector. Although national and international regulations emphasize sustainability, they often do not provide clear guidance on preferred practices due to commercial concerns. Therefore, airport operators and users around the world adopt various sustainability approaches. Consequently, the implementation of sustainability initiatives often requires significant initial investments, and the return on investment may be delayed. Therefore, information obtained from sustainability practices adopted by other countries and airports is of great importance (Aygun et al., 2023). The research primarily focused on the concept of sustainability. In the content of the section, new contents added to the concept of sustainability in aviation are discussed. Current sustainability strategies and projects were explained with examples. The main purpose of the research is to see the current functioning of sustainability practices and to encourage and develop their implementation. For this reason, a case study was conducted in which Istanbul Airport was selected as the sample group.

SUSTAINABILITY AT AIRPORTS: DEFINITION AND PRINCIPLES

The concept of sustainability came to the fore in the 1980s when growth-oriented economic models reached their limits. It was first used by the International Union for Conservation of Nature (IUCN) to protect natural resources. This concept became influential worldwide with the World Commission on Environment and Development. The definition of sustainability included in the Brundtland Report (1987), prepared under the leadership of former Norwegian Prime Minister Gro Harlem Brundtland, was widely accepted by the scientific community. The report defined sustainability and sustainable development as follows: "Sustainable development is the achievement of development to meet daily needs without compromising the capacity of nature to respond to the needs of future generations" (Brundtland, 1987). Various versions of sustainability were defined in the 1990s: broad and narrow, strong and weak, big S and small s sustainability. Therefore, in addition to a wide range of sustainable development projects, different technical meanings have found a place in the literature. 1992 was a critical year in terms of putting the concept of sustainability into practice. At the 1992 Rio Conference, organized by the United Nations and attended by 178 government representatives, many heads of state, and more than 1,000 NGOs, civil society, and campaign groups, important issues for the sustainability and development period were brought to the agenda (Scoones, 2007).

The concept of sustainability consists of three closely intertwined components: ecological, social, and economic. A new model for measuring sustainability called *"Triple Bottom Line"* (TBL) was proposed by John Elkington in the 1990s. According to this model, the success of a business depends on taking into account the society, environment, and regional and national impacts of the activities of the organization in which that business is carried out. The three basic measures of TBL are as follows: economic line, social line, and environmental line (Elkington, 1997). Although sustainability is primarily a determinant of environmental policies, it also covers economic and social development. Economic sustainability aims to change today's lifestyle, which threatens the quality of life, and to increase energy efficiency in production and consumption. Environmental sustainability includes efforts to protect natural resources and recycle waste. Social sustainability aims to reduce poverty and support cultural diversity. Therefore, environmental factors (air, water, and soil pollution) and social factors (health, education, and social services) should be taken into account when achieving sustainable economic development (Rodoplu & Gursel, 2022).

The basic concepts of development policies in the aviation sector are expressed as follows (Budd et al., 2013):

- Consumption of natural resources should be done in a way that meets the needs of future generations. It should not exceed the rate of use of renewable resources, such as biofuels, and the rate of use of renewable energy sources, non-renewable sources, such as petroleum fuels, should not exceed the rate of development of their substitutes (e.g. biofuels).
- The growth of the aviation industry should support a livable environment for future generations. To support this, pollutant emission rates should not exceed the absorptive capacity of the environment and the exposure to aircraft noise (the noise levels perceived by the population and the frequency of noise annoyance or arousal events).

ENVIRONMENTAL RISKS AND IMPACTS OF AIRPORTS

Environmental sustainability for airports should be evaluated when planning space and care should be taken to protect the existing infrastructure. Efficient utilization of new investments, particularly in the transformation of airports into eco-friendly facilities, can be achieved through the adoption of net zero carbon standards in infrastructure construction and airport renovation. Sustainability activities should therefore prioritize how to reduce the overall carbon footprint in the aviation sector (IATA, 2022).

Concerns about climate change are increasing worldwide. Sea level rise, temperature changes, weather, wind and storms can pose serious risks to airport operations. Approximately 70% of flight delays each year are due to bad weather conditions, and this rate is expected to increase in the future. In order to prevent such problems, both consumers and investors need to increase their awareness of social and environmental issues. The negativities experienced have led to an increase in net zero carbon emissions and emission reduction plans around the world (Learmonth, 2020).

The main reasons affecting the environmental performance of airports are as follows:

Emissions: Prominent emission sources at airports are vehicles operating both on land and in the air, ground support equipment, and electricity generation facilities. Ground-based airport greenhouse gas emissions come from gasoline and diesel fuel used for airport vehicles and ground support equipment (GSE), fossil fuel for electricity and heating, jet fuel for auxiliary power units (APUs) that power aircraft at airport gates, and other sources (Federal Aviation Administration, 2024). The reason airports reduce this is to reduce or eliminate greenhouse gases and reduce airport energy bills and operating costs. Airports can begin to reduce the amount of greenhouse gases coming from airport sources by estimating them (Federal Aviation Administration, 2024). Airport emissions fall into three categories: emissions from sources owned or controlled by the airport (Category 1), indirect emissions from purchased energy consumption (Category 2), and indirect emissions that the airport cannot control but can influence (Category 3). Some airports, such as San Francisco International Airport and Dallas-Fort Worth Airport, have significantly reduced their greenhouse gas emissions and achieved carbon neutrality targets. Monitoring and reducing emissions produced at the airport is an important responsibility for all airport authorities in order to comply with worldwide standards and reduce the carbon footprint (Dimitriou & Karagkouni, 2022a; Dimitriou & Karagkouni, 2022b; Federal Aviation Administration, 2024).

Noise: Aircraft noise is one of the most important problems affecting the airport interior and surroundings. The generation of aircraft noise is related to activities such as takeoff, landing, and movement of the aircraft (Sahrir et al., 2014). The first of two key European regulators for managing the impact of aircraft noise around airports is the Environmental Noise Directive (European Aviation Safety Agency, 2024). The Environmental Noise Directive (European Aviation Safety Agency, 2024) is the primary EU legislation aimed at identifying noise pollution levels, assessing their health impacts at individual residences, disseminating information to the public, mitigating and preventing environmental noise, and preserving noise quality in areas with favorable conditions (European Commission, 2024). The second is the Balanced Approach Regulation, which determines airport noise management elements (European Aviation Safety Agency, 2024). The European Aviation Safety Agency (EASA) undertakes several roles for these regulations. The first is to verify and publish aircraft noise and performance data used in models to calculate noise limits at the airport and evaluate the noise impact on the environment (European Aviation Safety Agency, 2024). The second is to collect noise certification documents from aircraft operating at European airports with a maximum take-off weight of more than 34,000 kg or with 19 or more passenger seats (European Aviation Safety Agency, 2022). Therefore, EASA launched the Aircraft Noise and Performance (ANP) database and Environment Portal (European Aviation Safety Agency, 2022), through which collaborating stakeholders can send and share information (European Aviation Safety Agency, 2024). To manage noise at airports: adoption of new aircraft technologies and designs that reduce the degree of noise generated, restricting the operation of certain aircraft that produce more noise, implementation of land use planning and management as well as operational improvement at the airport, and redistribution of noise through management of runways (Chourasia, 2021).

Energy Management: The majority of energy use in airports is based on heating, ventilation, air conditioning, and lighting. In addition, the aviation industry is completely dependent on liquid fuels for energy resources. Sources that are not completely safe, such as wind and solar energy, are not suitable for sustainable use. Although wind and solar energy are environmentally friendly, they may encounter various risks during installation and operation processes; for example, collisions with birds and environmental impacts. However, aviation is increasingly choosing sustainable alternative fuels for environmentally responsible mobility with renewable energy (ICAO, 2012). The energy used in airports is a significant source of CO_2 emissions, both on-site and externally sourced. Some recommended strategies to achieve energy efficiency include (IATA, 2022):

- Increasing transition activities to renewable energy sources (e.g. solar, wind, biomass, geothermal, hydroelectric) at airports,
- Adopting more efficient technologies to replace lighting and heating, ventilation, and air conditioning (HVAC) systems that are no longer in use,

- Arrangement of stairs, conveyor motors, and lighting systems that will automatically close when not in use,
- Solar energy, geothermal, displacement ventilation, etc. Using alternative heating and ventilation methods such as these can significantly reduce environmental impact and improve energy efficiency in buildings.
- Use of skylights and natural ventilation to save energy.

Water Management: In the context of sustainability, airports are paying more attention to water management in line with environmental plans and strategies. This is because aviation operations require large amounts of water. However, excessive water consumption also results in the generation of large amounts of wastewater. Wastewater containing pollutants poses a danger to both the surface and the ground. Airlines that handle passenger operations on the land side of airports cooperate with ground-handling companies and airport authorities. In addition, some air cargo operations are carried out in cargo terminals located on the land side of the airport. Many airports around the world also have hotels on the land side. Such stakeholders provide water consumption through the following factors: passengers, greeters, airport personnel, vehicle washing, toilet flushing, personal hygiene (e.g. hand washing and showers provided for passengers and airport personnel), cooking and beverage provision, airport landscaping, lawn and plant irrigation (Baxter et al., 2018). To manage water consumption, some airports follow the following methods (Dimitriou et al., 2021):

- Reducing water consumption in the airport area,
- Reusing water after treatment (wastewater and sewage treatment plants) in toilets or for irrigation purposes,
- Using rainwater to flush toilets,
- Protecting groundwater resources from pollution,
- Monitoring water consumption at the airport,
- Conducting surface and groundwater quality monitoring activities.

Waste Management: The waste generated by airport operations is significant and they need to embrace the 'polluter pays' principle. The amount of waste at airports depends on the number of passengers and aircraft. The sources of waste generated are solid urban waste, non-hazardous waste, and special hazardous waste produced in terminals or by airlines and other organizations operating at the airport. The amount of waste generated is determined by the number of passengers and aircraft operating at the airport. For a successful waste management process, separation of solid and liquid waste, hazardous and non-hazardous waste, waste reduction methods for the resulting garbage, and activities that increase reuse, recycling, and reprocessing are required (Dimitriou & Karagkouni, 2022b). To address issues such as land use, land density, and waste management, airport structures need to be aligned with appropriate planning strategies. Waste production should be reduced by using existing resources effectively, waste/sewage treatment plants need to be established, and planning and coordination need to be made to protect water resources and aquatic life. It is also essential to implement rainwater collection, systems harvesting systems, and groundwater recharge systems (Chourasiao et al., 2019).

According to the European Aviation Environment Report 2022, in 2020 the European Aviation Safety Agency (EASA) launched several portals to facilitate the sharing of aircraft noise certificates and performance data. In the same year, around half of operations in Europe were carried out with aircraft that met noise standards, and the Airport Carbon Accreditation Scheme added new levels to support airports to achieve net zero CO_2 emissions. The European Green Deal's Zero Pollution Action Plan aims to decrease the number of people impacted by transport noise by 30% and reduce early deaths due to air pollution by 55% (European Environment Report, 2022).

As a specialized agency of the United Nations, ICAO, and its member countries work to reduce greenhouse gas emissions from international aviationIn this context, ICAO collaborates closely with the United Nations Framework Convention on Climate Change (UNFCCC) and other UN agencies on environmental issues like aircraft noise and local air quality emissions (ICAO, 2012). ICAO reports international civil aviation CO_2 emissions to the UNFCCC, performs meteorological measurements with the World Meteorological Organization (WMO), partners with the International Maritime Organization (IMO) on greenhouse gas reduction, and works with the World Health Organization (WHO) on local air quality and noise concerns (ICAO, 2012).

ASSESSING ECONOMIC IMPLICATIONS OF SUSTAINABLE PRACTICES IN AIRPORT OPERATIONS

The goals of airport sustainability economic practices include providing sufficient profitability for investors, creating a high level of passenger satisfaction that will contribute to the national economy, and creating an economically sustainable operational environment. Airports are subject to various risks in terms of economic sustainability. These include fluctuations in travel demand, high operating costs, competitive pressures, increasing environmental regulations, technological changes, and political uncertainties. To mitigate these risks, airport operators need to develop strategies such as diversification, flexibility, cost-saving measures, and enhancing environmental sustainability efforts. The financial situation of airports in Europe has been degraded by the COVID-19 pandemic and is typically cost-intensive and revenue-poor. To increase regional economic potential, effective air transport services and infrastructure are essential. Air transport is closely linked to environmental and digitalization policies. The development of clean fuel infrastructure requires additional investment and re-evaluation of business models. Airports play a critical role in economic development, increasing productivity and reducing unemployment in their regions. They also support international trade, cultural exchange, education and tourism. However, airport expansion can also cause environmental and social challenges (Dimitriou & Karagkouni, 2022a).

According to ACI Europe's 2024 report, airports suffered significant revenue losses between 2020 and 2022 and received financial aid from governments. The pressure of high inflation on labor and public services was not reflected in user fees. Compared to before the pandemic, airport fees have only slightly increased. Rising debts and insufficient revenues have led to reduced airport investment, creating an investment gap in Europe. This makes it difficult for airports to provide the necessary financing for decarbonization, digitalization and capacity expansion. For this reason, airports aim to increase traffic volumes to ensure their financial sustainability, but this approach does not seem sustainable due to the climate crisis and capacity growth. The financial sustainability of airports in Europe should be made independent of volume growth, and this can be achieved by increasing unit revenues (ACI Europe Airport Industry Manifesto, 2024).

Airports can reduce greenhouse gas emissions and operating costs by implementing low-cost energy efficiency measures, such as improving building insulation. Other steps include purchasing renewable energy, installing renewable energy systems suitable for the airport, reducing energy consumption, and purchasing low- or zero-emission vehicles. State and federal incentives are available for energy efficiency measures, and the Federal Aviation Administration provides grants for certain emissions reduction projects (Federal Aviation Administration, 2024). Airports can create employment and contribute to the economy nationally. Airports that grow in scale reduce economic risk by employing at airports ethnics, women, individuals with certain disabilities, and minorities to provide a sustainable economic strategy. In addition, by including supply chain organizations at airports, it stimulates the local economy and reduces the carbon footprint caused by transportation from outside the region. Tourism associations, destination management companies, chambers of commerce, etc. contribute to economic sustainability. It can promote tourism in destinations by partnering with. Another strategy to reduce risk is to increase the availability of green financing (Desharnais, 2021). It may be a good time for airports to explore various options such as sustainability-linked bonds and loans for specific projects and long-term investments. Social bonds improve relations with a specific group, and green bonds contribute to decarbonization efforts or improve the resilience of the airport (Desharnais, 2021).

SOCIAL RISKS AND IMPACTS OF AIRPORTS

There is a consensus that being socially responsible in today's business environment goes beyond mere compliance with relevant legislation, involving continuous investment in human capital, environmental conservation, and relationships with stakeholders. However, how organizations translate these concepts into practice varies depending on the legal framework across countries, core competencies, available resources, stakeholders' interests, and cultural traditions of the business location (Jordão, 2009). Social dimensions encompass concepts such as education, equality, access to social resources, health, well-being, and quality of life. The Global Reporting Initiatives (GRI) have formulated a set of variables to gauge social impact and have disseminated guidelines based on these variables. These variables include employment practices, workforce management, employee welfare, occupational safety, provision of medical facilities, education and training initiatives, community engagement, ethical business conduct, human rights advocacy, engagement with residents, supplier/vendor management, public policy engagement, and health and safety standards, as well as customer relations (Chourasia et al., 2019). The social sustainability risks at airports can arise from various factors, including violations of workers' rights, issues in interacting with local communities, inadequate management of environmental impacts, employment practices, and societal isolation. These risks necessitate careful management by airport operators and stakeholders, employing appropriate policies and practices for mitigation. Social sustainability in airport operations involves ensuring employee development and supporting local communities by reducing noise disturbance to a minimum. Airports play a beneficial role in society's operational processes to increase social sustainability (Sreenath et al., 2021). In the context of social sustainability, airports must also ensure passenger health and safety (Desharnais, 2021). An example of this is to review food and beverage offerings and make room for healthy alternatives. To maintain social sustainability, the health, safety, and welfare measures provided for passengers must also be implemented for employees. The human resources policies adopted for airports include flexible and innovative working conditions, increasing the level of interaction with employees (Desharnais, 2021). A strong sense of community emerges in a work environment where the existing workforce feels safe and valued. In addition, strengthening airports' ties with local communities is also a part of social sustainability. To strengthen this bond, airports can follow ways such as sharing issues affecting the surrounding population, explaining the benefits of the airport, and discussing the consequences of future developments (Desharnais, 2021). The value attributed to airport employees plays a significant role in their contribution to social sustainability. Malaysia Airport, a prominent supporter in this regard, employs panel doctors and provides medical treatment to its workforce. Additionally, they offer various support programs such as development programs, leadership courses, managerial skill enhancement, and learning courses. Moreover, ensuring equal treatment of employees irrespective of race, gender, physical ability, or religion is an integral aspect of social sustainability (Sreenath et al., 2021). For instance, Aena, the Spanish airport operator, has incorporated principles of gender equality and non-discrimination into the company's collective agreement, ensuring their integration into all processes and actions. This initiative has led to a notable increase in the presence of women within Aena, from 32% to 37%. Furthermore, women now hold 45% of executive, middle management, and graduate positions within the organization. Aena's Senior Management Committee, comprising nine members, includes four women, constituting 44% of its composition. Similarly, the Extended Management Committee, consisting of 25 members, includes 10 women, representing 40% of its members. Aena aims to achieve a 40% female representation rate on its Board of Directors in the near future (ACI Europe Airport Industry Manifesto, 2024).

TECHNOLOGICAL AND INNOVATIVE SOLUTIONS IN AIRPORTS

In future technologies, research continues on new generation aircraft and engines for a zero-carbon solution for long-term sustainability in commercial aviation. Although electric aircraft are included in this research, these aircraft types will focus on electric vertical take-off and landing aircraft with limited range in small areas (IATA, 2022). For the use of these aircraft, airports need to improve their existing electrical networks. The utilization of hydrogen-powered propulsion systems for aircraft holds significant promise as a long-term solution for reducing aviation's CO_2 emissions. However, the integration of this technology faces numerous challenges that must be addressed before it can make a substantial impact. To enable widespread adoption, substantial investments in new aircraft fleets, infrastructure, and renewable energy sources are imperative for the production, liquefaction, and distribution of green hydrogen. The application of smart devices in airports is increasing day by day. The increasing number of passengers has led especially busy airports to digital transformation. Digital transformation aims to support economic growth and improve passenger experience (Sreenath et al., 2021). Using technologies developed to reduce the risks that may arise with technological transformation, computer-based systems that monitor, visualize, and respond to social, economic, and environmental problems of airports can be developed. Current digital transformation technologies in airports include augmented reality, big data analytics, blockchain technology, cloud services, cognitive computing, and the Internet of Things (IoT) (Brida et al., 2016; Sreenath et al., 2021). The need to continue sustainability activities in airport and flight operations creates the need for the future air transportation sector to be more customer-oriented, use time and cost-effectively, and be safer and environmentally sustainable than the current situation. For the aviation industry, digital technology and high levels of automation require the adoption of Cyber-Physical Systems (CPS) for increased air capacity and environmental sustainability (Sabatini & Gardi, 2023).

In risk strategies against technological transformation, the installation of Digital IoT beacons can facilitate passengers' navigation (Sreenath et al., 2021). Information such as flight delays, shuttle services, and queues at counters can be learned through Bluetooth geolocation (Sreenath et al., 2021). In addition, the use of IoT-enabled RFID tag technology facilitates the luggage and cargo transportation process and reduces the risk of bag loss (Halpern et al., 2021). Within the scope of risk strategies in technological transformation, digital IoT beacons can make it easier for passengers to find their way around the airport. Information about flight delays, service information, and counter queues can be obtained with Bluetooth geolocation technology. IoT-supported RFID tag technology facilitates baggage and cargo transportation and reduces the risk of loss. Airports such as London, Tokyo, and Singapore have initiated projects such as driverless vehicles and automated baggage handling systems. The guide and security robot named Reborg-Z, which works as a passenger assistant at Fuji Shizuoka Airport in Japan, is an example of this. A pilot project is being carried out at Tokyo Airport to monitor aircraft movements on the runway with digital infrared cameras (Sreenath et al., 2021). At Incheon Airport, robots provide passengers with guidance services at their departure gates. One of the digital transformations at Heathrow Airport in the UK is the introduction of automatic baggage drop machines and driverless baggage vehicles in the passenger terminal. This project serves to reduce queues at different toll booths and make passenger movements smoother and faster (Sreenath et al., 2021). Another example is robotic system trials at airports for loading passenger bags into trash bins to be transferred to the plane. Looking at this example in the context of sustainability, the Mototok green pushback tractor is one of the vehicles used at Madrid and Barcelona airports to push A320 family aircraft out of the gate and onto the taxiway. This device is electric and eliminates $CO2$ in operation. It can push back 28 planes before needing reloading. In addition, recent research has yielded findings on unmanned vehicles and Advanced Air Mobility (AAM), unveiling new prototype aircraft through their introduction and testing.Most of these are electric rotor-driven, electric vertical takeoff, and landing (eVTOL) aircraft (ICAO, 2023). Finally, it is important to strengthen digital infrastructure for preparedness and response to crises. Emergency management systems and communications platforms can help respond more effectively to events such as natural disasters or security breaches.

SUSTAINABILITY STRATEGIES IN AIRPORTS

Sustainability strategies at airports encompass digital, social, and economic factors as well as environmental impacts from airport operations and assets. The Airports Council International (ACI) established the Airport Carbon Accreditation Program to achieve the goal of net zero carbon emissions by 2050. In line with this goal, many environmentally friendly practices and technologies have been integrated into airport operations. Ground support equipment and vehicles have been upgraded with smart technologies, and energy production is based on wind and solar technologies. New technology aircraft provide greater fuel economy compared to older models. Energy efficiency has been increased in offices and other airport buildings through the implementation of smart building technologies. Energy efficiency has improved thanks to technological advances in baggage handling and lighting systems. Initiatives have been made to recover energy from waste materials (Alameeri et al., 2017).

RESEARCH METHOD

This study employed a longitudinal case study approach to examine Istanbul Airport in Turkey. The study aims to assess both the extent and the quality of sustainability reporting conducted by Istanbul Airport as documented in its sustainability reports. It uses content analysis to examine the use of the Global Reporting Initiative (GRI) standards (GRI, 2021), and United Nations (UN) Sustainable Development (SD) goals (UN SD, 2023). In qualitative research, non-numerical data are analyzed with the content analysis technique. While performing content analysis, the basis is to determine the codes and themes and to make inferences within the scope of the code-theme list of the data (Sigri, 2018). The coding was completed in MAXQDA22 using GRI standards (GRI, 2021), and United Nations Sustainability Development Goals that have been identified as most significant of the air transport industry.

In this study, a longitudinal study including the 2021-2022 annual sustainability report (https://www.istairport.com/en/corporate/sustainability/?locale=en) of Istanbul Airport was completed. Document analysis using reports includes the analysis of written materials containing information about the facts and phenomena targeted to be investigated (Yildirim & Simsek, 2021). in the qualitative research method. The benefits of this analysis are reaching subjects that cannot be easily reached, lack of reactivity, ease of long-term analysis, access to a large sample, providing individuality and originality, providing relatively low cost, and the fact that the organized documents are published by experts (Yildirim & Simsek, 2021). The reason why these years were taken as the basis for the research is that it is the most comprehensive sustainability report for Istanbul Airport among the sustainability reports that have been published since 2016. It is the most up-to-date report published as of April 2024, when the research was conducted. Istanbul Airport, which started its first operations in 2018, is one of the largest airports in Europe and the world. Istanbul Airport serves its passengers with its main terminal building of 1 million 400 thousand square meters. Four years after it entered service, it hosted more than 176 million passengers in total. More than one million two hundred thousand flights have taken place at Istanbul Airport, which provides flights to 265 destinations and 129 countries in the world, since its opening. The airport has a wide area not only in terms of flight operations but also for many related civil aviation activities and also offers a suitable settlement and activity opportunity for many local and foreign actors of the sector. According to OAG data, Istanbul Airport ranks 5th in the Top 10 Busiest Global Airports by Seats with 4,007,397 seats in 2023. Istanbul Airport is an international airport and the leading airline in terms of capacity measurement is the Turkish Airlines Company, with a capacity of 79.0%. The company's superiority is 98.9% on domestic flights, which is as close to a monopoly as any airline can achieve. At Istanbul Airport, domestic airlines' capacity is 80.1% and foreign airlines capacity is 19.9% (Figure 1) (CAPA, 2023).

Figure 1. Market share of the airlines operating at the Istanbul Airport (CAPA, 2023)

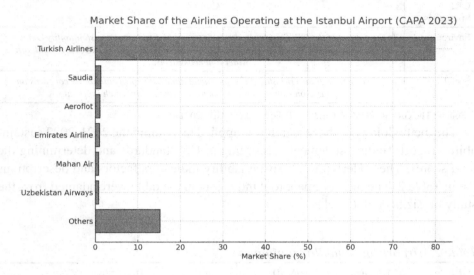

The GRI framework was adopted for this study with The Sustainable Development Goals (SDGs). Adopted by the United Nations in 2015, the Sustainable Development Goals (SDGs) aim to eliminate poverty, safeguard the environment, and ensure global peace and prosperity by 2030. These 17 interlinked goals highlight the importance of balancing social, economic, and environmental sustainability. Nations have pledged to advance particularly in critical areas such as eliminating discrimination against women and girls. Achieving the SDGs requires a collaborative effort, leveraging creativity, knowledge, technology, and financial resources from all societal sectors (UNDP, 2024). GRI Standards cover various topics on sustainability. These issues include relevant standards in economic, environmental, and social dimensions (Table 1), from anti-corruption to water and presevertion biodiversity, occupational health, and safety. Organizations choose among these goals to report their significant impacts (GRI, 2021):

Table 1. GRI Standards

GRI Standards	Content
Economic	*In the context of the GRI Standards, the economic dimension of sustainability concerns an organization's impacts on the economic conditions of its stakeholders, and on economic systems at local, national, and global levels. It does not focus on the financial condition of an organization.*

continued on following page

Table 1. Continued

GRI Standards	Content
Enviromental	*In the context of the GRI Standards, the environmental dimension of sustainability concerns an organization's impacts on living and non-living natural systems, including land, air, water and ecosystems.*
Social	*In the context of the GRI Standards, the social dimension of sustainability concerns an organization's impacts on the social systems within which it operates.*

Source: The GRI Standards A Guide for Policy Makers (GRI, 2021)

The methodology of the research was applied by reading the 2021-2022 sustainability report, finding statements according to UN standards and determining the total scores. The underlying UN sustainability indicators factors and descriptions are in Table 2. The measurement tool indicators in the table were adapted from the study of Zizka et al. (2021):

Table 2. Airport sustainability initiatives

GRI Standards	UN Goal Number	UN SD	Description
Social	5	Gender Equality	Gender hiring initiatives or projects Pay parity
Environmental	7	Affordable and Clean Energy	Renewable energy – solar, wind, geothermal Infrastructure improvements for energy projects Technology projects energy tracking –usage, reduction
Economic	8	Decent Work and Economic Growth	Employee engagement in projects on and off airport Benefits and Compensation Employee training and development
Economic	9	Industry Innovation and Infrastructure	Innovative technology investment, Safety enhancements – airside and landside Customer experience – innovative improvements – signage, wayfinding, efficiency in arrival/departure
Social	10	Reduced Inequalities	Diversity in vendors and contractors, Local culture understanding – exhibits, local business opportunities Projects that enhance disabled traveler experience
Environmental	12	Responsible Consumption and Production	Efficiency in aircraft ground handling equipment, parking garages, local transit Recycling programs Evidence of exceedance of environmental regulatory requirements in projects – LEED certification, wetlands mitigation
Environmental	13	Climate Action	Targeted carbon emissions reductions - low emissions vehicles, ATC, aircraft flow Investment in alternative fuels

Reference: Zizka et al. (2021)

BACKGROUND

Reporting, for the first time, has received significant academic and managerial attention in the social and environmental aspects of organizations. In this initial interest, US and Western European companies resorted to social reporting and accounting practices defined as *"identifying, measuring, monitoring and reporting the social and economic effects of an event"* (Kolk, 2005). Sectors such as tourism, transportation, mining, and energy have been the subject of sustainability reporting studies due to their sensitivity to the environment and human life (Agudelo, 2020; Jenkins & Yakovleva, 2006; Stevenson & Marintseva, 2019; Font & Lynes, 2018). The rapid growth of the airline sector in passenger and cargo transportation raises sustainability concerns by increasing hazardous waste and noise pollution (Karaman et.al., 2018). Due to the international nature of the sector, these negative impacts are not confined to the relevant countries but also affect other nations, contributing to global climate change (Karaman et al.,2018). The Airport Cooperative Research Program (ACRP) defines airport sustainability as *"practices that ensure the protection of the environment, including the conservation of natural resources"*. This definition of sustainability refers not only to progress in growing the economy and employment but also to stakeholders in airport management and the public (ACRP Report, 2012). Airports have been reporting on sustainability since the early 2000s to create an environmentally friendly corporate profile and provide a safe working environment for employees (Jordao, 2009). Researchers such as Jordao (2009), Koc and Durmaz (2015), and Karagiannis et al. (2019) have evaluated the sustainability activities and performances of airports according to GRI standards. These studies emphasize that airports need to increase their sustainability performance and provide more transparency in their reporting. In addition, Zizka et al. (2021) examined the sustainability reporting of Dublin Airport and proposed a disclosure model.

Although the literature on sustainability reporting in the airport sector is supported by some research, the increasing sector size and responsibility towards stakeholders show that this should be increased. In line with these references, the research will answer these questions:

RQ1: What is the quantity of Istanbul Airport's sustainability disclosures?
RQ2: What is the quality of Istanbul Airport's sustainability disclosures?

RESULTS

A total of 424 coding units were coded in the Istanbul Airport Sustainability 2022 report. Sentences and paragraphs (containing 4-5 sentences) that matched the relevant factor were used while coding. In these codes, 88 were found to be social, 154 environmental, and 182 economic. Details are given in Table 3, with SDG 8 and SDG 9 (Economic SDGs) having the highest quantity among UN indicators (RQ1):

Table 3. Istanbul airport sustainability report quantity

Categories	UN Sustainability Goals	Quantity	Total
Social	5- Gender Equality	16	88
	10- Reduced Inequalities	72	
Economic	8- Decent Work and Economic Growth	87	182
	9- Industry Innovation and Infrastructure	95	
Environmental	7- Affordable and Clean Energy	42	154
	12- Responsible Consumption and Production	72	
	13- Climate Action	40	

GRI reporting principles were used as the basis for the analysis of the quality of the sustainability report in the research. The GRI reporting principles for defining the report quality are categorized: as *reliability, timeliness, accuracy, balance, clarity,* and *comparability* (Table 4) (RQ2). The *accuracy* of qualitative information relates to the level of detail of the data and the consistency of the available evidence (GRI, 2021). *Balance* is ensuring that negative and positive impacts are fairly represented in the reporting of information. *Clarity* is data being accessible, understandable, and usable. *Comparability* is the analysis of changes in the impacts of institutions over time and the compilation and reporting of these impacts relative to the impacts of other organizations. *Timeliness* principle refers to how regularly and how soon after the reporting period the information is published (GRI, 2021). Reliability is determining the accuracy of the data and explaining its scope with data sources (GRI, 2021). The content analysis method was used to determine the frequencies in the table. In this method, the texts were first carefully examined according to established criteria. Then, the number of times each criterion was met was manually counted and these numbers were recorded in the table. This process enabled accurate calculation of frequencies.

Table 4. Istanbul airport sustainability report quality

GRI Standards Quality of Report	Social	Economic	Environmental	Total
Accuracy	12	12	18	42
Reliability	11	20	21	52
Balance	0	0	0	0
Comparability	6	1	5	12
Clarity	15	5	6	26
Timeliness	1	2	0	3

DISCUSSION

As a result of the research findings, a longitudinal picture of Istanbul Airport's current sustainability activities and targets was obtained. Because of the findings, it was observed that, in terms of quantity, the sustainability activities of Istanbul Airport were reported mostly in the economic dimension according to GRI standards. This finding was similar to studies conducted for similar purposes (Karagiannis et al., 2018; Wan et al., 2020; Zizka et al., 2021). This result was followed by environmental and social factors. Organizations, in most cases, make sustainability with financial criteria. In traditional decision-making, organizations consider only direct financial costs and benefits. In such cases, monetary consequences based on environmental and social impacts are ignored (Yuthas & Epstein, 2012).

Convenience at airports is also inextricably linked to economics. These are places that provide employment and revitalize national wealth. Therefore, they need to constantly increase their contribution, satisfy passengers, and meet the needs of employees. The economic importance of sustainability efforts in airlines is also reflected in the work of the relevant authorities. To improve the efficiency and cost-effectiveness of airport operations, ICAO developed the Airport Economics Manual (Doc 9562). This guide provides practical guidance to airport management to support sustainable development (ICAO, 2020).

Stakeholder theory suggests that when companies demonstrate high economic performance, they will face less urgent demands from their financial stakeholders. Additionally, higher growth potential increases a company's ability to incorporate sustainability issues into its strategies (Artiach et al., 2010). Rapidly growing companies are associated with social and environmental sustainability to ensure economic sustainability (Artiach et al., 2010; Karaman et al., 2018; Kuzey & Uyar, 2017). Companies are advised to deeply integrate sustainability efforts into their business activities; this enhances reputation and improves economic performance (Schaltegger et al., 2012). Companies can share their sustainability efforts through various channels, such as corporate reports, websites, press releases, and GRI data-bases (Karaman et al., 2018). Linking sustainability efforts to key business metrics, such as customer satisfaction, corporate governance, employee engagement, and risk management, can maximize firm value by positively influencing stakeholder perceptions (Du et al., 2010). These findings highlight the importance of companies combining sustainability efforts with their economic performance. Additionally, it appears that companies can increase the value of their sustainability efforts by communicating effectively with stakeholders. This situation reveals that businesses need to adopt a holistic approach for their sustainability strategies to be successful.

CONCLUSION AND PRACTICAL IMPLICATIONS

The primary areas of emphasis within airport sustainability practices include the implementation of robust environmental management policies, the optimization of energy utilization for enhanced efficiency, effective waste management strategies, endeavors to mitigate carbon emissions, the establishment of sustainable transportation systems, and the adoption of smart building technologies. Throughout this process, challenges such as limited financing options, regulatory constraints, shortage of skilled personnel, and the nascent environmental awareness within society emerge as significant hurdles hindering the advancement of sustainability initiatives. Istanbul Airport has taken an important step in sustainability. These study findings provide a summary of these efforts. The airport's sustainability strategies reflect a comprehensive approach covering environmental, economic, and social dimensions. The report shows that Istanbul Airport acts not only as a transportation hub but also as a catalyst for raising sustainability standards. However, these efforts need to continue and be improved. In practical implications, green infrastructure development, energy efficiency investments, improving social participation and communication, training and development programs for employees, and sustainable supply chain management practices should be implemented for the continuation of sustainability and risk management in airports.

REFERENCES

ACI Europe Airport Industry Manifesto. (2024). *Airport Industry Manifesto for the Next EU Political Cycle 2024-2029.* ACI Europe. https://www.aci-europe.org/downloads/resources/ACI%20EUROPE%20MANIFESTO.pdf

Agudelo, M. A. L., Johannsdottir, L., & Davidsdottir, B. (2020). Drivers that motivate energy companies to be responsible. A systematic literature review of Corporate Social Responsibility in the energy sector. *Journal of Cleaner Production*, 247, 119094. DOI: 10.1016/j.jclepro.2019.119094

Alameeri, A., Ajmal, M. M., Hussain, M., & Helo, P. T. (2017). Sustainability practices in the aviation sector: A study of UAE-based airlines. *International Journal of Sustainable Society*, 9(2), 119–147. DOI: 10.1504/IJSSOC.2017.086818

Artiach, T., Lee, D., Nelson, D., & Walker, J. (2010). The determinants of corporate sustainability performance. *Accounting and Finance*, 50(1), 31–51. DOI: 10.1111/j.1467-629X.2009.00315.x

Aygun, S., Sagbas, M., & Erdogan, F. A. (2023). Bibliometric Analysis of Sustainability in Civil Aviation. *Journal of Aviation*, 7(3), 448–456. DOI: 10.30518/jav.1358871

Baxter, G., Srisaeng, P., & Wild, G. (2018). An assessment of sustainable airport water management: The case of Osaka's Kansai international airport. *Infrastructures*, 3(4), 54. DOI: 10.3390/infrastructures3040054

Brida, J. G., Moreno-Izquierdo, L., & Zapata-Aguirre, S. (2016). Customer perception of service quality: The role of Information and Communication Technologies (ICTs) at airport functional areas. *Tourism Management Perspectives*, 20, 209–216. DOI: 10.1016/j.tmp.2016.09.003

Brundtland, G.H. (1987) Our Common Future Report of the World Commission on Environment and Development. Geneva, UN-Dokument A/42/427.

Budd, L., Griggs, S., & Howarth, D. (2013). Sustainable aviation futures: Crises, contested realities and prospects for change. In *Sustainable aviation futures* (pp. 3–35). Emerald Group Publishing Limited. DOI: 10.1108/S2044-9941(2013)0000004013

Burleson, C., & Maurice, L. (2003). Aviation and the environment: challenges and opportunities. In *AIAA International Air and Space Symposium and Exposition: The Next 100 Years* (p. 2554). DOI: 10.2514/6.2003-2554

CAPA. (2023). *Airports: Istanbul closes in on rejoining the 100 million annual air passengers by city club.*https://centreforaviation.com/analysis/reports/airports -istanbul-closes-in-on-rejoining-the-100-million-annual-air-passengers-by-city -club-664318

Chourasia, A. S., Jha, K., & Dalei, N. N. (2021). Development and planning of sustainable airports. *Journal of Public Affairs*, 21(1), e2145. DOI: 10.1002/pa.2145

Desharnais. (2021). *Recovering Sustainably: Why and How Airports Can Initiate, Maintain, or Enhance Their Sustainability Commitments.* ACI World Insights. https:// blog.aci.aero/recovering-sustainably-why-and-how-airports-can-initiate-maintain -or-enhance-their-sustainability-commitments/

Dimitriou, D., & Karagkouni, A. (2022a). Airports' Sustainability Strategy: Evaluation Framework Upon Environmental Awareness. *Frontiers in Sustainability*, 3, 1–11. DOI: 10.3389/frsus.2022.880718

Dimitriou, D., & Karagkouni, A. (2022b). Assortment of airports' sustainability strategy: A comprehensiveness analysis framework. *Sustainability*, 14(7), 1–18. DOI: 10.3390/su14074217 PMID: 36090804

Dimitriou, D., Sartzetaki, M., & Kalenteridou, I. (2021). Dual-level evaluation framework for airport user satisfaction. *International Journal of Operations Research and Information Systems*, 12(1), 17–30. DOI: 10.4018/IJORIS.2021010102

Du, S., Bhattacharya, C. B., & Sen, S. (2010). Maximizing business returns to corporate social responsibility (CSR): The role of CSR communication. *International Journal of Management Reviews*, 12(1), 8–19. DOI: 10.1111/j.1468-2370.2009.00276.x

Elkington, J. (1997). The triple bottom line. *Environmental management: Readings and cases*, 2, 49-66.

European Aviation Safety Agency. (2022). *A Look into Historic and Future Scenarios of Air Traffic, Noise and Emissions.* European Aviation Environmental Report 2022. https://www.easa.europa.eu/en/light/topics/european-aviation-environmental -report-2022

European Aviation Safety Agency. (2024). *Balanced Approach Regulation.* EASA Pro. https://www.easa.europa.eu/en/domains/environment/policy-support-and -research/balanced-approach-regulation

European Commission. (2024). *Environmental Noise Directive.* Energy, Climate change, Environment. https://environment.ec.europa.eu/topics/noise/environmental -noise-directive_en

European Environment Agency. (2022). *European Aviation Environmental Report 2022: Sustainability crucial for long-term viability of the sector*. European Environment Agency Newsroom. https://www.eea.europa.eu/en/newsroom/news/european-aviation-environmental-report-2022

Federal Aviation Administration. (2024). *Working to Build a Net-Zero Sustainable Aviation System by 2050*. Federal Aviation Administration. https://www.faa.gov/sustainability

Font, X., & Lynes, J. (2018). Corporate social responsibility in tourism and hospitality. *Journal of Sustainable Tourism*, 26(7), 1027–1042. DOI: 10.1080/09669582.2018.1488856

GRI. (2021). *The GRI Standards A Guide For Policy Makers*. GRI Standards How Policymakers Can Drive Sustainability Reporting. https://www.globalreporting.org/news/news-center/how-policymakers-can-drive-sustainability-reporting/

Halpern, N., Budd, T., Suau-Sanchez, P., Bråthen, S., & Mwesiumo, D. (2021). Conceptualising airport digital maturity and dimensions of technological and organisational transformation. *Journal of Airport Management*, 15(2), 182–203. DOI: 10.69554/MZJB2664

IATA. (2022). *Airport Environmental Sustainability*. IATA. chrome-extension://efaid-nbmnnnibpcajpcglclefindmkaj/https://www.iata.org/contentassets/d1d4d535bf1c4ba695f43e9beff8294f/airport-environmental-sustainability-policy.pdf

IATA. (2024, April). *Passenger Demand Up 21.5% in February*. Pressroom. https://www.iata.org/en/pressroom/2024-releases/2024-04-04-01/#:~:text=Geneva%20%2D%20The%20International%20Air%20Transport,21.5%25%20compared%20to%20February%202023

ICAO. (2012). *Global Aviation and Our Sustainable Future*. ICAO Rio +20. https://www.icao.int/environmental-protection/Documents/Rio+20_booklet.pdf

ICAO. (2020). *Airport Economics Manual Doc 9562*. ICAO Economic Development. https://www.icao.int/publications/Documents/9562_cons_en.pdf

Jenkins, H., & Yakovleva, N. (2006). Corporate social responsibility in the mining industry: Exploring trends in social and environmental disclosure. *Journal of Cleaner Production*, 14(3-4), 271–284. DOI: 10.1016/j.jclepro.2004.10.004

Jordão, C. T. (2009). A sustainability overview of the best practices in the airport sector. Scientific papers of the University of Pardubice. Series D, Faculty of Economics and Administration. 15.

Karagiannis, I., Vouros, P., Skouloudis, A., & Evangelinos, K. (2019). Sustainability reporting, materiality, and accountability assessment in the airport industry. *Business Strategy and the Environment*, 28(7), 1370–1405. DOI: 10.1002/bse.2321

Karaman, A. S., Kilic, M., & Uyar, A. (2018). Sustainability reporting in the aviation industry: Worldwide evidence. *Sustainability Accounting. Management and Policy Journal*, 9(4), 362–391. DOI: 10.1108/SAMPJ-12-2017-0150

Koç, S., & Durmaz, V. (2015). Airport corporate sustainability: An analysis of indicators reported in the sustainability practices. *Procedia: Social and Behavioral Sciences*, 181, 158–170. DOI: 10.1016/j.sbspro.2015.04.877

Kolk, A. (2005). Sustainability reporting. *VBA Journal, 21*(3), 34-42.

Kuzey, C., & Uyar, A. (2017). Determinants of sustainability reporting and its impact on firm value: Evidence from the emerging market of Turkey. *Journal of Cleaner Production*, 143, 27–39. DOI: 10.1016/j.jclepro.2016.12.153

Learmonth, I. (2020). *Clean energy and infrastructure: Pathway to airport sustainability*. CEFC. https://www.cefc.com.au/media/402343/cefc-pathway-to-airport-sustainability.pdf

Paraschi, E. P., & Poulaki, I. (2021). An Overview on Environmental Management in Aviation. *Challenging Issues on Environment and Earth Science*, 7, 31–43. DOI: 10.9734/bpi/ciees/v7/11732D

Report, A. C. R. P. (2012). *2012 Annual Report Of Progress*. Airport Cooperative Research Program. https://onlinepubs.trb.org/onlinepubs/acrp/acrpannual2012.pdf

Rodoplu, H., & Gursel, S. (2022). Sustainability Practices in Airport. In Karakoc, T. H., Colpan, C. O., & Dalkiran, A. (Eds.), *New Frontiers in Sustainable Aviation. Sustainable Aviation* (pp. 191–201). Springer. DOI: 10.1007/978-3-030-80779-5_10

Sabatini, R., & Gardi, A. (2023). Sustainable Aviation: An Introduction. In Sabatini, R., & Gardi, A. (Eds.), *Sustainable Aviation Technology and Operations* (pp. 1–28). DOI: 10.1002/9781118932599.ch1

Sahrir, S., Bachok, S., & Osman, M. M. (2014). Environmental and health impacts of airport infrastructure upgrading: Kuala Lumpur International Airport 2. *Procedia: Social and Behavioral Sciences*, 153, 520–530. DOI: 10.1016/j.sbspro.2014.10.085

Schaltegger, S., Lüdeke-Freund, F., & Hansen, E. G. (2012). Business cases for sustainability: The role of business model innovation for corporate sustainability. *International Journal of Innovation and Sustainable Development*, 6(2), 95–119. DOI: 10.1504/IJISD.2012.046944

Scoones, I. (2007). Sustainability. *Development in Practice*, 17(4-5), 589–596. DOI: 10.1080/09614520701469609

Sigri, U. (2018). *Nitel Araştırma Yöntemleri* (1st ed.). Beta Press.

Sreenath, S., Sudhakar, K., & Yusop, A. F. (2021). Sustainability at airports: Technologies and best practices from ASEAN countries. *Journal of Environmental Management*, 299, 439–451. DOI: 10.1016/j.jenvman.2021.113639 PMID: 34479146

Stevenson, I., & Marintseva, K. (2019). A review of Corporate Social Responsibility assessment and reporting techniques in the aviation industry. *Transportation Research Procedia*, 43, 93–103. DOI: 10.1016/j.trpro.2019.12.023

The Business Research Company. (2024, April 8). *Airlines Market Definition*. The Business Research Company. https://www.thebusinessresearchcompany.com/report/airlines-global-market-report

United Stations. (2023). *The Sustainable Development Goals Report*. United Nations Department of Economic and Social Affairs Statistics Division. https://unstats.un.org/sdgs/report/2023/

Wan, L., Peng, Q., Wang, J., Tian, Y., & Xu, C. (2020). Evaluation of airport sustainability by the synthetic evaluation method: A case study of Guangzhou Baiyun international airport, China, from 2008 to 2017. *Sustainability (Basel)*, 12(8), 3334. DOI: 10.3390/su12083334

Yildirim, A., & Simsek, H. (2021). *Sosyal Bilimlerde Nitel Araştırma Yöntemleri* (12th ed.). Seckin Press.

Zizka, L., McGunagle, D., & Clark, P. (2021). Sustainability Reporting on Dublin Airport: A Case Study. Retrieved from https://commons.erau.edu/publication/1687

KEY TERMS AND DEFINITIONS

Carbon Neutrality: Achieving a balance between emitting carbon and absorbing carbon from the atmosphere in carbon sinks.

Climate Adaptation: Adjusting practices, processes, and infrastructure to minimize the negative effects of climate change.

Economic Sustainability: The capacity of an airport to generate economic value and ensure long-term financial health.

Environmental Risks and Impacts: The potential negative effects of airport operations on the environment, including contributions to climate change, local pollution, and resource use.

Global Reporting Initiative (GRI): A set of global standards for sustainability reporting, helping organizations to communicate their impacts on critical sustainability issues. GRI standards aim to increase transparency and accountability.

Social Sustainability: The commitment of an airport to act in the best interests of its employees, local communities, and other stakeholders.

Sustainability Reporting: The process of disclosing and communicating an organization's environmental, social, and economic impacts and performance.

Technological and Innovative Solutions: The adoption of advanced technologies and innovative practices to enhance the sustainability and efficiency of airport operations.

Triple Bottom Line (TBL): A sustainability framework that includes three dimensions: economic, social, and environmental.

Chapter 12
Flight to Crisis, Navigating Operational Challenges:
A Case Study on Go First's Alleged Engine Failures

S. Baranidharan

https://orcid.org/0000-0002-7780-4045

Christ University, India

Sonal Devesh

Christ University, India

Dhakshayini K. N.

Christ University, India

G. Chandrakala

Dayananda Sagar University, India

EXECUTIVE SUMMARY

This case study explores the tumultuous journey of Go First, an airline marred by allegations of recurrent engine failures. Investigating the aftermath of these accusations, the case scrutinises the intricate interplay between safety, regulatory compliance, and financial viability in the aviation industry. Drawing from qualitative research and a comprehensive review of secondary sources, the narrative delves into the operational disruptions, safety concerns, financial strains, and reputational damage faced by the airline. The study contributes unique insights into crisis management, offering educators, researchers, and industry professionals a real-world context for

DOI: 10.4018/979-8-3693-2675-6.ch012

understanding and addressing operational challenges within the aviation sector.

FACTUAL BACKGROUND

Go First, previously known as GoAir, was founded in 2005 and has been operating as a low-cost carrier in India. The airline faced financial difficulties and struggled to compete with other airlines in the region. In recent years, it experienced operational challenges, including flight cancellations and delays. These issues have led to customer dissatisfaction and raised concerns about the airline's sustainability. Recent years have seen Go First grappling with operational challenges, including an increasing number of flight cancellations and delays. These issues have sparked concerns among passengers and industry observers, raising doubts about the airline's long-term sustainability and viability. Amidst these concerns, an aviation industry insider, requesting anonymity, has come forward to shed light on a significant underlying issue. The insider alleges that faulty engines were a major contributing factor to Go First's failure. According to the insider, the airline had been operating with engines prone to malfunctions, requiring frequent maintenance and leading to disruptions in flight operations.

The aviation industry has faced numerous challenges over the years, ranging from fluctuating fuel prices and regulatory changes to evolving consumer preferences and global crises. The case of Go First, an Indian low-cost airline, represents a complex scenario where multiple operational, financial, and strategic difficulties culminated in significant repercussions for the airline. In 2023, Go First filed for voluntary insolvency resolution due to its inability to sustain operations amid mounting financial burdens and operational challenges, exacerbated by alleged faulty engines and maintenance issues (Sharma et al., 2024). This case has garnered widespread attention, prompting a need to analyze the various factors leading to the airline's insolvency filing, as well as the broader implications for the aviation sector. Scholars have extensively examined the dynamics and crises in the aviation industry, including financial instability, management inefficiencies, and regulatory responses (Levine, 2006; Bawgi, 2022). Analyzing Go First's situation allows a deeper understanding of how airlines navigate their strategic decisions amidst financial turbulence and regulatory scrutiny. Given the global scale of the aviation industry, research has pointed to the importance of efficient financial management and strategic positioning for survival (Wibowo & Sutandi, 2018; Kaya et al., 2023). This study explored these aspects in the context of Go First, shedding light on the airline's approach to dealing with its operational setbacks and the cascading effects that led to its insolvency filing.

Go First, aiming to provide affordable travel options while maintaining efficient operational standards. However, the airline's journey was marred by a series of operational and financial setbacks that strained its capabilities. A significant challenge for Go First was the issue of faulty engines supplied by Pratt & Whitney, which led to frequent technical failures and grounded flights (Sharma et al., 2024). These recurring engine problems severely impacted the airline's operational efficiency, leading to a decline in customer satisfaction and trust, as well as escalating maintenance costs (Feitosa, 2002). The airline's financial health further deteriorated under these operational constraints. Reports indicate that Go First struggled to manage its financial ratios and liquidity due to the grounding of aircraft and increased operational costs (Wibowo & Sutandi, 2018). Despite attempts to restructure its finances, Go First faced a liquidity crunch that forced it to halt operations and seek insolvency resolution (Bian et al., 2022). This move highlighted the precarious nature of the airline's financial management and raised concerns about the effectiveness of its crisis response strategies (Harvey & Turnbull, 2010). The crisis at Go First has broader implications for the aviation sector, reflecting a recurring theme of operational and financial instability among low-cost carriers. The case also brings into focus the role of regulatory bodies, such as the Directorate General of Civil Aviation (DGCA), in maintaining oversight and ensuring compliance in the aviation sector (Décaudin & Lacoste, 2023). The regulatory response to Go First's issues emphasizes the need for a comprehensive framework to address operational deficiencies and protect stakeholders' interests in the aviation industry (Kaya et al., 2023).

The insider further claims that Go First's management failed to adequately address the engine problems. Allegedly, they neglected necessary investments in engine repairs, replacements, and maintenance programs. This alleged negligence exacerbated the situation, resulting in a decline in operational efficiency and a detrimental impact on the airline's reputation. To ascertain the veracity of these allegations, a thorough investigation is warranted. We must delve into Go First's maintenance records, examining any recurring engine issues and whether they were appropriately addressed. Additionally, testimonies from current and former employees, as well as industry experts, can provide insights into the airline's maintenance practices, engine reliability, and the potential impact of engine-related problems on operations.

Comparative analysis with other airlines operating similar aircraft models will also be crucial in determining whether the alleged engine issues were unique to Go First or indicative of broader industry challenges. If the allegations of faulty engines are proven true, it could have far-reaching consequences for Go First. The airline's reputation may suffer a significant blow as passengers lose confidence in its ability to provide safe and reliable air travel. Legal and financial ramifications, including compensation claims and potential penalties, may also arise.

Furthermore, rectifying the engine problems would require substantial investment and may result in disruptions to the airline's operations, further impacting its financial stability and market position. Ultimately, the investigation's findings will be pivotal in determining the accuracy of the allegations and guiding any necessary actions to address the issues raised. The case aims to provide a comprehensive understanding of the challenges faced by Go First and the potential implications for the airline and the aviation industry as a whole.

Go First, formerly known as GoAir, is currently not flying due to several factors and challenges it has faced recently. The primary reason for the airline's grounded operations is the indefinite bar imposed by the regulator, which prohibits Go First from selling tickets without its approval. This regulatory restriction has severely impacted the airline's ability to generate revenue and conduct its usual flight operations. Furthermore, Go First has faced financial difficulties, leading to the cancellation of all flights since May 3. The airline filed for insolvency on May 2, seeking protection from its creditors and attempting to restructure its financial obligations. This insolvency filing has further complicated the airline's operations and added to the uncertainty surrounding its future. Adding to Go First's challenges, lessors of the aircraft it operates approached the Directorate General of Civil Aviation (DGCA) under the Cape Town Convention. The Cape Town Convention is an international treaty that establishes rules for the leasing and financing of aircraft. Under this convention, lessors have the right to repossess their leased aircraft if the lessee, in this case, Go First, fails to fulfill its contractual obligations.

In Go First's case, the lessors sought to repossess 45 out of the 54 planes leased to the airline. This further exacerbated the airline's operational difficulties, as a significant portion of its fleet became subject to potential repossession. The combination of regulatory restrictions, financial challenges, and the potential repossession of leased aircraft has resulted in Go First's current grounding. The airline is undergoing insolvency proceedings, which involve the restructuring of its financial obligations and negotiations with stakeholders, including lessors and creditors.

METHODOLOGY

This study utilizes a qualitative research approach, mostly relying on secondary data sources to create a comprehensive account of Go First's operating difficulties stemming from purported engine malfunctions. There were numerous crucial milestones in the research process: The first step was conducting in-depth studies of the literature to get detailed background information on Go First's operating history and the particular engine failure instances. Relevant articles from newspapers, industry periodicals, and official reports were sourced for these reviews. In order to comprehend the regulatory reactions and compliance challenges experienced by the airline, regulatory papers and statements from aviation authorities, such as the Directorate General of Civil Aviation (DGCA), were then examined.

GO FIRST WOES: ALLEGED FAILURE DUE TO FAULTY ENGINES TROUBLES AND OPERATIONAL CHALLENGES: CRITICAL ANALYSIS

The case surrounding Go First's alleged failure due to faulty engines presents several important aspects that warrant a critical analysis. Here, we will delve into the key points and implications, assessing the evidence and potential consequences for the airline.

1. Allegations and Anonymous Source: The case primarily relies on allegations made by an anonymous aviation industry insider. While anonymous sources can provide valuable insights, their claims should be subjected to careful scrutiny. It is crucial to investigate the credibility and motivations of the source to ensure the accuracy of the information provided.
2. Validity of the Engine Issues: The case emphasizes the presence of faulty engines as a major factor contributing to Go First's failure. However, the information provided does not specify the exact nature of the engine problems or offer concrete evidence supporting the claims. Without detailed technical data and expert analysis, it becomes challenging to validate the severity and impact of the alleged engine issues.
3. Investigation and Industry Comparison: The proposed investigation, including reviewing maintenance records and conducting interviews, is necessary to substantiate or disprove the allegations. Additionally, comparing Go First's engine performance and maintenance practices with other airlines operating similar aircraft models can provide a broader perspective on the industry norms and identify any specific shortcomings of Go First.
4. Impact on Reputation and Customer Satisfaction: If the allegations are proven true, Go First's reputation would undoubtedly suffer a severe blow. Passengers place utmost trust in airlines to ensure their safety, and any compromise in this regard can have long-lasting effects. Customer satisfaction and loyalty would be significantly impacted, potentially resulting in a loss of passengers and reduced market share.
5. Legal and Financial Ramifications: In the event of proven negligence in addressing engine issues, Go First may face legal consequences, including lawsuits from affected passengers, shareholders, and regulatory penalties. These legal battles

can have substantial financial implications, leading to additional financial strain for an already struggling airline.

6. Operational Disruptions and Employee Morale: Rectifying the alleged engine problems would require substantial investments and could disrupt Go First's operations. Grounding aircraft for repairs or replacements can lead to flight cancellations and delays, further inconveniencing passengers and damaging the airline's operational efficiency. Additionally, employee morale may suffer, affecting productivity and potentially leading to increased turnover.

7. Industry-wide Implications: If the allegations of faulty engines are proven true, it could raise concerns about safety practices and maintenance standards within the aviation industry. This case could prompt a broader examination of maintenance protocols and regulatory oversight, impacting other airlines operating similar aircraft models.

Overall, while the case highlights serious allegations and potential implications for Go First, it is essential to approach the claims with caution and await the results of a thorough investigation. Only then can a definitive assessment be made regarding the role of faulty engines in the airline's failure and the subsequent consequences for its reputation, finances, and the broader industry.

Parties Involved

1. Go First (formerly known as GoAir): An Indian low-cost airline operating domestic and international flights.
2. Aviation Industry Insider (Anonymous): An individual with knowledge and experience in the aviation industry who claims that faulty engines played a crucial role in Go First's failure.

Allegations and Arguments

According to the anonymous aviation industry insider, faulty engines were a major contributing factor to Go First's failure. The insider alleges that the airline had been operating with engines that were prone to malfunctions and required frequent maintenance. These issues reportedly led to numerous flight cancellations and disruptions, causing significant inconvenience to passengers.

The insider further claims that Go First's management failed to address the engine problems adequately. Allegedly, they neglected to invest in necessary engine repairs, replacements, and maintenance programs. This alleged negligence worsened the situation, resulting in a decline in operational efficiency and a negative impact on the airline's reputation.

Problems and Challenges

1. Safety Concerns: The primary concern arising from the allegations of faulty engines is the potential compromise of safety. If Go First indeed operated with unreliable engines, it raises serious questions about the airline's commitment to ensuring the safety of its passengers and crew. Malfunctioning engines can lead to in-flight emergencies, loss of power, or even catastrophic failures, endangering the lives of those on board.
2. Reputation Damage: Accusations of operating with faulty engines can severely tarnish Go First's reputation. Passengers place significant trust in airlines to prioritize safety and reliability. If these allegations are substantiated, it can erode public confidence in the airline, resulting in a loss of customers and a decline in market share. Rebuilding trust and restoring the brand image would be an arduous task.
3. Customer Dissatisfaction: Flight cancellations and disruptions caused by engine problems can lead to frustrated and dissatisfied customers. Passengers rely on airlines to transport them to their destinations on time, and any disruptions can disrupt their travel plans, incur additional costs, and cause inconveniences. Customer dissatisfaction can result in negative word-of-mouth, reduced loyalty, and a negative impact on future bookings.
4. Legal and Regulatory Consequences: If the allegations of negligence in addressing engine issues are proven, Go First may face legal and regulatory repercussions. Passengers affected by flight cancellations or safety incidents could file lawsuits seeking compensation for damages, including inconvenience, financial losses, and emotional distress. Regulatory authorities may also initiate investigations and impose fines or penalties for violations of safety regulations.
5. Financial Implications: Operating with faulty engines can have significant financial implications for Go First. The airline may face increased maintenance costs due to frequent repairs or engine replacements. Additionally, flight cancellations and customer dissatisfaction can result in revenue losses. The need to rectify the engine problems and regain public trust may require substantial investments, further straining the airline's financial stability.
6. Operational Disruptions: Resolving the engine problems would likely lead to operational disruptions for Go First. Grounding aircraft for engine repairs or replacements could result in reduced flight schedules, cancellations, and delays. This would not only impact the airline's ability to serve its passengers but also

disrupt its overall operational efficiency. Recovering from such disruptions can be challenging and time-consuming.

7. Employee Morale and Retention: Allegations of negligence and operational difficulties can adversely affect employee morale within the organization. Employees may feel demotivated, anxious about safety concerns, or frustrated with the negative impact on customer satisfaction. It could lead to decreased productivity, increased turnover, and difficulty attracting new talent, further exacerbating operational challenges for the airline.

8. Industry Perception: Go First's alleged engine issues may not only impact its own operations but also affect the overall perception of the aviation industry. It could raise concerns among passengers and stakeholders about the safety practices and maintenance standards across the industry. Restoring confidence in the industry's ability to ensure safe air travel would require transparent investigations and proactive measures by regulatory bodies and airlines alike.

Investigation and Analysis

1. Reviewing Maintenance Records: A detailed examination of Go First's maintenance records would help identify any recurring engine issues and determine whether they were adequately addressed.

2. Interviews and Expert Opinions: Gathering testimonies from current and former employees, as well as industry experts, could shed light on Go First's maintenance practices, engine reliability, and the impact of any engine-related problems on the airline's operations.

3. Comparative Analysis: Comparing Go First's performance and engine-related issues with other airlines operating similar aircraft models would provide insights into whether the engine problems were specific to Go First or if they were prevalent across the industry.

Potential Impact

If the allegations of faulty engines are proven true, it could have significant consequences for Go First. These may include:

1. Reputation Damage: The airline's reputation may suffer as passengers lose confidence in its ability to provide safe and reliable air travel.

2. Legal and Financial Ramifications: Go First may face legal action from affected passengers, shareholders, or regulatory authorities if the alleged negligence in addressing engine issues is substantiated. The airline may also incur financial losses due to compensation claims and potential penalties.
3. Operational Challenges: Rectifying the engine problems would require substantial investment and possibly result in disruptions to the airline's operations, further impacting its financial stability and market position.

Key Findings

1. Allegations of Faulty Engines: The case study presents allegations made by an anonymous aviation industry insider that faulty engines played a significant role in Go First's failure. The insider claims that the airline operated with engines prone to malfunctions, resulting in frequent maintenance issues and flight disruptions.
2. Lack of Adequate Maintenance: According to the insider, Go First's management allegedly neglected necessary investments in engine repairs, replacements, and maintenance programs. This alleged negligence worsened the engine problems and led to a decline in operational efficiency.
3. Regulatory Restrictions: Go First faced regulatory restrictions imposed by the aviation regulatory authority, which indefinitely barred the airline from selling tickets without prior approval. This restriction severely impacted the airline's ability to generate revenue and conduct its usual flight operations.
4. Aircraft Repossession: Lessors of Go First's leased aircraft approached the Directorate General of Civil Aviation (DGCA) under the Cape Town Convention to repossess 45 out of the 54 planes leased to the airline. This action further complicated Go First's operations and added to its operational challenges.
5. Flight Cancellations and Insolvency Filing: Go First canceled all flights since May 3, following its filing for insolvency on May 2. The airline's financial difficulties and insolvency filing have contributed to the grounding of its operations and added uncertainty to its future.
6. Operational Challenges and Customer Dissatisfaction: The allegations of faulty engines and frequent flight cancellations have resulted in significant operational challenges for Go First. The disruptions to flight schedules and the inconvenience caused to passengers have led to customer dissatisfaction. This can have long-term implications for the airline, as customer loyalty and trust may be eroded.
7. Impact on Reputation: The allegations of operating with faulty engines and the subsequent flight disruptions can have a detrimental impact on Go First's reputation. Passengers expect airlines to prioritize safety and reliability, and any

compromise in these areas can severely damage the brand image. Rebuilding trust and restoring the airline's reputation would be a significant challenge.

8. Legal and Financial Ramifications: If the allegations of negligence in addressing engine issues are proven true, Go First may face legal action from affected passengers, shareholders, and regulatory authorities. Lawsuits seeking compensation for damages, fines, and penalties could have substantial financial implications for the airline. Resolving these legal and financial challenges would further strain the company's resources.

9. Employee Morale and Retention: The operational difficulties, negative publicity, and potential layoffs associated with the airline's failure could significantly impact employee morale. Disgruntled employees may become demotivated and potentially seek employment elsewhere. Retaining skilled and experienced staff members during this challenging period would be crucial for the airline's future operations.

10. Broader Industry Implications: If the allegations of faulty engines are substantiated, it could raise concerns within the aviation industry regarding safety practices and maintenance standards. Regulators and industry bodies may conduct investigations and implement stricter measures to ensure the safety and reliability of aircraft operated by various airlines.

DISCUSSION: GO FIRST

1. Conduct a Thorough Investigation: Go First should initiate a comprehensive investigation into the allegations of faulty engines. This investigation should involve a detailed review of maintenance records, technical analysis of engine performance, and interviews with relevant stakeholders, including employees and industry experts. The goal is to validate the claims, identify the root causes of the engine problems, and assess the extent of their impact on the airline's operations.

2. Address Maintenance Practices: If the investigation confirms the presence of maintenance issues, Go First should prioritize the improvement of its maintenance practices. This may include investing in robust maintenance programs, ensuring timely inspections and repairs, and implementing stringent quality control measures. Establishing a proactive maintenance culture will help prevent future engine problems and enhance operational efficiency.

3. Enhance Safety Measures: Regardless of the findings, Go First should place utmost importance on safety. The airline should review and strengthen its safety protocols, ensuring compliance with industry standards and regulatory require-

ments. This can involve comprehensive training programs for staff, regular safety audits, and the establishment of a safety management system to identify and mitigate risks effectively.

4. Rebuild Customer Trust: To rebuild customer trust, Go First should communicate transparently about the findings of the investigation and the steps taken to address any identified issues. Implementing a robust customer service program, offering compensation or alternative travel options for affected passengers, and ensuring reliable and timely operations in the future will be vital to restoring confidence and loyalty among passengers.

5. Strengthen Regulatory Compliance: Go First should work closely with the aviation regulatory authority to ensure full compliance with regulations and directives. This includes obtaining necessary approvals and adhering to maintenance and safety guidelines. By demonstrating a strong commitment to regulatory compliance, the airline can build credibility and mitigate any future regulatory concerns.

6. Financial Restructuring: Given Go First's insolvency filing and financial difficulties, the airline should work towards a comprehensive financial restructuring plan. This may involve negotiating with creditors, exploring potential partnerships or investments, and implementing cost-cutting measures to improve financial stability. Seeking professional guidance from financial experts or restructuring specialists can be beneficial in navigating this process.

7. Employee Engagement and Retention: Go First should prioritize employee engagement and retention during this challenging period. Open communication channels, providing support, and recognizing the efforts of employees can help boost morale and maintain a skilled workforce. Training programs and career development opportunities can also enhance employee loyalty and motivation.

8. Industry Collaboration and Best Practices: Go First should actively collaborate with industry peers, aviation associations, and regulatory bodies to share best practices and learn from others' experiences. Engaging in industry discussions and forums can provide valuable insights and guidance on maintaining safety, improving operational efficiency, and addressing maintenance challenges.

By implementing these suggestions, Go First can aim to address the findings of the case study, strengthen its operations, rebuild its reputation, and work towards long-term sustainability in the aviation industry.

PRACTICAL IMPLICATIONS

1. Safety and Maintenance: The case emphasizes the critical importance of prioritizing safety and robust maintenance practices in the aviation industry. Go First must invest in improving maintenance protocols, ensuring timely inspections, and implementing comprehensive safety measures. This will not only enhance the airline's operational efficiency but also contribute to ensuring the safety and well-being of passengers and crew.
2. Regulatory Compliance: Go First needs to strengthen its commitment to regulatory compliance. Adhering to industry standards and collaborating closely with the aviation regulatory authority will not only prevent potential penalties but also foster a culture of transparency, accountability, and trustworthiness.
3. Financial Stability: To secure its long-term viability, Go First should focus on financial restructuring. Working towards a comprehensive financial plan, negotiating with creditors, and implementing cost-cutting measures will help stabilize the airline's financial position and pave the way for sustainable growth.

SOCIAL IMPLICATIONS

1. Customer Trust and Satisfaction: Rebuilding customer trust is paramount for Go First. By effectively addressing the allegations, being transparent about findings, and prioritizing customer satisfaction, the airline can regain passenger confidence and loyalty. This will contribute to fostering a positive perception of the airline industry as a whole.
2. Employee Well-being: Ensuring employee well-being and engagement is essential for Go First's success. By providing support, recognition, and career development opportunities, the airline can boost employee morale, productivity, and retention. This will not only benefit the employees but also enhance the overall passenger experience.
3. Industry Best Practices: Collaboration and sharing best practices with industry peers will be instrumental in Go First's journey towards improvement. Engaging in industry discussions and forums will contribute to the adoption of standardized practices, increased safety, and enhanced operational efficiency across the aviation sector.

CONCLUSION

The case study surrounding Go First's alleged failure due to faulty engines high-lights significant challenges and implications for the airline. The allegations made by the aviation industry insider regarding faulty engines playing a major role in Go First's failure are serious and warrant a comprehensive investigation. If the claims are verified, they could have far-reaching consequences for the airline's reputation, legal standing, and financial viability. The investigation's findings will be crucial in determining the accuracy of the allegations and guiding any necessary actions to address the issues raised. Go First's alleged failure due to faulty engines serves as a reminder of the criticality of safety, maintenance, and regulatory compliance in the aviation industry. By implementing practical solutions and addressing social implications, Go First can rebuild its reputation, regain customer trust, and contribute to a safer and more reliable air travel experience. These actions will have a positive impact not only on the airline's future but also on the broader society, reinforcing the importance of passenger safety and satisfaction in the aviation industry.

REFERENCES

Bawgi, A. (2022). Go Airlines (India) Ltd-Go First's Insolvency Filing: Examining the Background, Challenges and Court Proceedings. *Jus Corpus LJ*, 3, 45.

Bian, J., Greenberg, J., Li, J., & Wang, Y. (2022). Good to go first? Position effects in expert evaluation of early-stage ventures. *Management Science*, 68(1), 300–315. DOI: 10.1287/mnsc.2021.4132

Décaudin, J. M., & Lacoste, D. (2023). Airlines: Standardize Your International Advertising! *Journal of Travel Research*, 62(5), 1090–1104. DOI: 10.1177/00472875221115176

Feitosa, W. R. (2002). Estratégias e políticas de preço no mercado de aviação: Caso da Gol transportes aéreos. *Revista Turismo em Análise*, 13(1), 48–65. DOI: 10.11606/issn.1984-4867.v13i1p48-65

Harvey, G., & Turnbull, P. (2010). On the Go: Walking the high road at a low cost airline. *International Journal of Human Resource Management*, 21(2), 230–241. DOI: 10.1080/09585190903509548

Kaya, G., Aydın, U., Ülengin, B., Karadayı, M. A., & Ülengin, F. (2023). How do airlines survive? An integrated efficiency analysis on the survival of airlines. *Journal of Air Transport Management*, 107, 102348. DOI: 10.1016/j.jairtraman.2022.102348

Levine, M. E. (2006). Why weren't the airlines reregulated. *Yale Journal on Regulation*, 23, 269.

Sharma, D., Totuka, A., Kumar, P., Yadav, A., & Jain, P. (2024). An analysis of go first airlines: A case study on voluntary insolvency resolution in the aviation industry. *Journal of Informatics Education and Research*, 4(2). Advance online publication. DOI: 10.52783/jier.v4i2.826

Wibowo, S., & Sutandi, S. (2018). Analisa Rasio Keuangan Garuda Indonesia Airlines, Singapore Airlines Dan Thailand Airlines Dengan Uji Non-Parametrik (Periode: 2010–2014). *eCo-Buss, 1*(2), 1-7. DOI: 10.32877/eb.v1i2.36

KEY TERMS AND DEFINITIONS

Aircraft Grounding: Aircraft grounding occurs when an airline is required to temporarily or permanently remove aircraft from service due to safety concerns, technical faults, or regulatory orders.

Customer Trust: Customer trust is the confidence passengers have in an airline's ability to provide safe, reliable, and timely service. Repeated operational failures and flight cancellations eroded customer trust in Go First, affecting its market reputation.

Engine Failures: Engine failures refer to the malfunctioning or breakdown of an aircraft's engine, which can lead to severe operational disruptions, safety risks, and potentially catastrophic incidents if not managed properly.

Fleet Management: Fleet management in aviation refers to the strategic oversight of an airline's aircraft inventory, including maintenance, scheduling, and financial management of the fleet.

Insolvency Protection: Insolvency protection is a legal status where a company seeks protection from creditors under insolvency laws to reorganize or restructure its debts.

Operational Disruptions: Operational disruptions are interruptions to an airline's regular service schedule, often caused by technical problems, maintenance issues, or external factors such as weather or regulatory interventions.

Regulatory Compliance: Regulatory compliance in aviation involves adhering to the rules, guidelines, and standards set by aviation authorities, such as the Directorate General of Civil Aviation (DGCA) in India.

Supply Chain Delays: Supply chain delays refer to the postponements in the delivery of critical components, such as spare parts or replacement engines, essential for maintenance and operational continuity.

Compilation of References

Aadhaar Now World's Largest Biometric Database. (2018). *5 Facts from UIDAI CEO's Presentation in Supreme Court You Must Know*. The Financial Express.

Abazari, F., Analoui, M., Takabi, H., & Fu, S. (2019). MOWS: Multi-objective workflow scheduling in cloud computing based on heuristic algorithm. *Simulation Modelling Practice and Theory*, 93, 119–132. DOI: 10.1016/j.simpat.2018.10.004

Abbasi, K., Alam, A., Brohi, N. A., Brohi, I. A., & Nasim, S. (2021). P2P lending Fintechs and SMEs' access to finance. *Economics Letters*, 204, 109890. DOI: 10.1016/j.econlet.2021.109890

Abdullahi, M., Baashar, Y., Alhussian, H., Alwadain, A., Aziz, N., Capretz, L. F., & Abdulkadir, S. J. (2022). Detecting Cybersecurity Attacks in Internet of Things Using Artificial Intelligence Methods: A Systematic Literature Review. In *Electronics (Switzerland)* (Vol. 11, Issue 2). DOI: 10.3390/electronics11020198

ACI Europe Airport Industry Manifesto. (2024). *Airport Industry Manifesto for the Next EU Political Cycle 2024-2029*. ACI Europe. https://www.aci-europe.org/downloads/resources/ACI%20EUROPE%20MANIFESTO.pdf

ACMA. (2020). Automotive Components Manufacturers Association of India. Retrieved from https://www.acma.in/annual-report.php

Aghajani, M., Ruge, G., & Jugdev, K. (2023). An Integrative Review of Project Portfolio Management Literature: Thematic Findings on Sustainability Mindset, Assessment, and Integration. *Project Management Journal*, 54(6), 629–650. DOI: 10.1177/87569728231172668

Agudelo, M. A. L., Johannsdottir, L., & Davidsdottir, B. (2020). Drivers that motivate energy companies to be responsible. A systematic literature review of Corporate Social Responsibility in the energy sector. *Journal of Cleaner Production*, 247, 119094. DOI: 10.1016/j.jclepro.2019.119094

Ahadiat, A., Ribhan, R., Maydiantoro, A., & Dwi Kesumah, F. S. (2021). The theory of planned behavior and marketing ethics theory in predicting digital piracy intentions. *WSEAS Transactions on Business and Economics*, 18, 679–702. DOI: 10.37394/23207.2021.18.68

Ahlemann, F., Bergan, P., Karger, E., Greulich, M., & Reining, S. (2024). Making Sense of Projects—Developing Project Portfolio Management Capabilities. *Schmalenbachs Zeitschrift fur Betriebswirtschaftliche Forschung = Schmalenbach Journal of Business Research*, 76(2), 293–325. DOI: 10.1007/s41471-023-00178-8

Ahmed, M. (2019). Data summarization: A survey. *Knowledge and Information Systems*, 58(2), 249–273. DOI: 10.1007/s10115-018-1183-0

Ahmetoglu, H., & Das, R. (2022). A comprehensive review on detection of cyber-attacks: Data sets, methods, challenges, and future research directions. In *Internet of Things (Netherlands)* (Vol. 20, p. 100615). Elsevier. DOI: 10.1016/j.iot.2022.100615

Ahonen, K., Seppänen, P., & Kallio, K. (2020). Project portfolio management in public sector organizations: Case studies in municipal organizations. *International Journal of Project Management*, 38(4), 237–251.

Ahsan, M., Nygard, K. E., Gomes, R., Chowdhury, M. M., Rifat, N., & Connolly, J. F. (2022). Cybersecurity Threats and Their Mitigation Approaches Using Machine Learning—A Review. In *Journal of Cybersecurity and Privacy* (Vol. 2, Issue 3, pp. 527–555). DOI: 10.3390/jcp2030027

Aiyanyo, I. D., Samuel, H., & Lim, H. (2020). A Systematic Review of Defensive and Offensive Cybersecurity with Machine Learning. *Applied Sciences (Basel, Switzerland)*, 10(17), 5811. Advance online publication. DOI: 10.3390/app10175811

Ajil, A., & Staubli, S. (2023). Predictive policing and negotiations of (in) formality: Exploring the Swiss case. *International Journal of Law, Crime and Justice*, 74, 100605. DOI: 10.1016/j.ijlcj.2023.100605

Ajzen, I. (1991). The theory of planned behavior. *Organizational Behavior and Human Decision Processes*, 50(2), 179–211. DOI: 10.1016/0749-5978(91)90020-T

Alameeri, A., Ajmal, M. M., Hussain, M., & Helo, P. T. (2017). Sustainability practices in the aviation sector: A study of UAE-based airlines. *International Journal of Sustainable Society*, 9(2), 119–147. DOI: 10.1504/IJSSOC.2017.086818

Albert, C., Baez, A., & Rutland, J. (2021). Human security as biosecurity: Reconceptualizing national security threats in the time of COVID-19. *Politics and the Life Sciences*, 40(1), 83–105. DOI: 10.1017/pls.2021.1 PMID: 33949836

Alcaraz, C., & Lopez, J. (2022). Digital twin: A comprehensive survey of security threats. *IEEE Communications Surveys and Tutorials*, 24(3), 1475–1503. DOI: 10.1109/COMST.2022.3171465

Alhakami, A. S., & Slovic, P. (1994). A psychological study of the inverse relationship between perceived risk and perceived benefit. *Risk Analysis*, 1(6), 1085–1096. DOI: 10.1111/j.1539-6924.1994.tb00080.x PMID: 7846317

Alharthi, Z. S. M., & Rastogi, R. (2020). An efficient classification of secure and non-secure bug report material using machine learning method for cyber security. *Materials Today: Proceedings*, 37(Part 2), 2507–2512. DOI: 10.1016/j.matpr.2020.08.311

Alhashmi, A., Darem, A., & Abawajy, J. (2021). Taxonomy of Cyber security Awareness Delivery Methods: A Countermeasure for Phishing Threats. *International Journal of Advanced Computer Science and Applications*, 12(10). Advance online publication. DOI: 10.14569/IJACSA.2021.0121004

Ali, I., & Gölgeci, I. (2019). Where is supply chain resilience research heading? A systematic and co-occurrence analysis. *International Journal of Physical Distribution & Logistics Management*, 49(8), 793–815. DOI: 10.1108/IJPDLM-02-2019-0038

Ali, I., & Hsu, L. (2023). Decision-making challenges in project portfolio management: A comprehensive review. *Journal of Project Management*, 39(2), 112–126.

Alli, B. O. (2008). Fundamental principles of occupational health and safety (2nd ed.). International Labour Organization.

Al-Mhiqani, M. N., Ahmad, R., Abidin, Z. Z., Ali, N. S., & Abdulkareem, K. H. (2019). Review of cyber attacks classifications and threats analysis in cyber-physical systems. *International Journal of Internet Technology and Secured Transactions*, 9(3), 282–298. DOI: 10.1504/IJITST.2019.101827

Almseidin, M., Zuraiq, A. A., Al-kasassbeh, M., & Alnidami, N. (2019). Phishing detection based on machine learning and feature selection methods. International Journal of Interactive Mobile Technology, 13(12), 171–183. DOI: 10.3991/ijim.v13i12.11411

Alsamiri, J., & Alsubhi, K. (2019). Internet of things cyber attacks detection using machine learning. *International Journal of Advanced Computer Science and Applications*, 10(12), 627–634. DOI: 10.14569/IJACSA.2019.0101280

Alswailem, A., Alabdullah, B., Alrumayh, N., & Alsedrani, A. (2019). Detecting Phishing Websites Using Machine Learning. 2nd International Conference on Computer Applications & Information Security (ICCAIS).

Andersen, T. J., & Schrøder, P. W. (2010). Strategic risk management. In *Strategic Risk Management Practice: How to Deal Effectively with Major Corporate Exposures* (pp. 200–224). Cambridge University Press. DOI: 10.1017/CBO9780511816017.010

Aneziris, O. N., Papazoglou, I. A., Mud, M. L., Damen, M., Kuiper, J., Baksteen, H., Ale, B. J., Bellamy, L. J., Hale, A. R., Bloemhoff, A., Post, J. G., & Oh, J. (2008). Towards risk assessment for crane activities. *Safety Science*, 46(6), 872–884. DOI: 10.1016/j.ssci.2007.11.012

Annam Pranitha, A. P. (2023). Detection Of Cyber Attack In Network Using Machine Learning Techniques. *Journal of Science and Technology*, 8(7), 133–139. DOI: 10.46243/jst.2023.v8.i06.pp133-139

Archer, N., & Ghasemzadeh, F. (1999). An integrated framework for project portfolio selection. *International Journal of Project Management*, 17(4), 207–216. DOI: 10.1016/S0263-7863(98)00032-5

Arias, J. C., & Stern, R. (2011). Review of risk management methods. *Business Intelligence Journal*, 4(1), 51–78.

Artiach, T., Lee, D., Nelson, D., & Walker, J. (2010). The determinants of corporate sustainability performance. *Accounting and Finance*, 50(1), 31–51. DOI: 10.1111/j.1467-629X.2009.00315.x

Aven, T. (2011). On some recent definitions and analysis frameworks for risk, vulnerability, and resilience. *Risk Analysis*, 31(4), 515–522. DOI: 10.1111/j.1539-6924.2010.01528.x PMID: 21077926

Aygun, S., Sagbas, M., & Erdogan, F. A. (2023). Bibliometric Analysis of Sustainability in Civil Aviation. *Journal of Aviation*, 7(3), 448–456. DOI: 10.30518/jav.1358871

Bai, C., & Sarkis, J. (2022). Integration of sustainability in project portfolio management: A systematic review and research agenda. *Journal of Cleaner Production*, 350, 131453.

Bai, C., Sarkis, J., & Dou, Y. (2021). Corporate sustainability development in the context of China's institutional environment: An integration of institutional and stakeholder theories. *Journal of Cleaner Production*, 312, 127749.

Baidoo, S., Donyina, J., & Alhassan, J. (2021). A review of project portfolio management methodologies: Trends and future directions. *Project Management Journal*, 52(1), 20–34.

Bai, L., Han, X., Wang, H., Zhang, K., & Sun, Y. (2021). A method of network robustness under strategic goals for project portfolio selection. *Computers & Industrial Engineering*, 161, 107658. DOI: 10.1016/j.cie.2021.107658

Balatbat, M., Al-Saidi, M., & Adams, J. (2022). Evaluating project portfolios: A new approach based on decision-making frameworks. *International Journal of Project Management*, 40(1), 60–74.

Bansal, R., Jenipher, B., Nisha, V., Makhan, R., Dilip, K., Pramanik, S., Roy, S., & Gupta, A. (2022). Big Data Architecture for Network Security. In Cyber Security and Network Security. Wiley. DOI: 10.1002/9781119812555.ch11

Basu, R. (2015). *Managing Projects in Research and Development*. Gower Publishing Limited.

Bawgi, A. (2022). Go Airlines (India) Ltd-Go First's Insolvency Filing: Examining the Background, Challenges and Court Proceedings. *Jus Corpus LJ*, 3, 45.

Baxter, G., Srisaeng, P., & Wild, G. (2018). An assessment of sustainable airport water management: The case of Osaka's Kansai international airport. *Infrastructures*, 3(4), 54. DOI: 10.3390/infrastructures3040054

BBC. (2018). *Typhoon Jebi forced the closure of Kansai Airport, near Osaka in Japan*. Available online at https://www.bbc.com/news/world-asia-45417035

BDO USA. (2023). TOP 10 business cyber security threats in 2023. Available at: https://surl.li/jaran

Bechtel, R., & Squires, J. (2001). Tools and Techniques to Facilitate Change. *Industrial and Commercial Training*, 33(7), 249–255. DOI: 10.1108/EUM0000000006001

Belanche, D., Casaló, L. V., & Flavián, C. (2014). The role of place identity in smart card adoption. *Public Management Review*, 16(8), 1205–1228. DOI: 10.1080/14719037.2013.792385

Below, A. (2019). Climate change: The existential threat multiplier. In Understanding new security threats. Routledge.

Bentele, G., & Nothaft, H. (2011). Trust and credibility as the basis of corporate social responsibility. The handbook of communication and corporate social responsibility, 208-230. DOI: 10.1002/9781118083246.ch11

Bernard, M., Rankin, C., Griggs, J., & Utzig, G. (2000). *Environmental Risk Assessment (ERA): an Approach for Assessing and Reporting Environmental Conditions*. Habitat Branch, Ministry of Environment, Lands and Parks.

Bhadouria, A. S. (2022). Study of: Impact of Malicious Attacks and Data Breach on the Growth and Performance of the Company and Few of the World's Biggest Data Breaches. *International Journal of Scientific and Research Publications*, 10(10), 1–11. DOI: 10.29322/IJSRP.X.2022.p091095

Bhattacharya, A., Bürkner, H.P., Bailey, A., & Verma, S. (2022). The organization of the future is fractal. https://www.bcg.com/publications/2022/fractal-companies -are-the-organizations-of-the-future

Bian, J., Greenberg, J., Li, J., & Wang, Y. (2022). Good to go first? Position effects in expert evaluation of early-stage ventures. *Management Science*, 68(1), 300–315. DOI: 10.1287/mnsc.2021.4132

Big Data Analytics for Cyber Security and Advance Persistent Threat Intelligence. (n.d.). Frontiers Media. https://www.frontiersin.org/research-topics/37830/big-data -analytics-for-cyber-security-and-advance-persistent-threat-intelligence

Bilen, A., & Özer, A. B. (2021). Cyber-attack method and perpetrator prediction using machine learning algorithms. *PeerJ. Computer Science*, 7, 1–21. DOI: 10.7717/ peerj-cs.475 PMID: 33954249

Blomquist, T., & Müller, R. (2006). Practices, roles, and responsibilities of middle managers in program and portfolio management. *Project Management Journal*, 37(1), 52–66. DOI: 10.1177/875697280603700105

Boiko, M., Bovsh, L., & Okhrimenko, A. (2022). Crisis resilience of the tourism business in martial law. *The International Scientific-Practical Journal: Commodities and Markets*, 42(2), 31–47. DOI: 10.31617/2.2022(42)03

Bolman, L., & Deal, T. (2017). *Reframing Organizations* (6th ed.). Jossey-Bass. DOI: 10.1002/9781119281856

Bosher, L., Chmutina, K., & van Niekerk, D. (2021). Stop going around in circles: Towards a reconceptualisation of disaster risk management phases. *Disaster Prevention and Management*, 30(4/5), 525–537. DOI: 10.1108/DPM-03-2021-0071

Bouarar, A. C., Mouloudj, S., & Mouloudj, K. (2022). Digital Transformation: Opportunities and Challenges. In Mansour, N., & Ben Salem, S. (Eds.), *COVID-19's Impact on the Cryptocurrency Market and the Digital Economy* (pp. 33–52). IGI Global. DOI: 10.4018/978-1-7998-9117-8.ch003

Bouarar, A. C., Stojczew, K., & Mouloudj, K. (2023). An Analytical Study on Digital Transformation in the Poland Hospitality Industry. In Fernandes, G., & Melo, A. (Eds.), *Handbook of Research on Innovation, Differentiation, and New Technologies in Tourism, Hotels, and Food Service* (pp. 32–50). IGI Global. DOI: 10.4018/978-1-6684-6985-9.ch002

Boukerche, A., & Coutinho, R. W. L. (2021). Design Guidelines for Machine Learning-based Cybersecurity in Internet of Things. *IEEE Network*, 35(1), 393–399. DOI: 10.1109/MNET.011.2000396

Boulton, E. G. (2022). PLAN E: A grand strategy for the twenty-first century era of entangled security and hyperthreats. *Journal of Advanced Military Studies*, 13(1), 92–128. DOI: 10.21140/mcuj.20221301005

Bove, V., Rivera, M., & Ruffa, C. (2020). Beyond coups: Terrorism and military involvement in politics. *European Journal of International Relations*, 26(1), 263–288. DOI: 10.1177/1354066119866499

Bovsh, L., Hopkalo, L., & Rasulova, A. (2023). The concept of investment risk management by subjects of the hotel business in the conditions of martial law. In M. Sahaidak & T. Sobolieva (Eds.), Management: Challenges in global world (pp. 236-247). Kyiv National Economic University named after Vadym Hetman. http://doi.org/doi.org/10.35668/978-966-926-425-1

Bovsh, L., Mouloudj, K., Rasulova, A. M., & Tkachuk, T. M. (2024c). Viral Content in Event Management of Hospitality and Socio-Cultural Activities. In S. Kulshreshtha & C. Webster (Eds.), *New Technologies in Virtual and Hybrid Events* (pp. 228-257). IGI Global. DOI: 10.4018/979-8-3693-2272-7.ch012

Bovsh, L., Bosovska, M., & Okhrimenko, A. (2021). Compliance-strategizing of economic security of the business in digitalization conditions. *Herald of KNUTE.*, 6(6), 42–60. DOI: 10.31617/visnik.knute.2021(140)03

Bovsh, L., Hopkalo, L., Tonkonoh, I., Mouloudj, K., Bouarar, A. C., & Mechta, M. (2024a). Sustainable Competitive Edge in Rehabilitation Hospitality: Insights From Ukraine. In Rodrigues, P., Borges, A., Vieira, E., & Tavares, V. (Eds.), *Compelling Storytelling Narratives for Sustainable Branding* (pp. 343–365). IGI Global. DOI: 10.4018/979-8-3693-3326-6.ch018

Bovsh, L., Mouloudj, K., Bosovska, M., Alla, R., & Boiko, M. (2024b). Reputational Compliance in the Communicative Online Environment of a Hotel Entity. In Rouco, J., & Figueiredo, P. (Eds.), *Business Continuity Management and Resilience: Theories, Models, and Processes* (pp. 199–219). IGI Global. DOI: 10.4018/979-8-3693-1658-0.ch009

Bovsh, L., Rasulova, A., & Muravyova, I. (2022). *The impact of the war on the tourism brand of Ukraine. Creative space of Ukraine and the world*. Collective Monograph. Available at https://www.newroute.org.ua/wp-content/uploads/2022/11/6.pdf

Bradley, G. (2016). *Benefit Realisation Management: A Practical Guide to Achieving Benefits Through Change*. Gower Publishing. DOI: 10.4324/9781315569055

Brida, J. G., Moreno-Izquierdo, L., & Zapata-Aguirre, S. (2016). Customer perception of service quality: The role of Information and Communication Technologies (ICTs) at airport functional areas. *Tourism Management Perspectives*, 20, 209–216. DOI: 10.1016/j.tmp.2016.09.003

Bridge, J. (2023, Dec. 5). Warfare ruins the environment – and not just on the front lines. https://theconversation.com/warfare-ruins-the-environment-and-not-just-on-the-front-lines-218853

British Business Bank. (2023). *Annual report and accounts 2023*. Retrieved from https://www.british-business-bank.co.uk/about/research-and-publications/annual-report-and-accounts-2023

Brooke, J., & Pagnanelli, F. (2014). Integrating sustainability into innovation project portfolio management – A strategic perspective. *Journal of Engineering and Technology Management*, 34, 46–62. DOI: 10.1016/j.jengtecman.2013.11.004

Brundtland, G.H. (1987) Our Common Future Report of the World Commission on Environment and Development. Geneva, UN-Dokument A/42/427.

Brynjolfsson, E., & McAfee, A. (2014). *The Second Machine Age: Work, Progress, and Prosperity in a Time of Brilliant Technologies*. W. W. Norton & Company.

Budd, L., Griggs, S., & Howarth, D. (2013). Sustainable aviation futures: Crises, contested realities and prospects for change. In *Sustainable aviation futures* (pp. 3–35). Emerald Group Publishing Limited. DOI: 10.1108/S2044-9941(2013)0000004013

Burleson, C., & Maurice, L. (2003). Aviation and the environment: challenges and opportunities. In *AIAA International Air and Space Symposium and Exposition: The Next 100 Years* (p. 2554). DOI: 10.2514/6.2003-2554

Byrne, B. M. (2013). *Structural equation modeling with Mplus: Basic concepts, applications, and programming*. Routledge.

Callahan, C., & Soileau, J. (2017). Does enterprise risk management enhance operating performance? *Advances in Accounting*, 37, 122–139. DOI: 10.1016/j.adiac.2017.01.001

Camarota, S. A. (2016). New Data: Immigration Surged in 2014 and 2015. More than three million legal and illegal immigrants settled in the United States in the last two years. Center for Migration Studies. https://cis.org/Report/New-Data-Immigration -Surged-2014-and-2015

CAPA. (2023). *Airports: Istanbul closes in on rejoining the 100 million annual air passengers by city club.*https://centreforaviation.com/analysis/reports/airports -istanbul-closes-in-on-rejoining-the-100-million-annual-air-passengers-by-city -club-664318

Carfora, V., Cavallo, C., Catellani, P., Del Giudice, T., & Cicia, G. (2021). Why do consumers intend to purchase natural food? Integrating theory of planned behavior, value-belief-norm theory, and trust. *Nutrients*, 13(6), 1904. DOI: 10.3390/nu13061904 PMID: 34205879

Centobelli, P., Cerchione, R., Esposito, E., Passaro, R., & Shashi, . (2021). Determinants of the transition towards circular economy in SMEs: A sustainable supply chain management perspective. *International Journal of Production Economics*, 242, 108297. DOI: 10.1016/j.ijpe.2021.108297

Chandon, P., Wansink, B., & Laurent, G. (2000). A benefit congruency framework of sales promotion effectiveness. *Journal of Marketing*, 64(4), 65–81. DOI: 10.1509/jmkg.64.4.65.18071

Chao, R., & Kavadias, S. (2008). A Theoretical Framework for Managing the New Product Development Portfolio: When and How to Use Strategic Buckets. *Management Science*, 54(5), 907–921. DOI: 10.1287/mnsc.1070.0828

Chapman, C., & Ward, S. (2003). *Project Risk Management: Processes, Techniques and Insights* (2nd ed.). John Wiley & Sons.

Chapman, R. J. (1998). The effectiveness of working group risk identification and assessment techniques. *International Journal of Project Management*, 16(6), 333–343. DOI: 10.1016/S0263-7863(98)00015-5

Chartres, N., Bero, L. A., & Norris, S. L. (2019). A review of methods used for hazard identification and risk assessment of environmental hazards. *Environment International*, 123, 231–239. DOI: 10.1016/j.envint.2018.11.060 PMID: 30537638

Chen, C., & Cheng, H. (2009). A comprehensive model for selecting information system project under fuzzy environment. *International Journal of Project Management*, 27(4), 389–399. DOI: 10.1016/j.ijproman.2008.04.001

Chen, Z., Li, H., Ren, H., Xu, Q., & Hong, J. (2011). A total environmental risk assessment model for international hub airports. *International Journal of Project Management*, 29(7), 856–866. DOI: 10.1016/j.ijproman.2011.03.004

Chernikova, E. G., & Tarasyeva, L. V. (2010). The main directions of ensuring economic security of the enterprise. Problems of Ensuring Economic Security: Materials of the International Scientific and Practical Conference. Donetsk, DonNTU, 163-165.

Chłodnicka, H., & Zimon, G. (2020). Bankruptcu risk assessment measures of polish SMEs. *WSEAS Transactions on Business and Economics*, 17(3), 14–20. DOI: 10.37394/23207.2020.17.3

Chourasia, A. S., Jha, K., & Dalei, N. N. (2021). Development and planning of sustainable airports. *Journal of Public Affairs*, 21(1), e2145. DOI: 10.1002/pa.2145

Christodoulou, A., & Demirel, H. (2018). *Impacts of climate change on transport. A Focus on Airports, Seaports and Inland Waterways*. European Union Publication Office. DOI: 10.2760/378464

Chrusciel, D., & Field, D. (2006). Success Factors in Dealing with Significant Change in an Organization. *Business Process Management Journal*, 12(4), 503–516. DOI: 10.1108/14637150610678096

Clain, G. (2023, Apr. 14). What are compound climate risks and how might they impact companies? Ecoact. https://eco-act.com/blog/compound-risks-climate/

Clegg, S., Killen, C., Biesenthal, C., & Sankaran, S. (2018). Practices, projects and portfolios: Current research trends and new directions. *International Journal of Project Management*, 36(5), 762–772. DOI: 10.1016/j.ijproman.2018.03.008

Committee of Sponsoring Organizations of the Treadway Commission (COSO). (2017). Retrieved from https://www.coso.org/_files/ugd/3059fc_61ea5985b03c4293960642fdce408eaa.pdf

Cooper, R., Edgett, S., & Kleinschmidt, E. (2002). *Portfolio Management: fundamental for new product success*. Stage-Gate International and Product Development Institute Inc. Available at http://stage-gate.net/downloads/ working_papers/wp_12.pdf

Cooper, C., Dewe, P., & O'Driscoll, M. (2001). *Organizational Stress: A review and critique of theory, research, and applications*. Sage. DOI: 10.4135/9781452231235

Cooper, R. (2005). Portfolio Management for Product Innovation. In Levine, H. A. (Ed.), *Project Portfolio Management: A Practical Guide to Selecting Projects, Managing Portfolios and Maximizing Benefit* (pp. 318–354). John Wiley and Sons.

Cooper, R. (2008). Perspective: The Stage-Gate® Idea-to-Launch Process—Update, What's New, and NexGen Systems. *Journal of Product Innovation Management*, 25(3), 213–232. DOI: 10.1111/j.1540-5885.2008.00296.x

Cooper, R. G., & Sommer, A. F. (2023). Dynamic Portfolio Management for New Product Development. *Research Technology Management*, 66(3), 19–31. DOI: 10.1080/08956308.2023.2183004

Cooper, R., Edgett, S., & Kleinschmidt, E. (2000). New Problems, New Solutions: Making Portfolio Management More Effective. *Research Technology Management*, 16(2), 180–186. DOI: 10.1080/08956308.2000.11671338

Cooper, R., Edgett, S., & Kleinschmidt, E. (2001). Portfolio Management in New Product Development: Results of an Industry Practices Study. *R & D Management*, 31(4), 361–381. DOI: 10.1111/1467-9310.00225

Cotroneo, A. & Triggiano, M. (2024, March 13). Exploring the intersection of armed conflict, climate risks and mobility: the ICRC's experience.

Cró, S., Calisto, M. D., Martins, A. M., & Simões, J. M. (2020). Safety and Security Perception as Strategic Issues for Hospitality Companies. In Carvalho, L., Calisto, L., & Gustavo, N. (Eds.), *Strategic Business Models to Support Demand, Supply, and Destination Management in the Tourism and Hospitality Industry* (pp. 134–149). IGI Global. DOI: 10.4018/978-1-5225-9936-4.ch007

Dallat, C., Salmon, P. M., & Goode, N. (2017). Risky systems versus risky people: To what extent do risk assessment methods consider the systems approach to accident causation? A review of the literature. *Safety Science*.

Davis, K. (2014). Different stakeholder groups and their perceptions of project success. *International Journal of Project Management*, 32(2), 189–201. DOI: 10.1016/j.ijproman.2013.02.006

Davolio, M. E., Banfi, E., Gehrig, M., Gerber, B., Luzha, B., Mey, E., ... Wicht, L. (2015). School of Social Work Research and Development Background to jihadist radicalisation in Switzerland.

de Araújo Lima, P. F., Crema, M., & Verbano, C. (2020). Risk management in SMEs: A systematic literature review and future directions. *European Management Journal*, 38(1), 78–94. DOI: 10.1016/j.emj.2019.06.005

De la Torre, R., Hsu, K., & Chiang, H. (2020). Project portfolio management: A review and a new framework for balancing strategic value and risk. *Journal of Strategic and Performance Management*, 11(3), 55–72.

De Lima Filho, F. S., Silveira, F. A. F., De Medeiros Brito, A.Junior, Vargas-Solar, G., & Silveira, L. F. (2019). Smart Detection: An Online Approach for DoS/DDoS Attack Detection Using Machine Learning. *Security and Communication Networks*, 2019(1), 1574749. DOI: 10.1155/2019/1574749

De Vivo, C., Barbato, G., Ellena, M., Capozzi, V., Budillon, G., & Mercogliano, P. (2023). Climate-Risk Assessment Framework for Airports under Extreme Precipitation Events: Application to Selected Italian Case Studies. *Sustainability (Basel)*, 15(9), 7300. DOI: 10.3390/su15097300

De Vivo, C., Ellena, M., Capozzi, V., Budillon, G., & Mercogliano, P. (2021). Risk assessment framework for Mediterranean airports: A focus on extreme temperatures and precipitations and sea level rise. *Natural Hazards*, 1–20.

Décaudin, J. M., & Lacoste, D. (2023). Airlines: Standardize Your International Advertising! *Journal of Travel Research*, 62(5), 1090–1104. DOI: 10.1177/00472875221115176

Deloitte. (2014). *Enterprise risk management*. Retrieved from https://www2.deloitte.com/gr/en/misc/litetopicpage.global-topic-tags.enterpriseriskmanagement.html

Denisov, O. E. (2019). Methods of ensuring the economic security of industries in the system of economic security of Ukraine. *State and Regions*, 6(111), 29–34. DOI: 10.32840/1814-1161/2019-6-6

Department of Technical Cybernetics(CPC). (2015). Electronic synopsis of lectures on the discipline "Empirical methods of software engineering". National Technical University of Ukraine "Kyiv Polytechnic Institute. Available at: https://surl.li/iwxjf

Desharnais. (2021). *Recovering Sustainably: Why and How Airports Can Initiate, Maintain, or Enhance Their Sustainability Commitments*. ACI World Insights. https://blog.aci.aero/recovering-sustainably-why-and-how-airports-can-initiate-maintain-or-enhance-their-sustainability-commitments/

DeVore, M. R., & Stähli, A. (2011). From armed neutrality to external dependence: Swiss security in the 21st century. *Schweizerische Zeitschrift für Politikwissenschaft*, 17(1), 1–26. DOI: 10.1111/j.1662-6370.2011.02003.x

Di Bona, G., Silvestri, A., Forcina, A., & Petrillo, A. (2018). Total efficient risk priority number (TERPN): A new method for risk assessment. *Journal of Risk Research*, 21(11), 1384–1408. DOI: 10.1080/13669877.2017.1307260

Díaz-Díaz, R., & Pérez-Bustamante, G. (2020). Digital innovation, ecosystem configurations, and the mediating role of absorptive capacity. *Journal of Business Research*, 120, 12–21.

Dietrich, P., & Lehtonen, P. (2005). Successful Management of Strategic Intentions through Multiple Projects – Reflections from Empirical Study. *International Journal of Project Management*, 23(5), 386–391. DOI: 10.1016/j.ijproman.2005.03.002

DiGiovanni, C.Jr. (2003). The spectrum of human reactions to terrorist attacks with weapons of mass destruction: Early management considerations. *Prehospital and Disaster Medicine*, 18(3), 253–257. DOI: 10.1017/S1049023X00001138 PMID: 15141866

Dimitriou, D., & Karagkouni, A. (2022a). Airports' Sustainability Strategy: Evaluation Framework Upon Environmental Awareness. *Frontiers in Sustainability*, 3, 1–11. DOI: 10.3389/frsus.2022.880718

Dimitriou, D., & Karagkouni, A. (2022b). Assortment of airports' sustainability strategy: A comprehensiveness analysis framework. *Sustainability*, 14(7), 1–18. DOI: 10.3390/su14074217 PMID: 36090804

Dimitriou, D., Sartzetaki, M., & Kalenteridou, I. (2021). Dual-level evaluation framework for airport user satisfaction. *International Journal of Operations Research and Information Systems*, 12(1), 17–30. DOI: 10.4018/IJORIS.2021010102

Distefano, N., & Leonardi, S. (2014). Risk assessment procedure for civil airport. *IJTTE. International Journal for Traffic and Transport Engineering*, 4(1), 62–75. DOI: 10.7708/ijtte.2014.4(1).05

Dolman, N., & Vorage, P. (2020). Preparing Singapore Changi Airport for the effects of climate change. *Journal of Airport Management*, 14(1), 54–66. DOI: 10.69554/VETC9210

DSNS. (2023). Emergency events. https://dsns.gov.ua/news/nadzvicaini-podiyi

Duarte, R. P. G. M. (2020). Case Study: Facebook in face of crisis (Doctoral dissertation).

Du, S., Bhattacharya, C. B., & Sen, S. (2010). Maximizing business returns to corporate social responsibility (CSR): The role of CSR communication. *International Journal of Management Reviews*, 12(1), 8–19. DOI: 10.1111/j.1468-2370.2009.00276.x

Dutra, C., Ribeiro, J., & Carvalho, M. (2014). An economic-probabilistic model for project selection and prioritization. *International Journal of Project Management*, 32(6), 1042–1055. DOI: 10.1016/j.ijproman.2013.12.004

EEA (2016). *Map book urban vulnerability to climate change Factsheets*. European Environment Agency.

EEA (2017b). *Climate change adaptation and disaster risk reduction in Europe.* European Environment Agency.

EEA. (2017a). *Climate change, impacts and vulnerability in Europe 2016. An indicator-based report.* European Environment Agency.

EEA. (2019). European Aviation. European Environment Agency.

Eilat, H., Golany, B., & Shtub, A. (2006). Constructing and evaluating balanced portfolios of R&D projects with interactions: A DEA based methodology. *European Journal of Operational Research*, 172(3), 1018–1039. DOI: 10.1016/j.ejor.2004.12.001

Elkington, J. (1997). The triple bottom line. *Environmental management: Readings and cases*, 2, 49-66.

Elonen, S., & Artto, K. (2003). Problems in managing internal development projects in multi-project environments. *International Journal of Project Management*, 2(6), 395–402. DOI: 10.1016/S0263-7863(02)00097-2

Enz, C. A. (2009). The physical safety and security features of U.S. hotels. *Cornell Hospitality Quarterly*, 50(4), 553–560. DOI: 10.1177/1938965509345963

Ershadi, M., Jefferies, M., Davis, P., & Mojtahedi, M. (2020). Towards successful establishment of a project portfolio management system: business process management approach. *Journal of Modern Project Management*, 23. .DOI: 10.19255/JMPM02302

Eser Davolio, M. (2019). Background of Jihadist radicalisation and measures for prevention and intervention in Switzerland. Sozialpolitik. ch, 2(2.2).

EU-CIRCLE. (2016). Impacts of climate change and extreme weather events on critical infrastructure state of the art review and taxonomy of existing knowledge. http:// www. eu- circle. eu/ for.

EUROCONTROL. (2013). *Challenges of growth 2013 - Task 8: Climate Change Risk and Resilience.*

EUROCONTROL. (2018). *European aviation in 2040. Challenges of Growth.*

EUROCONTROL. (2024). *Safety.* Available online at: https://www.EUROCONTROL .int/safety

European Aviation Safety Agency. (2022). *A Look into Historic and Future Scenarios of Air Traffic, Noise and Emissions.* European Aviation Environmental Report 2022. https://www.easa.europa.eu/en/light/topics/european-aviation-environmental-report-2022

European Aviation Safety Agency. (2024). *Balanced Approach Regulation.* EASA Pro. https://www.easa.europa.eu/en/domains/environment/policy-support-and-research/balanced-approach-regulation

European Commission. (2018). *Streamlining and strengthening corporate governance within the European Commission.* Retrieved from https://commission.europa.eu/system/files/2018-11/streamlining-strengthening-corporate-governance-european-commission_en.pdf

European Commission. (2024). *Environmental Noise Directive.* Energy, Climate change, Environment. https://environment.ec.europa.eu/topics/noise/environmental-noise-directive_en

European Environment Agency. (2022). *European Aviation Environmental Report 2022: Sustainability crucial for long-term viability of the sector.* European Environment Agency Newsroom. https://www.eea.europa.eu/en/newsroom/news/european-aviation-environmental-report-2022

Evans, K., & Reeder, F. (2010). *A human capital crisis in cybersecurity: Technical proficiency matters.* CSIS.

Eydeland, A., & Wolyniec, K. (2003). *Energy and power risk management: New developments in modeling, pricing, and hedging* (Vol. 206). John Wiley & Sons.

Fagarasan, C., Cristea, C., Cristea, M., Popa, O., & Pisla, A. (2023). Integrating Sustainability Metrics into Project and Portfolio Performance Assessment in Agile Software Development: A Data-Driven Scoring Model. *Sustainability (Basel)*, 15(17), 13139. DOI: 10.3390/su151713139

Faramarzi, M., Azizi, M., & Zeynalzadeh, S. (2020). Multi-criteria decision-making approaches for project portfolio management: A systematic review. *Journal of Strategic and International Studies*, 15(2), 72–88.

Farooq, U., Tariq, N., Asim, M., Baker, T., & Al-Shamma'a, A. (2022). Machine learning and the Internet of Things security: Solutions and open challenges. *Journal of Parallel and Distributed Computing*, 162, 89–104. DOI: 10.1016/j.jpdc.2022.01.015

Federal Aviation Administration. (2024). *Working to Build a Net-Zero Sustainable Aviation System by 2050.* Federal Aviation Administration. https://www.faa.gov/sustainability

Feitosa, W. R. (2002). Estratégias e políticas de preço no mercado de aviação: Caso da Gol transportes aéreos. *Revista Turismo em Análise*, 13(1), 48–65. DOI: 10.11606/issn.1984-4867.v13i1p48-65

Fichman, R. G., Dos Santos, B. L., & Zheng, Z. (2014). Digital innovation as a fundamental and powerful concept in the information systems curriculum. *Management Information Systems Quarterly*, 38(2), 329–A15. DOI: 10.25300/MISQ/2014/38.2.01

Financial Reporting Council. (2014). *Guidance on risk management, internal control and related financial and business reporting* (1st ed.). The Financial Reporting Council Limited. Retrieved from https://www.frc.org.uk/news-and-events/news/2014/09/frc-updates-uk-corporate-governance-code/

Financial Reporting Council. (2018). *Guidance on risk management, internal control and related financial and business reporting*. Retrieved from https://www.frc.org.uk/getattachment/d672c107-b1fb-4051-84b0-f5b83a1b93f6/Guidance-on-Risk-Management-Internal-Control-and-Related-Reporting.pdf

Financial Reporting Council. (2020). *Company guidance (Updated 20 May 2020) (COVID-19)*. Retrieved from https://www.frc.org.uk/news-and-events/news/2020/05/covid-19-update-7-may-2020/

Fishbein, M., & Ajzen, I. (1974). Attitudes towards Objectives as Predictors of Single and Multiple Behavorial Criteria. *Psychological Review*, 81, 1–59.

Fong, P. S., Ng, C. K., & Ho, S. K. (2023). Strategic alignment in project portfolio management: Emerging trends and practices. *International Journal of Project Management*, 41(1), 54–67.

Font, X., & Lynes, J. (2018). Corporate social responsibility in tourism and hospitality. *Journal of Sustainable Tourism*, 26(7), 1027–1042. DOI: 10.1080/09669582.2018.1488856

Fornell, C., & Larcher, D. F. (1981). Evaluating Structural Equation Models with Unobservable Variables and Measurement Error. *JMR, Journal of Marketing Research*, 25, 186–192.

Fraley, J. B., & Cannady, J. (2017). The promise of machine learning in cybersecurity. *Conference Proceedings - IEEE SOUTHEASTCON*. DOI: 10.1109/SECON.2017.7925283

Frankelius, P. (2009). Questioning two myths in innovation literature. *The Journal of High Technology Management Research*, 20(1), 40–51. DOI: 10.1016/j.hitech.2009.02.002

Franssen, E. A., Staatsen, B. A., & Lebret, E. (2002). Assessing health consequences in an environmental impact assessment: The case of Amsterdam Airport Schiphol. *Environmental Impact Assessment Review*, 22(6), 633–653. DOI: 10.1016/S0195-9255(02)00015-X

Frigo, M. L. (2018). Strategic Risk Management. In Augier, M., & Teece, D. J. (Eds.), *The Palgrave Encyclopedia of Strategic Management*. Palgrave Macmillan. DOI: 10.1057/978-1-137-00772-8_522

Galatchi, L. D. (2006). Environmental risk assessment. *Chemicals as intentional and accidental global environmental threats*, 1-6.

Gale, N. K., Heath, G., Cameron, E., Rashid, S., & Redwood, S. (2013). Using the framework method for the analysis of qualitative data in multi-disciplinary health research. *BMC Medical Research Methodology*, 13(1), 1–8. DOI: 10.1186/1471-2288-13-117 PMID: 24047204

Gaziano, C., & McGrath, K. (1986). Measuring the concept of credibility. *The Journalism Quarterly*, 63(3), 451–462. DOI: 10.1177/107769908606300301

Geller, E. S., Roberts, D. S., & Gilmore, M. R. (1996). Predicting Propensity to Actively Care for Occupational Safety. *Journal of Safety Research*, 27(1), 1–8. DOI: 10.1016/0022-4375(95)00024-0

Gemünden, H.G., Lehner, P., & Kock, A. (2018). The project-oriented organization and its contribution to innovation. *International Journal of Project Management*, 36(1), 147–160. https://doi.org/.ijproman.2017.07.009.DOI: 10.1016/j

Ghazi, K. (2016). Safety and security measures in Egyptian hotels. *Journal of Association of Arab Universities for Tourism and Hospitality*, 13(1), 165–190. DOI: 10.21608/jaauth.2016.49721

Giacomin, M., Wang, J., & Kuo, Y. (2021). Fuzzy logic applications in project portfolio management: A review and future directions. *International Journal of Project Management*, 39(6), 645–659.

Gligor, D., Bozkurt, S., Russo, I., & Omar, A. (2019). A look into the past and future: Theories within supply chain management, marketing, and management. *Supply Chain Management*, 24(1), 170–186. DOI: 10.1108/SCM-03-2018-0124

Graebner, M. E. (2021). Evolution of Qualitative Research Methods in Strategic Management. In Duhaime, I. M., Hitt, M. A., & Lyles, M. A. (Eds.), *Strategic Management: State of the Field and Its Future* (pp. 99–114). Academic. DOI: 10.1093/oso/9780190090883.003.0006

Graydon, P. J., & Holloway, C. M. (2017). An investigation of proposed techniques for quantifying confidence in assurance arguments. *Safety Science*, 92, 53–65. DOI: 10.1016/j.ssci.2016.09.014

Green, S., & Harris, M. (2023). Integrating project selection frameworks with business intelligence tools. *Journal of Information Technology*, 38(1), 89–104.

GRI. (2021). *The GRI Standards A Guide For Policy Makers*. GRI Standards How Policymakers Can Drive Sustainability Reporting. https://www.globalreporting.org/news/news-center/how-policymakers-can-drive-sustainability-reporting/

Grigoroudis, E., Orfanoudaki, E., & Zopounidis, C. (2012). Strategic performance measurement in a healthcare organisation: A multiple criteria approach based on balanced scorecard. *Omega*, 40(1), 104–119. DOI: 10.1016/j.omega.2011.04.001

Grigoroudis, E., & Siskos, Y. (2012). Decision Support Systems for the Selection of Projects: A Review of Multi-Criteria Methods. *European Journal of Operational Research*, 220(2), 305–317.

Hadjinicolaou, N., Kader, M., & Abdallah, I. (2022). Strategic Innovation, Foresight and the Deployment of Project Portfolio Management under Mid-Range Planning Conditions in Medium-Sized Firms. *Sustainability*, 14(80). Advance online publication. DOI: 10.3390/su14010

Hagmann, J., Davidshofer, S., Tawfik, A., Wenger, A., & Wildi, L. (2018). The programmatic and institutional (re-) configuration of the Swiss national security field. *Schweizerische Zeitschrift für Politikwissenschaft*, 24(3), 215–245. DOI: 10.1111/spsr.12304

Haimes, Y. Y. (2009). On the definition of resilience in systems. *Risk Analysis*, 29(4), 498–501. DOI: 10.1111/j.1539-6924.2009.01216.x PMID: 19335545

Hair, J., Hollingsworth, C. L., Randolph, A. B., & Chong, A. Y. L. (2017). An updated and expanded assessment of PLS-SEM in information systems research. *Industrial Management & Data Systems*, 117(3), 442–458. DOI: 10.1108/IMDS-04-2016-0130

Halawa, W., Abdelalim, A., & Elrashed, I. (2013). Financial evaluation program for construction projects at the pre-investment phase in developing countries: A case study. *International Journal of Project Management*, 31(6), 912–923. DOI: 10.1016/j.ijproman.2012.11.001

Halpern, N., Budd, T., Suau-Sanchez, P., Bråthen, S., & Mwesiumo, D. (2021). Conceptualising airport digital maturity and dimensions of technological and organisational transformation. *Journal of Airport Management*, 15(2), 182–203. DOI: 10.69554/MZJB2664

Hartono, E., Holsapple, C. W., Kim, K. Y., Na, K. S., & Simpson, J. T. (2014). Measuring perceived security in B2C electronic commerce website usage: A re-specification and validation. *Decision Support Systems*, 62, 11–21. DOI: 10.1016/j. dss.2014.02.006

Harvey, G., & Turnbull, P. (2010). On the Go: Walking the high road at a low cost airline. *International Journal of Human Resource Management*, 21(2), 230–241. DOI: 10.1080/09585190903509548

Haynie, B. (2021). *Climate Change Migration: Developing a Security Strategy for All*. RAND. (https://www.rand.org/well-being/portfolios/mass-migration.html)

Hedberg, T. D., Bajaj, M., & Camelio, J. A. (2019). Using Graphs to Link Data Across the Product Lifecycle for Enabling Smart Manufacturing Digital Threads. *ASME Journal of Computing and Information Science in Engineering*, 1, 213–224.

Hellenic Corporate Governance Council. (2021). Code of corporate governance for listed companies. Retrieved from https://www.esed.org.gr/en/code-listed

Henderson, T., & Boje, D. M. (2018). *Organizational development and change theory managing fractal organizing processes*. Routledge.

Henseler, J., Ringle, C. M., & Sinkovics, R. R. (2009). The use of partial least squares path modeling in international marketing. In *New challenges to international marketing*. Emerald Group Publishing Limited. DOI: 10.1108/S1474-7979(2009)0000020014

Hillson, D. (2012). *Managing risk in projects*. Gower Publishing, Ltd.

Holmes-Smith, P. (2006). *School socio-economic density and its effect on school performance*. Mceetya.

Holzmann, R., & Jorgensen, S. (1999). *Social protection as social risk management*. The World Bank.

Hossain, M. D., Ochiai, H., Doudou, F., & Kadobayashi, Y. (2020). SSH and FTP brute-force attacks detection in computer networks: Lstm and machine learning approaches. *2020 5th International Conference on Computer and Communication Systems, ICCCS 2020*, 491–497. DOI: 10.1109/ICCCS49078.2020.9118459

Ho, W. (2008). Integrated analytic hierarchy process and its applications – A literature review. *European Journal of Operational Research*, 186(1), 211–228. DOI: 10.1016/j.ejor.2007.01.004

Hsu, S., Weng, K., Cui, Q., & Rand, W. (2015). Understanding the complexity of project team member selection through agent-based modeling. *International Journal of Project Management*, 34(1), 82–93. DOI: 10.1016/j.ijproman.2015.10.001

Huang, Y., McMurran, R., Dhadyalla, G., & Jones, R. P. (2008). Probability based vehicle fault diagnosis: Bayesian network method. *Journal of Intelligent Manufacturing*, 19(3), 301–311. DOI: 10.1007/s10845-008-0083-7

Huesig, S., & Endres, H. (2018). Exploring the digital innovation process: The role of functionality for the adoption of innovation management software by innovation managers. *European Journal of Innovation Management*, 22(2), 302–314. DOI: 10.1108/EJIM-02-2018-0051

Hughes, G. (2023). War in the grey zone: Historical reflections and contemporary implications. In Survival: Global Politics and Strategy June-July 2020 (pp. 131-157). Routledge.

Hull, T. (2010), April. A deterministic scenario approach to risk management. In *2010 Enterprise Risk Management Symposium* (pp. 1-7).

Husted, J. A., Cook, R. J., Farewell, V. T., & Gladman, D. D. (2000). Methods for assessing responsiveness: A critical review and recommendations. *Journal of Clinical Epidemiology*, 53(5), 459–468. DOI: 10.1016/S0895-4356(99)00206-1 PMID: 10812317

Hutchison-Krupat, J., & Kavadias, S. (2014). Strategic Resource Allocation: Top-Down, Bottom-Up, and the Value of Strategic Buckets. *Management Science*, (September), 391–412.

Iamratanakul, S., Patanakul, P., & Milosevic, D. (2008). Project portfolio selection: From past to present. *4th IEEE International Conference on Management of Innovation and Technology*.

IATA. (2022). *Airport Environmental Sustainability*. IATA. chrome-extension://efaid-nbmnnnibpcajpcglclefindmkaj/https://www.iata.org/contentassets/d1d4d535bf1c4 ba695f43e9beff8294f/airport-environmental-sustainability-policy.pdf

IATA. (2024). *Safety*. Available online at: https://www.iata.org/en/programs/safety/

IATA. (2024, April). *Passenger Demand Up 21.5% in February*. Pressroom. https://www.iata.org/en/pressroom/2024-releases/2024-04-04-01/#:~:text=Geneva%20 %2D%20The%20International%20Air%20Transport,21.5%25%20compared%20 to%20February%202023

IBEF. (2021). Indian Brand Equity Foundation. https://www.ibef.org/economy/indian-economy-overview

IBEF. (2022). Indian Brand Equity Foundation. https://www.ibef.org/economy/economic-survey-2021-22

IBEF. (2024). Indian Brand Equity Foundation. https://www.ibef.org/industry/india-automobiles

ICAO. (2012). *Global Aviation and Our Sustainable Future*. ICAO Rio +20. https://www.icao.int/environmental-protection/Documents/Rio+20_booklet.pdf

ICAO. (2013). *Annex 19 - Safety Management*. International Civil Aviation Organization.

ICAO. (2020). *Airport Economics Manual Doc 9562*. ICAO Economic Development. https://www.icao.int/publications/Documents/9562_cons_en.pdf

ICAO. (2022). *Key Steps for Aviation Organisation Climate Change Risk Assessment and Adaptation Planning: Key Steps for Aviation Organisation Climate Change Risk Assessment and Adaptation Planning*. International Civil Aviation Organization.

IOM. (2018). About the Niamey declaration. Niamey Declaration. https://www.niameydeclarationguide.org/#:~:text=ABOUT%20THE%20NIAMEY%20DECLARATION&text=At%20the%20meeting%2C%20a%20joint,migrants%20and%20victims%20of%20trafficking

Irwin, L. (2024, January 16). *Almost 2,000 flights canceled as airports deal with snow, ice*. The Hill. Available online at https://thehill.com/policy/transportation/4411649-winter-storm-flights-canceled-la-guardia-reagan/

ISO. (2018). *ISO 31000*. Retrieved from https://www.iso.org/obp/ui#iso:std:iso:31000:ed-2:v1:en

Ittner, C. D., & Larcker, D. F. (2021). The audit committee's role in overseeing and ensuring effective risk management. *Journal of Accounting Research*, 59(2), 455–485. DOI: 10.1111/1475-679X.12350

Iwendi, C., Rehman, S. U., Javed, A. R., Khan, S., & Srivastava, G. (2021). Sustainable Security for the Internet of Things Using Artificial Intelligence Architectures. *ACM Transactions on Internet Technology*, 21(3), 1–22. DOI: 10.1145/3448614

Jackob, N. (2008). *Credibility effects*. The International Encyclopedia of Communication. DOI: 10.1002/9781405186407.wbiecc153

Jacxsens, L., Uyttendaele, M., & De Meulenaer, B. (2016). Challenges in risk assessment: Quantitative risk assessment. *Procedia Food Science*, 6, 23–30. DOI: 10.1016/j.profoo.2016.02.004

Jain, V., Rastogi, M., Ramesh, J. V. N., Chauhan, A., Agarwal, P., Pramanik, S., & Gupta, A. (2023). FinTech and Artificial Intelligence in Relationship Banking and Computer Technology. In Saini, K., Mummoorthy, A., Chandrika, R., Gowri Ganesh, N. S., & Global, I. G. I. (Eds.), *AI, IoT, and Blockchain Breakthroughs in E-Governance*. DOI: 10.4018/978-1-6684-7697-0.ch011

Janz, M. R., Soi, N., Russell, R., & the World Vision International. (2009) Collaboration and partnership in humanitarian action. Humanitarian Practice Network, *45*(15). https://odihpn.org/publication/collaboration-and-partnership-in-humanitarian-action/

Jenkins, H., & Yakovleva, N. (2006). Corporate social responsibility in the mining industry: Exploring trends in social and environmental disclosure. *Journal of Cleaner Production*, 14(3-4), 271–284. DOI: 10.1016/j.jclepro.2004.10.004

Jeong, C. B., Kang, H. M., Lee, Y. H., Kim, M. S., Lee, J. S., Seo, J. S., Wang, M., & Lee, J. S. (2018). Nanoplastic ingestion enhances toxicity of persistent organic pollutants (POPs) in the monogonont rotifer Brachionus koreanus via multixenobiotic resistance (MXR) disruption. *Environmental Science & Technology*, 52(19), 11411–11418. DOI: 10.1021/acs.est.8b03211 PMID: 30192528

Jepsen, A. L., & Eskerod, P. (2009). Stakeholder analysis in projects: Challenges in using current guidelines in the real world. *International Journal of Project Management*, 27(4), 335–343. DOI: 10.1016/j.ijproman.2008.04.002

Jones, R. N. (2001). An environmental risk assessment/management framework for climate change impact assessments. *Natural Hazards*, 23(2-3), 197–230. DOI: 10.1023/A:1011148019213

Jonsson, P., & Mårtensson, M. (2018). Dynamic capabilities in project portfolio management: A conceptual framework. *International Journal of Project Management*, 36(4), 602–617.

Jordão, C. T. (2009). A sustainability overview of the best practices in the airport sector. Scientific papers of the University of Pardubice. Series D, Faculty of Economics and Administration. 15.

Jore, S. H., Utland, I.-L. F., & Vatnamo, V. H. (2018). The contribution of foresight to improve long-term security planning. *Foresight*, 20(1), 68–83. DOI: 10.1108/FS-08-2017-0045

Junkes, M. B., Tereso, A. P., & Afonso, P. S. (2015). The importance of risk assessment in the context of investment project management: A case study. *Procedia Computer Science*, 64, 902–910. DOI: 10.1016/j.procs.2015.08.606

Jyh, D. (2015). Strategic project portfolio selection for national research institutes. *Journal of Business Research*, 68(11), 2305–2311. DOI: 10.1016/j.jbusres.2015.06.016

Kaldor, M. (2014). Human security: Political authority in a global era. In Martin, M., & Taylor, O. (Eds.), *Routledge Handbook of Human Security*. Routledge.

Kaplan, R., & Norton, D. (1992). The balanced scorecard-measures that drive performance. *Harvard Business Review*, 70, 71–79. PMID: 10119714

Karagiannis, I., Vouros, P., Skouloudis, A., & Evangelinos, K. (2019). Sustainability reporting, materiality, and accountability assessment in the airport industry. *Business Strategy and the Environment*, 28(7), 1370–1405. DOI: 10.1002/bse.2321

Karaman, A. S., Kilic, M., & Uyar, A. (2018). Sustainability reporting in the aviation industry: Worldwide evidence. *Sustainability Accounting. Management and Policy Journal*, 9(4), 362–391. DOI: 10.1108/SAMPJ-12-2017-0150

Kaya, G., Aydın, U., Ülengin, B., Karadayı, M. A., & Ülengin, F. (2023). How do airlines survive? An integrated efficiency analysis on the survival of airlines. *Journal of Air Transport Management*, 107, 102348. DOI: 10.1016/j.jairtraman.2022.102348

Kendall, G., & Rollins, S. (2003). *Advanced Project Portfolio Management and the PMO, Multiplying ROI at Warp Speed*. J. Ross Publishing, Inc.

Kersten, A., & Budowski, M. (2016). A gender perspective on state support for crime victims in Switzerland. *International Journal of Conflict and Violence*, 10(1), 127–140.

Kerzner, H. (2023). *Project Management: A Systems Approach to Planning, Scheduling, and Controlling*. Wiley.

Keskin, D. (2020). A two-stage fuzzy approach for Industry 4.0 project portfolio selection within criteria and project interdependencies context. *Journal of Multi-Criteria Decision Analysis*, 27(1–2), 65–83. DOI: 10.1002/mcda.1691

Kester, L., Griffin, A., Hultink, E. J., & Lauche, K. (2009). Portfolio decision-making genres: A case study. *Journal of Engineering and Technology Management*, 26(4), 327–341. DOI: 10.1016/j.jengtecman.2009.10.006

Ketabdari, M., Giustozzi, F., & Crispino, M. (2018). Sensitivity analysis of influencing factors in probabilistic risk assessment for airports. *Safety Science*, 107, 173–187. DOI: 10.1016/j.ssci.2017.07.005

Khalili-Damghani, K., & Tavana, M. (2014). A comprehensive framework for sustainable project portfolio selection based on structural equation modelling. *Project Management Journal*, 45(2), 83–97. DOI: 10.1002/pmj.21404

Khalili-Damghani, K., & Tavana, M. (2022). Project portfolio management: A review and future research directions. *European Journal of Operational Research*, 299(3), 815–832. DOI: 10.1016/j.ejor.2021.07.023

Khanh, P. T., Ng c, T. H., & Pramanik, S. (2023). Future of Smart Agriculture Techniques and Applications. In Khang, A., & Global, I. G. I. (Eds.), *Advanced Technologies and AI-Equipped IoT Applications in High Tech Agriculture*. DOI: 10.4018/978-1-6684-9231-4.ch021

Khan, W. Z., Rehman, M. H., Zangoti, H. M., Afzal, M. K., Armi, N., & Salah, K. (2020). Industrial internet of things: Recent advances, enabling technologies and open challenges. *Computers & Electrical Engineering*, 81, 1–13. DOI: 10.1016/j.compeleceng.2019.106522

Kilincer, I. F., Ertam, F., & Sengur, A. (2021). Machine learning methods for cyber security intrusion detection: Datasets and comparative study. *Computer Networks*, 188, 107840. Advance online publication. DOI: 10.1016/j.comnet.2021.107840

Killen, C. P., Hunt, R. A., & Kleinschmidt, E. J. (2008). Project portfolio management for product innovation. *International Journal of Quality & Reliability Management*, 25(1), 24–38. DOI: 10.1108/02656710810843559

Kim, J. J., Panton, A., & Schwerhoff, G. (2024). Energy security and the green transition.

Kim, H., & Park, H. (2021). A Hybrid Approach for Sustainable Project Portfolio Management: Integration of Machine Learning and Multi-Criteria Decision-Making. *Journal of Cleaner Production*, 303, 127021.

Kinyua, J., & Awuah, L. (2021). AI/ML in Security Orchestration, Automation and Response: Future Research Directions. *Intelligent Automation & Soft Computing*, 28(2), 527–545. DOI: 10.32604/iasc.2021.016240

Kizito, R., Abolhasani, M., & Cohen, J. (2021). Enhancing project portfolio management through a hybrid multi-criteria decision-making approach. *International Journal of Operations & Production Management*, 41(7), 1246–1272.

Kochan, C. G., & Nowicki, D. R. (2018). Supply chain resilience: A systematic literature review and typological framework. *International Journal of Physical Distribution & Logistics Management*, 48(8), 842–865. DOI: 10.1108/IJPDLM-02-2017-0099

Kock, A., & Gemünden, H. G. (2016). The effects of project portfolio management on project success: A longitudinal study. *International Journal of Project Management*, 34(2), 119–133.

Koç, S., & Durmaz, V. (2015). Airport corporate sustainability: An analysis of indicators reported in the sustainability practices. *Procedia: Social and Behavioral Sciences*, 181, 158–170. DOI: 10.1016/j.sbspro.2015.04.877

Kolk, A. (2005). Sustainability reporting. *VBA Journal, 21*(3), 34-42.

Kompanets, K., Antonyuk, I., & Medvedeva, A. (2022). Marketing techniques in the organization of the restaurant business of Ukraine during the war. *Science and Technology Today*, 5(5). Advance online publication. DOI: 10.52058/2786-6025-2022-5(5)-78-86

Korstanje, M. E. (2020). Tourism Security: A Critical Insight, Korstanje, M.E., & Seraphin, H. (Eds.) *Tourism, Terrorism and Security: Tourism Security-Safety and Post Conflict Destinations* (pp. 1-20). Emerald Publishing Limited, Leeds. DOI: 10.1108/978-1-83867-905-720201002

Koufteros, X. A. (1999). Testing a model of pull production: A paradigm for manufacturing research using structural equation modeling. *Journal of Operations Management*, 17(4), 467–488. DOI: 10.1016/S0272-6963(99)00002-9

Krasnomovets, V. (2023). Theoretical foundations of hotel safety within the system of sustainable development. *Visegrad Journal on Bioeconomy and Sustainable Development*, 12(2), 54–59. DOI: 10.2478/vjbsd-2023-0011

Kristoff, M., & Panarelli, L. (2010). Haiti: A republic of NGOs? In *Peace Brief*. United States Institute of Peace.

Kruck, A., & Weiss, M. (2023). The regulatory security state in Europe. *Journal of European Public Policy*, 30(7), 1205–1229. DOI: 10.1080/13501763.2023.2172061

KSE. (2023). A report on the direct damage to the infrastructure from the destruction caused by Russia's military aggression against Ukraine a year after the start of the full-scale invasion. https://kse.ua/wp-content/uploads/2023/03/UKR_Feb23_FINAL_Damages-Report.pdf

Kudratova, S., Huang, X., & Zhou, X. (2018). Sustainable project selection: Optimal project selection considering sustainability under reinvestment strategy. *Journal of Cleaner Production*, 203, 469–481. DOI: 10.1016/j.jclepro.2018.08.259

Kumar, P.S., Ravi, M. & Vijayakumar, K.C.K. (2016). Risk Assessment for Machinery Shop in Automobile Industry. *International Journal of Mathematical Sciences and Engineering, 5.*

Kumar, R., & Lightner, R. (2007). Games as an interactive classroom technique: Perceptions of corporate trainers, college instructors and students. *International Journal on Teaching and Learning in Higher Education*, 19(1), 53–63.

Kumar, S., Xiao, J. J., Pattnaik, D., Lim, W. M., & Rasul, T. (2022). Past, present and future of bank marketing: A bibliometric analysis of International Journal of Bank Marketing (1983–2020). *International Journal of Bank Marketing*, 40(2), 341–383. DOI: 10.1108/IJBM-07-2021-0351

Kusiak, A. (2019). Fundamentals of smart manufacturing: A multi-thread perspective. *Annual Reviews in Control*, 47, 214–220. DOI: 10.1016/j.arcontrol.2019.02.001

Kuzey, C., & Uyar, A. (2017). Determinants of sustainability reporting and its impact on firm value: Evidence from the emerging market of Turkey. *Journal of Cleaner Production*, 143, 27–39. DOI: 10.1016/j.jclepro.2016.12.153

Kuzmenko, O., Makliuk, O., & Chernyshova, O. (2022). Business cybersecurity in a time of war. *Economy and Society*, 44. Advance online publication. DOI: 10.32782/2524-0072/2022-44-21

Kyiv School of Economics (KSE). (2023). Report on damages to infrastructure caused by Russia's war against Ukraine: One year after the start of the full-scale invasion. Available at: https://kse.ua/wp-content/uploads/2023/03/ENG_FINAL_Damages-Report_.pdf

Lappe, M., & Spang, K. (2014). Investments in project management are profitable: A case study-based analysis of the relationship between the costs and benefits of project management. *International Journal of Project Management*, 32(4), 603–612. DOI: 10.1016/j.ijproman.2013.10.005

Learmonth, I. (2020). *Clean energy and infrastructure: Pathway to airport sustainability.* CEFC. https://www.cefc.com.au/media/402343/cefc-pathway-to-airport-sustainability.pdf

Lee, J., & Kim, S. (2000). An integrated approach for interdependent information system project selection. *International Journal of Project Management*, 2000(19), 111–118.

Lee, M. C. (2009). Predicting and explaining the adoption of online trading: An empirical study in Taiwan. *Decision Support Systems*, 47(2), 133–142. DOI: 10.1016/j.dss.2009.02.003

Leung, Y. (2013). Perceived benefits. Encyclopedia of behavioral medicine, 1450-1451. DOI: 10.1007/978-1-4419-1005-9_1165

Levine, H. A. (2005). *Project portfolio management: A Practical Guide to Selecting Projects, Managing Portfolios, and Maximizing Benefits.* Pfeiffer Wiley.

Levine, M. E. (2006). Why weren't the airlines reregulated. *Yale Journal on Regulation*, 23, 269.

LHR. (2011). *HAL final report*. Heathrow Airport Limited.

Liao, Z., & Shi, X. (2017). Web functionality, web content, information security, and online tourism service continuance. *Journal of Retailing and Consumer Services*, 39, 258–263. DOI: 10.1016/j.jretconser.2017.06.003

Liaw, J., De Silva, N., Ibrahim, N., Moiden, A. H., Razak, M. A., & Abd Khalil, A. (2021). The Impact on Non-Traditional Security Threats in Sri Lanka. Akademika, 91(3).

Lien, C. H., Hsu, M. K., Shang, J. Z., & Wang, S. W. (2021). Self-service technology adoption by air passengers: A case study of fast air travel services in Taiwan. *Service Industries Journal*, 41(9-10), 671–695. DOI: 10.1080/02642069.2019.1569634

Lim, M. K., Bahr, W., & Leung, S. C. (2013). RFID in the warehouse: A literature analysis (1995–2010) of its applications, benefits, challenges and future trends. *International Journal of Production Economics*, 145(1), 409–430. DOI: 10.1016/j.ijpe.2013.05.006

Lin, C., & Chen, Y. (2004). Bid/no-bid decision-making - a fuzzy linguistic approach. *International Journal of Project Management*, 22(7), 585–593. DOI: 10.1016/j.ijproman.2004.01.005

Lin, E., Chen, Q., & Qi, X. (2020). Deep reinforcement learning for imbalanced classification. *Applied Intelligence*, 50(8), 2488–2502. DOI: 10.1007/s10489-020-01637-z

Linstone, H., & Turoff, M. (2002). *The Delphi Method - Techniques and applications. The delphi method - Techniques and applications*. Adison Wesley.

Lin, Y., Wang, Y., & Yu, C. (2010). Investigating the drivers of the innovation in channel integration and supply chain performance: A strategy orientated perspective. *International Journal of Production Economics*, 127(2), 320–332. DOI: 10.1016/j.ijpe.2009.08.009

Liu, B. (2006). A survey of credibility theory. *Fuzzy Optimization and Decision Making*, 5(4), 387–408. DOI: 10.1007/s10700-006-0016-x

Liu, Q., & Xu, J. (2023). Continuous monitoring in project portfolio management: Strategies and best practices. *International Journal of Operations & Production Management*, 43(1), 32–48.

Liu, W., Wang, X., & Zhao, Y. (2022). Dynamic Project Portfolio Management in the Age of Sustainability: A Systematic Review and Future Research Agenda. *International Journal of Project Management*, 40(3), 153–170.

Lopez Perez, R., Adamsky, F., Soua, R., & Engel, T. (2018). Machine Learning for Reliable Network Attack Detection in SCADA Systems. *Proceedings - 17th IEEE International Conference on Trust, Security and Privacy in Computing and Communications and 12th IEEE International Conference on Big Data Science and Engineering, Trustcom/BigDataSE 2018*, 633–638. DOI: 10.1109/TrustCom/BigDataSE.2018.00094

Lopez, A. (2016). Vulnerability of airports on climate change: An assessment methodology. *Transportation Research Procedia*, 14, 24–31. DOI: 10.1016/j.trpro.2016.05.037

López-Chaua, A., Cervantes, J., López-García, L., & Lamont, F. (2013). Fisher's decision tree. *Expert Systems with Applications*, 40(16), 6283–6291. DOI: 10.1016/j.eswa.2013.05.044

Lu, Liu, Wang, Huang, & Xu. (2020). Smart manufacturing: Connotation, reference model, applications and research issues. Robotics and Computer-Integrated Manufacturing, 61, 1-14.

Luna, R., Rhine, E., Myhra, M., Sullivan, R., & Kruse, C. S. (2016). Cyber threats to health information systems: A systematic review. In *Technology and Health Care* (Vol. 24, Issue 1, pp. 1–9). IOS Press. DOI: 10.3233/THC-151102

Mahn, T. (2013). *Country-Level Aid Coordination at the United Nations – Taking the ResidentCoordinator System Forward*. The German Development Institute.

Malathi, C., & Padmaja, I. N. (2023). Identification of cyber attacks using machine learning in smart IoT networks. *Materials Today: Proceedings*, 80, 2518–2523. DOI: 10.1016/j.matpr.2021.06.400

Mane, N., Verma, A., & Arya, A. (2020). A Pragmatic Optimal Approach for Detection of Cyber Attacks using Genetic Programming. *20th IEEE International Symposium on Computational Intelligence and Informatics, CINTI 2020 - Proceedings*, 71–76. DOI: 10.1109/CINTI51262.2020.9305844

Manuele, F. A. (2016). Root-Causal Factors: Uncovering the Hows & Whys of Incidents. *Professional Safety*, 61(05), 48–55.

Marhavilas, P. K., Koulouriotis, D., & Gemeni, V. (2011). Risk analysis and assessment methodologies in the worksites: On a review, classification and comparative study of the scientific literature of the period 2000–2009. *Journal of Loss Prevention in the Process Industries*, 24(5), 477–523. DOI: 10.1016/j.jlp.2011.03.004

Markovska, A. V., & Zholobnyuk, D. O. (2023). Restaurant business during the war. *Black Sea Scientific Studies*, 65-67, 65–67. Advance online publication. DOI: 10.36059/978-966-397-300-5-18

Martinsuo, M. (2013). Project portfolio management in practice and in context. *International Journal of Project Management*, 31(6), 794–803. DOI: 10.1016/j.ijproman.2012.10.013

Martinsuo, M., Korhonen, T., & Laine, T. (2014). Identifying, framing and managing uncertainties in project portfolios. *International Journal of Project Management*, 32(5), 732–746. DOI: 10.1016/j.ijproman.2014.01.014

Martinsuo, M., & Lehtonen, P. (2007). Role of single-project management in achieving portfolio management efficiency. *International Journal of Project Management*, 25(1), 56–65. DOI: 10.1016/j.ijproman.2006.04.002

Maryam, S. Z., Ahmad, A., Aslam, N., & Farooq, S. (2022). Reputation and cost benefits for attitude and adoption intention among potential customers using theory of planned behavior: An empirical evidence from Pakistan. *Journal of Islamic Marketing*, 13(10), 2090–2107. DOI: 10.1108/JIMA-03-2021-0059

Mazaraki, A. A., & Bosovska, M. V. (2013). Theoretical and methodological foundations of the formation of the integration strategy of enterprises. *Business Info*, 7, 299–308.

McKinsey & Company. (2020). *Investors remind business leaders: Governance matters*. Retrieved from https://www.mckinsey.com/business-functions/strategy-and-corporate-finance/our-insights/investors-remind-business-leaders-governance-matters

Mclaughlin, S., & Cooper, J. A. G. (2010). A multi-scale coastal vulnerability index: A tool for coastal managers? *Environmental Hazards*, 9(3), 233–248. DOI: 10.3763/ehaz.2010.0052

Merz, F. (2021). Improving National PVE Strategies: Lessons Learned from the Swiss Case. Researching the Evolution of Countering Violent Extremism, 22.

Meskendahl, S. (2010). The influence of business strategy on project portfolio management and its success - A conceptual framework. *International Journal of Project Management*, 28(8), 807–817. DOI: 10.1016/j.ijproman.2010.06.007

Milis, K., & Mercken, R. (2004). The use of the balanced scorecard for the evaluation of Information and Communication Technology projects. *International Journal of Project Management*, 22(2), 87–97. DOI: 10.1016/S0263-7863(03)00060-7

Mishra, B. K., Kumar, P., Saraswat, C., Chakraborty, S., & Gautam, A. (2021). Water security in a changing environment: Concept, challenges and solutions. *Water (Basel)*, 13(4), 490. DOI: 10.3390/w13040490

Mittal, S., Khan, M. A., Purohit, J. K., Menon, K., Romero, D., & Wuest, T. (2020). A smart manufacturing adoption framework for SMEs. *International Journal of Production Research*, 58(5), 1555–1573. DOI: 10.1080/00207543.2019.1661540

Mohagheghi, V., Mousavi, S., Antucheviciene, J., & Mojtahedi, M. (2019). Project portfolio selection problems: A review of models, uncertainty approaches, solution techniques, and case studies. *Technological and Economic Development of Economy*, 25(6), 1380–1412. DOI: 10.3846/tede.2019.11410

Mohammad, J., & Pan, Y. (2021). Sustainability, the Fourth Pillar of Project Portfolio Management: A Holistic Approach. *Journal of Modern Project Management*, 27(9), 199-215. DOI: DOI: 10.19255/JMPM02714

Mohammad, A., Maen, A., Szilveszter, K., & Mouhammd, A. 2017. Evaluation of machine learning algorithms for intrusion detection system. In *Proceedings of the IEEE 15th International Symposium on Intelligent Systems and Informatics (SISY'17)*. IEEE.

Mondal, D., Ratnaparkhi, A., Deshpande, A., Deshpande, V., Kshirsagar, A. P., & Pramanik, S. (2023). Applications, Modern Trends and Challenges of Multiscale Modelling in Smart Cities. In *Data-Driven Mathematical Modeling in Smart Cities*. IGI Global. DOI: 10.4018/978-1-6684-6408-3.ch001

Morris, P. W. G., & Jamieson, A. (2005). *Moving from corporate strategy to project strategy*. Project Management Institute. DOI: 10.1177/875697280503600402

Moskalenko, V. V., & Godlevskyi, M. D. (2018). Modeli ta metody stratehichnoho upravlinnia rozvytkom pidpryiemstva [Models and methods of strategic management of enterprise development]. Ministry of Education and Science of Ukraine, National Technical University "Kharkiv Polytechnic Institute". Kharkiv: Tochka. http://library.kpi.kharkov.ua/en/node/8774

Mueller, K. L., Lauvaux, T., Gurney, K. R., Roest, G., Ghosh, S., Gourdji, S. M., Karion, A., DeCola, P., & Whetstone, J. (2021). An emerging GHG estimation approach can help cities achieve their climate and sustainability goals. *Environmental Research Letters*, 16(8), 084003. DOI: 10.1088/1748-9326/ac0f25

Müller, R., Martinsuo, M., & Blomquist, T. (2008). Project portfolio control and portfolio management performance in different contexts. *Project Management Journal*, 39(3), 28–42. DOI: 10.1002/pmj.20053

Müller, R., & Turner, J. R. (2013). Leadership competency profiles of successful project managers. *International Journal of Project Management*, 31(1), 40–50.

Myers, S., Brealy, R., & Allen, F. (2014). Principles of Corporate Finance (10^a ed.). New York: McGraw-Hill Irwin.

Nagariya, R., Kumar, D., & Kumar, I. (2020). Service supply chain: From bibliometric analysis to content analysis, current research trends and future research directions. *Benchmarking*, 28(1), 333–369. DOI: 10.1108/BIJ-04-2020-0137

Naji, N., & Schildknecht, D. (2021). Securing Swiss Futurity: The Gefährder Figure and Switzerland's Counterterrorism Regime. *Social Sciences (Basel, Switzerland)*, 10(12), 484. DOI: 10.3390/socsci10120484

Nambisan, P. (2017). *An introduction to ethical, safety and intellectual property rights issues in biotechnology*. Academic Press.

Nasierowski, W., & Arcelus, F. J. (2012). What is innovativeness: literature review. *Foundations of Management, 4*(1), 63-74.

Neely, A., Gregory, M., & Platts, K. (2021). Performance Measurement System Design: A Literature Review and Research Agenda. *International Journal of Operations & Production Management*, 41(9), 88–112.

Nir, K. (2021). Economics of artificial intelligence in cybersecurity. *IT Professional*, 23(5), 73–77. DOI: 10.1109/MITP.2021.3100177

Nolte, I. M. (2018). Interorganizational collaborations for humanitarian aid: An analysis of partnership, community, and single organization outcomes. *Public Performance & Management Review*, 41(3), 596–619. Advance online publication. DOI: 10.1080/15309576.2018.1462212

Norton, S. B., Rodier, D. J., van der Schalie, W. H., Wood, W. P., Slimak, M. W., & Gentile, J. H. (1992). A framework for ecological risk assessment at the EPA. *Environmental Toxicology and Chemistry*, 11(12), 1663–1672. DOI: 10.1002/ etc.5620111202

NOVA. (2008). A Radical Mind. https://www.pbs.org/wgbh/nova/article/mandelbrot -fractal/

Nowak, M. (2013). Project portfolio selection using interactive approach. *Procedia Engineering*, 57, 814–822. DOI: 10.1016/j.proeng.2013.04.103

Nunnally, J. C. (1978). An overview of psychological measurement. *Clinical diagnosis of mental disorders: A handbook*, 97-146.

OECD. (2015). *G20/OECD principles of corporate governance*. OECD Publishing., DOI: 10.1787/9789264236882-

OECD. (2019). *Lives in Crises: What Do People Tell Us About the Humanitarian Aid They Receive?* OECD Publishing. DOI: 10.1787/9d39623d-

OECD. (2019). *OECD corporate governance factbook 2019*. OECD Publishing. Retrieved from https://www.oecd.org/corporate/Corporate-Governance-Factbook.pdf

OECD. (2020). Executive summary. In *Implementing the OECD guidelines on corporate governance of state-owned enterprises: Review of recent developments*. OECD Publishing. DOI: 10.1787/deac8436-

Olsson, R. (2006). Management of flexibility in projects. *International Journal of Project Management*, 24(1), 66–74. DOI: 10.1016/j.ijproman.2005.06.010

Oppenheimer, M., Campos, M., Warren, R., Birkmann, J., Luber, G., O'Neill, B., & Hsiang, S. (2015). Emergent risks and key vulnerabilities. In *Climate change 2014 impacts, adaptation and vulnerability: part a: global and sectoral aspects* (pp. 1039–1100). Cambridge University Press.

Orosz, G., Duran, A., & Merz, C. (2021). Managing project portfolio conflicts: A framework for handling discrepancies and alignment issues. *Journal of Strategic and International Studies*, 16(1), 33–45.

Ostrom, L. T., & Wilhelmsen, C. A. (2019). *Risk assessment: tools, techniques, and their applications*. John Wiley & Sons. DOI: 10.1002/9781119483342

Padovani, M., Muscat, A., Camanho, R., & Carvalho, M. (2008). Looking for the right criteria to define projects portfolio: Multiple case study analysis. *Product: Management & Development*, 6(2), 127–134.

Pahrudin, P., Chen, C. T., & Liu, L. W. (2021). A modified theory of planned behavioral: A case of tourist intention to visit a destination post pandemic Covid-19 in Indonesia. *Heliyon*, 7(10), e08230. DOI: 10.1016/j.heliyon.2021.e08230 PMID: 34708160

Pajares, J., & López, A. (2014). New Methodological Approaches to Project Portfolio Management: The Role of Interactions within Projects and Portfolios. *Procedia: Social and Behavioral Sciences*, 119, 645–652. DOI: 10.1016/j.sbspro.2014.03.072

Paraschi, E.P., Poulaki, I., Papageorgiou, A. (2022). From Environmental Management Systems to Airport Environmental Performance: A Model Assessment. *Journal of Environmental Management and Tourism, (Volume XIII*, Summer), 3(59): 831-852. https://doi.org/DOI: 10.14505/jemt.v13.3(59).22

Paraschi, E. P. (2022). Current Aviation challenges and opportunities. *Journal of Airline Operations and Aviation Management*, 1(2), 7–14. DOI: 10.56801/jaoam.v1i2.6

Paraschi, E. P. (2023). Aviation and Climate change: Challenges and the way forward. *Journal of Airline Operations and Aviation Management*, 2(2), 86–95. DOI: 10.56801/jaoam.v2i1.5

Paraschi, E. P., & Poulaki, I. (2021). An overview on Environmental Management in Aviation. In *Challenging Issues on Environment and Earth Science*. International Book Publishing. DOI: 10.9734/bpi/ciees/v7/11732D

Park, J. H., & Kwon, H. Y. (2022). Cyberattack detection model using community detection and text analysis on social media. *ICT Express*, 8(4), 499–506. DOI: 10.1016/j.icte.2021.12.003

Patanakul, P. (2015). Key attributes of effectiveness in managing project portfolio. *International Journal of Project Management*, 33(5), 1084–1097. DOI: 10.1016/j.ijproman.2015.01.004

Patel, S., & Kumar, R. (2022). Data reliability in project portfolio management: Current challenges and solutions. *Data and Information Management*, 6(4), 211–225.

Pei, Y., Wang, S., Fan, J., & Zhang, M. (2015, August). An empirical study on the impact of perceived benefit, risk and trust on e-payment adoption: Comparing quick pay and union pay in China. In *2015 7th international conference on intelligent human-machine systems and cybernetics* (Vol. 2, pp. 198-202). IEEE.

Penzenstadler, B., Raturi, A., Richardson, D., & Tomlinson, B. (2014). Safety, security, now sustainability: The nonfunctional requirement for the 21st century. *IEEE Software*, 31(3), 40–47. DOI: 10.1109/MS.2014.22

Peralta, M.E.& Soltero, V.M. (2020). Analysis of fractal manufacturing systems framework towards industry 4.0. *Journal of Manufacturing Systems, 57*, 46–60.

Petit, Y., & Hobbs, B. (2010). Project portfolios in dynamic environments: Sources of uncertainty and sensing mechanisms. *Project Management Journal*, 41(4), 46–58. DOI: 10.1002/pmj.20201

Petro, Y., & Gardiner, P. (2015). An investigation of the influence of organizational design on project portfolio success, effectiveness and business efficiency for project-based organizations. *International Journal of Project Management*, 33(8), 1717–1729. DOI: 10.1016/j.ijproman.2015.08.004

Pietrzak, P. (2017). The US Foreign Policy towards Syria under the Donald Trump Administration. RESEARCH GATE. https://www. researchgate. net/publication/310599117_The_US_Foreign_Policy_towar ds_Syria_under_the_Donald_Trump_Administration

Pietrzak, P. (2021). Immanuel Kant and Niccolò Machiavelli's Traditions and the Limits of Approaching Contemporary Conflicts—The Case Study of the Syrian Conflict (2011–Present). *Statu Nascendi Journal of Political Philosophy and International Relations*, 2, 53–84.

Piletska, S. T., Korytko, T. Yu., & Tkachenko, E. V. (2021). A model of integrated assessment of the enterprise economic security. *Economic Herald of Donbass*, 65(3), 56–66. DOI: 10.12958/1817-3772-2021-3(65)-56-65

Pitsis, T., Kornberger, M., & Clegg, S. (2004). The art of managing relationships in inter-organizational collaboration. *Management*, 7, 47–67.

Plattfaut, R. (2022). On the importance of project management capabilities for sustainable business process management. *Sustainability (Basel)*, 14(13), 7612. DOI: 10.3390/su14137612

PM. Mell, T.Grance, NIST Definition of Cloud Computing. (2011). (pp. 800–145). National Institute., DOI: 10.6028/NIST.SP.800-145

PMI. (2013). A Guide to the project management body of knowledge, PMBoK Guide (5th ed.). Project Management Institute, Inc.

PMI. (2017). The Standard for Portfolio Management (4th ed.). Project Management Institute, Inc.

Podsakoff, P. M., MacKenzie, S. B., Lee, J. Y., & Podsakoff, N. P. (2003). Common method biases in behavioral research: A critical review of the literature and recommended remedies. *The Journal of Applied Psychology*, 88(5), 879–903. DOI: 10.1037/0021-9010.88.5.879 PMID: 14516251

Prasad, A. (2023). Google predicts an increase in Russian cyberattacks on Ukraine and NATO members in 2023. Forbes.ua. Available at: https://surl.li/jaqxk

Probst, T. M., Gold, D., & Caborn, J. (2008). A preliminary evaluation of SOLVE: Addressing psychosocial problems at work. *Journal of Occupational Health Psychology*, 13(1), 32–42. DOI: 10.1037/1076-8998.13.1.32 PMID: 18211167

PWC's Global Economic Crime and Fraud Survey. (2022). Protecting the perimeter: A new frontier of platform fraud. https://www.pwc.com/gx/en/forensics/gecsm-2022/pdf/PwC%E2%80%99s-Global-Economic-Crime-and-Fraud-Survey-2022.pdf

Qi, Q., & Tao, F. (2019). A Smart Manufacturing Service System Based on Edge Computing, Fog Computing, and Cloud Computing. *IEEE Access : Practical Innovations, Open Solutions*, 7, 86769–86777. DOI: 10.1109/ACCESS.2019.2923610

Radaelli, P. (2021). Enterprise Risk Management in Practice: A European Perspective, Maffei, M. (Ed.) *Enterprise Risk Management in Europe* (pp. 261-278). Emerald Publishing Limited. DOI: 10.1108/978-1-83867-245-420211015

Raghunath, K. M. K., & Devi, S. T. (2022). Risk Assessment in the Information Technology Industry: An Imperative Phenomenon. In *Global Risk and Contingency Management Research in Times of Crisis* (pp. 122-141). IGI Global.

Raghunath, K. M. K., Devi, S. T., & Patro, C. S. (2018). Impact of Risk Assessment Models on Risk Factors: A Holistic Outlook. In *Research, Practices, and Innovations in Global Risk and Contingency Management* (pp. 134-153). IGI Global DOI: 10.4018/978-1-5225-4754-9.ch008

Raghunath, K. M. K., & Devi, S. L. T. (2018). Supply Chain Risk Management: An Invigorating Outlook. *International Journal of Information Systems and Supply Chain Management*, 11(3), 87–104. DOI: 10.4018/IJISSCM.2018070105

Raghunath, K. M. K., Devi, S. L. T., Anuradha, K., & Veni, K. V. S. K. (2021). Reinvigorating Organizational Effectiveness and Sustainability Through Risk Assessment Tools Within the Construction Industry. In *Remote work and sustainable change for the future of global business*. IGI Global. DOI: 10.4018/978-1-7998-7513-0.ch009

Raghunath, K. M. K., Devi, S. L. T., & Patro, C. S. (2017). An empirical take on qualitative and quantitative risk factors. *International Journal of Risk and Contingency Management*, 6(4), 1–15. DOI: 10.4018/IJRCM.2017100101

Raghunath, K. M. K., & Devi, S. T. (2021). Effectiveness of risk assessment models in business decisions: Reinforcing knowledge. In *Research Anthology on Small Business Strategies for Success and Survival* (pp. 1076–1096). IGI Global. DOI: 10.4018/978-1-7998-9155-0.ch053

Raghunath, K. M. K., Patro, C. S., & Sirisha, K. (2019). Paraphernalias of Entrepreneurship–A Contemplating Outlook. *International Journal of E-Entrepreneurship and Innovation*, 9(1), 47–62. DOI: 10.4018/IJEEI.2019010105

Ranjan, R., & Karmakar, S. (2024). Compound hazard mapping for tropical cyclone-induced concurrent wind and rainfall extremes over India. *NPJ Natural Hazards*, 1(1), 15. DOI: 10.1038/s44304-024-00013-y

Rao, P., Mehta, R., & Zhang, J. (2023). Developing dynamic capabilities for competitive advantage in large organizations. *Journal of Business Research*, 143, 290–302.

Rapid 7. (2020). Catching modern threats: InsightIDR detection methodologies. Available: https:// www.rapid7.com/resources

Rashid, M. M., Kamruzzaman, J., Hassan, M. M., Imam, T., & Gordon, S. (2020). Cyberattacks detection in iot-based smart city applications using machine learning techniques. *International Journal of Environmental Research and Public Health*, 17(24), 1–21. DOI: 10.3390/ijerph17249347 PMID: 33327468

Rausand, M. (2013). *Risk assessment: theory, methods, and applications* (Vol. 115). John Wiley & Sons.

Rawat, D. B., Doku, R., & Garuba, M. (2021). Cybersecurity in Big Data Era: From Securing Big Data to Data-Driven Security. *IEEE Transactions on Services Computing*, 14(6), 2055–2072. DOI: 10.1109/TSC.2019.2907247

Raye, J. (2013). Fractal Organization Theory. *Proceedings of the 56th Annual Meeting of the ISSS - 2012, San Jose, CA, USA*. Retrieved from https://journals.isss.org/index.php/proceedings56th/article/view/1796

Rego, P., Souto, C., & Oliveira, J. (2018). The relationship between project portfolio management and project success: A systematic review. *Journal of Strategic and International Studies*, 14(1), 92–110.

Renn, O. (2017). *Risk governance: coping with uncertainty in a complex world*. Routledge. DOI: 10.4324/9781849772440

Report, A. C. R. P. (2012). *2012 Annual Report Of Progress*. Airport Cooperative Research Program. https://onlinepubs.trb.org/onlinepubs/acrp/acrpannual2012.pdf

République et canton de Neuchâtel. (2023, October 16). *Antennes MPV - neuchâtel*. Police Neuchâteloise Antennes MPV. https://www.ne.ch/autorites/DESC/PONE/GCM/Documents/Antennes.pdf

République et canton de Neuchâtel. (2024). La Gestion Cantonale des menaces (GCM). https://www.ne.ch/autorites/DESC/PONE/GCM/Pages/accueil.aspx

Ribeiro Ramos, O., Mironenko, E., Britchenko, I., Zhuk, O., & Patlachuk, V. (2022). Economic security as an element of corporate management. *Financial and Credit Activity: Problems of Theory and Practice*, 1(42), 304–312. DOI: 10.55643/fcaptp.1.42.2022.3698

Ring, D. (2019). Definition OKRs (Objectives and Key Results). Techtarget. Available at: https://www.techtarget.com/searchhrsoftware/definition/OKRs-Objectives-and-Key-Results (10/9/2023)

Riyako, E. (2023). Law Firm Metrics and KPIs: Management through Digital. Ligazakon.net. https://surl.li/jbiam

Rodoplu, H., & Gursel, S. (2022). Sustainability Practices in Airport. In Karakoc, T. H., Colpan, C. O., & Dalkiran, A. (Eds.), *New Frontiers in Sustainable Aviation. Sustainable Aviation* (pp. 191–201). Springer. DOI: 10.1007/978-3-030-80779-5_10

Rosenberg, M. (2018). How Trump Consultants Exploited the Facebook Data of Millions. *The New York Times*. https://www.nytimes.com/2018/03/17/us/politics/cambridge-analytica-trump-campaign.html

Rosen, F. (1977). Basic needs and justice. *Mind*, 86(341), 88–94. DOI: 10.1093/mind/LXXXVI.341.88

Rudenko, R., Pires, I. M., Oliveira, P., Barroso, J., & Reis, A. (2022). A Brief Review on Internet of Things, Industry 4.0 and Cybersecurity. *Electronics (Basel)*, 11(11), 1742. Advance online publication. DOI: 10.3390/electronics11111742

Rume, T., & Islam, S. D. U. (2020). Environmental effects of COVID-19 pandemic and potential strategies of sustainability. *Heliyon*, 6(9), e04965. DOI: 10.1016/j.heliyon.2020.e04965 PMID: 32964165

Saaty, T. (2008). Decision making with the analytic hierarchy process. *International Journal of Services Sciences*, 1(1), 83–98. DOI: 10.1504/IJSSCI.2008.017590

Sabatini, R., & Gardi, A. (2023). Sustainable Aviation: An Introduction. In Sabatini, R., & Gardi, A. (Eds.), *Sustainable Aviation Technology and Operations* (pp. 1–28). DOI: 10.1002/9781118932599.ch1

Saheed, Y. K., & Arowolo, M. O. (2021). Efficient Cyber Attack Detection on the Internet of Medical Things-Smart Environment Based on Deep Recurrent Neural Network and Machine Learning Algorithms. *IEEE Access : Practical Innovations, Open Solutions*, 9, 161546–161554. DOI: 10.1109/ACCESS.2021.3128837

Sahoo, S., & Goswami, S. (2023). A Comprehensive Review of Multiple Criteria Decision-Making (MCDM) Methods: Advancements, Applications, and Future Directions. *Decision Making Advances*, 1(1), 25–48. DOI: 10.31181/dma1120237

Sahrir, S., Bachok, S., & Osman, M. M. (2014). Environmental and health impacts of airport infrastructure upgrading: Kuala Lumpur International Airport 2. *Procedia: Social and Behavioral Sciences*, 153, 520–530. DOI: 10.1016/j.sbspro.2014.10.085

Sanchez-Franco, M. J., & Rondan-Cataluña, F. J. (2010). Virtual travel communities and customer loyalty: Customer purchase involvement and web site design. *Electronic Commerce Research and Applications*, 9(2), 171–182. DOI: 10.1016/j.elerap.2009.05.004

Sarbanes-Oxley Act of 2002: Conference report (to accompany H.R. 3763). (2002). U.S. G.P.O.

Sarker, I. H. (2021). CyberLearning: Effectiveness analysis of machine learning security modeling to detect cyber-anomalies and multi-attacks. *Internet of Things : Engineering Cyber Physical Human Systems*, 14, 100393. DOI: 10.1016/j.iot.2021.100393

Sataloff, R.T., Johns, M.M., & Kost, K.M. (2019). Industry 4.0 and cybersecurity Managing risk in an age of connected production. Academic Press.

Schaltegger, S., Lüdeke-Freund, F., & Hansen, E. G. (2012). Business cases for sustainability: The role of business model innovation for corporate sustainability. *International Journal of Innovation and Sustainable Development*, 6(2), 95–119. DOI: 10.1504/IJISD.2012.046944

Schipper, R., & Silvius, G. (2018). Towards a conceptual framework for sustainable project portfolio management. *International Journal of Project Organisation and Management*, 10(3), 191–221. DOI: 10.1504/IJPOM.2018.093977

Schlatt, V., Guggenberger, T., Schmid, J., & Urbach, N. (2022). Attacking the Trust Machine: Developing an Information Systems Research Agenda for Blockchain Cybersecurity. *International Journal of Information Management*. Advance online publication. DOI: 10.1016/j.ijinfomgt.2022.102470

Scoones, I. (2007). Sustainability. *Development in Practice*, 17(4-5), 589–596. DOI: 10.1080/09614520701469609

Self, C. C. (2014). Credibility. In *An integrated approach to communication theory and research* (pp. 449–470). Routledge.

Shabani, N., & Munir, A. (2020). A review of cyber security issues in hospitality industry. In Arai, K., Kapoor, S., & Bhatia, R. (Eds.), *Intelligent Computing. SAI 2020. Advances in Intelligent Systems and Computing* (Vol. 1230, pp. 482–493). Springer. DOI: 10.1007/978-3-030-52243-8_35

Sharitov, O. (2023). Rockets instead of visitors. The war damaged more than 1,000 restaurants, cafes and hotels. How does business restore them and how can the state help. ForbesUkraine. https://surl.li/ixncp

Sharma, D., Totuka, A., Kumar, P., Yadav, A., & Jain, P. (2024). An analysis of go first airlines: A case study on voluntary insolvency resolution in the aviation industry. *Journal of Informatics Education and Research*, 4(2). Advance online publication. DOI: 10.52783/jier.v4i2.826

Shashwat, K., & Rani, M. (2023). Technological Transformation in Hospitality Industry: An Overview. In Nadda, V., Tyagi, P., Moniz Vieira, R., & Tyagi, P. (Eds.), *Sustainable Development Goal Advancement Through Digital Innovation in the Service Sector* (pp. 133–151). IGI Global. DOI: 10.4018/979-8-3693-0650-5.ch009

Shaver, J. M. (2021). Evolution of Quantitative Research Methods in Strategic Management. In *Strategic Management: State of the Field and Its Future* (pp. 83-98). Oxford Academic. DOI: 10.1093/oso/9780190090883.003.0005

Shenhar, A., Dvir, D., Levy, O., & Maltz, A. (2001). Project Success: A Multidimensional Strategic Concept. *Long Range Planning*, 34(6), 699–725. DOI: 10.1016/S0024-6301(01)00097-8

Shiro, E. (2024, Jan. 8). The Current Migrant Crisis Is a Collective Trauma. Time. https://time.com/6553088/venezuelan-migrant-crisis-collective-trauma-essay/

SIAM. (2020). Society of Indian Automobile Manufacturers. Retrieved from https://www.siam.in/uploads/filemanager/319SIAMAnnualReport2020-21.pdf

Sigri, U. (2018). *Nitel Araştırma Yöntemleri* (1st ed.). Beta Press.

Silvius, G., & Marnewick, C. (2022). Interlinking Sustainability in Organizational Strategy, Project Portfolio Management and Project Management: A Conceptual Framework. *Procedia Computer Science*, 196, 938–947. DOI: 10.1016/j.procs.2021.12.095

Simonovic, S. P., Kundzewicz, Z. W., & Wright, N. (2021). Floods and the COVID-19 pandemic-A new double hazard problem. *WIREs. Water*, 8(2), e1509. DOI: 10.1002/wat2.1509 PMID: 33786171

Singh, J., Wazid, M., Das, A. K., Chamola, V., & Guizani, M. (2022). Machine learning security attacks and defense approaches for emerging cyber physical applications: A comprehensive survey. *Computer Communications*, 192, 316–331. DOI: 10.1016/j.comcom.2022.06.012

Sinha, S. (2023). State of IoT 2023: Number of connected IoT devices growing 16% to 16.7 billion globally. IoT Analytics. https://iot-analytics.com/number-connected -iot-devices/

Skulmoski, G., & Hartman, F. (2007). The Delphi Method for Graduate Research. *Journal of Information Technology Education*, 6, 1–21. DOI: 10.28945/199

Slovic, P. (2016). Understanding perceived risk: 1978–2015. *Environment*, 58(1), 25–29. DOI: 10.1080/00139157.2016.1112169

Smith, G. (2021). Overcoming barriers to coordinating across social protection and humanitarian assistance—building on promising practices.

Smith, J., & Johnson, R. (2023). Aligning Project Portfolio Management with Organizational Sustainability: New Perspectives and Approaches. *Sustainability*, 15(4), 2124.

Smith, K. (2013). *Environmental hazards: assessing risk and reducing disaster*. Routledge. DOI: 10.4324/9780203805305

Sok, H., Ooi, M., & Kuang, Y. (2015). Sparse alternating decision tree. *Pattern Recognition Letters*, 60-61, 57–64. DOI: 10.1016/j.patrec.2015.03.002

Soliman, M., Gulvady, S., Elbaz, A. M., Mosbah, M., & Wahba, M. S. (2023). Robot-delivered tourism and hospitality services: How to evaluate the impact of health and safety considerations on visitors' satisfaction and loyalty? *Tourism and Hospitality Research*, 24(3), 393–409. DOI: 10.1177/14673584231153367

Souder, W. E., & Bethay, D. (1993). The risk pyramid for new product development: An application to complex aerospace hardware. *Journal of Product Innovation Management*, 10(3), 181–194. DOI: 10.1111/1540-5885.1030181

Spencer, A., & Tarlow, P. (2021). *Tourism Security to Tourism Surety and Well-being, Tourism Safety and Security for the Caribbean (Tourism Security-Safety and Post Conflict Destinations)*. Emerald Publishing Limited. DOI: 10.1108/978-1-80071-318-520211004

SpencerStuart. (2019). *Corporate governance in the UK*. Retrieved from https://www.spencerstuart.com/-/media/2019/ukbi-2019/uk_board_index_2019_final_version.pdf

Sreenath, S., Sudhakar, K., & Yusop, A. F. (2021). Sustainability at airports: Technologies and best practices from ASEAN countries. *Journal of Environmental Management*, 299, 439–451. DOI: 10.1016/j.jenvman.2021.113639 PMID: 34479146

Statista. (2021). Potential scenarios of AI-enabled cyberattacks worldwide as of 2021. https://www.statista.com/statistics/1235395/worldwide-ai-enabled-cyberattackscompanies/

Stevenson, I., & Marintseva, K. (2019). A review of Corporate Social Responsibility assessment and reporting techniques in the aviation industry. *Transportation Research Procedia*, 43, 93–103. DOI: 10.1016/j.trpro.2019.12.023

Stolzer, A. J., Sumwalt, R. L., & Goglia, J. J. (2023). *Safety Management Systems in Aviation* (3rd ed.). CRC Press. DOI: 10.1201/9781003286127

Suárez-Orozco, M. M. (2019). Introduction: Catastrophic migrations. In Suárez-Orozco, M. M. (Ed.), *Humanitarianism and Mass Migration: Confronting the World Crisis* (1st ed., pp. 1–40). University of California Press. DOI: 10.2307/j.ctv9zchv9.5

Subramanian, N., & Ramanathan, R. (2022). Analytic Network Process: A review of applications and methodology. *Omega*, 106, 102458.

Suresh, P., Logeswaran, K., Keerthika, P., Devi, R. M., Sentamilselvan, K., Kamalam, G. K., & Muthukrishnan, H. (2022). Contemporary survey on effectiveness of machine and deep learning techniques for cyber security. In *Machine Learning for Biometrics: Concepts, Algorithms and Applications* (pp. 177–200). Academic Press. DOI: 10.1016/B978-0-323-85209-8.00007-9

Sweet, A. S. (2000). *Governing with judges: constitutional politics in Europe*. OUP Oxford. DOI: 10.1093/0198297718.001.0001

Taddeo, M., & Bosco, F. (2019). We Must Treat Cybersecurity as a Public Good: Here's Why. Accessed at https://www.weforum.org/agenda/2019/08/we-must-treat-cybersecurity-like-public-good/

Tajeddini, K., Rasoolimanesh, S. M., Gamage, T. C., & Martin, E. (2021). Exploring the visitors' decision-making process for Airbnb and hotel accommodations using value-attitude-behavior and theory of planned behavior. *International Journal of Hospitality Management*, 96, 102950. DOI: 10.1016/j.ijhm.2021.102950

Tavana, M., Santos-Arteaga, F. J., & Fadaei, M. (2018). Project portfolio selection: A review of methods and applications. *International Journal of Project Management*, 36(6), 775–787. DOI: 10.1016/j.ijproman.2018.04.004

Teller, J. (2013). Portfolio Risk Management and Its Contribution to Project Portfolio Success: An Investigation of Organization, Process, and Culture. *Project Management Journal*, 44(2), 36–51. DOI: 10.1002/pmj.21327

Teller, J., & Kock, A. (2013). An empirical investigation on how portfolio risk management influences project portfolio success. *International Journal of Project Management*, 31(6), 817–829. DOI: 10.1016/j.ijproman.2012.11.012

Teller, J., Unger, B. N., Kock, A., & Gemünden, H. G. (2012). Formalization of project portfolio management: The moderating role of project portfolio complexity. *International Journal of Project Management*, 30(5), 596–607. DOI: 10.1016/j.ijproman.2012.01.020

The Business Research Company. (2024, April 8). *Airlines Market Definition*. The Business Research Company. https://www.thebusinessresearchcompany.com/report/airlines-global-market-report

The Directorate-General for European Civil Protection and Humanitarian Aid Operations (ECHO). (2023). Forgotten Crises. https://civil-protection-humanitarian-aid.ec.europa.eu/what/humanitarian-aid/needs-assessment/forgotten-crises_en

The Website of Dziennik Gazeta Prawna. (2023). Jak samorządy poradziły sobie z kryzysem uchodźczym i co jeszcze je czeka? (https://www.gazetaprawna.pl/perlysamorzadu/artykuly/8665348,jak-samorzady-poradzily-sobie-z-kryzysem-uchodzczym-i-co-jeszcze-je-czeka.html)

The Website of The Republic of Poland (2022). Support for Poland to help refugees from Ukraine.

The White House. (2021). Report on The Impact of Climate Change on Migration.

Thomas, M. A., Michaelis, A. C., Oakley, N. S., Kean, J. W., Gensini, V. A., & Ashley, W. S. (2024). Rainfall intensification amplifies exposure of American Southwest to conditions that trigger postfire debris flows. *npj. Npj Natural Hazards*, 1(1), 14. DOI: 10.1038/s44304-024-00017-8

Thompson, L., & Smith, R. (2022). Managing stakeholder interests in project selection: A comprehensive review. *Project Management Journal*, 53(6), 101–115.

Trautman, L. J., & Ormerod, P. C. (2016). Corporate directors' and officers' cyber-security standard of care: The Yahoo data breach. *The American University Law Review*, 66(5), 1231.

Trilles, S., Hammad, S. S., & Iskandaryan, D. (2024). Anomaly detection based on Artificial Intelligence of Things: A Systematic Literature Mapping. In *Internet of Things (Netherlands)* (Vol. 25). Elsevier B.V. DOI: 10.1016/j.iot.2024.101063

Trim, P., & Lee, Y.-I. (2022). *Strategic Cyber Security Management* (1st ed.). Rout-ledge., DOI: 10.4324/9781003244295

Tuna, A. A., & Türkmendağ, Z. (2022). Cyber Business Management. In *Conflict Management in Digital Business* (pp. 281-301), Emerald Publishing Limited. DOI: 10.1108/978-1-80262-773-220221026

Turunen, S. (2020). Accountability. In de Lauri, A. (Ed.), *Humanitarianism*. Brill.

Ukrainian Truth. (2023). Everything you need to know about the Kakhovskaya HPP disaster. Available at: https://www.pravda.com.ua/articles/2023/06/6/7405590/

UNISDR. (2017). C. Cross-Sectoral and Multi-Risk Approach to Cascading Disasters.

United Nations. (2015, December 9). Security Council, unanimously adopting resolution 2250 (2015), urges member states to increase representation of youth in decision-making at all levels | meetings coverage and press releases. https://press .un.org/en/2015/sc12149.doc.htm

United Stations. (2023). *The Sustainable Development Goals Report*. United Nations Department of Economic and Social Affairs Statistics Division. https://unstats.un .org/sdgs/report/2023/

US Department of Homeland Security. (n.d.). Complex coordinated attacks. https:// www.cisa.gov/sites/default/files/2022-11/Action%20Guide%20CCA%20508%20 FINAL%2020190905.pdf)

Van der Meer-Kooistra, J., & Vosselman, E. (2023). The impact of human biases on project selection: Evidence from recent studies. *Management Accounting Research*, 55, 123–135.

Vasile, E., & Croitoru, I. (2012). Integrated risk management system–key factor of the management system of the organization. Risk management-Current issues and challenges. InTech.

Veeraiah, V., Talukdar, V., Manikandan, K., Talukdar, S. B., Solavande, V. D., Pramanik, S., & Gupta, A. (2023). Machine Learning Frameworks in Carpooling. In Handbook of Research on AI and Machine Learning Applications in Customer Support and Analytics. IGI Global.

Verezomska, I., Bovsh, L., Prykhodko, K., & Baklan, H. (2022). Cyber protection of hotel brands. *Restaurant and hotel consulting.Innovation*, 5(2), 190–209. DOI: 10.31866/2616-7468.5.2.2022.270089

Verma, A., & Shri, C. (2022). Cyber Security: A Review of Cyber Crimes, Security Challenges and Measures to Control. *Vision (Basel)*. Advance online publication. DOI: 10.1177/09722629221074760

Verma, V., & Sinha, P. (2018). Managing project portfolio in a dynamic environment. *International Journal of Project Management*, 36(7), 995–1007.

Vidal, L., Marle, F., & Bocquet, J. (2011). Using a Delphi process and the Analytic Hierarchy Process (AHP) to evaluate the complexity of projects. *Expert Systems with Applications*, 38(5), 5388–5405. DOI: 10.1016/j.eswa.2010.10.016

Vieira, G., Oliveira, H., Almeida, J., & Belderrain, M. (2024). Project Portfolio Selection considering interdependencies: A review of terminology and approaches. *Project Leadership and Society*, 5, 100115. DOI: 10.1016/j.plas.2023.100115

Vinodkumar, M. N., & Bhasi, M. (2010). Safety Management Practices and Safety Behaviour: Assessing the Mediating Role of Safety Knowledge and Motivation. *Accident; Analysis and Prevention*, 42(6), 2082–2093. DOI: 10.1016/j.aap.2010.06.021 PMID: 20728666

Vogiatzis, K., Kassomenos, P., Gerolymatou, G., Valamvanos, P., & Anamaterou, E. (2021). Climate Change Adaptation Studies as a tool to ensure airport's sustainability: The case of Athens International Airport (AIA). *The Science of the Total Environment*, 754, 142153. DOI: 10.1016/j.scitotenv.2020.142153 PMID: 33254882

Walker, H., Armenakis, A., & Bernerth, J. (2007). Factors influencing organizational change efforts: An integrative investigation of change content, context, process and individual differences. *Journal of Organizational Change Management*, 20(6), 761–773. DOI: 10.1108/09534810710831000

Walsh, K. (2019). Continuous Monitoring Drives Sustainable Cybersecurity. Accessed at https://www.zeguro.com/blog/continuous-monitoring-sustainable-cybersecurity

Wang, Y., Zhong, R. Y., & Xu, X. (2018). A decision support system for additive manufacturing process selection using a hybrid multiple criteria decision-making method. *Rapid Prototyping Journal*, 24(9), 1544–1553. DOI: 10.1108/RPJ-01-2018-0002

Wan, L., Peng, Q., Wang, J., Tian, Y., & Xu, C. (2020). Evaluation of airport sustainability by the synthetic evaluation method: A case study of Guangzhou Baiyun international airport, China, from 2008 to 2017. *Sustainability (Basel)*, 12(8), 3334. DOI: 10.3390/su12083334

Ward, J., & Daniel, E. (2012). *Benefits Management: How to Increase the Business Value of Your IT Projects*. John Wiley & Sons. DOI: 10.1002/9781119208242

Watson, C. C. (2011, August). Risk assessment using the three dimensions of probability (likelihood), severity, and level of control. In *29th International Systems Safety Conference* (No. M11-0220).

Weber, O., Scholz, R. W., & Michalik, G. (2010). Incorporating sustainability criteria into credit risk management. *Business Strategy and the Environment*, 19(1), 39–50. DOI: 10.1002/bse.636

Weber, T. (2014). On the (non-) equivalence of IRR and NPV. *Journal of Mathematical Economics*, 52, 25–39. DOI: 10.1016/j.jmateco.2014.03.006

Wehbi, K., Hong, L., Al-Salah, T., & Bhutta, A. A. (2019). A Survey on Machine Learning Based Detection on DDoS Attacks for IoT Systems. *Conference Proceedings - IEEE SOUTHEASTCON, 2019-April*. DOI: 10.1109/SoutheastCon42311.2019.9020468

Wibowo, S., & Sutandi, S. (2018). Analisa Rasio Keuangan Garuda Indonesia Airlines, Singapore Airlines Dan Thailand Airlines Dengan Uji Non-Parametrik (Periode: 2010–2014). *eCo-Buss, 1*(2), 1-7. DOI: 10.32877/eb.v1i2.36

Wilson, D. J., Takahashi, K., Smith, D. R., Yoshino, M., Tanaka, C., & Takala, J. (2006). Recent trends in ILO conventions related to occupational safety and health. *International Journal of Occupational Safety and Ergonomics*, 12(3), 255–266. DOI: 10.1080/10803548.2006.11076688 PMID: 16984785

Woodruff, J. M. (2005). Consequence and likelihood in risk estimation: A matter of balance in UK health and safety risk assessment practice. *Safety Science*, 43(5-6), 345–353. DOI: 10.1016/j.ssci.2005.07.003

World Bank. (n.d.). *GFDRR Annual Report2022: Bringing Resilience to Scale (English)*. World Bank Group. https://documents.worldbank.org/curated/en/099904102272326411/IDU0242fa9a607c8804e9a0b0d404a431f9a65a9

Woźniak, A. (2022). Fala uchodźców zaczyna już paraliżować polskie dworce. The Website of Rzeczposoplita Newspaper. https://www.rp.pl/transport/art35835921 -fala-uchodzcow-zaczyna-juz-paralizowac-polskie-dworce

Wu, C. Y., Kuo, C. C., & Yang, C. S. (2019). A phishing detection system based on machine learning. *2019 International Conference on Intelligent Computing and its Emerging Applications (ICEA)*, 28–32. DOI: 10.1109/ICEA.2019.8858325

Yao, X., Zhou, J., Lin, Y., Li, Y., Yu, H., & Liu, Y. (2019). Smart manufacturing based on cyber-physical systems and beyond. *Journal of Intelligent Manufacturing*, 30(8), pp2805–pp2817. DOI: 10.1007/s10845-017-1384-5

Yelin, K. (2005). Linking Strategy and Project Portfolio Management. In Levine, H. A. (Ed.), *Project Portfolio Management: A practical guide to selecting projects, managing portfolios and maximizing benefit* (pp. 137–145). Pfeiffer Wiley.

Yeo and yeo. (2023). Cybercrime to cost the World 8 trillion annually in 2023. Accessed from https://www.yeoandyeo.com/resource/cybercrime-to-cost-the-world -8-trillion-in-2023

Yeung, A. B. (2004). The octagon model of volunteer motivation: Results of a phenomenological analysis. *Voluntas*, 15(1), 21–46. DOI: 10.1023/B:VO-LU.0000023632.89728.ff

Yigit, S. (2021, December 10). Hybrid war: Addition to the IR lexicon. Retrieved February 29, 2024, from https://www.geopolitic.ro/2021/12/hybrid-war-addition -ir-lexicon/

Yigit, S. (2023). Multi-Dimensional Understandings of Migration: Threats or Opportunities? In Handbook of Research on the Regulation of the Modern Global Migration and Economic Crisis (pp. 239-256). IGI Global.

Yigit, S. (2021). The Concept of Citizenship and the Democratic State. *Electronic Journal of Social and Strategic Studies*, 2, 5–25.

Yildirim, A., & Simsek, H. (2021). *Sosyal Bilimlerde Nitel Araştırma Yöntemleri* (12th ed.). Seckin Press.

Yin, R. K. (2018). *Case Study Research and Applications: Design and Methods*. Sage Publications.

Yohannes, A., & Mauritsius, T. (2022). Critical success factors in information technology projects. *International Journal of Emerging Technology and Advanced Engineering*, 12(7), 45–67. DOI: 10.46338/ijetae0722_06

Yoon, B., & Chung, Y. (2018). The effects of corporate social responsibility on firm performance: A stakeholder approach. *Journal of Hospitality and Tourism Management*, 37, 89–96. DOI: 10.1016/j.jhtm.2018.10.005

Yoo, Y., Boland, R. J.Jr, Lyytinen, K., & Majchrzak, A. (2012). Organizing for innovation in the digitized world. *Organization Science*, 23(5), 1398–1408. DOI: 10.1287/orsc.1120.0771

Zailani, S., Iranmanesh, M., Masron, T. A., & Chan, T. H. (2016). Is the intention to use public transport for different travel purposes determined by different factors? *Transportation Research Part D, Transport and Environment*, 49, 18–24. DOI: 10.1016/j.trd.2016.08.038

Zaitchik, B. F., Omumbo, J., Lowe, R., van Aalst, M., Anderson, L. O., Fischer, E., Norman, C., Robbins, J., Barciela, R., Trtanj, J., von Borries, R., & Luterbacher, J. (2022). Planning for compound hazards during the COVID-19 pandemic. *Bulletin of the American Meteorological Society*, 103(3), E704–E709. DOI: 10.1175/BAMS-D-21-0215.1

Zamir, A., Khan, H. U., Iqbal, T., Yousaf, N., Aslam, F., Anjum, A., & Hamdani, M. (2019). Phishing web site detection using diverse machine learning algorithms. *The Electronic Library*, 38(1), 65–80. DOI: 10.1108/EL-05-2019-0118

Zarjou, M., & Khalilzadeh, M. (2022). Optimal project portfolio selection with reinvestment strategy considering sustainability in an uncertain environment: A multi-objective optimization approach. *Kybernetes*, 51(8), 2437–2460. DOI: 10.1108/K-11-2020-0737

Zhang, J., Wang, M., & Chen, Y. (2021). Strategic alignment and portfolio management: A conceptual framework for successful project selection. *Project Management Journal*, 52(3), 47–61.

Zhang, Y., & Yang, X. (2022). Managing risk-reward balance in project portfolios: Recent advances and methodologies. *Risk Management*, 24(2), 99–114.

Zhao, H., Zhang, L., & Wang, X. (2023). Forecasting benefits in project portfolio management: Techniques and challenges. *Operations Research Perspectives*, 10, 100–112.

Zhao, X., & Wang, L. (2023). Challenges in establishing criteria for project evaluation and selection. *European Journal of Operational Research*, 295(3), 715–728.

Zhivko, Z. B., Cherevko, O. V., Zachosova, N. V., Zhivko, M. O., Bavorovska, O. B., & Zanora, V. O. (2019). Organization and management of the economic security system of the enterprise: Educational and methodological manual. Yu.A. Chabanenko Publisher. https://surl.li/hmcbr

Zhou, X., Lu, G., Xu, Z., Yan, X., Khu, S., Yang, J., & Zhao, J. (2022). Influence of Russia-Ukraine War on the Global Energy and Food Security. *Resources, Conservation and Recycling*, 188, 106657. DOI: 10.1016/j.resconrec.2022.106657

Zizka, L., McGunagle, D., & Clark, P. (2021). Sustainability Reporting on Dublin Airport: A Case Study. Retrieved from https://commons.erau.edu/publication/1687

Zopounidis, C., & Doumpos, M. (2021). Multi-criteria decision analysis in project portfolio management: Trends and developments. *European Journal of Operational Research*, 290(3), 827–839. DOI: 10.1016/j.ejor.2007.11.026

Zou, P. X., & Sunindijo, R. Y. (2015). *Strategic safety management in construction and engineering*. John Wiley & Sons. DOI: 10.1002/9781118839362

About the Contributors

Aleksandra Zając received her PhD in 2019 on the basis of a dissertation on attempts to implement community policing in Poland. From 2016-2021, she was a lecturer at the State Higher Vocational School in Racibórz, where she educates policemen and other state service officers. Her research interests concern the work of police and other governmental institutions in a democratic society, threats in modern societies, secutiry issues inflence upon business. In 2022 she joined the American Institute of Applied Sciences in Switzerland.

Giuseppe Catenazzo is the Head of Research & Adjunct Lecturer at AUS American Institute of Applied Sciences in Switzerland and an Affiliate Professor in Marketing at ICN Business School, a French Grande École. He also teaches Market Research & Consumer Behaviour, Economics & Management, Operations Management and Statistics at several institutions in Switzerland. Giuseppe is an Italian and Swiss citizen. He studied in France, Italy, Switzerland, and the United Kingdom and speaks several languages. Dr Catenazzo is also an editor of international research books; his research on quality perceptions, service recovery, and complaining behavior has been published in Production Planning and Control, International Journal of Quality and Reliability Management, and the Journal of Consumer Satisfaction, Dissatisfaction & Complaining Behavior.

Emmanuel Fragnière, CIA (Certified Internal Auditor), is a professor of service science at the University of Applied Sciences of Western Switzerland – HEG Valais. He is also a lecturer in enterprise risk management at the Management School of the University of Bath. His research focuses on the development of risk management models for decision-makers in the service sector. He has published several papers in academic journals, including Environmental Modelling and Assessment, Interfaces, Management Science and Service Science. He is the co-author (with George Sullivan) of the book Risk Management: Safeguarding Company Assets (Fifty-Minute Crisp Series, November 2006).

* * *

Ahmed Chemseddine Bouarar is a Professor of English, accounting, and marketing at University of Medea, Algeria. He received his Ph.D. in sciences commerciales from the University of Algiers 3 at Algiers in 2016. Bouarar has made over 40 scholarly contributions, including nearly 25 peer-reviewed research papers.

Sonal Devesh is an Associate Professor at the School of Business and Management, Christ University, Bangalore, India. She holds a PhD in Statistics from UTHM Malaysia and has over 24 years of experience in teaching and research. Her expertise lies in areas such as social sciences, economics, banking, and ergonomics. Dr. Devesh has published extensively in peer-reviewed journals and has a notable academic presence, with contributions to international conferences and various research projects (IRINS) (Frontiers Loop).

Yianni Doumenis, an accomplished academic and a forward-thinking professional in investment management and Fintech, boasts a wealth of experience across corporate and public pension funds, banking and technology sectors. His proficiency in multilingual communication has propelled him to excel in business development and client services, catering to prestigious entities like ADIA and CalPERS. Notably, his adeptness extends to originating and executing currency mandates, fostering substantial asset growth. Currently serving as the Course Leader for the MSc in Finance and Risk Management and a Senior Lecturer in the MSc in Business Analytics at the Claude Littner Business School, University of West London, Yianni's academic journey traverses renowned institutions including LSE, UCL and Queen Mary University of London, where he earned BSc, MPhil, MSc and PhD degrees in Economics and Econometrics and Mathematical Economics. Beyond academia, his entrepreneurial spirit shone through as the co-founder of Quantimetrica, a cutting-edge technology company based in the UK. Yianni's fervour lies in applied research, particularly in risk management, governance and data analytics, as he passionately addresses contemporary issues vital for business success and societal impact. His comprehensive expertise and pioneering contributions make Yianni a formidable force at the intersection of academia, finance and technology.

Jorge Gomes is Professor of Strategy and Management at Universidade Lusófona and researcher at ADVANCE/CSG/ISEG - University of Lisbon. He holds a PhD in Management from ISEG and a Master's in Management Sciences from ISCTE-IUL, a postgraduate degree in Project Management from INDEG / ISCTE and a degree in Geographic Engineering from the Faculty of Sciences of the University of Lisbon. For the last 35 years he has worked as an engineer, project manager, quality auditor and consultant. His research interests include Strategy and Operations, Benefits Management, Project Management, Project Success, Maturity Models, IS/IT Investment Management.

Ankur Gupta has received the B.Tech and M.Tech in Computer Science and Engineering from Ganga Institute of Technology and Management, Kablana affiliated with Maharshi Dayanand University, Rohtak in 2015 and 2017. He is an Assistant Professor in the Department of Computer Science and Engineering at Vaish College of Engineering, Rohtak, and has been working there since January 2019. He has many publications in various reputed national/ international conferences, journals, and online book chapter contributions (Indexed by SCIE, Scopus, ESCI, ACM, DBLP, etc). He is doing research in the field of cloud computing, data security & machine learning. His research work in M.Tech was based on biometric security in cloud computing.

Dhakshayini K. N. is an Assistant Professor at the School of Business and Management at Christ University, Bangalore. She holds multiple academic qualifications, including MCom, MBA, MPhil, and a PhD from Bangalore University. Her research and teaching focus on areas within business and management, and she has contributed to various academic publications and conferences. Dr. Dhakshayini has also been involved in several workshops and faculty development programs, further enhancing her expertise in her field.

Danuta Kaźmierczak is Prof. Assoc. at University of The National Education Commission, Krakow, Poland, a researcher in human security, civil protection, safety education management.

Stanisław Kowalkowski is Colonel, Professor, The Military Engineering, Camouflaging and Force Protection Faculty at War Studies University in Warsaw, Poland. Engineering and technology specialist at engineering support and crisis management

Bovsh Liudmyla is PhD, associate professor, associate professor of the Department of Hotel and Restaurant Business, State University of Trade and Economics, Kyiv, Ukraine. Field of scientific interests: economics and business organization, investments in tourism and hotel and restaurant business, tax policy of business entities.

K. Madhu Kishore Raghunath has obtained his Ph.D. in Management from the National Institute of Technology-Warangal and he is currently working as an Assistant Professor in the Department of Finance, GITAM institute of management, in GITAM (Deemed to be University) Visakhapatnam Campus. He has a Post-graduate degree in Management with Finance and Marketing specializations from Jawaharlal Nehru Technological University and has over 5 years of teaching experience in higher education along with CBSE-NET & AP & TS- SLET qualification. His research interests include subjects like Finance, Marketing, Risk Management, and Supply Chain Management.

Kamel Mouloudj is a Professor in the College of Economic at University of Medea (Algeria). His researches have focused primarily on studies predicting the behavior of individuals (including customers, employees, students, etc.). He earned her Bachelor of Science in Commercial Sciences and Master of Marketing from University of Blida, and Doctor of Marketing from University of Algiers 3. He has over 19 years of teaching experience and has over 45 publications. He participated in three research projects at the University of Medea on industrial marketing, energy, and green start-ups. He is Chair of Doctoral Training Committee at department of commercial sciences from 2019 to now (2024).

Anusha N. is currently working as Associate Professor in Department of IoT, School of Computer science and Engineering, VIT Vellore. She has 20 years of teaching experience. She has completed PhD from Anna University in 2017,M.E in 2007 and B.E in 2000.Her areas of interest include Low power VLSI, Embedded Systems, Artificial Intelligence, IoT. She has published her research articles in reputed journals and also published 2 patents.

Keerthika P. is currently working as Associate Professor in the School of Computer Science and Engineering, Vellore Institute of Technology, Vellore. She has a work experience of 17 years in teaching. She has completed her Ph.D in Anna University, Chennai. She is contributing towards research in the area of Grid and Cloud Computing for the past 14 years. She has published around 50 research papers in reputed journals indexed by Scopus and SCI and presented 30 papers in National and International Conferences. Her areas of interest are Machine Learning, Data Science and Cloud Computing. She was one of the recognized Supervisors in the Faculty of Information and Communication Engineering under Anna University, Chennai. She is currently one of the recognized supervisors in VIT University. She has guided 5 Ph.D scholars in the areas of Machine Learning and Cloud under Anna University. She has received grants from various funding agencies like DRDO and DST. She is currently acting as Reviewer and Editorial Board member in reputed journals.

Sheela P. is an academician with over 30 years of teaching experience. Her Core interest lies in subjects of Accounting and Finance. In the span of her career, she taught various finance and accounting subjects garnering great name and reputation for her teaching skills and pedagogy.

Suresh P. is currently working as Associate Professor in the School of Computer Science and Engineering, Vellore Institute of Technology, Vellore, Tamil Nadu, India. He has 17 years of teaching and academic experience. He has completed Ph.D in Anna University, Chennai. He has published 50 research papers in reputed international journals indexed by Scopus/SCI/WoS and presented 35 papers in National and International Conferences. He has authored 6 books and 15 book chapters. His areas of interest include Networks, Cloud Computing, Data Science, Machine Learning and Deep Learning. He has received grants from various funding agencies like DRDO, ICMR, and CSIR towards the conduct of seminars and workshops. He has received Best Faculty Award and Best Performer in Academics, Research and consultancy from Kongu Engineering College, Erode, Tamilnadu. He is acting as Reviewer and Editorial Board member in reputed journals.

Elen Paraskevi Paraschi is an Assistant Professor at the Department of Tourism Management of the University of Patras, Greece. She also has several years of managerial experience at Zakynthos international airport. Her research focuses on air transport and tourism management, with particular emphasis on safety and security issues, crisis management, environmental performance and sustainability, as well as patterns of interactions between multiple stakeholders in the tourism industry. She has developed and patented the Airport Business Excellence Model (ABEM),™ a holistic model for evaluating airport performance. She has also developed a Quality-of-Life Tourism Model (QoLTM) for the Greek islands. Moreover, she participates in the European Network on Impact of Climate Change on Aviation (EN-ICCA) of the European Aviation Safety Agency (EASA), which aims to ensure aviation safety against risks related to climate change. Furthermore, she is a member of the International Society for Development and Sustainability (ISDS). Her scientific work has been published in prestigious peer-reviewed journals (Tourism Management, Economic and Industrial Democracy, Transport Policy, Transport Economics and Management, Journal of Airline Operations and Aviation Management, Journal of Aviation, Journal of Environmental Management and Tourism, International Journal of Cultural and Digital Tourism, etc.) and has been presented in international conferences.

Sabyasachi Pramanik is a professional IEEE member. He obtained a PhD in Computer Science and Engineering from Sri Satya Sai University of Technology and Medical Sciences, Bhopal, India. Presently, he is an Associate Professor, Department of Computer Science and Engineering, Haldia Institute of Technology, India. He has many publications in various reputed international conferences, journals, and book chapters (Indexed by SCIE, Scopus, ESCI, etc). He is doing research in the fields of Artificial Intelligence, Data Privacy, Cybersecurity, Network Security, and Machine Learning. He also serves on the editorial boards of several international journals. He is a reviewer of journal articles from IEEE, Springer, Elsevier, Inderscience, IET and IGI Global. He has reviewed many conference papers, has been a keynote speaker, session chair, and technical program committee member at many international conferences. He has authored a book on Wireless Sensor Network. He has edited 8 books from IGI Global, CRC Press, Springer and Wiley Publications.

Manjula Devi R. is an Assistant Professor (Senior Grade) in the Department of of Computer Science and Engineering (CSE) at Kongu Engineering College, Perundurai. . She has a work experience of 13 years in teaching. She received her B.E. (CSE) Karunya Institute of Technology, Coimbatore (2004) and her M.E. (CSE) from Kongu Engineering College, Perundurai (2006). She completed her PhD (Information and Communication Engineering) from Anna University, Chennai (2015). Her research interests are Machine Learning, Soft Computing, Computer Graphics, and Artificial Intelligence. She has published over 45 technical papers on Neural Network, Intrusion Detection System, Data Mining and Cloud Computing. She is currently acting as Reviewer and Editorial Board member in reputed journals. She is authored more than 15 books edited by Charulatha Publications, Chennai. She has been honored with various award such as Best Faculty Award, Shri P. K. Das Memorial Best Faculty Award & Life Time Achievement Award–2015, Best Author Award, GRABS Best Young Teacher Award, Young Woman Educator & Scholar Award, etc.

Mário José Batista Romão is an Associate Professor of Information Systems at ISEG – University of Lisbon. He is Director of the Masters program in Computer Science and Management. He holds a PhD in Management Sciences by ISCTE-IUL and by Computer Integrated Manufacturing at Cranfiel University (UK). He also holds a MsC in Telecommunications and Computer Science, at IST - Instituto Superior Técnico, University of Lisbon. He is Pos-Graduated in Project Management and holds the international certification Project Management Professional (PMP), by PMI – Project Management International. He has a degree in Electrotecnic Engineer by IST.

Baranidharan S. specialized in Finance Economics and Econometrics. Having 5 years research experience, 2 years of Industrial experience and 6 years of teaching experience. Published 6 patent, 45 research articles in international and national journal which are indexed in Scopus, WoS, Proquest, ABDC, etc.

Maheswaran S. has completed his B.E (EIE) from Bharathiyar University in the year 2002, M.E (Applied Electronics) from Anna University in the year 2004 and Ph.D in the field of Embedded Systems from Anna University in the year 2016. He has about 18 years of teaching experience at various levels and presently working as an Associate Professor in the Electronics and Communication Engineering Department, Kongu Engineering College, Perundurai. He has obtained one Patent, published one Patent, 25 papers at International Journals. He presented papers in 28 International and 6 National conferences. He is a reviewer in more than 20 international journals and conferences. His area of research includes Embedded Systems, Embedded IoT, Instrumentation and Automation. He is member of IETE, The Institution of Engineers (India) and ISTE. He is the recipient of many award includes Young Scientists' conclave Best hall presentation award 2016 (IISF-2016) – under the theme of "Innovative Agriculture Practices and Livestokes Management" organized by Ministry of Science & Technology, Ministry of Earth Sciences, Vijnana Bharati (VIBHA), CSIR, Science & Technology and Earth Sciences, Government of India. Recipient of best reviewer from IEEE journal.

Kishor Kumar Sadasivuni is an accomplished Research Assistant Professor and the esteemed leader of the SmartNano Solutions group at the Center for Advanced Materials, Qatar University. With a strong foundation in analytical chemistry, he embarked on his academic journey, earning a Master's degree from Andhra University, India. His pursuit of knowledge led him to the University of South Brittany in Lorient, France, where he earned his Ph.D. in Materials Science and Engineering in 2012 under the guidance of Professor Yves Grohens. This marked the beginning of his impressive career in academia and research. Dr. Kishor Kumar Sadasivuni's contributions to the scientific community have been exceptional. His groundbreaking work earned him recognition as one of the world's top 2% scientists, a distinction conferred by Stanford University in 2019, 2020, 2021 and 2023. Qatar University has also acknowledged his remarkable achievements with honors. Boasting over 15 years of active research experience, Dr. Kishor has made significant strides in his field. His prolific publication record includes more than 450 research articles in esteemed international peer-reviewed journals, accumulating an impressive total citation count of 14000 and an h-index of 64. He has also authored 20 book chapters and served as the editor of 11 books, with several of his works featured in Springer's prestigious Top 25 e-book downloads of 2020. Dr. Kishor's innovative mindset is evident through his patent portfolio. He holds three US patents and two Indian patents, with five patent disclosures currently under consideration. As a visionary leader, he spearheads 13 research projects, encompassing grants from the Qatar National Research Fund, including NPRP, UREP, IRCC grants, as well as projects supported by Qatar University, collectively amounting to an impressive 5 million USD. A true collaborator, Dr. Kishor has actively engaged with researchers from diverse disciplines worldwide, boasting over 450 co-authors in fields such as computer science, biomedical sciences, industrial engineering, and electrical engineering. His global collaborations span countries like the USA, France, South Korea, Oman, Spain, Italy, Australia, and Malaysia.

Shreeya Sanjeev Gokhale is currently doing her Bachelor Degree in Computer Science and Engineering at Vellore Institute of Technology, Vellore, Tamilnadu, India. Her areas of interest include Data Science, NLP, Cyber Security, Machine Learning and Deep Learning.

Tetiana Tkachuk is a PhD in Economics, Assistant professor Conducts fundamental and applied research in the field of tourism and hotel and restaurant business, including modern trends and features of the formation and functioning of franchise networks of hospitality enterprises, digitization of hotel and restaurant activities, functioning of hotel and restaurant business entities in the luxury service segment.

S. L. Tulasi Devi is an Associate Professor in School of Management from National Institute of Technology- Warangal. She has over 25 years of experience in academic teaching in Finance. Her areas of research interest are financial management, corporate finance, and financial econometrics.

Shilpy Verma is PhD in Economics from Centre for International Trade and Development, Jawaharlal Nehru University. Presently, she is working with the Amity School of Economics, Amity University, Noida as Assistant Professor. Previously she has worked in Public Debt Management Cell, Department of Economic Affairs, Ministry of Finance as a Consultant prior to this she has worked with the Ministry of Textiles, Government of India as a Young Professional, Department of Commerce, Ministry of Commerce and Industry as a Consultant, Indian Institute of Foreign Trade as Research Associate. she has a close to 2 years experience of teaching in Delhi University as lecturer. 4 Scopus indexed paper and 1 book chapter.

Kirti Hemant Wanjale, Associate Dean Quality, Associate Professor, Computer Engineering Department, Vishwakarma Institute of Information Technology. She has published 140 papers in reputed International Journals, Conferences etc. She has authored 7 books on various topics. She is a reviewer of Elsevier, Springer WPC, IJCSNS, IJCA, IJCSI, and many more. She has chaired many international conferences. She has also filed and published 17 patents in India and the UK out of that 7 are granted. She is a Fellow member of ISTE (India), IAENG (Hongkong), CSI (Pune). Her area of research is Cloud Computing, Quantum Computing, Cloud Security, High Performance Computing, Internet of Things, Artificial Intelligence.

Marek Wrzosek is Colonel, Professor, War Studies University in Warsaw, Poland. Engineering and technology specialist at information security and crisis management.

Sureyya Yigit is Professor of Politics and International Relations School of Politics and Diplomacy New Vision University Tbilisi, Georgia.

Nataliya Zikii is a PhD in Economics, assistant professor Conducts fundamental and applied research in the field of tourism and hotel and restaurant business, in particular regarding modern trends and features of restructuring of tourist enterprises, formation of digitalization of hospitality enterprises, digitalization of service enterprises.

Index

S

Safety 4, 18, 25, 26, 27, 44, 48, 75, 81, 82, 83, 84, 89, 90, 117, 118, 122, 126, 140, 141, 142, 145, 147, 159, 160, 205, 206, 207, 208, 209, 210, 211, 212, 214, 219, 221, 222, 224, 225, 227, 229, 230, 231, 236, 245, 248, 249, 250, 252, 255, 256, 258, 260, 265, 266, 272, 277, 281, 282, 283, 284, 285, 286, 287, 288, 289, 290, 291

Sarbanes-Oxley Act 91, 92, 96, 100, 101, 110, 113

Security 1, 2, 3, 4, 5, 6, 8, 9, 12, 13, 14, 16, 17, 18, 20, 21, 22, 23, 24, 25, 26, 27, 29, 34, 36, 38, 41, 42, 43, 44, 45, 46, 47, 48, 49, 51, 52, 54, 55, 56, 59, 60, 63, 64, 65, 66, 67, 68, 69, 70, 71, 72, 77, 79, 83, 85, 86, 87, 88, 89, 90, 122, 123, 126, 130, 132, 137, 143, 145, 148, 149, 151, 159, 160, 161, 164, 166, 167, 169, 171, 184, 185, 203, 204, 205, 206, 207, 208, 209, 210, 211, 212, 213, 214, 215, 216, 217, 218, 219, 220, 221, 222, 223, 224, 225, 262, 263

Security Management Strategy 204, 206, 210, 212, 216, 217, 218

Social Responsibility 91, 111, 113, 141, 148, 179, 271, 272, 273, 275

ST 21, 22, 34, 36, 37

Sustainability Reporting 104, 105, 106, 251, 263, 267, 273, 274, 275, 276

Sustainable Aviation 245, 252, 271, 273, 274

Switzerland 17, 54, 68, 69, 71, 72, 73, 74, 87, 88, 91

T

Terrorism 60, 62, 63, 66, 68, 69, 72, 85, 87, 90, 207, 212, 218, 222

Transparency 14, 91, 92, 93, 95, 96, 99, 100, 101, 102, 103, 104, 105, 106, 107, 110, 111, 113, 157, 234, 267, 276, 288

W

West Africa 59, 63, 77, 78

Printed in the United States
by Baker & Taylor Publisher Services

Printed in the United States
by Baker & Taylor Publisher Services